HARMONY & DISCORD

A modernised view of J. S. Bach, produced by Dr Caroline Wilkinson, Senior Lecturer in Forensic Anthropology at the University of Dundee, Scotland, commissioned by the Bachhaus Museum, Eisenach, Germany.

Harmony & Discord

The Real Life of Johann Sebastian Bach

Julian Shuckburgh

To my daughter Hannah

www.harmonydiscord.com

First published in 2009 by Old Street Publishing Ltd
40 Bowling Green Lane, London London EC1R 0NE
www.oldstreetpublishing.co.uk
Copyright © Julian Shuckburgh 2009

ISBN 978-1-906525-34-7

10 9 8 7 6 5 4 3 2 1

The right of Julian Shuckburgh to be identified as the author of this work has been asserted by him in accordance with the Copyright, Designs and Patents Act 1988.

All rights reserved. No part of this publication may be reproduced, stored in or introduced into a retrieval system, or transmitted, in any form, or by any means (electronic, mechanical, photocopying, recording or otherwise) without the prior written permission of the publisher.

A CIP catalogue record for this title is available from the British Library.

Typeset by Martin Worthington

Printed and bound in Great Britain

Contents

	List of illustrations	vii
	Acknowledgements	ix
	Introduction	1
1	Childhood and Trauma	13
2	Orphanhood	27
3	Starting Out	43
4	Marriage in Mühlhausen	63
5	Competition in Weimar	77
6	Death in Cöthen	105
7	Schoolmaster in Leipzig	129
8	The Heights of Composition	157
9	Surviving Disasters	181
10	Professional Crisis	199
11	Resuscitation	217
12	Looking Back	241
13	Fame and Triumph	269
14	Towards the End	283
	Epilogue	301
	Endnotes	309
	Appendix 1: The Compositions	315
	Appendix 2: Works and Movements: A Personal Choice	369
	Select bibliography	375
	Index	379

Illustrations

First plate section
Page

i   Modernised view of Bach (Dr Caroline Wilkinson/Bachhaus Museum)

ii   *Johann Ambrosius Bach*, Johann David Herlicius (Staatsbibliothek, Berlin/Bridgeman Art Library)

ii   The Harz Mountains, painted by Georg Heinrich Crola (Sammlung Georg Schäfer, Schweinfurt/AKG Images)

iii   Lüneburg, engraving by Conrad Buno (Stadtarchiv der Hansestadt Lüneburg)

iii   St Michael's Church, Lüneburg, engraving by Joachim Burmester (AKG Images/De Agostini)

iv   *Wilhelm Ernst, Duke of Saxe-Weimar*, unknown artist (Schlossmuseum Weimar/Bridgeman Art Library)

iv   Mühlhausen, engraving by Matthæus Merian (AKG Images)

v   Johann Adam Reincken playing harpsichord, Jan Voorhout (Museum für Hamburgische Geschichte/AKG Images)

vi   New Church, Arnstadt (Foto Bach-Archiv, Leipzig/Constantin Beyer)

vii   *Georg Frideric Handel*, Thomas Hudson (Gerald Coke Handel Collection, Foundling Museum, London/Bridgeman Art Library)

vii   *Georg Philipp Telemann*, unknown artist (Private Collection/Bridgeman Art Library)

viii   Church, Dornheim (Foto Bach-Archiv, Leipzig)

Page

viii Wilhelmsburg Palace, Weimar (Zentralbibliothek, Weimar/ Bridgeman Art Library)

Second plate section

ix The palace church, Weimar, painted by Christian Richter (Klassik Stiftung Weimar)

x *Prince Leopold of Anhalt-Cöthen*, unknown artist (Bach-Gedenkstaat Schloss Köthen/Historisches Museum fur Mittelanhalt)

x Central market square, Leipzig, engraving by Johann Georg Schreiber (Stadtgeschichtliches Museum, Leipzig)

xi St Thomas's Church, Leipzig, engraving by G. Bodenehr (Kupferstich Bach-Archiv, Leipzig)

xi St Thomas's Church, Leipzig today (Leipzig Tourismus und Marketing GmbH (LTM)/ Schmidt)

xii Leipzig in 1722, map painted by Amy Shuckburgh in 2009

xiv St Nicholas's Church, Leipzig (Leipzig Tourismus und Marketing GmbH (LTM)/Schmidt)

xiv *Johann August Ernesti*, Anton Graff (Kunstbesitz der Universität Leipzig/foto Marion Wenzel)

xv Zimmerman's coffee-house, Leipzig, engraving by Johann Georg Schreiber (Stadtgeschichtliches Museum, Leipzig)

xv St John's Church, outside Leipzig (Kupferstich Bach-Archiv, Leipzig)

xvi *Johann Sebastian Bach*, Elias Gottlob Haußmann Stadtgeschichtliches Museum, Leipzig)

Acknowledgements

I became interested in Bach as a classical composer in my childhood, particularly at the Cothill House prep school in Oxfordshire where the remarkable music teacher, R. A. L. Ogston, introduced me to the keyboard music. Indeed, in July 1951 Mr Ogston gave me, as a birthday present, a book entitled *The Music Companion: A Compendium for All Lovers of Music* which contains very interesting comments on Bach's music. And since those days long ago I have constantly continued to read, play and hear the huge range of compositions. In 1969 I became a bass singer in the Bach Choir in London, enabling me to participate in annual performances of the *St Matthew Passion* over several decades, as well as frequent Mass in B Minor concerts and occasional cantatas and *St John Passion*s.

Over the years I read the standard and traditional biographies of Bach dating back to the 19th century (listed here in the Bibliography), and was increasingly aware that, unlike his many famous contemporaries such as Handel and Telemann, Bach did not achieve mastership during his life. This seemed mysterious, since so much of his music was the finest of all time. As Simon Russell Beale said in his recent BBC4 *Sacred Music* programme, Bach was 'now thought to be one of the greatest composers in history, but then unknown to anyone outside a small part of Germany'.

Among the many musicians, academics and other music-lovers with whom I have discussed various mysteries and complexities regarding the standard view of Bach's life, I am especially grateful to and acknowledge Sir David Willcocks, Sir John Eliot Gardiner, David Hill, Katharine Richman, Dr Basil Keen, Professor Christoph Wolff, Anthony Roland,

Dr Richard Zegers,[1] the late Sir Paul Wright, Stephen Cleobury,[2] David Reynolds, Robert Gray, Philip Stevens, Pauline Asquith, Gila Falkus, and my daughter Hannah Shuckburgh.

---

1 Dr Zegers, of the Academic Medical Centre in the University of Amsterdam, responded to my suggestion that Bach's body is not in St Thomas's Church in Leipzig (see page 301). He wrote, 'Indeed I do think that the remnants in Leipzig are not, unfortunately, those of J. S. Bach. As we are speaking, we are about to complete an article that reviews all the known aspects concerning the alleged remnants of Bach, and all evidence points into the direction that it is very unlikely the remnants are what we think (and hope) they are. For us as well, the reason Leipzig does not want to give permission to examine the remnants is that they also suspect the remnants are somebody else's. It's a pity that they rejected our proposition, since we had even a mobile CT-scan arranged to photograph the whole skeleton, and also one of the world-leading experts in DNA research willing to co-operate in this matter.'
2 Stephen Cleobury is Director of Music at King's College, Cambridge. As a superb organist, he made valuable contributions to my account of Bach's obsession with the instrument.

Introduction

In the run-up to the third millennium in the year 2000, there was much focus around the world on the life and work of Johann Sebastian Bach, because it was the 250th anniversary of his death. A great range of his music was performed in churches and concert halls, many radio and television programmes about him were broadcast, and several biographies were published or reprinted. During that year the distinguished conductor Sir John Eliot Gardiner performed the entire surviving range of Bach's church cantatas, with his Monteverdi Choir and the English Baroque Soloists, in suitable churches around Europe. As Gardiner wrote at the time, 'Bach is probably the only composer whose musical output is so rich, so challenging to the performer and so spiritually uplifting to performer and listener alike, that one would gladly spend a year in his exclusive company.'

Also in 2000, the equally distinguished professor of music at Harvard University Christoph Wolff published his biography of Bach, subtitled 'The Learned Musician'.[1] This work was widely praised as the 'definitive' account of Bach's life, and fully and comprehensively summarises the vast amount of scholarly research conducted by musicologists throughout the second half of the 20th century. Professor Wolff is widely appreciated as one of the world's leading participators in Bach scholarship, and has been involved in most of the discoveries and advances in knowledge over the last thirty years. He is co-editor of the research journal *Bach-Jahrbuch*, co-author of the *Bach Compendium*, and editor of *The New Bach Reader**. No one could be better qualified to present the most up-to-date and richly detailed Bach chronicle. Like most readers of *Johann Sebastian Bach: The Learned Musician*, I was extremely impressed by his work, its highly organised structure, his intense appreciation and respect for Bach's life

---

* This book is mentioned in later footnotes as NBR.

and work, and his overview of what the huge range of modern research has revealed about one of the world's greatest composers.

But I was also struck by various factors and elements that led me to wonder if the whole truth was really available to ordinary readers like myself. In his Preface, Professor Wolff writes that Bach's life 'lacks exciting dimensions and does not lend itself to a narrative that focuses on and is woven round a chronological list of dates and events'. It is indeed the case that Bach kept no diaries, wrote no memoirs – or if he did they do not survive – and seems to have exchanged rather few letters with his friends and family. But we certainly have much more information about him than about, for example, William Shakespeare. It should be possible to explore his human qualities, his character, his frailties as well as his strengths, rather than to resort to the overall impression conveyed by Professor Wolff that Bach was a touching, almost god-like hero, endowed with unique musical and scholarly abilities, and with an intensely virtuous and largely unblemished personality.

Another factor that led me to speculate that a new view of Bach could be constructed was the famous story that his music, and indeed his reputation, almost sank without trace within a few years of his death in July 1750, not to be restored until nearly eighty years later when Mendelssohn performed the *St Matthew Passion* in Berlin in March 1829. This is an exaggeration: in fact his reputation, such as it was – and most although far from all of his compositions – did survive in the German music world, not least promoted by his son Carl Philipp Emanuel Bach. But it does bring to mind some fundamental questions which never seem to have been fully addressed by the experts. Bach clearly is one of the greatest composers of all time. In that case, why was practically none of his music printed and published in his lifetime, or indeed for half a century after his death? Why was no inscribed gravestone erected when he was buried in the cemetery at the Johanneskirche in Leipzig? Why did his children fall out with one another after his death, and his wife, Anna Magdalena, die in poverty ten years later?

One clear explanation for the absence of these personal questions in the Bach scholarship may lie in the fact that, unlike his contemporaries Georg Frideric Handel and Georg Philipp Telemann, he had clearly not become an international superstar. I was particularly struck by this when, some years ago, I read an anonymous book published in 1789 entitled *Introduction to the Knowledge of Germany*. Its author may be unknown, but it provides a convincing and positive account of the structure of German society in the 18th century, including German citizens' achievements in the fields of arts and architecture. Here are some examples:

> Germany is the undoubted soil from which some of the most celebrated discoveries have been produced in latter ages. The arts of printing and gunnery had their birth in this country, as well as several others; such, for instance, as the divers methods of engraving, which were either invented there, or first reduced to utility.
>
> In all these, as well as the polite arts of painting, architecture, and music, the Germans make a respectable figure even among the most expert. They were, during the middle ages, esteemed as complete architects as any in Europe. The durability of their edifices is particularly remarkable, as well as their spaciousness, and the ingenuity of their contrivance. Their painters have been so numerous and eminent as to have constituted a school inferior, in the opinion of some, to none but the Italian. In music their talents are highly valued. The name of a Handel stands on a par with that of a Corelli, and in some countries above it.

The author has his criticisms too, of which an interesting one is this:

> It is rather surprising that, with so decided an aptitude for such of the fine arts as fall under the eye and ear, they should so long have remained in a state of inferiority to their neighbours, in those that relate to wit and

fantasy. It is only of late that they have begun to emerge, for which no cause appears assignable but that already hinted, the neglect during so long a time to cultivate and polish their own language.

In any event, it is surely significant that throughout this well-researched and affirmative account of German culture, there is no mention of Bach, or indeed any other composer apart from Handel.

To be fair, there is quite a lot of surviving information about what Bach's contemporaries in Thuringia, and indeed elsewhere, thought of him during his lifetime, mostly recorded by fellow musicians or professional writers about music. As early as 1717, in his last year in Weimar, he was briefly referred to by the journalist Johann Mattheson (1681–1764)[2] as 'the famous organist of Weimar' – and indeed many if not most of people's remarks over the succeeding years are about his exceptional organ-playing skills. Unfortunately very few of them convey any sense of his personal character; practically the only one that does is from the organist Johann Balthasar Reimann (1702–49), who wrote in a brief account of his own life that in 1729 'I travelled to Leipzig in order to hear the famous Joh. Sebast. Bach play. This great artist received me amicably and so delighted me with his exceptional skill that I have never regretted the journey.'[3] Not all comments, however, are unmitigated praise. Mattheson, for instance, criticised his text setting in 1725,[4] and Johann Adolph Scheibe (1708–76), a composer and music critic, wrote a famous article in his journal *Critische Musikus* in 1737 in which he accused some of Bach's compositions of lacking 'amenity', with a 'bombastic' and 'confused' style.[5] This article inspired several of Bach's fans to leap to his defence over the following two years – an event we shall explore further on.

And it is also the case that, after his death, within the specialist world of music Bach's reputation survived – for several reasons. Two of his sons, Carl Philipp Emanuel and Johann Christian, had done unusually well in their musical careers. All Bach's pupils continued to use his music, particularly the 48 Preludes and Fugues, for teaching purposes, and this became a continuing tradition at least in some musical circles. And every now and then a young musical genius would encounter his work, as Mozart did in 1789, realise its extraordinary quality, and spread the word around. This knowledge was confined to specialists and connoisseurs, and to a limited range of Bach's compositions, but as time passed it became apparent to music teachers, not just in Germany but elsewhere in Europe, that Bach featured prominently in virtually every published scholarly survey of music theory and composition. In 1800 this persuaded the recently founded Leipzig publishers Hoffmeister & Kühnel that they would find a market if they began the issue of a complete edition of Bach's keyboard works.

To assist this project, they decided to consult a much respected professor at Göttingen University, named Johann Nikolaus Forkel, who was known to be an expert on music of the period, and an enthusiast for Bach. They began by sending him in 1801 their first volume of the complete works, asking for his comments. He was viciously critical of the choices, pointing out many inaccuracies and errors, but very keen to encourage the project, and in due course he persuaded them that it would benefit the music sales if they commissioned him to write the first ever biography of the composer.

Forkel was then in his early fifties, and his career had curiously paralleled some aspects of Bach's and Handel's. He was born in 1749 in a tiny village in Saxe-Coburg called Meeder, the son of the local cobbler. He had a passionate obsession with music, encouraged by the village schoolmaster, and at the age of 13 he was admitted to the choir of the parish church at Lüneburg (the northern town where Bach attended school in 1700–02). At 20 he entered Göttingen University as a law student, supporting himself there by taking on music students. While still in his twenties, he was appointed Director of Music, a job he held for forty years until his death in 1818. Over this time he attracted much scholarly approval for his critical skills and literary activities, publishing over a twelve-year period a two-volume *General History of Music* (1788 and 1801) from ancient Greek and Roman times to the end of the 16th century, and several other learned books on music.

As a professional musicologist Forkel was well qualified for the task of promoting Bach, but he had added advantages. He had been in touch for some time in the 1770s with two of Bach's sons, Carl Philipp Emanuel and Wilhelm Friedemann, from whom he obtained a lot of useful personal recollections and professional information. He was also a passionate believer in the uniqueness of Bach's work, and resolved to present him as a German national hero of monumental significance. His book, subtitled 'For Patriotic Admirers of Fine Musical Art', ends with these words:

> And this man, the greatest musical poet and the greatest musical orator that ever existed and probably ever will exist, was a German. Let his country be proud of him; let it be proud, but, at the same time, worthy of him!

1802 was a good year for this kind of patriotic tone in Germany, as nationalist feelings rose under the pressure of Napoleonic France. And Forkel wrote well, with plenty of convincing and often touching details about Bach's personal and professional life. The book is a model of hagiography. It was very successful, and remained in print in various editions throughout the succeeding two centuries (although Bach's music sales and performances did not expand for another three or more decades). As Charles Stanford Terry wrote in 1920:

> That Forkel is remembered at all is due solely to his monograph on Bach. Written at a time when Bach's greatness was realised in hardly any quarter, the book claimed for him pre-eminence which a tardily enlightened world has conceded him.

The book itself is actually quite brief, only 110 pages long. Many of these pages contain repeated eulogies and references to the 'sublime' and 'transcendent' genius of this 'prince of musicians', and paint a much romanticised picture of the life of the time. One cannot escape the sense of Forkel's determination to present a positive impression, indeed to 'sell' Bach, to his readers. For example, when writing about his forebears, Forkel says:

> The Bachs not only displayed a happy contentedness, indispensable for the cheery enjoyment of life, but exhibited a clannish attachment for each other...

and follows this with a jolly account of annual family reunions in Erfurt or Eisenach or Arnstadt. No mention is made of Bach's troubled childhood, or of the tensions and dissents that occurred in his early years in the music profession, particularly at Arnstadt and Mühlhausen. Forkel repeats the already locally well-known story about how the Elector of Saxony invited Bach to compete in a contest against a distinguished French keyboard player called Louis Marchand, and how Bach triumphed because Marchand ran home to France before the competition took place.

In fact Forkel's book depends heavily on a long (4,000-word) obituary of Bach which had appeared in 1754 in a magazine published by a former student of his called L. C. Mizler (1711–78).[6] Although it was unsigned, Forkel discovered that it had been written by C. P. E. Bach, assisted by J. F. Agricola, another former pupil who had since achieved success in the music profession. The magazine had a small readership and the obituary would have been long forgotten by its readers, so Forkel evidently felt free to make much use of it, in places simply repeating its words more or less verbatim. Clearly the pattern of Bach's life that Forkel presented in 1802 was itself drawn from Carl Philipp Emanuel's memoir of his father.

There is nothing disreputable or improper about a son's setting out the pattern of his father's life, and no reason to suspect deliberate deceptions. But Emanuel was not a researcher or a historian, nor indeed any kind of professional writer, and it seems clear that he relied wholly on his own memories of events (some of which he misremembered, such as the death of his uncle Christoph), and on anecdotes told him by his father. Emanuel may not have shared Forkel's wish to transform his father into a national superstar, but he certainly conveyed a strong sense of Bach's under-appreciated excellence (a quarter of the piece is devoted to the Marchand story mentioned above), and played down the details of his personal life. The structure of Forkel's book also set a pattern which has been broadly followed ever since by Bach's biographers, including Philipp Spitta, whose massive and enormously detailed two-volume study of Bach's life and music appeared between 1873 and 1880, Albert Schweitzer (1908), C. S. Terry (1928), Christoph Wolff (2000) and many others in between.

The essential assumptions are that Bach was an archetypal German genius under-appreciated in his day; that his personal life was irrelevant or of no significance; that he was a devoted husband to his two wives and father of twenty children, several of whom obtained public fame in the music profession; that he attained his incomparable achievements not through the rebelliousness that was the 19th-century view of artistic genius, but through his obsessive devotion to study and work; that despite setbacks in his career path he never lost an absolute belief in his own unique talents; and that he was an unquestioning believer in Lutheran Christianity. As a consequence the biographer's task has generally been to concentrate on the music rather than on its composer's personality.

This is not to deny that the writers mentioned above have uncovered much interesting personal information over the last two centuries, particularly in recent years, and corrected a number of factual errors in Forkel's book (and one another's). Mountains of research have been undertaken over this time, not all of it musicological in nature. Examination of local council archives, the discovery of letters and documents, the uncovering of lost or forgotten references to Bach or his family or his friends or music pupils – all this has created a considerably more detailed picture of what actually went on through that 65-year life. But the approach remains musicological, rather than human or psychological, and most of the basic assumptions outlined by Emanuel in the obituary and repeated by Forkel remain unquestioned.

Born in Weimar in 1714, Carl Philipp Emanuel Bach evidently enjoyed an energetic, balanced and busy childhood there, in Cöthen from the age of three to nine and thereafter in Leipzig, where he attended St Thomas's School before proceeding to higher education at Leipzig University and then at Frankfurt an der Oder. Later, he succeeded Telemann as cantor at the Johanneum in Hamburg. Like his father, he was raised in a home where he was constantly surrounded by music, and no doubt benefited from keyboard and other instrumental teaching from his father; but as a musician and composer he demonstrated an independence and self-confidence about finding his own style – which supports the proposition that his childhood was stable and pleasant. So it is hardly surprising that in his late thirties he should have chosen to paint his father's life in rose-tinted colours – and indeed continued to do so in his old age when communicating with the young music professor Johann Nikolaus Forkel. But it remains a mystery why the delightful man and master composer so applauded in his obituary should have more or less sunk without trace from the public view for half a century – a fate that certainly did not befall his lesser contemporaries, men like Handel and Telemann.

The final step in the sanctification of Bach as a composer, as mentioned above, came several decades after Forkel's book was published, and the event that brought it about was a performance of the *St Matthew Passion* in Berlin in 1829, arranged and conducted by Felix Mendelssohn, who had only just celebrated his 20th birthday. Mendelssohn had a deep-rooted passion for Bach, partly inherited from his grandparents, two of whom had studied music with J. P. Kirnberger, one of Bach's pupils, and partly encouraged by his own teacher at the Berlin Singakademie, C. F. Zelter. These connections, all involving the close and specialised world of musical training, are not only a vivid example of how Bach's works survived his disappearance from the public view; they also made possible the most dramatic event in the long process of his fame's development. But that is another story, which we shall examine later.

One other issue comes to mind: that the vast range of Bach's compositions known today could very probably reveal a wide range of information about his life. All the works are listed from 1 to 1,120 under the title BWV (*Bach-Werke-Verzeichnis*),* starting with more than 200 cantatas, and moving on to other church music, motets, oratorios and passions, chorales, several hundred organ works, many other keyboard works, and chamber, ensemble and orchestral music. But they are listed entirely by category rather than chronologically, and the crucial factor is that in recent years musicologists have discovered when virtually all of them were composed and performed; and this information, when considered side by side with the events of Bach's life, should provide us with a huge range of opportunities to surmise what the composer felt as the days, weeks, months and years passed.†

Furthermore, it should be understood that the number of surviving compositions is much greater than 1,120, since a number of them contain many movements. There are 78 in the *St Matthew Passion*, 68 in the *St John Passion*, 64 in the Christmas Oratorio, 27 in the Mass in B Minor, and an average of seven or eight in the more than 200 cantatas. Reading and listening

---

* *Bach-Werke-Verzeichnis* was produced by Wolfgang Schmieder under the title *Thematisch-systematisches Verzeichnis der musikalischen Werke von Johann Sebastian Bach* in 1950, and revised in 1990.

† The compositions are listed chronologically in Appendix 1.

to them all takes a long time, but provides us with an opportunity to reach a new assessment of his musical skills as well as his personal emotions.*

Lurking around within the established facts are many hints that Bach's life and character were more subtle and complex than we think. Since Forkel created his image of Bach at the beginning of the 19th century, no one has sought to question its basic assumptions, mostly derived from the obituary. But the truth may be different. In order to unravel it we somehow have to remove these assumptions from our minds, take ourselves back to the last decade of the 17th century when Bach was a child, and follow the events of his life as they actually took place; then we can draw our own conclusions.

---

* The author has studied them all and chosen to star-rate a considerable number. A list of his personal assessments appears in Appendix 2.

Chapter 1

CHILDHOOD AND TRAUMA

(1685–95)

The Germany in which Bach was born in March 1685, and where he lived the whole of his life, was not a nation, but a loose confederation of some 300 separate sovereign states, mostly governed by dukes and princes and hereditary electors. Rather like Italy, but unlike France and Britain, these neighbours had failed since the 13th century to seek the advantages of unification. They had no common law, no effective 'national' taxation system, no literature to reflect the life of the whole country in a language understandable by all, and no unifying industry like the French wine or the English cloth trade. Unification in 18th-century Europe, encouraged by the growth of monetary systems, of increasingly professional bureaucratic classes, of standing armies, of the broadening of education and many other factors, in Germany simply strengthened the hands of the territorial princes.

There were none the less some large, commercially energetic cities, particularly Hamburg, Frankfurt and Leipzig, throughout the German states whose success dated back at least to medieval times and usually resulted from their position on the key trading routes across Europe to the near east. It was in these cities that modern ideas progressed, that merit from whatever social class might be recognised and rewarded, and where the best hopes for a German future might seem to lie. But where the absolute rulers sat, in towns such as Cassel, Hanover, Berlin and Dresden, the feudal age lived on, and social and economic traditions died hard.

In these smaller towns, social divisions were fixed and rigid. Middle-class citizens insisted on maintaining every distinction that separated them from the peasantry, and were among themselves more subtly divided by factors such as their level of education. Those who had attended a grammar school and university, and entered a respected profession such as the law, were regarded as infinitely superior to shop owners and craftsmen, however well off or successful, and were entitled to enter – usually by marriage – the higher ranks of the patricians of their town. But any form of social advancement of this kind was rare and hard to achieve. Below the levels of the aristocracy and wealthy upper-class families, three other social categories could be defined. First there were notaries and advocates, shopkeepers, artists and civil servants. Then there were small stall-holders and street hawkers, shop assistants and craftsmen – including musicians. And finally, in the vast majority, were all the rest – coachmen, servants, labourers and the rural peasantry. The Protestant clergy were almost entirely from middle-class or peasant backgrounds. At universities, theology students were the poorest and most despised, and when they finally graduated and obtained employment in the Lutheran church, they had little social standing.

Johann Sebastian Bach was born on 21 March 1685, in Eisenach, a small, ancient walled town in the centre of Thuringia, with a population of around 6,000; it had only 13 years previously become the capital of an independent principality when the Duke of Saxe-Eisenach moved there. His father, Johann Ambrosius Bach, was a professional musician, and sprang from a line of Bachs dating back to the beginning of the 17th century,* almost all of whom had also worked in the music world.

---

* According to a family genealogy compiled by Johann Sebastian Bach in 1735 (see page 241), his father's great-grandfather, Vitus Bach, was a Hungarian white-bread baker who, because of his Lutheran religion, fled to Germany in the mid-16th century, and died in 1619. Over the next 150 years his descendants included some 60 professional musicians.

His mother, Elisabeth, was the daughter of a former furrier in neighbouring Erfurt, named Valentin Lämmerhirt (1585–1665). Ambrosius and Elisabeth were married in 1668, and by the time of Sebastian's birth already had six children; another child – their first – had died as a small baby, 15 years before Sebastian was born.* They had been living in Eisenach for 14 years by then, were both in their early forties, and Ambrosius had firmly established his position there as a popular† and successful director of town music. So they saw themselves as secure members of the middle classes, a step above the craftsmen and musicians Ambrosius employed.

In towns like Eisenach, professional musicians filled a number of roles in the local community. There were four main sources of income for them. The town council employed so-called town pipers (*Stadt Pfeiferei*) – whose job was to perform at official civic functions, funerals and wedding celebrations (for which they were paid extra by the people organising the event). In Eisenach, their main task was to perform twice a day, at 10 a.m. and 5 p.m., on the balcony of the town hall, facing out over the market square, for the pleasure of passing citizens. Then there were the churches, all of which employed a full-time organist to provide the music appropriate to each service. He recruited, on a freelance basis, whatever players and singers were required by his choice of music. Then there were music teachers at the local schools – music being regarded as a major subject in the curriculum, second only to theology. And finally, if there was a local duke or elector – as was the case in Eisenach after 1672 – there were jobs for court musicians. Even in the most modest courts there would be several permanent music staff, led by a director

---

* Their surviving children were Johann Christoph (b. 1671), Johann Balthazar (b. 1673), Johannes Jonas (b. 1675), Marie Salome (b. 1677), Johanna Juditha (b. 1680) and Johann Jacob (b. 1682). Their first son, Johann Rudolf, was born in 1670 and died aged six months. Their last-born son will generally be referred to as Sebastian in this account.

† The Eisenach town chronicle reported, in Easter 1672, that 'the new town musician made music with organ, violins, voices, trumpets and military drums, as had never before been done by any cantor or town musician as long as Eisenach stood'. (See *NBR* 1.)

(kapellmeister), who performed regular church music, concerts and entertainments for the duke and his guests, also recruiting freelancers – known as beer fiddlers – whenever required. Some were much grander: Augustus the Strong in Saxony in 1716 employed a 20-strong choir and 17 Polish orchestral players, as well as 60 ballet dancers and 27 actors.

The streets of Eisenach, as in most medieval towns, were narrow and crooked, lined with a few hundred tall *Fachwerk*, half-timbered houses, many of which were already two or three centuries old, grim-looking from the outside but sometimes improved and comfortable within. Most of them were three storeys high, with the ground floor built around a big *Flur* or hall, entered from the street through a wide door and leading to a courtyard behind, with outbuildings around it. Ambrosius had bought his house, on *Fleischgaße* (now the *Lutherstraße*) in the town centre, ten years before, funding it no doubt partly from his wife's dowry and partly from his own income. He hardly earned a huge salary from his job as the local town musician, but was able to bolster his income – indeed more than double it – from teaching and performing, for civic events and receptions, and private weddings and funerals.

On the ground floor Ambrosius would conduct his teaching sessions, and in the cellars below store his musical instruments and other household possessions. Upstairs were reception rooms and bedrooms around the upper hall, where large chests stood containing the family linen (enough to last for months without a washing day), and the remaining bedrooms on the top floor. There were no baths, but probably a rough-and-ready drainage system. Water had to be fetched from the public fountain in the street.

The house was packed full, day and night, with students and fellow musicians, and with the couple's six children. The eldest was Christoph, born just four months before his parents moved to Eisenach from Erfurt, now aged 14. Then there was twelve-year-old Balthasar, Jonas aged ten, Marie aged eight, Juditha aged five, and Jacob aged three. And that was not all. The couple also housed two close relations: three-year-old Johann

Nicolaus Bach, who had been orphaned when his father – Ambrosius's second cousin – died of the plague in 1682 and his mother a year later; and Johann Jacob Bach, the 17-year-old son of another of Ambrosius's numerous cousins, whom he had taken on as an apprentice a year or two before. So Sebastian's birth brought the household to eleven. Music was a constant presence. Christoph was already a skilled keyboard player, about to leave home to go back to Erfurt and study with the well-known musician Johann Pachelbel, an old family friend. Balthasar was about to be nominated apprentice to his father.

Two days later, on 23 March, the little baby was taken to St George's, the main church in Eisenach, to be christened.[7] Elisabeth was not allowed to be there, as the church rules proscribed the entry of any mother until she had undergone the purification ceremony six weeks after giving birth, a ritual known in the Anglican Church as the Churching of Women. By the font stood Ambrosius, together no doubt with his eldest son Christoph and perhaps Balthasar, Jonas and Nicolaus, watching as the vicar, Johann Christoph Zerbst, conducted the brief ceremony. Standing there with them were two godfathers: the local duke's chief forester, Johann Georg Koch, and Sebastian Nagel, a town musician from nearby Gotha and an old friend of Ambrosius, after whom the baby was named.

Until this point Ambrosius had led quite a rewarding and energetic life. Born in 1645 in Erfurt (where his father too was a town musician), he and his twin brother Christoph had been brought up in Arnstadt. He spent seven years of his youth doing his apprenticeship as a musician, before being appointed to the Erfurt town music company as a violinist. At 23 he stepped up the social ladder by marrying Elisabeth, whose late father, the furrier, had been a much respected member of the town council. Family connections were an enormous help in this neighbourhood, and Ambrosius had all the ones he needed: his father, his uncles and numerous Bach cousins all held posts as town or court musicians in Weimar, Erfurt, Arnstadt, Eisenach and further afield, and in accordance with family tradition they helped one another in finding employment for their male offspring and husbands for their daughters. When Ambrosius took on the post at Eisenach in 1671, the town council upped his salary by more than a third compared with his predecessor's, and he repaid them by staging hundreds of enjoyable and highly praised performances in the town over the next 15 years. Another sign of his musical versatility was his appointment as trumpeter in the duke's* court orchestra. And he was the proud father of seven talented children.

It was not usual at the time to have so large a family, the average being four or five. Ambrosius and Elisabeth were clearly good and caring parents, and found rewards in the process: enjoyment and pleasure from their children's company, pride in their skills, and the ambition to extend the family tradition in the music profession. Elisabeth took day-to-day care of the children, but Ambrosius was at home a lot of the time and closely involved in their lives.

But Sebastian's birth signalled the start of a grim transformation in the family's fate. A year or two before, in 1682–3, the large nearby town of Erfurt had been assaulted by the plague, which had killed a great many inhabitants – including young Johann Nicolaus's father – and reduced its population by nearly half. Quite apart from the misery of so many deaths, this had had a severe effect on the local economy, substantially affecting the welfare and earnings of the middle and working classes throughout Thuringia. The Bachs had come through relatively unscathed (apart from the death of their eldest son at the age of only six months, in 1670). But only two months after Sebastian was born, their son Jonas died, aged ten. And then, a year later, his little six-year-old sister Juditha also died. That same year, Christoph left home to go and study with Pachelbel in Erfurt. So, soon after Sebastian's first birthday, the lively household of young Bachs was much reduced. Though they left no written evidence to prove it, these events must have had a crushing effect on Ambrosius and Elisabeth, and hence on their youngest child. Worse was to come.

---

* Duke Johann Georg I of Saxe-Eisenach, who ruled there from 1672, succeeded by his son Johann Georg II in 1686.

HARMONY AND DISCORD

As Sebastian grew up, surrounded constantly by music-making and musicians and musical instruments, he observed himself at the heart of a genetic pattern which went back unaltered over many decades. He saw himself as destined to join this family tradition, and his father gave him every opportunity to do so, teaching him how to sing and play, involving him in rehearsals and performances (many of which took place in the house), and in copying out music, repairing and maintaining musical instruments, and all the other activities that professional musicianship involves. He was three when his brother Balthasar (by then 15) was appointed to an apprenticeship with his father, and no doubt he spent much time watching the two of them at work, observing and learning what the life of professional musicians was like. There was also a tradition among Ambrosius's brothers and cousins (the grandsons of Hans Bach, who had died in 1626) that the Bach relations would get together once a year to celebrate their pride in the family's exceptional dominance of the music profession in their neighbourhood, meeting in Erfurt or Arnstadt or Eisenach, singing and playing music together. Sebastian was taken by his parents, probably several times, to these family reunions, and they made a deep impression on him.[8] He would remember his great-uncle Heinrich (1615–92) and Heinrich's two sons, Johann Michael (1648–94) and Johann Christoph (1642–1703); his father's two brothers, Johann Christoph (1645–93) and Georg Christoph (1642–97); and another uncle, Johann Aegedius (1645–1716). And he had at least twelve cousins, mostly in their teens and early twenties.

Sebastian's education began in 1690, at the local German primary school. In the following spring, on 5 April 1691, through unknown causes Balthasar died, the third of Sebastian's siblings to die, and one he most admired and loved. Death, or the threat of it, was clearly ever-present, forcing itself to the front of his young mind. When we imagine life in the late-17th century, when the average age of death was so much younger than now, we tend to assume that people were more accepting of it than we are; but there is no evidence for this, and indeed plenty that grief and mourning at the loss of loved ones was just as searing as it is for us. It has even been suggested by historians that parents then were indifferent when their children died, and that parental neglect and abuse may not infrequently have caused the death. Perhaps we have been brought up to believe that in past centuries parents were not as close to their children as in our day, and that their relations with one another were far more formal and detached.[9] But such assumptions must be discarded. More recent research, particularly examining the diaries, notebooks and autobiographies written by the actual people who lived in those times,[10] shows vividly that parents and children cared as deeply for one another then as now.

Ambrosius and Elisabeth had by 1691 lost four of their children, three of them in less than six years – and the misery was by no means over yet. Twelve months later another death struck the household: that of young Johann Jacob, the 24-year-old cousin who had become Ambrosius's apprentice nearly ten years before. Little Sebastian had now experienced two deaths at home within a year, Christoph had moved away, and Ambrosius and Elisabeth were left with only three children of their own (Marie, now 15, ten-year-old Jacob, and Sebastian), and their ten-year-old step-cousin Johann Nicolaus. Then in 1693 there was yet more grief, when Ambrosius's beloved identical twin brother, Johann Christoph, a town musician in neighbouring Arnstadt, fell ill and died.

In May 1692, aged seven, Sebastian joined Jacob at the local Latin boys' school of St George's, attached to the church where he had been christened. This was not a very distinguished school – it was eventually promoted to the status of gymnasium 15 years later, in 1707 – and clearly Sebastian was thought to be brighter than average, because he began in the *quinta* class where most boys were eight or older. School was an all-year-round affair, the only holiday allowed being during harvest time. Classes were held six days a week, starting at 6.00 a.m. and running until 9.00 (7.00 to 10.00 in winter) before the boys went home for a three-hour break. They returned at 1.00 p.m. for an hour of music lessons, followed by two more hours of other studies – reading, writing, grammar, scripture, arithmetic and Latin. On Wednesdays and Saturdays they had the afternoon off.

The school's surviving records show both the number of days in the year each pupil missed, and where they ranked in the class.[11] In his first year, Sebastian missed 48 days – an exceptional level of truancy. Only one explanation makes sense: his father must have been unconcerned about his formal education, and found it useful to have him at home assisting with practical musical tasks, and perhaps even singing in the town choir. The boy was certainly talented, and willing to work hard when he had to. Despite these absences, he ended the year in 47th place in his class of 81 pupils, only a little more than half-way down. He clearly wasn't exactly a prodigy, but he had enough energy and intelligence to catch up with his older classmates. In his second year in the *quinta* he was absent less – a mere 29½ days – and by Easter 1694, just after his ninth birthday, he had risen to 14th in the class of 74.

School was competitive. Boys were conscious every week of their rise or fall in the class. Sebastian was confident that he could do well at music, but less so with other subjects. The regular scripture lessons involved interminable readings of the Bible, and no doubt he was struck over and over again by passages in the New Testament about human life and death, and how the Gospels recounted Jesus' references to it: assertions like 'Verily, verily, I say unto you, except a corn of wheat fall into the ground and die, it abideth alone: but if it die, it bringeth forth much fruit. He that loveth his life shall lose it; and he that hateth his life in this world shall keep it unto life eternal.'* Death for Sebastian was not some distant thing imagined, as it is for most young children, but already a very present horror. Jesus must have seemed to offer the only solace, the promise of paradise after life.

In Eisenach at this time, Ambrosius was not the only professional musician called Bach. His slightly older cousin Johann Christoph

---

* John 12: 24–5.

(1642–1703) had been the town organist there for nearly 30 years, as well as organist and harpsichordist in the court *Kapelle*. His chief job was to manage music in the services of the three main town churches, including St George's. By the time Sebastian got to know him well, he was living alone with his wife Elisabeth, his four sons having grown up and recently left home. Christoph missed his own sons, and was impressed by Sebastian's interest in music. The boy was constantly at St George's, not only as a member of the school choir, but because this church was also where Ambrosius regularly performed with his town musicians, on all Sundays and feast days. Sebastian became fascinated by the organ, and Christoph began to teach him not only how to play but how this extraordinarily complex instrument worked.

When you are eight, the organ is a mysterious giant with inexplicable strength. It can utter a vast range of sounds, from gentle whistling to ear-splitting, strident bombastics. The dozens of pulleys at the sides, with strange names, are hard to grasp. Hundreds of pipes range above you, some 16 feet high and others as tiny as your fingernail. Your legs are too short to reach the row of long wooden pedals below your feet. But the instrument exudes power, enables the player, one person alone, to be an entire orchestra. Sebastian must have been entranced, not just by playing it, but by the challenge of understanding its mechanics.

The organ in St George's was a huge, three-manual instrument, and in a state of decay. It had been erected more than a century earlier, and renovated and enlarged several times before Christoph took it over in 1665. He had instigated some repairs at that stage, but now the duke had accepted his submission that an entirely new instrument should be installed, at a cost of 2,000 florins.* It was to be the largest organ in Thuringia, designed by an organ builder from Ohrdruf called G. C. Stertzing, with four manuals and 58 stops – a seriously ambitious project which was not completed until

---

* About £84,000 in today's money (2009). Where money is mentioned hereafter, the sum in square brackets is an approximate current sterling equivalent.

three years after Christoph's death ten years later. Meanwhile, he had to make do with the existing one. With Stertzing's help, he was constantly having to make repairs and adjustments.

Its defects were extremely enlightening to anyone interested in how organs work. Here, moving around behind the grand frontage, Sebastian could see all the variations of pipe design, some metal and some wood, some open on top and others closed or half-closed with a lid, the different shapes and sizes, the alloys used, and the hundreds of tangled rods that connected the pipes to the keys. Here he could observe the bellows and their connection to the soundboards, and distinguish how the three keyboards related to different sounds, and how the couplers allowed you to play on two manuals at once. Every time a repair was needed, Sebastian could learn something new about the technical complexities of this extraordinary instrument.

He learned the meanings and the sounds of all the stop knobs – the Principal, Viol di Gamba, Quintatön, Grobgedackt, Quinta, Octave, Gemshorn, Cymbal, Trumpet – and how some sounded an octave or more higher or lower than others. He discovered the mixtures, with their peculiar names – Cornet, Sharp, Sesquialtera – and how they added resonance and colour to the tone. He found out why some notes sounded out of tune, and how this could be corrected. He learned how the air from the bellows came through to the soundboards, and why in cold weather, if not protected in frames, they would produce uncontrollable wailing sounds.

The source of all the organ's sounds is air, or wind, generated by bellows. Today the air is provided by an electric fan, but until the end of the 19th century all organs were blown by hand, and large organs required several men to pump them. Each group of pipes, with its individual sound, is called a stop; and each stop requires a pipe for each note on the keyboard. So for each stop there are between 54 and 61 pipes. Each group of pipes stands on its own soundboard, to which the wind is fed from the bellows below, and held under pressure. If you want to play a particular group of pipes, you pull out the stop knob, which releases the sliders below them and lets the air through. When you press a key on the keyboard, a valve opens in the soundboard and allows the pipe to sing.

There are two main sorts of pipes, called flues and reeds. Flues are the simpler ones, not unlike flutes. The wind comes up through the base, past a small plate and out through the mouth above. The length of the pipe determines the pitch it sounds – the shorter the pipe, the higher the note. If it is covered at the top with a lid, this lowers its note by an octave. Reed pipes are slightly more elaborate and produce a more resonant sound. They have a metal tongue just above the base, which vibrates against the open side of a little brass tube when the air comes through. The tongue is secured by a small tuning spring, made of wire, which can be raised or lowered to modify the pitch. There are many sorts of flue and reed pipes, producing the great variety of sounds that an organist can project.

Sebastian was equally fascinated by Christoph's playing. He not only was a skilled organ player, but had an exceptional ability to improvise. Inventing music as you go along is something we can all try, but to develop it needs a good deal of confidence and mental agility. Classical musicians in our time rarely build up this skill, seeing their main task as understanding and interpreting what the composer imagined in his head, and wrote out in detail at his desk. Organists still do it to some extent – and of course so do jazz musicians, and performers of Indian, Chinese and other eastern musics. But 300 years ago in Europe improvisation was still regarded as an extremely important branch of musical art. Organists in particular, since they had before them such a huge range of sounds and effects, were expected to create music to fill the gaps in the course of long church services, or before and after them – and indeed to some extent they still do.

If you ask an organist where his ideas for improvisation come from, he is likely to suggest several answers. One is the instrument itself, and its particular qualities and capacities; another might be the building he's performing in or the general atmosphere surrounding him, the nature of the audience or congregation and their expectations, and the type of the service, such as wedding or funeral. More specifically, he will be sparked off by a tune from a hymn about to be or just sung, or the content of a biblical reading. The tune usually comes first, and then its harmony and rhythm, then counterpoint and fugue, and a general desire to create a mood appropriate to the situation. Sometimes the start goes nowhere, and after a minute or two the improviser will realise this and start again.

But if *ad lib(itum)* playing goes well it is a thrilling experience, full of spontaneity and excitement, inspiring to the player and a bolster to his confidence. It leads to two thoughts: that he should remember as much as possible of what he invented, to use again; and that he should try to write it down so others can play it too. Improvisation is the starting-point for composition. Sebastian watched his elderly second cousin skilfully operate the defective organ in St George's Church, listened to his inventive musical extemporisation, and felt inspired.

But the traumas of Sebastian's childhood were now reaching their climax. On 21 March 1694 he celebrated his ninth birthday, and shortly afterwards joined the *quarta* class at the Latin school. Easter was celebrated on 11 April. Three weeks later, his mother died. She was 50. No one knows the cause of Elisabeth's death, or whether she was ill beforehand, or how the family tried to cope, or where she was buried. The only evidence that survives is an entry in the local death register: '3 May 1694. Buried, Johann Ambrosius Baach's [*sic*] wife – without fee'.[12]

For many children this might have been the last straw. Imagine it: you are nine years old. Almost from your birth the dear ones in your family have died like flies around you – your little sister Juditha, your brother Balthasar, your cousin Johann Jacob, your uncle. And now your mother. How can you bear this life if everyone who loves you deserts you, and if those who survive around you are in perpetual mourning? Sebastian had a strong will to live, but it must already have been clear in his mind that life on earth was temporary and painful, that he could tolerate it only if he held an unshakeable belief in a better life hereafter. But at least he had music around him, music which expresses emotions that words cannot, music which may provide some consolation for grief. He was absent from school for 51½ days that year, ending 23rd in the class of 45 boys.

Ambrosius was no doubt devastated by his wife's death, and panic-stricken about the effect on his three young children and his step-cousin Johann Nicolaus. There must have seemed to him only one way out – to find himself another wife as quickly as possible. With his usual devotion to the concept of family support, he cast around among his relations, and remembered the widow of his Arnstadt cousin Johann Günther Bach, who had died eleven years earlier. Barbara Margaretha was the daughter of the former mayor of Arnstadt, Caspar Keul. A year after Günther's death she remarried, but then her second husband also died, in 1688, and still in her mid-thirties she was left with two young daughters aged twelve and ten. Within a few weeks of Elisabeth's burial Ambrosius proposed to her, and she accepted. They married on 27 November, in a small formal ceremony in his home, surrounded by his children* and hers, and no doubt some relations and friends.[13] Johann Nicolaus was not there: he had left shortly after Elisabeth's death, moving to live with some other Bach relations in Erfurt, where he later studied medicine and became a doctor in east Prussia. But Sebastian never forgot him.

So by the end of the year some stability in the family had been reestablished, the children had a new mother and two new sisters, and Christmas could be celebrated with a touch of the old domestic flair. For professional musicians Christmas was a busy time, and Ambrosius put his usual energy into church performances throughout the week and into the new year. But the strain had taken its toll, and only a few weeks later he fell seriously ill. Margaretha brought in doctors, spending the family savings on their prescriptions of a range of herbal medicines to save him. But it was no use. He died on 20 February 1695, aged 49, and was buried four days later.[14] Nine-year-old Sebastian was now an orphan.

---

* Probably including his eldest son Johann Christoph, who only five weeks earlier, on 23 October, had himself got married, in Ohrdruf, to Johanna Dorothea Vonhoff.

Chapter 2

ORPHANHOOD

(1695–1702)

Barbara Margaretha Bach, at 36, was now a widow for the third time in 13 years, and bore two heavy responsibilities. She was the mother of two daughters – aged ten and eleven – by her first two husbands, and the stepmother of Ambrosius's children. And as widow of the town music director, she was obliged to be in charge of town music for the next six months, until the council had time to appoint a new director. Although during these months she continued to receive Ambrosius's modest salary, she was hardly in a position to bolster it with freelance work as he had done, and she had to go on paying the wages of Ambrosius's four employees. There were severe money problems, and with help from the cantor of St George's School she presented a petition to the town council for a bounty.[15] But it was not enough. She struggled on in Eisenach for two or three months, increasingly aware that, once a new town music director was appointed, she would be unable to support these five young children and herself with no income. There was no choice but to break up the family.

She decided to return to Arnstadt with her two daughters, and persuaded Marie Salome, now 18, to move to Erfurt to live with her mother's family, the Lämmerhirts.* There was only one choice for the two boys, Jacob and Sebastian, and she contacted their 24-year-old brother Johann Christoph in Ohrdruf, where he had recently married and been appointed organist at St Michael's Church, and persuaded him to take them in. The house was put up for sale, and its proceeds† divided between the four heirs, three of whom would now live together.

Sebastian barely knew his elder brother, though no doubt he had met him from time to time, most recently at his wedding and the funerals of their parents. Christoph was 15 when he left home in 1686, when Sebastian was only a year old, and lived for three years 50 miles away in Erfurt as an apprentice to the much respected organist and composer Johann Pachelbel, who when Christoph was 17 secured him an appointment there as organist at the local church of St Thomas's. Christoph held this rather poorly paid job for several months, but then resigned and moved to Arnstadt to assist his elderly great-uncle Heinrich Bach, who was struggling in his seventies to continue as organist at three churches there. Heinrich had been in poor health for nearly a decade, and two other musicians had helped him out – his son Günther until he died in 1683, and his son-in-law (and Christoph Bach's godfather) Christoph Herthum. But Christoph Bach performed this act of family support for only a year, before applying for the job in Ohrdruf.[16]

Ohrdruf was an even smaller town than Eisenach, one of the most ancient in Thuringia, originally built around an eighth-century Benedictine monastery along the valley by the river Ohr, and the residence of the Counts of Gleichen. It was noted for its flourishing economy based on artisans and manufacturers, and had suffered severely destructive fires several times over the preceding centuries, most recently in 1661;[17] but

---

* Marie Salome soon married a successful Erfurt furrier named Johann Andreas Wiegand, a business partner of her mother's family the Lämmerhirts; she died in 1728 in her fifties.

† Probably about 120 florins [£5,000].

the counts had rebuilt it, and St Michael's Church was a modest 17th-century building with a tall tower at the eastern end (only part of which now survives), built on the site of the monastery chapel. Soon after taking up his post Christoph had met and married the daughter of an Ohrdruf town councillor, Johanna Dorothea Vonhoff, and she was about to give birth to their first child, Tobias Friedrich. Her mother-in-law had died only 14 months earlier, but it would not have occurred to Johanna Dorothea then that she would soon become responsible for the care of two young brothers-in-law – a task that was to prove somewhat burdensome. Christoph's pay was far from lavish, 45 florins [£1,890] a year plus a few piles of grain and firewood. Although they did in due course benefit from the proceeds from the sale of his father's house in Eisenach, and the following year, in 1696, Christoph secured a huge pay increase of nearly 80 per cent, clearly taking on the upbringing of the two boys would not be easy.

Christoph negotiated a deal with the lyceum in Ohrdruf to provide the two boys with free board. This was a rather more respected school than St George's in Eisenach, founded in 1560 by the current Count of Gleichen, and attracting students from other towns. Sebastian, now aged ten, enrolled in the *tertia* class along with Jacob, now thirteen. Over the next twelve months Sebastian's performance at school improved dramatically.[18] He was the youngest in the class, but after the exams in July 1696 he was in fourth place – an exceptional achievement for anyone, let alone a child recently orphaned and living somewhat unwelcomed in his brother's home. He had evidently resolved that the only way to survive these constant losses and deprivations was hard work, carrying out one's duties to one's best ability, and set himself high standards, based on family tradition. He no doubt remembered all those uncles and cousins he used to meet at annual gatherings when his parents were still alive, with their respectable posts throughout Thuringia as organists and town musicians, and concluded that Bachs should be proud of themselves, confident in their talents, satisfied with what life offered them, respectful of their aristocratic employers, and upholding of the moral and ethical standards of Lutheran society: modesty, honesty, frugality and industry. He would have trouble with some of these standards in his adult life, as we shall see – not least because some of them embody inherent contradictions – but they must have helped him build up a level of self-confidence which steered him through the teenage years ahead.

At the end of Sebastian's first year at the lyceum, his brother Jacob departed. He was only 14, but Christoph must have felt troubled by the burden of caring for these two boys, particularly as he now had his own baby son, Tobias Friedrich, and he arranged for Jacob to be taken on as apprentice to the newly appointed successor to their father as director of the Eisenach town music. Jacob moved back to Eisenach in July 1696. Christoph might have justified this dismissal of his brother on the basis that he himself had been sent away from home by his father, as an apprentice to Pachelbel – though admittedly he was already 15 at the time. So now Sebastian was the only remaining burden.

Christoph shortly came up with another scheme to improve his income. Pachelbel had recently resigned from the post of town organist at Gotha, moving to Nuremberg, and recommended his former student as his successor. Christoph confronted his Ohrdruf employers with the prospect of his departure, telling them of the much improved pay he had been offered, and this persuaded them to up his annual income from 45 to 70 florins, plus additional in-kind payments of grain and wood. As he recorded in an autobiographical note written four years later:

> Since during my stay here I always experienced good will, from both high and low, and having beseeched God's wisdom, I resolved to remain here and be content with the smaller pay and benefits.[19]

But it seems likely that he was not really content. At some level he probably resented still having to support Sebastian, and inwardly sought to secure some way of expelling the boy as soon as it could respectably be done. Next year, aged twelve, Sebastian was still the youngest in the *tertia* class, and came first in the exams – including Latin and Greek – in July, moving up to the *secunda*. He sang in the school choir, and three times a year they performed around the town streets, each singer pocketing a useful share of the money donated. Sebastian, in a bid to retain the security of his home, delivered his share to Christoph.

In the main downstairs room in Christoph's house there was a harpsichord,* and a locked cupboard where Christoph kept his music manuscripts. One summer after Jacob and Sebastian moved in, the latter became aware that in the cupboard was a manuscript containing a collection of keyboard pieces by leading contemporary composers, which Christoph had copied during his time as Pachelbel's apprentice. Although Sebastian was allowed access to other music owned by Christoph, and frequently practised it on the harpsichord, for some reason which he could not understand Christoph refused, 'despite all his pleading', to allow him to read or play the pieces in this particular manuscript. The experience was a huge frustration. Did Christoph believe Sebastian was too young, too poor a player? Was he jealous of Sebastian's precocious keyboard skills? Did he regard the manuscript as so valuable that it could not be touched?

Sebastian decided to rebel. Everyone in the house was usually in bed by 9.00 or 10.00 p.m., after dark. He got up, went downstairs, and succeeded in extracting the paper-covered manuscript through the lattice-work in the front of the cupboard. He began to copy it out, assisted only by the moonlight. Then he squeezed it back through the grill, and returned to bed for a few hours' sleep, before rising to be at school by 6.00 a.m. He continued with this extraordinarily demanding project for six months, until he finally possessed his own copy of the entire manuscript.

---

*   Or possibly a virginal or spinet, or even a clavichord. The story of the 'moonlight manuscript' is recounted in C. P. E. Bach's 1754 obituary of his father, where the instrument is described as a *Klavier*, which means any domestic keyboard instrument. The anecdote is also repeated in J. N. Forkel's biography (1802).

But then disaster struck. At lunchtime one day he was playing it on the harpsichord when Christoph unexpectedly returned from work and recognised the music. He snatched Sebastian's hard-earned copy, confiscated it, and never returned it.* Whatever profound frustration and anger Sebastian felt at the time about the meanness and brutality of his brother's behaviour, when in later life he told his children the story, its purpose was to illustrate his own devotion to music and his intense energy and capacity for hard work. But he couldn't resist adding a revealing allegory. As his son recounted:

> We may gain a good idea of our little Johann Sebastian's sorrow over this loss by imagining a miser whose ship, sailing for Peru, has foundered with its cargo of a hundred thousand thaler.

The manuscript's value to Sebastian was inestimable,† and it may have had considerable influence on his approach to composing.

Nor was music entirely satisfactory at the lyceum. The cantor (teacher in charge of music), Johann Heinrich Arnold, was highly unpopular, accused of a range of improper behaviour – including excessive severity – in the school, in church and in the town generally. In June 1696 a new young rector was appointed, Johann Christoph Kiesewetter, who sacked Arnold a year later and replaced him in January 1698 with a much more capable teacher from Gotha named Elias Herda, who had been a choral scholar at St Michael's School in Lüneburg – a connection that

---

* Scholars who wish to see Johann Christoph Bach in a positive light have frequently suggested, as Christoph Wolff does in *Johann Sebastian Bach: The Learned Musician* (2000), that: 'It seems likely … that Christoph returned the copy to Sebastian when the latter left for Lüneburg.' But there is no evidence for this. If he had, Sebastian would almost certainly not have told his children, as the obituary states, that 'he did not recover the book until after the death of this brother'.

† 100,000 thaler, in today's money, is £5 million. Sebastian no doubt read at school about the Spanish kingdom of Peru, the main source of Europe's gold and silver.

would before long play a crucial role in Sebastian's life. That summer, aged thirteen, Sebastian came fifth in the *secunda* class. Herda had studied theology at Jena University, and although his role at the lyceum was as cantor he was also responsible for general teaching. In scripture lessons the class would have read Leonhard Hutter's book *Compendium locorum theologicorum* (1610), a concise outline of Lutheran orthodox theology which was used in schools throughout Germany.

Through these readings and lessons, Sebastian became imbued with the fundamental Christian understanding of human life, death, the soul, resurrection and immortality. Mankind is a combination of body and soul, and death is the penalty for sin. Those who believe in God and in his son Jesus will continue to exist after their physical death. Death for them is not a painless transition to a perfect world, but destruction, the obliteration of the sinful flesh so that believers can be renewed and rise again. As Leonhard Hutter writes, 'the souls of the believers in Christ are in the hands of God, awaiting there the glorious resurrection of the body and the full enjoyment of the eternal blessedness'. If your beloved parents are snatched away from you by death before you are ten, it is at least some consolation to imagine that they are in heaven and that eventually, if you maintain your faith, you will be with them again. Ask anyone who has been orphaned at that age. Sebastian seized on this concept, and – as we shall see – adhered to it throughout his life.

When Christoph took up his job as organist at St Michael's in Ohrdruf, he was no doubt attracted by the fact that it contained two organs. The small one dated back to the previous century, but it had been renovated in 1683 and a pedal board added. The main organ was built in 1675, and had been quite recently enlarged to include two keyboards, a pedal board and 21 stops.[20] Christoph must have assumed they would both be in good condition, but after only a year or two things began to go wrong, particularly on the *Rückpositiv* keyboard. He complained to the town council, and in 1693 Pachelbel was summoned from Gotha to inspect the instrument, producing a detailed and highly critical report. The organ builder who had installed the extensions five years before, Heinrich Brunner, undertook to do the repairs, but continued to make a poor job if it; and in 1698 another organ builder, Christian Rothe, from Salzungen, was brought in to assess the problems and stipulate what further repairs were needed. He brought with him one of his apprentices, Heinrich Nicolaus Trebs, with whom Sebastian struck up a lasting friendship. Through this experience he learned a lot more about organ technology, how repairs could be undertaken and what reports to the owners should deal with. It was to prove another useful and productive source of learning to add to what he had observed with his elderly cousin in Eisenach.

But he could have given only a passing thought to the idea that he might train to become an organ builder like Trebs. The most immediate option would be to follow his father and eldest brother and aim to be an organist or a town piper, but his teachers might well have encouraged him with more ambitious plans, including the possibility of going to university. If he could imagine himself as a school cantor like Elias Herder, a university degree would be required; and he could even then contemplate studying law, or theology, either of which could raise him further up the social ladder. Although rather few Bachs had actually attended university, several in their social circle had, including Pachelbel and Christoph's father-in-law, Johann Bernhard Vonhoff, the Ohrdruf town councillor. Certainly by this age Sebastian had an exceptional range of musical skills. He had devoted endless hours to developing his keyboard-playing on the harpsichord. He could write and copy music rapidly and accurately, in both the German keyboard tablature and conventional notation. He had an exceptionally beautiful treble voice, and much experience of using it in choirs. He could play the violin and viola (and probably also the cello). He already had an expert knowledge of organ technology, which gave him the ability not only to mend defective organs but to extemporise on this instrument, with all its fascinatingly complex sound effects. And he had imbued in himself a commitment to hard work, which all musicians need to acquire in early life.

But in Thuringia, and indeed throughout Germany, climbing up the social ladder was no easy task. The population of some 18 million people was basically divided into three groups, of which 75 per cent were the rural peasantry. At the top end the nobility numbered some 200,000, and in between was the bourgeoisie. This middle class was itself divided, the upper comprising wealthy merchants, brewers, business agents, lawyers and the most prosperous master artisans, and the lower being ordinary shopkeepers, commercial employees, subordinate officials and the rest of the artisans. In some towns and cities there were also minority groups such as Dutch Calvinists, the Huguenots who had fled France after 1685, and Jews. But throughout German society there was a basic assumption that the circumstances of your birth would determine your social position for the rest of your life.[21]

In his second year in the *secunda* class at school Sebastian did even better than before, ending up second overall after the exams in July 1699, and being promoted to the *prima* at the extraordinarily young age of 14 years and four months.* In the class with him, starting after harvest time, was Georg Erdmann, an 18-year-old in similarly impoverished circumstances whose career would turn out to be far more distinguished than Sebastian's – he would become a baron (a rare and remarkable social advancement), and the Imperial Russian Resident Minister in Danzig. Both boys were dependent for their school fees on grants, known as *hospitia liberalia*, donated by affluent locals, and for some unknown reason in January 1700, half-way through the school year, both boys' stipends were withdrawn. Despite the fact that Sebastian had inherited his share of the proceeds from the sale of his parents' house in Eisenach, and that he rigorously participated in whatever money-making activities were

---

* The average age was 17½, and the oldest boy in the class was 21.

available to a schoolboy of his age (such as the triennial *Currende* singing in the streets of the town), he was now broke, and Christoph was neither able nor prepared to fund him. As Forkel wrote in his 1802 biography, Sebastian was 'thus again left destitute'. Discussions were opened with the school about where he should go from there. Certainly one option for Sebastian was to follow in the family tradition, give up his education, and take on a musical apprenticeship with one of the many Bachs in the Thuringian neighbourhood.

But the cantor, Elias Herda, had heard that there were vacancies for able choral scholars at St Michael's School in Lüneburg – which he had himself attended – and proposed the two boys to fill them, reporting on their musical and vocal talents.[22] Normally, the school accepted only younger boys able to serve for several years, or youths of 17 or 18 whose voices were mature; but with help from his colleague the school rector – who no doubt provided strong academic recommendations – Herda succeeded, and both Georg and Sebastian were immediately awarded places.

Sebastian was now confronted with the opportunity to leave his brother Christoph's home, after five years there; but it would involve an arduous journey because Lüneburg is way up in northern Germany, more than 200 miles away from Ohrdruf, and there was no way to travel except on foot. The boys prepared themselves, obtaining with the school's assistance the necessary passports and travel documents, and working out the route, what possessions they would be able to carry with them, and how they would get there in time for Easter so that they could participate in the three-day church festival as the school requested. Sebastian decided to take with him the Stainer violin he had inherited from his father.

Georg Erdmann left the lyceum in January, but Sebastian hung on until March (February that year was when Germany finally adopted the Gregorian calendar, and was therefore only 18 days long). They set off together for Lüneburg on 15 March. Sebastian celebrated his 15th birthday a week later as they toiled their way through the eastern Harz mountains to Brunswick, where in all likelihood they were given a bed and food by Sebastian's distant cousin Johann Stephan Bach, who was cantor at the cathedral. But there was no time to hang around – 95 miles still to go before they reached Lüneburg.* The vast Harz mountains area has not much changed over the last three centuries, with its huge ranges of high hills in the west, its dark forests and meadows, wide lakes, unusual plants and animals such as wild cats, owls, black storks and kingfishers.

Georg and Sebastian made it to St Michael's in Lüneburg before the end of the month, and were already singing in the school choir for the evening service on Saturday 3 April, and the 6.00 a.m. matins the following morning. They were immediately plunged into a heavy schedule of rehearsals and performances at services in the week leading up to Easter, as core members of the matins choir of 15 singers who lodged in the school.[23] Sebastian had every reason to feel singularly appreciated by the cantor, August Braun, who made it clear from the start that his treble voice and singing ability were exceptional.

Lüneburg, part of the Hanseatic League, was much the largest town Sebastian had yet seen, with a population of around 10,000, set in countryside very different from Thuringia where he had spent his childhood. North of the town, along the river Elbe, were acres of marshland, sandy soil and swampy heaths covered with small, long-haired sheep, and beehives producing honey and wax. Salt springs and limestone provided the town with a profitable trade, on the route as it was between Hanover and Hamburg.[24] The centre of the town was dominated by a newly-built castle, the secondary residence of the Duke of Brunswick-Lüneburg. St Michael's was a Latin school founded in the 14th century, serving the boys of the town and neighbourhood.

---

* They were fortunate to leave Ohrdruf when they did, because soon afterwards another plague struck the town, killing many inhabitants. Johann Christoph and his family survived it.

Forty years earlier the school had been expanded. In 1656 the duke had created next door to it a *Ritter-Academie*, a knights' school, designed to provide aristocratic boys with training in riding, shooting, dancing and fencing, as well as their normal education. The residential scholars at the school slept in a dormitory alongside the *Ritter-Academie*, and the upper-class boys were allowed to hire them to clean their clothes and polish their shoes – a small but useful additional source of income. This was Sebastian's first direct encounter with the nobility, with their etiquette, their French language and their expectations and patterns of behaviour. The diplomatic skills he learned here in ingratiating himself with aristocrats were to prove useful in his career.

He must have become aware that the nobility considered themselves virtually a different race, and that some of them even thought that later in life too they would receive differential treatment. He observed that on every public occasion they made sure their social inferiors were kept at a distance, they had their own separate pews in church, and in school their uniforms had distinctive silver epaulettes and they ate at different tables. Even when swimming in the river, they bathed in an area separated off by a raised bank. He may also have quickly realised that on the whole the nobility did not contribute very much to intellectual life, either creatively or by encouraging the work of others, and that in other countries such as France and England their peers regarded most of them as ignorant boors. But it was an inescapable fact that they controlled a very large proportion of Germany's resources, and if you were ambitious in any field you would have no choice but to seek their patronage.

But at St Michael's there was more than music, and more than acquiring social skills. The curriculum included religion, philosophy, Latin and Greek history and literature, mathematics, history, French, Italian, geography, physics, poetry, genealogy and heraldry; and most boys by the age of 18 or 19 would move on to a university to study theology, jurisprudence or medicine and thereafter take up careers as priests, lawyers or doctors. Georg Erdmann did indeed later follow this line, studying law at university and in due course ending up in the Russian diplomatic service.*

Not long after Sebastian's arrival, he was singing in the choir one day when:

> without his knowledge or will, there was once heard, with the soprano tones that he had to execute, the lower octave of the same. He kept this quite new species of voice for eight days, during which he could neither speak nor sing except in octaves. Thereupon he lost his soprano tones and with them his fine voice.[25]

Every boy has to accommodate himself at some stage to the breaking of his voice, but it is alarming if you are dependent on singing for your board and lodging. Usually a treble like Sebastian, once the upper notes became unreachable, would be able to manage for quite a while as an alto. And certainly the average age at which boys' voices broke was considerably older than his, more like 17½ or 18.[26] Clearly Sebastian was reaching puberty, as well as the completion of his education, well ahead of his contemporaries.† But he hung on to his membership of the matins choir, now singing as a bass.

In the central square of Lüneburg stood the town's main church, St John's, where the organist was Georg Böhm, born 40 years earlier in a town near Ohrdruf.[27] For some years before landing this job in 1698, Böhm had worked in Hamburg, and had become fascinated by north German music styles and the cosmopolitan atmosphere of this great city, where modern Italian and French styles of music were highly popular, including operas and theatrical dance music. He took to composition, most of it providing for the needs of St John's Church, but much

---

* See page 181. How he managed to afford to attend university remains a mystery.

† This is substantially older than the average age at which boys reach puberty today, which is around 13 or 14.

influenced by his attraction to new musical styles, writing preludes and fugues, elaborate variations on familiar hymn tunes, and keyboard suites with dance movements.

Because the musical community in the town was quite small, it was not long before Böhm encountered young Sebastian; he was immediately struck by his unusual talent, his strong devotion to the profession, and his already advanced organ skills. He befriended him, introduced him to his compositions (many of which Sebastian copied out), and recommended that he make a trip to Hamburg to explore the new styles for himself. He introduced him in particular to the pastor at St Catherine's Church there, Heinrich Elmenhorst, a successful theologian and poet, and a supporter of the Hamburg opera house which had opened in the Goose Market in 1678, and for which he had written a number of opera librettos. Sebastian soon found time to make the 30-mile trip to meet Elmenhorst, who immediately introduced him to the church's organist, Johann Adam Reincken.

Reincken was something of a local star in Hamburg. He had been organist at St Catherine's for almost 40 years, and was one of the founders of the celebrated Hamburg opera in 1678, while his orchestral and chamber compositions were much enjoyed at the informal *collegium musicum* performances that were increasingly taking place in coffee-houses and other places in the city, involving amateur as well as professional players. Sebastian found Reincken's playing highly impressive, and made several other trips to Hamburg to hear him, and to admire the huge and magnificent organ on which he played, and which he kept in almost perfect playing condition.[28] It was another revelation for Sebastian, setting standards that he was inspired to maintain for himself. Equally revelatory were the works he heard, and he began to collect them, making his own copies of pieces by Italian composers such as Corelli, Gabrieli, Vivaldi, Frescobaldi and Albinoni, and French composers such as Lully and Couperin, as well as works by his own countrymen, Schütz, Buxtehude,

Reincken himself and many others. He was becoming extremely well acquainted with the whole range of European baroque music, in addition to works from previous centuries.

After one of these trips, having stayed longer than he had planned, he was on his way back to Lüneburg with no money in his pocket when he arrived, extremely hungry, at an inn where he could smell the aroma of tempting food wafting through the air. He went around to the back, hoping to find something edible thrown out of the kitchen, but with no luck. As he sat there, feeling rather miserable, he suddenly heard a window open above, and saw two herring heads being chucked out on to the rubbish pile beside him. 'Ah,' he thought, 'at least I can chew a bit of that.' He picked them up, and to his amazement discovered that inside each head was a Danish ducat coin. Evidently some kindly person staying in the inn – perhaps one of the aristocratic students at the *Ritter-Academie* – had recognised him and decided to come to his rescue, but Sebastian never identified his benefactor. He pocketed one of the coins, and spent the other on an uplifting meal of roast beef. The other coin enabled him in due course to afford a further trip to hear Reincken in Hamburg.[29]

Although opera was becoming increasingly popular in Hamburg, and his new friends Reincken and Elmenhorst were intimately involved in it, for some reason Sebastian felt little connection with this particular genre, and no desire to tackle composition or libretto-writing, or to see himself as a performer in this field. He was certainly well aware that some kind of potentially lucrative musical career was attainable in this lively and affluent city. His exact contemporary Georg Frideric Handel, who had been born in Halle just two months before Sebastian, took the very opposite view. As one of Handel's earliest biographers put it, at almost exactly this time he began 'to discover that spirit of emulation, and passion for fame, which urged him strongly to go out into the world, and try what success he should have in it'.[30] He quickly got a job in an orchestra in Hamburg, and the path to his eventual fame was set. Sebastian, on the other hand, though he had no shortage of energy and devotion to hard work, felt an inescapable trepidation about going 'out into the world'. What he was desperate for was some source of security. The only way he could envisage this was to return to Thuringia, to follow the pattern of his forebears, and remain in contact with his numerous worthy but modest relations.

In April 1702, aged 17, Sebastian ended his schooling at St Michael's – and was now dependent for his survival on finding a job. Family connections would probably be the best way to achieve this, and repairing his somewhat damaged relationship with his brother Johann Christoph was a necessary first step. He wrote a quite long and lively capriccio in E major,[31] and inscribed on the front page 'in honorem Johann Christoph Bachii Ohrdrufiensis'. Although no doubt he still felt secretly furious at the way Christoph had stolen his laboriously-made copy of the 'moonlight manuscript',* he had to accept that family loyalty was the only dependable source of security in a troubled world; and Christoph and his wife Johanna Dorothea were suitably impressed by the piece.

But if he was to placate Johann Christoph, he should also honour his loyal friend Georg Erdmann, who had toiled all the way to Lüneburg with him two years earlier. Another much more emotional keyboard capriccio he wrote at this time was 'sopra la lontananza de il fratro dilettissimo',† probably dedicated to Georg. This is true 'programme music', with a plot line illustrating how his friends try to persuade him not to leave, warn him of the dangers of travel, and wish him *bon voyage*. The third movement, a passacaglia in F minor marked 'Adagissimo', expresses true grief.

---

* This is highly probable, since Bach clearly told the story several times to his sons, with the result that Emanuel wrote about it in detail half a century later (see pages 302-04).

† 'On the absence of the most beloved brother', BWV 992. It has long been assumed that this piece was dedicated to Sebastian's brother Johann Jacob, and its name adjusted from *fratro* (based on the Latin word *frater*) to *fratello*. But even *fratello* in Italian can mean 'comrade' as well as 'brother', and Sebastian still addressed Georg Erdmann as 'Mr Brother' in a letter to him in 1726 (see page 182).

Chapter 3

STARTING OUT

(1702–07)

Three months later, Sebastian applied for the post of organist at the main church in Sangerhausen, another ancient little Thuringian town north-east of Ohrdruf. The job became available in July 1702, after the existing organist, who was also the town judge, had died. Sebastian's application was accepted, and he prepared himself to impress the town council by composing some organ works to perform at the audition. It is not clear precisely when he went for the audition, nor which pieces these were, but one plausible possibility and probably typical example is the Prelude and Fugue in C major, BWV 531. The prelude opens with a startling solo on the foot pedals, which would have certainly impressed the councillors, although it is not very interesting harmonically, barely leaving the initial key of C. The fugue that follows is impressive too, and also contains a lively bass to demonstrate the player's skills with his feet. Another competently composed and more gentle piece he may have played for them that day is BWV 764, an arrangement (what is known as a chorale setting) of the hymn *Wie schön leuchtet uns der Morgenstern*, which follows the standard north-German style for this kind of work. He had already by then written out a large repertoire of organ pieces to choose from, many copied from other composers' works and many devised by him from his improvisations in different styles modelled on works he had studied and heard in Lüneburg.

In any event, the officials were thoroughly and unanimously impressed, and the 17-year-old was offered the job. It was an encouraging achievement for a young man of his age to land a job previously held by a veteran organist and distinguished lawyer, and clearly not only his organ skills but his hard-working and dedicated character appealed to them. But then the local duke of Saxe-Weißenfels, whose secondary residence was in Sangerhausen, intervened, deciding that he wanted the job to go to a young musician called Johann Augustin Kobelius, who had been part of his court orchestra and trained by his kapellmeister. In the unlikely event that Sebastian had not previously been aware of the aristocracy's power to manipulate the lives of ordinary people, he certainly was now. His anger and humiliation at the hands of 'the highest authority of the land' was becoming a permanent mindset. Kobelius was appointed in November, and Sebastian had to resume job-searching.[32]

No doubt his Bach relations throughout the neighbourhood put out signals for anything that might be available, and perhaps in the light of the Saxe-Weißenfels experience Sebastian was inclined to aim for a job in a court *Kapelle*, on the basis that if you have a duke as your employer you will be more secure. The elderly court organist in Weimar, Johann Effler, had known several members of the Bach family over the years, including two of Ambrosius's cousins, and it was probably through him that Sebastian finally secured his first job in January 1703, working for the ducal court of Saxe-Weimar. Family connections and string-pulling were the only way, or so it must have appeared to Sebastian, to advance one's career.

Weimar in the 17th century was a small town in a valley on the river Ilm, the capital of a principality belonging to the dukes of Saxe-Weimar since 1569. It had a rather curious and troublesome regime, owing to a family law passed in 1629 which required there to be joint rulers. When Duke Johann Ernst I died in 1683, he was succeeded by his 21-year-old son Wilhelm Ernst; and two years later his second son, Johann Ernst II, also reached the age of 21 and became joint duke. Joint rule, however, is a difficult concept even between close and affectionate siblings, and from the start these two brothers were antagonistic and competitive with each other, engaging in frequent disputes about their respective rights. Johann Ernst became so frustrated by his elder brother's dominating intentions that, in 1698, he appealed to the emperor to resolve matters by dividing the duchy between them, a proposal that after four years' consideration the emperor rejected. So the power struggles continued.

The elder brother, Wilhelm Ernst, now in his forties, led a somewhat austere and lonely life in the town's main palace, the Wilhelmsburg. In his youth he had married Princess Charlotte Marie of Saxe-Jena; they had no children, they separated, and she had recently died. His younger brother, Johann Ernst II, on the other hand, had been twice married and had several children now aged from 6 to 15. They inhabited the adjoining *Rotes Schloß* (Red Castle), with a distinctly less puritanical lifestyle.

Sebastian was housed in the Wilhelmsburg, an impressive castle erected in 1651–4 by the dukes' father, and housing a museum, an art gallery, and an exceptionally valuable library containing the archives of the dukes of Saxony of the Ernestine line. But his job was menial, involving as much valeting and other chores as playing music. In the surviving financial records of the Weimar court he is referred to as a lackey, and he was paid a measly 6 fl 18 gr [£288] a quarter, with free board and lodging.[33] This was not an optimistic start to a musical career, particularly compared with his brothers' who had landed jobs as organists by his age.

But there were some compensations. His colleagues in the *Kapelle* were an impressive group, and in particular he found himself working with an exceptionally able violinist, Johann Paul von Westhoff, whose solo violin partitas – still performed today – had been published in 1696. Von Westhoff was an international star, now in his late forties, and had performed throughout his career around much of Europe, including Italy, France and England. This was perhaps Sebastian's first encounter with a musician who had achieved Europe-wide appreciation and success, and knowing him personally and working with him may well have inspired Sebastian's own extraordinary compositions for unaccompanied violin, the six sonatas and partitas.* In charge of the whole court musical establishment, as kapellmeister, was Johann Samuel Drese, now in his late sixties, who was also a respected composer, as was his assistant, the vice-kapellmeister Georg Christoph Strattner.

The court organist, Johann Effler – who was also the dukes' financial secretary – was another asset: he had strong links with the Bach family stretching back over several decades. And not least, Sebastian felt appreciated by the younger duke, Johann Ernst, who officially oversaw the court *Kapelle* and encouraged its players to perform secular music in the Red Castle.

By the middle of the summer, after Sebastian had been lackeying in Weimar for six months, he had a stroke of luck. In Arnstadt, less than 20 miles south-east of Weimar, one of the medieval town churches, St Boniface, had burned down in 1581, and was eventually rebuilt in a new style by 1683, and renamed the Neuekirche (New Church). By the end of the century sufficient funds† had been raised to commission a new organ for the New Church, designed by Johann Friedrich Wender, a successful organ designer whose business was based in Mühlhausen. The new organ was now completed. The town's mayor, Martin Feldhaus, who was in charge of the construction of both church and organ, was an affluent businessman and property owner, now aged 69. In his mid-forties he had married Margaretha Wedemann, the daughter of the town clerk and treasurer, and two of his wife's sisters had married members of the Bach family, Johann Christoph (1642–1703) and Johann Michael (1648–1694).

---

* BWV 1001–1006. The ciaccona in the Partita in D minor (the fifth movement in BWV 1004) is a clear sign that the composer is a potential genius. In comparison with the 30 other skilful movements in this series, it reaches an extraordinary level of emotional potency.

† 800 florins [£33,600].

The normal form when a new organ was constructed, or an old one restored, was to have it tested and approved by a professional organist before the contract with the organ builder was finalised. The town and court organist, Christoph Herthum, was not only kitchen manager for the local Count of Schwarzburg-Arnstadt, Anton Günther II, but also a friend of the late Ambrosius Bach and godfather to his son Johann Christoph, Sebastian's eldest brother. Here was a further opportunity for string-pulling. Feldhaus and Herthum persuaded the count that J. S. Bach should be summoned to conduct the test. They managed this by misinforming him that Sebastian was 'Court Organist to the Prince of Saxe-Weimar'.[34]

Sebastian now had another opportunity to prepare organ pieces designed not only to test the instrument but to impress those present in the church. The kind of piece he would have regarded as appropriate was a toccata, based on improvised demonstrations of what the organ keyboard can produce, and designed to show the virtuoso capacities of the player. This was a common tradition in northern Germany, followed by composers he had encountered such as Buxtehude and Reincken. A perfect example which he may have played on this first day in the New Church in Arnstadt is the opening toccata of BWV 565, which is now one of the most famous organ pieces ever composed – not least because of its inclusion in Walt Disney's film *Fantasia* (1940).*

Sebastian was collected from Weimar in late June by a messenger with two horses, and was generously paid three separate fees: for 'compensation', for food and lodging at Arnstadt, and for testing and performing on the organ. The total came to 9 fl 4 gr [£386], a third of his annual salary in Weimar. His performance was impressive, and a month later, with the approval of the count, Feldhaus offered him the

---

* Some modern scholars have contested whether this piece was written by Bach. But Christoph Wolff, in his recent biography *Johann Sebastian Bach: The Learned Musician* (2000), argues convincingly that it was.

job of organist in the New Church. This was an important breakthrough, his first opportunity to enter the music profession in a serious post, a real compensation for the disappointment of being rejected by the Sangerhausen council, and an escape from his inferior role as a lackey in Weimar. On 9 August 1703 a contract of employment was drawn up by the count's consistory,[35] which he happily accepted; and the dukes of Saxe-Weimar raised no objection.

The contract listed his obligations, and set out his pay: 50 fl a year, plus 30 thalers [£3,560] for board and lodging – more than doubling his income. The salary was funded half from beer taxes and half from the church treasury; and the 30 thalers came from the town hospital, an old people's home where he was expected to play the organ at services. Oddly enough, there is no surviving evidence that he actually did regularly attend services at the hospital, and it seems curious that this charitable institution was required to fund more than 40 per cent of a church organist's wages. Perhaps we must conclude that it was a misappropriation of charity funds.[36]

Sebastian's other duties and responsibilities, set out in a form that was conventional for church organists, were as follows:

> Be true, faithful and obedient to the Count of Schwarzburg-Arnstadt, and show yourself industrious and reliable in the office, vocation and practice of art and science that are assigned to you.
>
> Do not mix into other affairs and functions.
>
> Appear promptly on Sundays, feast days, and other days of public divine service at the organ entrusted to you.
>
> Play the organ as is fitting.
>
> Keep a watchful eye over it and take faithful care of it.
>
> Report in time if any part of it becomes weak and give notice that the necessary repairs should be made.
>
> Do not let anyone have access to it without the foreknowledge of the Superintendent.

In general see that damage is avoided and everything kept in good order and condition.

In your daily life, cultivate the fear of God, sobriety, and the love of peace.

Avoid bad company and any distractions from your calling, and in general conduct yourself in all things towards God, High Authority, and your superiors, as befits an honour-loving servant and organist.[37]

Arnstadt is one of the oldest towns in Thuringia, dating back at least as far as the beginning of the eighth century, in the valley north of the mountainous Thuringian Forest and only a few miles east of Ohrdruf. The Counts of Schwarzburg had bought it in 1332, and over the centuries walled and enlarged it with a second church, an elegant Mannerist town hall, the Neideck Castle and other buildings, and a handsome six-arched stone bridge over the river Gera.[38] Its population was now about 3,800, and when the New Church was restored it was big enough to accommodate more than 1,000 in its broad nave, with double galleries along each side. The splendid new organ stood high up on a third gallery at the west end, with space at the sides for the choir and instrumentalists.

This really was an exceptional job for an 18-year-old organist to have acquired, in the biggest church in town, with a brand-new organ at his disposal, and a reasonably light workload confined to four services a week plus feast days. Moreover, he was almost as well paid as the town and court organist Christoph Herthum, who had played a vital part in his recruitment. And he was also provided with his own bellows operator, Michael Ernst Frobenius, paid for by the consistory.[39] Sebastian plunged into his role with energy and enthusiasm, devoting a lot of his time to writing out organ compositions, particularly chorale preludes played at the beginning and end of services and introducing the hymns sung by the congregation.

The choir for the New Church was a group of students at the town's lyceum, boys mostly in their early teens, selected by the cantor of the town's main church, Ernst Dietrich Heindorff, and supervised by Andreas Börner, the organist at the Lower Church. Why Sebastian was not required to be in charge of his own church's choir – as is clear from the terms of his contract of employment – is a mystery, perhaps explicable only on the grounds that Börner had served as interim organist there before Sebastian was appointed. But the arrangement had a strange effect on him. He must have felt alienated, detached, and irritated by the boastfulness and overconfidence of some of the older students, particularly those already in their twenties. The local community began to be aware that the New Church organist did not get on well with his own choir.

By the middle of 1705 Sebastian was just beginning his third year in the job. Late in the evening of 4 August he was walking past the town hall in the main square, on his way home from the castle, accompanied by his cousin Barbara Catharina Bach, when he saw six students sitting on a wall known as the *Langenstein* (long stone).[40] Suddenly one of them, a young man called Geyersbach who was a bassoon player, jumped up holding a stick, and angrily shouted at Sebastian:

'Why the hell did you abuse me, Herr Bach?'

'What do you mean? I haven't abused you. I don't abuse people, I go my way in peace.'

'You did, you called me a prick of a bassoonist,' said Geyersbach.*
'Or do you think you weren't insulting me but insulting my bassoon? That's an insult to me. Why the hell are you such a dirty dog?'

Geyersbach lunged at him with his stick, and Sebastian tried to draw his sword, but the two ended up struggling on the ground until the other

---

* Geyersbach accused Sebastian of calling him a *Zippelfagottist*, which is traditionally translated as 'nanny-goat bassoonist'. Christoph Wolff (p. 84) translates it as 'greenhorn bassoonist'. But the 32-volume *Deutsches Wörterbuch* (dictionary) makes clear that *Zippel*, in Thuringian dialect, means penis. This is confirmed by Klaus Eidam in *Das wahre Leben des Johann Sebastian Bach* (Munich, 1999).

students managed to separate them.

'You're in serious trouble, Geyersbach,' said Sebastian as he rose to his feet. 'I won't condescend to have duels with you. I'm going to report you to the consistory tomorrow.'

And so he did. Ten days later there was a hearing in the town hall, and Geyersbach was asked to respond to Sebastian's statement of what had occurred that night. He vehemently denied that he had attacked him. All he acknowledged was that he had seen Sebastian, smoking his pipe, walking across the street, and asked him whether he admitted that he had called him a prick of a bassoonist. Unable to deny it, Sebastian had proceeded to draw his dagger, and Geyersbach had had no choice but to defend himself. One of the other students, called Hoffmann, stated that it was not clear to him who had made the first physical assault. The hearing was adjourned, and resumed five days later. Of course, small dagger- and sword-carrying was normal among grown-up men throughout Europe in the early 18th century. And at the end of Sebastian's life he stilled owned a silver dagger.*

On 19 August, the council asked Sebastian to provide proof that Geyersbach, and not he, had initiated the brawl. Clearly Barbara Catharina was in a position to provide this, and Sebastian rather sarcastically asked them if they thought a female person's evidence would be sufficient. The members felt somewhat affronted, and threw another accusation at him. 'You should certainly have refrained from calling Geyersbach a prick of a bassoonist. Such gibes always lead to this kind of unpleasantness, particularly since you're known not to get on well with the school pupils, and you claim that you're not responsible for their orchestral playing – which is not the case because your duty is to help out in all music-making.'

Sebastian was on his back foot. 'I wouldn't refuse, if only there was a musical director in charge of them,' he said, to which one of the

---

* See page 219.

councillors replied, 'You must learn to live with imperfections, Herr Bach. You must get on better terms with the students, and avoid making their lives miserable.' It was agreed that Barbara Catharina should be summoned to the next meeting.

On 21 August she was sworn in, and gave her account of the event. She fully supported Sebastian's version, adding that Geyersbach had first hit him in the face, that Sebastian had then thrust up his dagger without removing it from its scabbard, they had scuffled, Geyersbach had dropped his stick, and then the other students had pulled them apart. She also denied that Sebastian had been smoking a pipe.

Geyersbach spoke up again, this time admitting that he had struck out, but claiming that he could prove Sebastian had also struck him because his vest still showed the holes caused by the punctures. By this time the councillors were feeling thoroughly frustrated by the inquiry, and announced that, since no town ministers were present, Sebastian and Geyersbach would both be temporarily released, and informed in due course if a formal verdict was reached.

It seems likely that Sebastian's sense of insecurity in the face of his elders was a growing feature of his character. He wanted their approval, but he was damned if he would bend over backwards to get it. He must have felt much the same about his employers, whose judgements he often thought trivial and petty, although he was only too aware of the power they held over people of his social class. He had no choice but to try to repress the harsh resentments building up inside him. His resolve was to stick rigidly to the rules, and in any future disputes to rely on his adherence to them.

And soon there was indeed another dispute. In the autumn of 1705 he resolved to make a trip to Lübeck, a town even further north than Hamburg, where his hero the Danish-born Dietrich Buxtehude, the best-known representative of the north German school of music, was organist and administrator at the church of St Mary. Buxtehude's regular 'evening music' concerts in the church, in which he performed organ pieces, cantatas and oratorios, were famously popular events, and Sebastian was determined to find an opportunity to hear some of them. He obtained permission from his superintendent to be absent for four weeks, on the basis that his competent cousin Johann Ernst Bach, the eldest son of Ambrosius's late twin brother, would take his place.

But the permission was obtained by deceit. Sebastian knew perfectly well that he did not have the funds to travel this long distance – 50 miles further than his epic journey from Ohrdruf to Lüneburg when he was 15 – on horseback or by stage-coach, that he would therefore have to walk, and that the journey there and back would by itself take a month. The trouble was that he also knew his employers would not grant him more than four weeks' absence, if only on principle; but he was determined to do it none the less, whatever the consequences.

In terms of his musical education, the trip was hugely productive. He attended a number of Buxtehude's concerts, probably including performances of two cantata-like works commemorating the death of Leopold I and the accession of his son Joseph I as Holy Roman Emperor. These had a powerful effect on Sebastian's own conception of how to compose works celebrating human events and relationships. He had already composed two such keyboard pieces himself, the capriccios dedicated to Georg Erdmann and his brother Christoph.* Also in Lübeck he heard many of Buxtehude's performances on the organ, and transcribed a number of his compositions. But it was Buxtehude as an overall role model that most affected Sebastian: his fame as an organist and composer, his entrepreneurial energy in promoting and managing concert performances, the originality and inventiveness of his compositions, his organ skills, and the broad range of his contacts in the music profession.

Two years earlier, Buxtehude, by then in his mid-sixties, had spread the word that he planned to retire and was seeking a suitable successor

---

* See page 42.

at St Mary's. Among the applicants interested in taking over from this distinguished organist and composer in the free imperial city of Lübeck were two talented young musicians from Hamburg, who paid him a visit in 1703: Johann Mattheson and Georg Frideric Handel. The problem was that Buxtehude required that whoever took on the role should also marry his eldest daughter, Anna Margaretha. This may seem a curious prerequisite for an organist, but Buxtehude himself had begun the tradition when he secured the post in 1668 by marrying the daughter of his predecessor, Franz Tunder. Neither Mattheson nor Handel succumbed to the temptation, possibly because Anna Margaretha Buxtehude was considerably older than either of them, and the post was eventually assigned after Buxtehude's death in 1707 to his assistant, Johann Christian Schieferdecker, who did indeed marry her. It is far from implausible that during his visit in 1705 Sebastian too was offered a chance to secure this lucrative and highly reputable post. He didn't take it, possibly because like Handel he did not want to marry an older woman, or more probably because he did not feel confident enough to emigrate again to northern Germany.

Although he had been permitted absence of four weeks only, he was in Lübeck for almost eight, and did not return to Arnstadt until nearly three months after leaving. His cousin Johann Ernst had done nothing wrong in acting as his substitute at the New Church during his absence, but the consistory – aggravated by the previous dispute over the Geyersbach fight and Sebastian's dismissal of responsibility for the choir – summoned him to a hearing, on 21 February 1706. It became clear that the issue in their minds was less to do with the prolonged absence, or the deception about his travelling time, than about the way he was actually carrying out his job.

Sebastian stated to the council that he had made the journey 'in order to comprehend one thing and another about his art',[41] and that he hoped that the organ-playing had been so taken care of by the one he had engaged for the purpose (Johann Ernst) that no complaint could be entered on that account. This response struck them immediately as arrogant and unapologetic, and elicited a heap of criticisms about the way he conducted the church services and performed on the organ. There were too many 'curious' variations on the chorale, too many strange tones 'mingled in it', and too many elaborations in his accompaniment of the hymn tunes, which left the congregation confused.

> In the future, if he wished to introduce a *tonus peregrinus*, he was to hold it out, and not to turn too quickly to something else or, as had hitherto been his habit, even play a *tonus contrarius*.

This was not the first time he had been censured; his superintendent had some time before told him not to play such long and elaborate introductions to the hymns, and he had responded by immediately 'falling into the other extreme' and making them too short. But the main charge against him was the lack of choir-singing and orchestral playing in the church services, which could only be the consequence of his unwillingness to take on the students. This will not do, they said. 'If you are unwilling to take responsibility for the concerted music, you must state this categorically so we can make other arrangements and employ someone who will.'

Sebastian finally began to see that not only were his musical talents unappreciated, but his job was under threat; and he rather weakly responded by saying that if he were provided with a competent conductor he would perform well enough. The consistory announced that he would be given eight days in which to make his decision and declare it to them.

They then called up the student who was prefect and choir leader, Johann Andreas Rambach, and reproved him too, not only for contributing to the disorderly relations between Bach and the choir, but for going down into the wine cellar the previous Sunday while the superintendent was preaching his sermon. Rambach earnestly apologised for the latter, but claimed that it was not fair that Bach should blame him for the choir's deficiencies, because the conducting was actually carried out by another student, called Schmidt. Their response was to tell him that unless his behaviour radically improved he would lose his prefecture; that if he had complaints against the organist he should declare them to the authorities and 'not take the law into his own hands'; and finally that he was to be punished with a two-hour detention for the next four days. But they were certainly not siding with Bach, nor considering his request for a competent conductor.

So how was Sebastian to deal with these repeated fracas with what must have seemed a thoroughly unsympathetic body of employers? His reluctance to take on responsibility for the choir was clearly unwise, but he could not bring himself to compromise. He could only concentrate on his own music-making, and keep his ear open for opportunities to find another job. His post as organist at the New Church might seem secure to some, and indeed enviable to many young musicians of his generation, but he was increasingly resentful of and irritated by the limitations imposed on him, and the lack of appreciation of the work he did and the music he composed. He began to see Arnstadt as an oppression rather than a source of personal security.

Later that year, since the issue about the New Church choir had still not been resolved, the consistory summoned him again. This time they gave him a final opportunity to declare 'whether he is willing to make music with the students as he has already been instructed to do, or not'. They tried to express the matter in more conciliatory terms, pointing out that there was no shame or disgrace in a church organist's making music with the students assigned to him, and how beneficial it was to their musical education. But once again he would not compromise, and only stated that he would consider the matter and reply to them in writing in due course.

HARMONY AND DISCORD

This was not a wise or diplomatic response, and immediately drew another accusation from the consistory: what right did he have to have recently allowed a strange young woman to enter the choir loft and let her make music there? To this he simply stated that he had informed the church vicar, Justus Christian Uthe, about this, implying that he had his permission.

No one knows the identity of the young woman Sebastian took up to the organ loft. She may just have been a professional singer whom he could have met at one of the count's concerts or opera performances at Neideck Castle. Sebastian never revealed her identity. But women were clearly much in his mind now. Martin Feldhaus, the mayor who had secured Sebastian's job in the first place, had three girls living with him, the orphaned daughters of his sister-in-law Catharina Wedemann, who had married Johann Michael Bach, and died in 1704. One of these girls was Barbara Catharina Bach, who had witnessed Sebastian's brawl with Geyersbach when they were walking home together from Neideck Castle. Her younger sister, Maria Barbara Bach, was Feldhaus's god-daughter, and it was she with whom he was now beginning to fall in love.

Or was it love? The inescapable fact was that Sebastian's traumatic experience of deaths in his family, becoming orphaned at the age of nine, being undermined and rejected by his brother Christoph and sent 200 miles away to Lüneburg, had left him with a profound sense of insecurity and a desperate need to establish some kind of stable life. The only way he could conceive of achieving this was through the myriad Bach family connections, and Feldhaus was the ideal source.

We need a family tree (see p. 59) to comprehend the complexities of these connections – and Sebastian began to compile one[42] (which, as we shall later see, he would subsequently extend to cover at least all the male and musical members of the Bach family).

Johann Wedemann, who had been town scribe in Arnstadt until his death in 1684, was the father of five daughters, the two eldest of whom married first cousins of Sebastian's father Ambrosius (sons of Heinrich Bach [1615–

57

92]). Maria Elisabeth married Johann Christoph Bach, the Eisenach organist with whom Sebastian had spent such instructive time in his early years;[43] and Catharina married his younger brother Johann Michael Bach, organist at Gehren. It was their three orphaned daughters, Friedelena Margaretha, Barbara Catharina and Maria Barbara, who were now living with Martin Feldhaus. The third Wedemann daughter, Margaretha, Catharina's twin, was Martin Feldhaus's wife. The fourth Wedemann daughter, Susanna Barbara, married her town-scribe father's assistant, Johann Gottfried Bellstedt (whose brother Hermann, the town scribe in Mühlhausen, was shortly to contribute usefully to Sebastian's career). And finally the fifth Wedemann daughter, Regina, would later marry the vicar of St Bartholomew's in the neighbouring village of Dornheim, who was to preside at Sebastian's wedding.

Marriage was what he had in mind, not only escape from Arnstadt. And it was a brave idea, because he was well aware that married life involved many new responsibilities, children, many new financial demands – and 22 was an exceptionally young age for a man to marry.[44] But it seemed to offer the security and stability for which he yearned. Maria Barbara was nearly a year older than Sebastian, clearly fond of him, and her close connection with the Feldhaus family was a potential asset. She was his second cousin, she was an orphan like him, and like him she had been brought up on music. And it was perfectly normal for marriage to be seen as an affair of good sense rather than romantic love.

What provided his escape from Arnstadt was the death in December 1706 of the organist at St Blasius's Church in Mühlhausen, news of which reached him through Johann Hermann Bellstedt. He immediately sent word to his Mühlhausen contacts – who included Johann Friedrich Wender, the organ builder who had created the instrument in the New Church – that he was willing to be auditioned for the post, and he was requested to appear, with vocal compositions of his own making, on Easter Sunday, 24 April 1707. He likely once again recruited his cousin Johann Ernst to take over the organ-playing in the New Church in his absence.

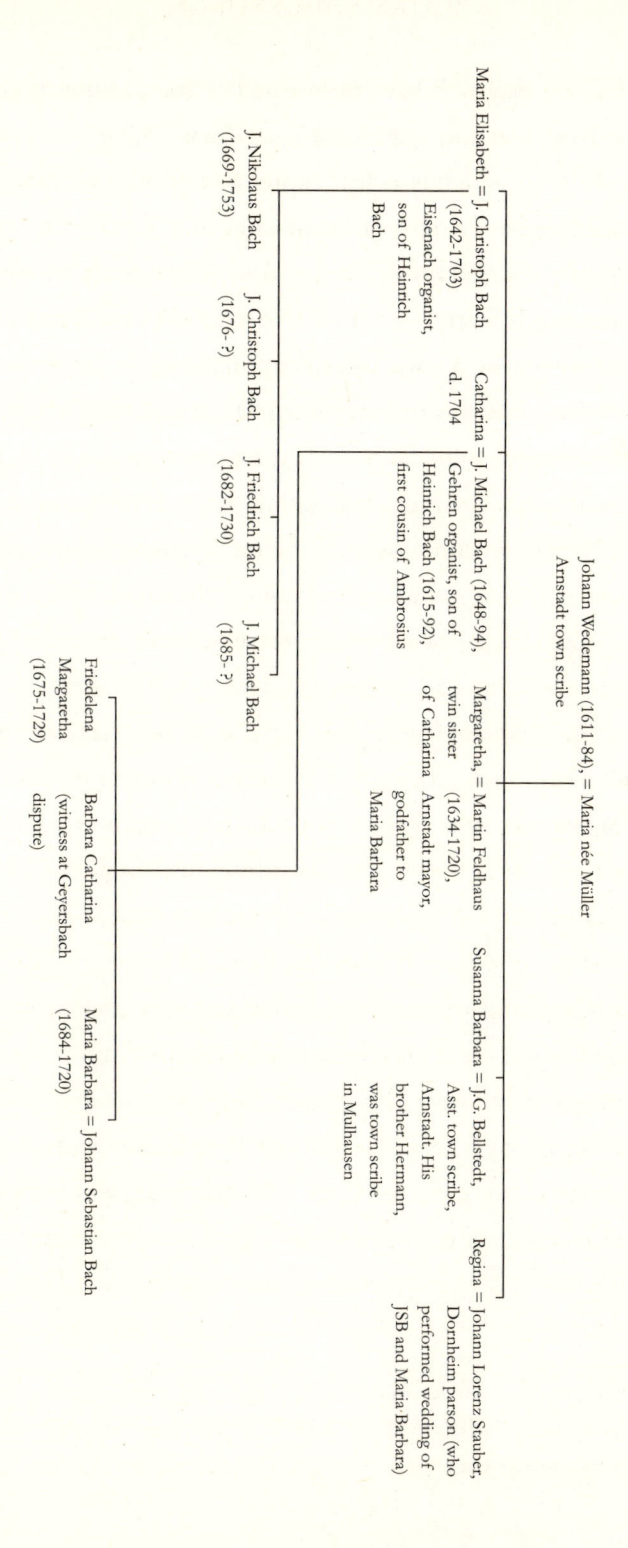

Johann Wedemann (1611-84), = Maria née Müller
Arnstadt town scribe

Maria Elisabeth = J. Christoph Bach (1642-1703), Eisenach organist, son of Heinrich Bach

Catharina = J. Michael Bach (1648-94), d. 1704 Gehren organist, son of Heinrich Bach (1615-92), first cousin of Ambrosius

Margaretha, twin sister of Catharina

= Martin Feldhaus (1634-1720), Arnstadt mayor, godfather to Maria Barbara

Susanna Barbara = J.G. Bellstedt, Asst. town scribe, Arnstadt. His brother Hermann, was town scribe in Mulhausen

Regina = Johann Lorenz Stauber, Dornheim parson (who performed wedding of JSB and Maria Barbara)

J. Nikolaus Bach (1669-1753)

J. Christoph Bach (1676-?)

J. Friedrich Bach (1682-1730)

J. Michael Bach (1685-?)

Friedelena Margaretha (1675-1729)

Barbara Catharina (witness at Geyersbach dispute)

Maria Barbara (1684-1720) = Johann Sebastian Bach

The piece he may well have performed at the audition is one of his earliest surviving cantatas, *Christ lag in Todes Banden* ('Christ lay in the bonds of death', BWV 4), which is a clear expression of how his compositional skills had developed. There is no great originality or inventiveness in the piece, although it is skilfully constructed in the standard mode of 17th-century cantatas. It starts with a brief orchestral introduction (called a sinfonia), followed by a variation of settings of the seven verses of a traditional Easter hymn written by Martin Luther: for the choir, a treble* and alto duet, a tenor solo, the chorus again, a bass solo, a treble and tenor duet, and finally a four-part chorale setting of the kind that became typical in all his later cantatas and passions. The most striking of the movements is the bass solo, number 6, which has quite a theatrical, operatic feel to it, surely influenced by the words of the verse, which ends thus:

Das Blut zeichnet unsere Tür,	The blood marks our doors,
Das hält der Glaub dem Tode für,	Faith holds it before death,
Der Würger kann uns nicht mehr schaden.	The murderer can no longer harm us.
Hallelujah!	Alleluia!

This is the notion to which Sebastian felt such a close connection: that for the faithful, death is a triumphant escape from the miseries of life. The moment of surprise comes with the mention of death, when the bass voice plunges from C down to F an octave and a half below. And immediately there is a sense of triumph and joy in the expression of the following line, with *nicht* ('no') repeated four times, followed by 'Alleluia'.

---

* Although 'soprano' merely means the higher voice, it is now generally associated with female singers. So 'treble' is used to remind us that only male singers were allowed to perform in 18th-century church services.

The Mühlhausen council were suitably impressed by Sebastian's performance, and he was offered the job after a further meeting with them in June, to negotiate his employment terms. The church authorities in Arnstadt appear to have been rather relieved by his decision to resign, and at a consistory meeting on 29 June he expressed his thanks to them for his past employment, and formally returned the keys of the New Church organ.

Chapter 4

MARRIAGE IN MÜHLHAUSEN

(1707–08)

By the time Sebastian took over the post of organist at St Blasius's Church in Mühlhausen in June 1707, at the age of 22, he had already accumulated an extensive collection of compositions, based on his own organ improvisations and on the wide range of works by composers he had studied at Lüneburg, including not only his countrymen such as Reincken, Buxtehude and Pachelbel, but many French and Italian composers too. He immersed himself in these works because he was completely addicted to mastering the intricacies of contrapuntal music – music involving the combination and interweaving of melodies. He had a natural ability for exploring and performing the musical structures of his time, and this increasingly encouraged him to study them, copy them, and develop them further. He was constantly testing his own skills, for example by taking a theme and its countersubject, and developing it in a number of ways to produce different pieces based on the same original theme. The most vivid example of his passion for exploring the creative potential of themes can be found in his hundreds of harmonisations of simple hymn tunes and folk-songs. The chorales in his masses and cantatas are the most familiar of these creations, but he had already written a great many arrangements of familiar hymn tunes, mostly for organ accompaniment.

The fugue, which had been much explored by the 17th-century composers he admired and studied, had a particular intellectual attraction for him because it was constructed according to a range of quite strict rules. A fugue begins with the 'exposition', which means the entry of the individual voices with the opening melody one by one; and then one or more 'episodes' in which the voices develop new themes or variations of the original one; and finally a return to the original opening melody and key. There are many other intricate and elaborate rules for the construction of fugues, and part of the joy of fugal composition is to explore ways of breaking them constructively, something Sebastian increasingly found himself able to do. In many of his early fugal compositions, such as the organ and harpsichord fugues based on works by Albinoni, Torelli, Reincken and Legrenzi,* he developed combined or double counterpoint, in which the different voices followed different themes at the same time, and interchanged or inverted them as they proceeded.

So for him these musical developments were a kind of intellectual challenge, involving fixed rules that can be subtly and creatively expanded, and existing music by respected composers that can be redesigned and developed within the rules. His early compositions are full of laudable merits – vitality, meticulous workmanship, with sound and well-knit harmonies, and ingenious and effective counterpoint. What is largely absent, as is the case for many composers in their early stages, is true originality, and true emotion. For him these qualities lay ahead, and the roots from which they sprang would be his exploration of the cantata, motivated by the words of the text.†

Mühlhausen was one of the largest towns in Thuringia, a free city under the direct control of the emperor, located on the river Unstrut, 35 miles northwest of Arnstadt. The upper town, originally called the *Neustadt* (new town), contained an Augustine convent and several Lutheran churches, of which the *Marienkirche* (St Mary's Church), one of the largest and grandest sacral

---

* BWV 579, 944, 946, 950, 954, 965 and 966.

† His earliest surviving cantata, *Nach der, Herr, verlanget mich* (BWV 150), was probably written while he was in Arnstadt, and is clearly influenced by Buxtehude, with its ciaccona for choir, bassoon and strings. This cantata is technically skilful, but a gloomy work, reflecting a text about the burdens of life on earth.

buildings in Thuringia, was the principal; and in the lower town, the *Altstadt*, the main church was St Blasius's.[45] Both had schools attached to them, each with their own pastor, organist and choirmaster. In a narrow street between the old and new towns stood the vast *Rathaus* (town hall). The town was partly walled, with tall towers, and its winding streets were lined with timber-framed houses. But a month before Sebastian's arrival there, in May 1707, a devastating fire had destroyed a large part of the town, and caused much economic and political distress among the inhabitants and their leaders.

Sebastian's basic tasks at St Blasius's were not dissimilar to those he had performed at the New Church in Arnstadt, and nor was his pay: 85 gulden [£3,750] a year, plus an allowance of grain, wood and kindling.[46] But there were additional duties which he inherited from his predecessors, Johann Georg Ahle and his father Johann Rudolf, who between them had held the job non-stop for the preceding 52 years until Johann Georg's death in December 1706. Both the Ahles had been prolific composers of vocal music and had also served as town councillors, and Johann Georg had even been appointed poet laureate by Emperor Leopold I in 1680. So one of the traditions in the town was that the organist at St Blasius's was responsible for musical celebrations of civic events, such as the annual election of the town council. Sebastian welcomed this, seeing it not only as a step up the social ladder but as an opportunity to extend his composing skills, and to earn extra income.

Money was increasingly crucial: Maria Barbara Bach had accepted his proposal of marriage and they had begun to plan their wedding in October. In August there was a further stroke of luck: Sebastian's uncle Tobias Lämmerhirt, his mother's brother, died and left him the sum of 50 florins [£2,100]. Maria Barbara was still living in Arnstadt with her aunt Margaretha Feldhaus, so the marriage banns were read there, and a wedding licence issued by Count Anton Günther II in which the normal fees were remitted – a sign that Sebastian's Arnstadt troubles had not undermined Martin Feldhaus's or his own reputation in the town. The wedding took place on 17 October,[47] conducted by the widowed Reverend Lorenz Stauber, pastor at the village of Dornheim, less than a mile to the east of Arnstadt. Stauber himself later married Maria Barbara's aunt, Regina Wedemann.

Another important difference between Arnstadt and Mühlhausen was that Sebastian was responsible not to the clergy and schoolmasters, under the authority of the count, but to the free city's elected council. Elections took place annually, and in early 1708 he was commissioned to compose a large-scale work to celebrate the inauguration of the new city council, and in particular the two town mayors, Adolf Strecker and Georg Adam Steinbach. The piece was performed on Saturday 4 February in the Marienkirche, a week later he was paid a generous 3 thalers [£150] for it, and the council had it published at their own expense by the local printer, Tobias David Brückner.* It was described on the title page as a 'Congratulatory Church Motet', though it is now known as a cantata, BWV 71, entitled *Gott ist mein König* ('God is my king'), a quotation from Psalm 74: 12. He set it for an exceptionally large range of instruments: three trumpets, two recorders, two oboes, bassoon, strings (violins, violas, cellos and bass), timpani and organ, accompanying a choir with four soloists.

As with a great many of Bach's surviving cantatas, no evidence exists as to who produced or compiled the text. Some historians have speculated that he might have written the unattributed libretti himself, but the generally accepted view today is that, although from time to time he made his own alterations to existing texts, he usually obtained them from local poets whose identities are unknown. The possibility that he actually considered himself capable of writing poems or any other form of literature that would inspire a vocal work is for some reason no longer thought plausible. And yet it is hard to read the text for *Gott ist mein König* without speculating that there is an extraordinarily autobiographical echo throughout the first six movements.

The libretto is a combination of short quotations from the Bible, a stanza from a well-known hymn written in 1630 by Johann Heermann entitled *O Gott, du frommer Gott*, and three other original verses. Bear in mind as you read it that it

---

* Only two choral works by Bach were published in his lifetime, and this was the first.

is designed to celebrate the election of two elderly chief town magistrates, and to honour Emperor Joseph I to whom they were responsible.

1. God is my King of old, working salvation in the midst of the earth. (Psalm 74: 12)

2. I am this day fourscore years old … wherefore then should thy servant be yet a burden? Let thy servant turn back again, that I may die in mine own city, and be buried by the grave of my father and of my mother. (II Samuel 19: 35, 37)

Should I in this world
carry my life further,
through many sour steps
pressing forward into old age,
than grant mercy for sin
and protect me from shame,
so that I might bear
my grey hair with honour.
(v. 6 of Johann Heermann's hymn *O Gott, du frommer Gott*)

3. As thy days, so shall thy strength be, and God is with thee in all that thou doest. (Deuteronomy 33: 25, and Genesis 21: 22)

4. The day is thine, the night also is thine: thou hast prepared the light and the sun. Thou hast set all the borders of the earth. (Psalm 74: 16–17)

5. Through powerful strength
You maintain our borders,
here peace must glow,
though murder and the storm of war

are raised up everywhere.
Though crown and sceptre tremble,
You have caused salvation
through powerful strength.

6. O deliver not the soul of thy turtledove unto the multitude of the wicked. (Psalm 74: 19)

7. The new regime
in every course
crown with blessing!
Peace, quiet and good health
must always stand by the side
of the new regime.
Happiness, health, and great victory
must newly and daily
delight you, Joseph,
so that all lands and places
may constantly enjoy
happiness, health, and great victory!

In any event, whether or not Bach chose the biblical quotations and hymn verse and wrote the other verses himself, what his settings make abundantly clear is the significance the words had for him, particularly their references to God's role as the ancient king, working for human salvation; to ageing, and the yearning to be reunited with his parents in the town of his birth; and to his faith in God as protection from the wicked. Much the most beautiful movement, interestingly, is the sixth, a harmonically adventurous and haunting chorus in C minor, based on the first half of Psalm 74: 19 with its references to the poor and needy. It is as if these words had suddenly affected Sebastian's own feelings about the town council and its role in society, about the ruthless selfishness of government and the vulnerability of ordinary people.

Another cantata he wrote around this time, probably for a funeral, is known as the 'Actus Tragicus',* entitled *Gottes Zeit ist die allerbeste Zeit* ('God's time is the best of all times', BWV 106). Here too the text comprises a number of short quotations from the Bible, and verses from two familiar hymns; and here too there is no evidence as to who compiled it. But what is clear is that Sebastian felt inspired again by the lesson that death lies all around us, and the only solace is our faith in Jesus. A very striking passage appears in the fourth section of the second movement, where the three lower voices in the chorus sing the words from Ecclesiasticus 14: 17 'The decree from of old is, "You must surely die!"', and then the treble soloist enters with an uplifting arioso, singing almost the last words in the entire Bible, from Revelation 22: 20: 'Even so, come, Lord Jesus.' And the way this short piece ends is intensely dramatic, with the treble's prayer unaccompanied for two whole bars, followed by a prolonged bar of silence.

'Actus Tragicus' is indeed an extraordinarily sophisticated expression, through music, of how human beings have always tried to reconcile life and death by their belief in an after-life. The biblical quotations, in the order in which he uses them, reveal all too clearly how he has been struggling over 14 years to come to terms with the loss of his parents, by believing that the world of pain and tribulation in which we live is in essence a preparation for paradise hereafter. In the opening chorus, the first four statements are as follows:

> For in him we live, and move, and have our being. (Acts 17: 28)
>
> So, teach us to number our days, that we may apply our hearts unto wisdom. (Psalm 90: 12)
>
> Set thine house in order, for thou shalt die, and not live. (Isaiah 38: 1)
>
> For the covenant from the beginning is, Thou shalt die the death. (Ecclesiasticus 14: 17)

---

* This title was probably not Bach's. It appears in the earliest surviving manuscript of the work, which was copied by an unknown musician and dated 'Leipzig, 1768'.

Then the treble sings 'Even so, come, Lord Jesus', and all the other voices and instruments die out and leave him in lonely fragility, followed by silence – for which Sebastian inserted a blank bar with a pause written over it (known as *fermata*). We are now exactly at the centre of the cantata.

The second half focuses on the only optimism that grieving Christians can attain: an alto sings 'Into thine hand I commit my spirit; thou hast redeemed me, O Lord God of Truth'. (Psalm 31: 5); and a tenor quotes Jesus' words from Luke 23: 43, 'Today shalt thou be with me in paradise'. Then the chorus re-enters, singing the first verse of Martin Luther's famous hymn *Mit Fried und Freud ich fahr dahin* ('With peace and joy I depart'), followed by a chorale from another hymn, ascribing glory to God, and ending with an exuberant and lively amen.

So it would be wrong to assume that gloom and despondency were Sebastian's only inspirations, or that his working life in Mühlhausen was only devoted to handling the church music. The surviving parts of his Quodlibet (BWV 524) vividly reveal some more conventional characteristics, including his sense of humour, his views of family and social life, and his enjoyment of controversy and political incorrectness. The piece is written for treble, alto, tenor and bass accompanied by harpsichord, and the burlesque text is packed with comic references to daily life, travel by sea, clothes, food, horses, money, foxes and much else. It must have been composed for a wedding – and possibly a family wedding, because there is a mention of Salome (*wie sieht die Salome so sauer um den Schnabel?* – 'why does Salome look so down in the mouth?'), who could be his sister. The riotous words represent the style of Thuringian humour, and the accompanying music neatly reflects this.*

Quodlibet, based on Latin, means 'what pleases you'. There was a long tradition in Germany, going back at least to the 15th century, of weaving familiar tunes into musical performances as a kind of joke, a representation of humour that able jazz players still effect today. The

---

* Some academics suggest this piece was not composed by Bach, but copied by him.

Bachs, at their annual family reunions,* are reported by J. N. Forkel to have performed a quodlibet each year. As he puts it:

> They sang popular songs, the contents of which were partly comic and partly naughty, all together and extempore, but in such a manner that the several parts thus extemporised made a kind of harmony together, the words, however, in every part being different.[48]

So Sebastian was thoroughly familiar with this medium.

He also earned extra income by performing regularly at several neighbouring churches, including the St Mary and Magdalen School for girls, where the church housed a new single-manual organ built by Johann Friedrich Wender, the designer of the excellent instrument in the Arnstadt New Church. But money remained a source of continuing anxiety, particularly since he was now married and Maria Barbara was keen to start having children. No contraceptives then existed, and their only way of postponing her getting pregnant – which she did five months later, in April 1708 – was through what we might now call 'natural family planning', which required tough restrictions on their intercourse. But Sebastian had the will-power to impose them.

He was also well aware that the organ in St Blasius's, though much larger, was in a somewhat deficient state, despite having been rebuilt and enlarged by Wender in the 1690s, and that it was his responsibility under his conditions of employment to report these defects. In February 1708, soon after the performance of his Congratulatory Church Motet *Gott is mein König,* he produced an eleven-point written summary of the repairs he considered either essential or to be recommended, involving improvements in the wind supply, and the replacement of various stops with new ones to improve the organ's variety of sounds.[49] The most drastic change he proposed was the installation of a third manual keyboard, called the *Brustpositiv*, with seven varied wood and tin stops designed to increase the organ's range for solo

---

* See page 19.

performances. He presented the document on the 21st to the parish council, who immediately asked Wender to quote for the labour and material costs involved. His estimate was a massive 250 thalers [£12,000]. Only two days later a deal was negotiated, involving the acquisition by Wender of a second small organ in the choir loft, for a total of 200 thalers. Sebastian had every reason to feel that he had earned much respect from the parish council during the eight months he had been working for them, since they were immediately willing to spend such a large sum on his recommendations, and had clearly appreciated his Motet earlier in the month.

Another cantata he wrote that spring, at the request of his friend Georg Christian Eilmar, the pastor at the Marienkirche, is *Aus der Tiefen rufe ich, Herr, zu dir* ('Out of the depths have I cried unto thee, O Lord', BWV 131), based on all eight verses of Psalm 130, and two verses from the hymn *Herr Jesu Christ, du höchstes Gut*. The whole piece is an extraordinary expression of gloom. Although the psalm has an element of optimism with its references to God's forgiveness and the possibility of redemption, the two hymn verses are all about grief, death, sin and lamentation. These words are set in G minor virtually throughout, in a complex series of movements for chorus and bass and tenor arias, with fugal passages and changes of tempo; and to express a touch of optimism the final choral fugue ends in G major, with the words *Und er wird Israel erlösen aus allen seinen Sünden* ('And he shall redeem Israel from all his iniquities'), and long, flowing passages on the word 'redeem'.

But when, only four months later, in June, Sebastian heard word of a new job opportunity in Weimar, he could not resist the temptation to apply for it. Two factors would have played a key part in his mind. First, the salary on offer for the post of court organist to the Duke Wilhelm Ernst, 150 florins [£6,300] a year, would mean a massive 75 per cent increase in his income; and secondly, to return with a respectable job to the town where only five years earlier he had been employed as a ducal lackey would surely improve his self-respect. Another influential factor was the prospect of working with fellow professionals. At least this would avoid the tiresome responsibilities of coping with school choirs and irritating clerics which had caused him such stress in Arnstadt.

This step forward was, of course, due once again to family connections. Johann Effler, who had held the post for many years, and secured Sebastian's first job there in 1703, had finally decided to retire. The organ in the castle church had recently been restored, and Effler invited Sebastian to come and inspect and approve it. Duke Wilhelm Ernst was present when he performed on it, and was suitably impressed; then and there he was offered the job.

Sebastian returned to Mühlhausen and immediately wrote a long – and revealing – letter of resignation to his employers:[50]

> To the everywhere honoured and most highly esteemed parishioners of the Church of St Blasius, a humble memorial: Your magnificence, honoured and noble sirs, honoured and learned sirs, honoured and wise sirs, most gracious patrons and gentlemen!
>
> The manner in which Your Magnificence and my most respected patrons most graciously engaged my humble self for the post of organist of the Church of St Blasius when it became vacant a year ago, and your graciousness in permitting me to enjoy a better living, I must ever acknowledge with obedient thanks. Even though I should always have liked to work towards the goal, namely, a well-regulated church music, to the glory of God and in conformance with your wishes, and would, according to my small means, have helped out as much as possible with the church music that is growing up in almost every township, and often better than the harmony that is fashioned here, and therefore have acquired from far and wide, not without cost, a good store of the choicest church compositions, just as I have always fulfilled my duty in delivering the project for remedying the faults of the organ and should gladly have discharged every other duty of my office – yet it has not been possible to accomplish all this without hindrance, and there are, at present, hardly

any signs that in the future a change may take place (although it would rejoice the souls belonging to this very church); to which I should humbly add that, however simple my manner of living, I can live but poorly, considering the house rent and other most necessary expenses.

Now, God has brought it to pass that an unexpected change should offer itself to me, in which I see the possibility of a more adequate living and the achievement of my goal of a well-regulated church music without further vexation, since I have received the gracious admission of His Serene Highness of Saxe-Weimar into his court *Kapelle* and chamber music.

Accordingly, I have felt I must bring my intention in this matter, with obedient respect, to the notice of my most gracious patrons, and at the same time beg them to content themselves for the time being with the modest services I have rendered to the Church and to furnish me at the earliest moment with a gracious dismissal. If I can contribute anything further to the service of Your Honours' Church, I will do so more in deed than in words, remaining for ever, Honoured Sir, most gracious patrons and gentlemen, your honours' most obedient servant,

Joh. Seb. Bach
Mühlhausen, 25 June 1708

Leaving aside the obsequious tone, which was fairly standard at the time in formal correspondence of this kind (and which we will later find over and over again), the letter shows that many of the frustrations and irritations that had so affected his four-year stint in Arnstadt had not vanished in Mühlhausen. And money remained a major issue too: there are five references to it ('permitting me to enjoy a better living', 'my small means', 'not without cost', 'however simple my manner of living, I can live but poorly', and 'a more adequate living'), as well as four to his sense that his musical skills were unappreciated ('the goal [of] a well-regulated church music' (twice), 'without hindrance', and 'without further vexation'). But perhaps there's more to it than that: there is surely a hint, from the long account of how he had carried out his duties, his accumulation of 'a good store of the choicest church compositions', and the deficiencies 'in the harmony that is fashioned here', that he hoped St Blasius might try to persuade him to stay, in particular by raising his salary.

But they did not. In the parish records on 26 June it is reported that 'the organist Pach [*sic*] received a call to Weimar and accepted the same', and 'since he could not be made to stay, consent must doubtless be given to his dismissal'.[51] But they did seek his assurance that he would see through the massively expensive organ renovation that he had initiated, to which he agreed. And he also suggested a replacement, his distant relation Johann Friedrich Bach, the third son of the late Johann Christoph, the Eisenach organist. Eight days later the parish records state that 'there had presented himself for the vacant post of organist Mr Pache's [*sic*] cousin, also named Pache, a student'. Johann Friedrich landed the job, but at a salary significantly lower than Sebastian's.

Chapter 5

COMPETITION IN WEIMAR

(1708–17)

The decision to return to Weimar was, on reflection, a curious one. Sebastian had already taken on three jobs since graduating from St Michael's in Lüneburg, two of which had been working for the aristocracy, and one for a town council. Mühlhausen had been a substantial improvement on his troubled four years in Arnstadt: it was a democratic free city with a substantial population and a long tradition of lively and distinguished music; and there had been much appreciation of his own performances and compositions over his thirteen months there. Going back to Weimar was not exactly a step forward. If your ambition as a musician was to become rich and famous, it was obvious that you had to travel, certainly to the larger cities in Germany like Hamburg, Berlin, Leipzig, Cologne and Frankfurt, if not to Rome, Vienna, Milan and Paris. This was what Handel understood all too clearly – and it would shortly lead to his appointment as kapellmeister to the Elector of Hanover, the future George I. Of course this required courage, and the ability to detach yourself from your place of birth. But Sebastian's self-doubt and insecurity must have held him back. He knew that Italy was the home of the most active and fashionable musical developments in Europe, he knew that Vivaldi, Albinoni and Corelli were world-famous composers of his father's and his own generation – but he lacked the nerve to compete with them. By returning to Weimar he was admitting, to himself at least, that he would feel safer remaining in the heart of Thuringia, surrounded by his Bach relations and following their generational traditions. One comforting fact must have been the presence there of his cousin the 23-year-old Johann Gottfried Walther, related to his mother's family the Lämmerhirts, who had recently taken the post of organist in the town church. Walther would certainly become a friend.

The main attraction, however, was the money. Maria Barbara was now four months pregnant, and clearly if the Mühlhausen town council were not willing to improve his 'small means' he had no choice, in the short term anyway, but to find somewhere to live and work where he could afford to bring up a family. The annual 150 florins [£6,300], paid quarterly, was a sharp improvement; and it was enhanced with a yearly allowance of 18 bushels of wheat, 12 bushels of barley, 4 cords of wood and 30 pails of beer from the castle brewery, free of beverage tax.[52]

Sebastian and Maria Barbara arrived in Weimar in July 1708, and were allocated a flat in a house belonging to Adam Immanuel Weldig, a falsetto singer in the court *Kapelle*, master of the pages and dancing teacher, whom Sebastian knew from his previous time there. The ducal secretary handed him a 'benevolent entry allowance' of ten florins [£420] to cover the costs of the move.[53] The flat was in the market square in the centre of the town, a few hundred yards from the Wilhelmsburg Palace where Duke Wilhelm Ernst had previously employed him.

But despite the financial improvements, the Bachs were soon aware that the post of court organist was not exactly a step up the social ladder. There were twelve permanent employees in the court *Kapelle*, still headed by the kapellmeister Johann Samuel Drese, assisted by his son Johann Wilhelm. Several of them, including the Bachs' landlord Weldig, had at least one additional job in the court, such as secretary, court cantor or chamber valet.[54] Sebastian was almost the lowest in rank. He was above a coachman or a groom, but below a ducal valet or a gardener. As for friendships, another sad discovery was that the brilliant violinist Johann

Paul von Westhoff, whom Sebastian had so admired in his previous period in Weimar, had died three years earlier, in 1705. But the old family friend Johann Effler, who had done so much to assist Sebastian's career and whom he was now succeeding as court organist, was still there, now in retirement in his early seventies.

Duke Johann Ernst II, Wilhelm Ernst's younger brother, had died in July 1707, and his widow Charlotte Dorothea Sophia was the temporary co-ruler, to be regent until his son Ernst August reached the age of 21 in April the next year. Wilhelm Ernst got on no better with his sister-in-law than he had with his brother, and had recently issued a decree that the court musicians were allowed to perform in the Red Castle, the neighbouring mansion where she and her children lived, only if they had obtained his written permission. This was the kind of trivial domestic dispute that the two rulers had exchanged for decades, and Kapellmeister Drese was careful to explain to Sebastian and his fellow employees how essential it was to avoid exacerbating such issues, and what conflicting views about musical functions were predominant in each palace.

Wilhelm Ernst had conducted Sebastian's audition, had been impressed by his organ skills, and was therefore in effect his patron. But it soon became apparent to Sebastian that the duchess Charlotte and her family were enthusiastic and talented secular music-lovers. Ernst August was himself an amateur trumpeter and violinist, and had begun to accumulate a fine collection of instruments and manuscripts. His half-brother Prince Johann Ernst, now aged eleven, was even more precociously talented, and was keenly studying the violin and composition. Clearly the Red Castle was where enjoyable chamber music could be played, whereas the Wilhelmsburg would be confined largely to church music.

As court organist, Sebastian's prime function was to handle the two weekly church services, one on Sunday and the other mid-week. The services took place in the narrow but splendidly tall baroque church that was part of the palace, designed by the architect Johann Moritz Richter.

The organ and musicians' space was right at the top, carved into the ceiling some 60 feet above the ground in a cupola with a dome above it, decorated with paintings of heaven and flying angels. Down below sat the congregation, consisting of the ducal family, their household members, court officials, selected local gentry and other employees. Despite the unusual structure of the building, the acoustic effects afforded by the vault above them were profoundly impressive, and the organ itself, just visible on the east side of the cupola, had recently been restored and improved* and was in excellent condition.

The standard Lutheran service comprised an opening hymn, appropriate to the season, sung by the congregation accompanied by the organ, followed by a setting of *Kyrie eleison* ('Lord have mercy') sung by the choir.† Then the pastor, standing at the altar, would intone the Gloria and the congregation would follow with the traditional Gloria hymn *Allein Gott in der Höh sei Ehr* (Only to God on high be glory). The tune of this hymn may be familiar to Anglicans as 'O sinner, lift the eye of faith', hymn 104 in *Hymns Ancient and Modern*:

Geistlicher Lieder, 1539

O Sinner, lift the eye of faith, To true repentance turning;

Sebastian would shortly write at least four harmonic keyboard settings of it, as well as a chorale organ prelude (BWV 715) which contains in the last two bars an extraordinary harmonic route through all twelve chromatic notes before returning to G major – another of the many examples of his intellectual, almost mechanical, approach to adventuring through the possibilities of harmony.

---

* By the Weimar organ builder Heinrich Nicolaus Trebs, with whom Sebastian continued to co-operate over the next few years (see page 34, and *NBR* 42).

† One such Kyrie which Bach probably wrote at this time is the opening movement of the Mass in F major, BWV 233.

The rest of the service included readings from the Epistles and the Gospels, a sermon, holy communion, and two or three further hymns. The organist accompanied the hymns, and was expected to play preludes and postludes before and after the service, either improvising or performing existing pieces. Any organist would regard himself as a crucial element in the church service, particularly if he could contribute adventurous and attractive versions of familiar and beloved hymn tunes. This was a motivation not just to develop his improvisational skills, but to explore the infinite possibilities of harmonic settings.

So Sebastian began, soon after his arrival in Weimar, to compile a written collection of his organ settings of traditional Lutheran hymns. He had come across a number of similar compilations, such as Johann Pachelbel's *Chorale-Fugen durch gantze Jahr*, and *Chorale zum Praeambuliren*, a collection of 44 short fugues by his elderly cousin the Eisenach organist Johann Christoph Bach who had so influenced his childhood interest in the organ. The first step was to buy a small bound volume of 180 pages, on each of which he drew six staves. His plan was to fit into this space a comprehensive range of 164 hymn settings, the first 60 covering the entire church year beginning with Advent, and the remainder appropriate for liturgical seasons, including hymns for the catechism, thanksgiving, temptation, death and the last judgement. He began by selecting the hymn tunes and writing their titles at the top of each page, and then copied nine or ten that he had previously composed. This was an ongoing project.

The earlier chorales are fairly conventional, four-part arrangements with the hymn tune at the top, a steady 'walking' base and lively motifs in the centre. *In dulci jubilo* (BWV 608) is a familiar example. But later ones were more adventurous, with the chorale tune appearing in lower voices or moving between them. In all, the collection reveals Sebastian's fascination with the capabilities of harmonisation and the organ's capacity to express them, and the progress he made over these early years in developing such skills. When he eventually (probably in 1720) wrote a title page at the front of the book, he inscribed it '*Orgel-Büchlein,* in which a beginner at the organ is given instruction in developing a chorale in many diverse ways, and at the same time in acquiring facility in the study of the pedal since in the chorales contained therein the pedal is treated as wholly obbligato'.[55]

Duke Ernst August clearly enjoyed Sebastian's organ-playing, which encouraged him to extend his organ compositions very substantially over the next few years; at least 100 survive – preludes and fugues, toccatas, fantasias, a passacaglia, concertos, and a great many based on chorales. Even though much of his weekly performance in the church was improvised, he felt that a lot of these inventions should be preserved, either because they could later be developed and extended, or because they might be useful for teaching purposes.

For teaching was another activity to which Sebastian had become attracted, not least because it provided additional income. His irritation and embarrassment at failing to allure the students and choir members in Arnstadt had receded somewhat over the last few years, and he had indeed begun to recruit one or two pupils to whom he taught keyboard skills. Two of them, Johann Martin Schubart and Johann Caspar Vogler, had demonstrated their appreciation of his teaching by following him to Mühlhausen, and then to Weimar, to continue studying with him. The appeal for him, apart from the fees they paid, was their capacity for hard work and their acceptance of his standards; and indeed they both later became professional organists. What appealed to them was the way he conveyed his own passion for music, his willingness to proceed gently through the beginner's stages, and his capacity to surprise and excite them with adventurous improvising. Sebastian was not skilled at social intercourse or intimate friendships with his contemporaries, but with these earnest young students he felt connected. As we shall see, teaching was to become a central part of his life.*

And then there were other jobs Drese soon asked him to undertake, such as repairing various instruments that belonged to the court *Kapelle*. Harpsichords particularly became his speciality, and over the next few months he earned some useful fees for repairing several of them in the Wilhelmsburg and the Red Castle.[56] Harpsichords are not as complex as organs, but like organs they contain stops at various pitches. Typically there are three sets of strings, two of them tuned to eight-foot pitch and the third an octave higher, the four-foot pitch. There are usually two manuals (keyboards), enabling the player to use the different string choirs either individually or together. The strings are plucked (rather than struck, as in clavichords and pianos) by plectra made of quill, the hollow basal part of a bird's feather, usually the crow's. Each plectrum is inserted in a complex structure called a jack, resting on the back of the key lever, and containing a damper made of felt or leather, which mutes the string when the player's finger comes off the key.

Although well-made harpsichords are surprisingly stable instruments, they are sensitive to the weather and need constant tuning, and fairly frequent repairs. Every now and then a string will snap and need replacing, a tricky task involving twisting one end of it to make an eye which will hook around the hitch pin at the far end of the instrument, and then winding the other end into the wrest pin which is turned to tune the string. The plectra usually need replacing every few years, a laborious process involving removing the jacks, extracting the plectra and cutting new quills with a sharp knife. Once the new ones are inserted, the harpsichord needs to be played for a few days to flex them, and then the whole set must be 'voiced' to produce an even and proper tone.

---

* Duke Ernst August employed him in 1711 and 1712 to give keyboard lessons to his page, Adam von Jagemann; but he paid him in cords of timber rather than money (see *NBR* 43).

The regular tuning of the duke's harpsichords opened Sebastian's mind to the complexities of temperament. All musicians at this time were aware that pitch was not a simple question – unlike today, when we have a universally accepted A' (the A above middle C) = 440 Hz (cycles per second). There had been a long tradition in Europe throughout the 16th and 17th centuries that instruments were pitched at A' = 465 Hz, a tone above our standard, but towards the end of the 17th century, under French influence and the production of their widely played woodwinds, the standard, known as *Cammerton* or *Kammerton* (chamber tone), became much lower, A' being roughly 415 Hz. But existing organs, brass and woodwind could not easily be re-tuned, and so a variety of pitches survived, and much music had to be adapted and re-notated so these instruments could play together in tune.

But that is just about the pitch. Equally troublesome at the time was the fact that if you divide an octave into twelve exactly equal semitones, there is an intrinsic acoustic defect – the minor and major thirds are somewhat impure, and this becomes more apparent the more you play in the remote and abstruse keys. So it became an issue whether to go for equal or unequal temperament – in other words whether, and how far, to adjust the gaps between the semitones within each octave. Increasingly, as he adjusted the harpsichord strings and played his keyboard improvisations on their manuals, it became clear to Sebastian how to vary the intervals between different notes in order for remote keys to sound pure. The term *wohltemperirt* (well-tempered) had entered his mind.

******

In December 1708 Maria Barbara gave birth to their first child, a girl, whom they named Catharina Dorothea. Sebastian's sister-in-law, Johanna Dorothea Bach, who had looked after him in his teenage years in Ohrdruf, was godmother, as was Martha Lämmerhirt, the widow of his maternal uncle Tobias. The godfather was Sebastian's old friend the clergyman Georg Christian Eilmar, who as archdeacon of the Marienkirche in Mühlhausen had commissioned one of his earliest cantatas.* The baptism took place on 29 December, in the late-Gothic church of St Peter and St Paul, across the town square from Weldig's house where the Bachs lived. Also at the ceremony was Maria Barbara's unmarried elder sister, Friedelena Margaretha Bach, who had come to live with them to help bring up the family.

Sebastian, aged only 23, was now a father, and his mind was filled with pride and satisfaction at the way he had achieved a secure and stable life reminiscent of his early years in Eisenach. The flat in the town square was packed tight, with the two students, Schubart and Vogler, his sister-in-law Friedelena, his wife, baby daughter and himself all living together in the few rooms available to them. There was every motivation to enlarge the family, and happiness now filled his mind with positive emotions.

Back in Mühlhausen, the town council had recalled how impressed they had been by Sebastian's Congratulatory Church Motet composed to celebrate their annual election (*Gott ist mein König*), and as the new election approached they contacted him to commission a new piece. He completed it by the beginning of February 1709, and travelled to Mühlhausen to perform it on the 7th, being paid 6 thalers [£288] for the composition and his travel costs. As with the previous piece, the council had it published by the local printer† a few days later. Sebastian's 24th birthday was approaching, and in March 1709 there was an encounter with two talented and ambitious young musicians who gave him a clear picture of how commitment and energy could forward your musical career.

In Eisenach, Sebastian's second cousin Johann Bernhard Bach (1676–1749) had succeeded Johann Christoph (who died in 1703) as organist at

---

* *Aus der Tiefen rufe ich, Herr, zu dir*, BWV 131. See page 72.

† But unfortunately no copy has survived, and the title and content of the work are unknown.

St George's and harpsichordist in the town *Kapelle*. Three years later the ducal court of Saxe-Eisenach had employed a new concertmaster named Georg Philipp Telemann, a man of great energy and exceptional musical talent whose career would make fascinating comparison with Sebastian's.[57] Telemann was born on 14 March 1681, so he was now 28. His father, a deacon and preacher in the town of Magdeburg, had died when he was only four, and he had been brought up by his widowed mother Maria. Although it was obvious even in his earliest years that he had innate musical ability, Maria Telemann took the view that to make his way in the world her son should train for the priesthood like his father, and she tried to suppress his passion for learning to play various instruments, including harpsichord, flute, violin and cittern (lute). But he persevered in secret, with much help from his schoolteachers, and by the time he was twelve he had written a large amount of music – arias, motets and even an opera, called *Sigismundus*, which was performed at his school in Magdeburg. In 1698 Telemann attended the gymnasium at Hildesheim to prepare for university, an experience not dissimilar to Sebastian's at St Michael's in Lüneburg. Telemann studied natural sciences, Latin, Greek and other subjects at Hildesheim, but like Sebastian he pursued his music in every available spare moment, expanding his playing skills to the oboe, viola da gamba, double bass and trombone, and even (despite his Lutheran background) taking on the organ-playing in the local Catholic monastery of St Godehard.

In 1701 he went to Leipzig University to study law, and on his way there he stopped at Halle, where he met the 16-year-old genius Georg Frideric Handel, with whom he established a friendship that lasted all their lives, enlivened by constant correspondence and occasional meetings, even after Handel moved to London. Telemann began his legal studies at Leipzig, but within a few weeks even the chief magistrate, burgomaster Dr Franz Conrad Romanus, had discovered his musical talents and commissioned him to write a choral piece every fortnight for performance in St Thomas's Church. His musical activities expanded dramatically over the next three years, and

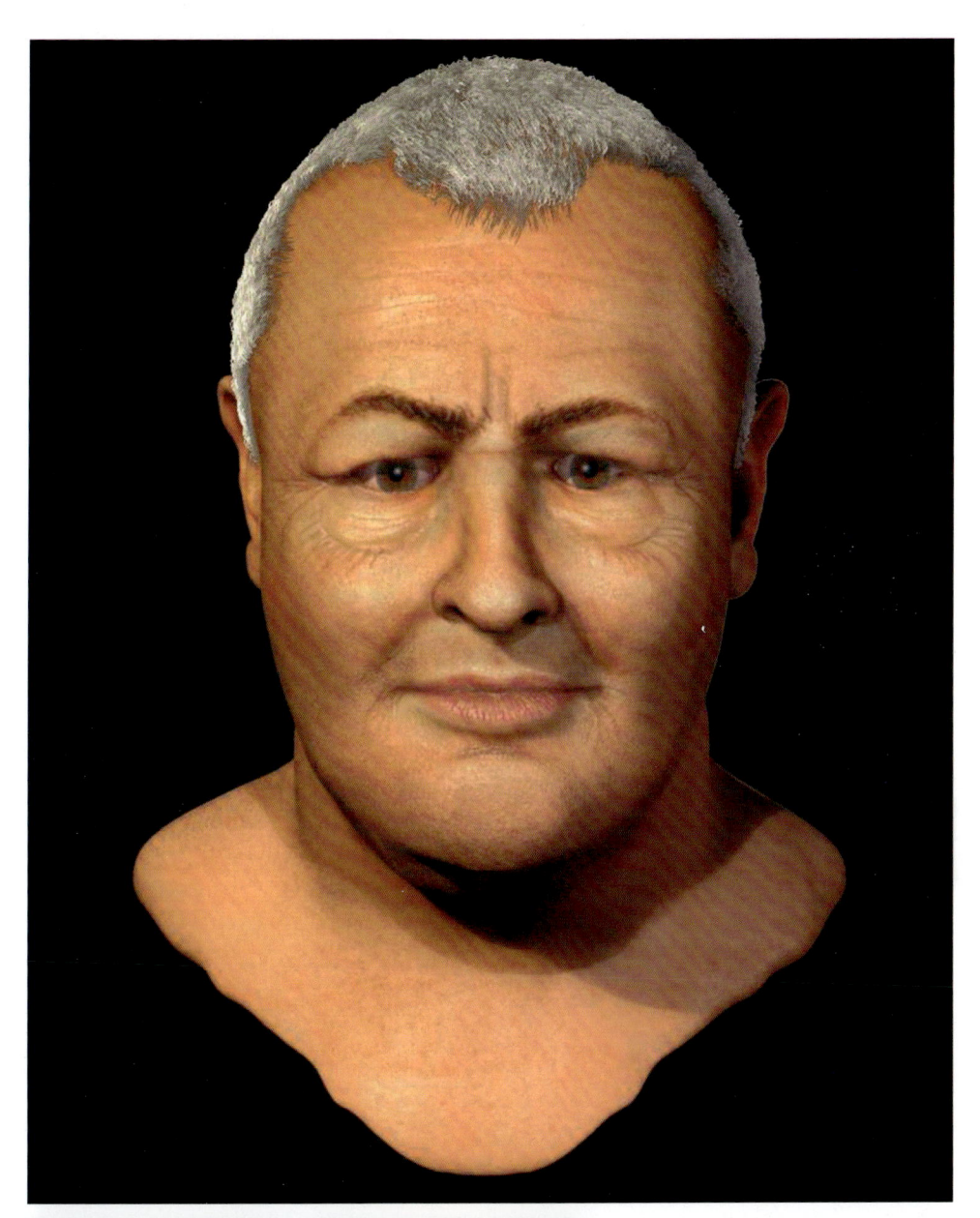

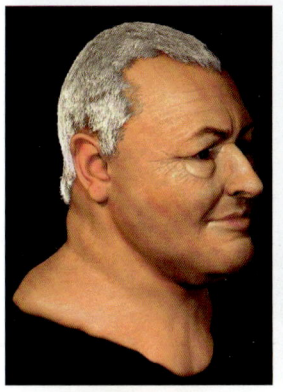

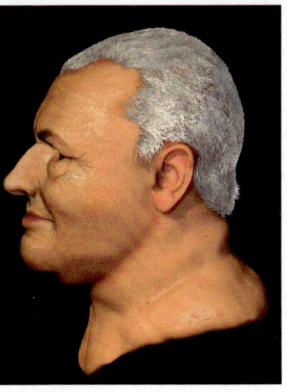

Three versions of the only existing modernised view of Bach, based on the Haußmann portrait painted in his old age (1746). This was recently commissioned by the Bachhaus Museum and produced by Dr Caroline Wilkinson, Senior Lecturer in Forensic Anthropology at the University of Dundee in Scotland.

The only existing portrait of Bach's father, Johann Ambrosius (1645–95), believed to date from about 1685 (the year in which Bach was born). It is attributed to the artist called Johann David Herlicius.

BELOW
The Harz mountains, through which in March 1700 the 14-year-old Bach and his friend Georg Erdmann (1682–1736) walked more than 200 miles for two weeks, from Ohrdruf all the way north to Lüneburg.

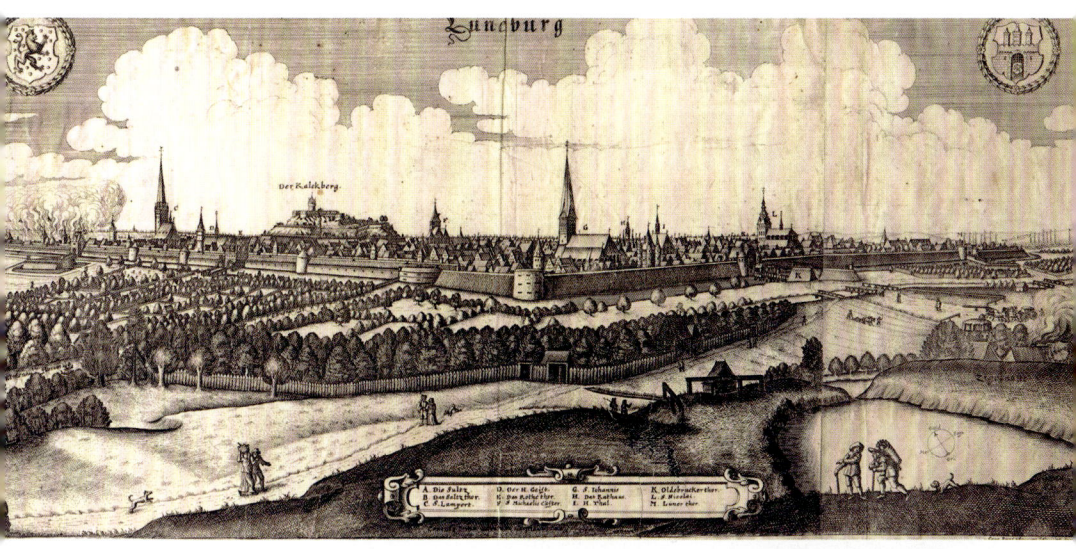

The town of Lüneburg, engraved in the 18th century by Conrad Buno. In the centre is St Michael's School, where Bach and Erdmann became choir members in April 1700.

RIGHT
St Michael's Church in Lüneburg, where Bach regularly sang for two years, first as a treble and then as a bass. This engraving was made around that time by Joachim Burmester.

Wilhelm Ernst, Duke of Saxe-Weimar (1662–1723), from whom Bach obtained his first post as a lackey in Weimar. The portraitist is unknown.

BELOW
Mühlhausen, the town west of Weimar where Bach became organist at St Blasius's Church in 1707. This engraving was created in 1650 by Matthæus Merian.

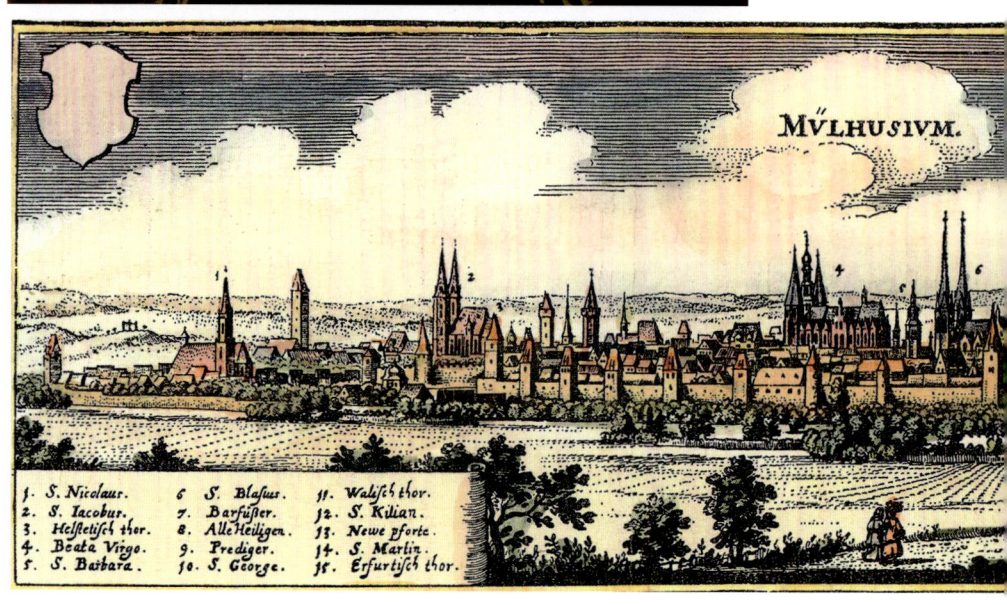

A 1674 painting by Jan Voorhout of Johann Adam Reincken, the locally famous organist in Hamburg who strongly encouraged Bach's skills. Here he is playing the harpsichord, with other players and singers.

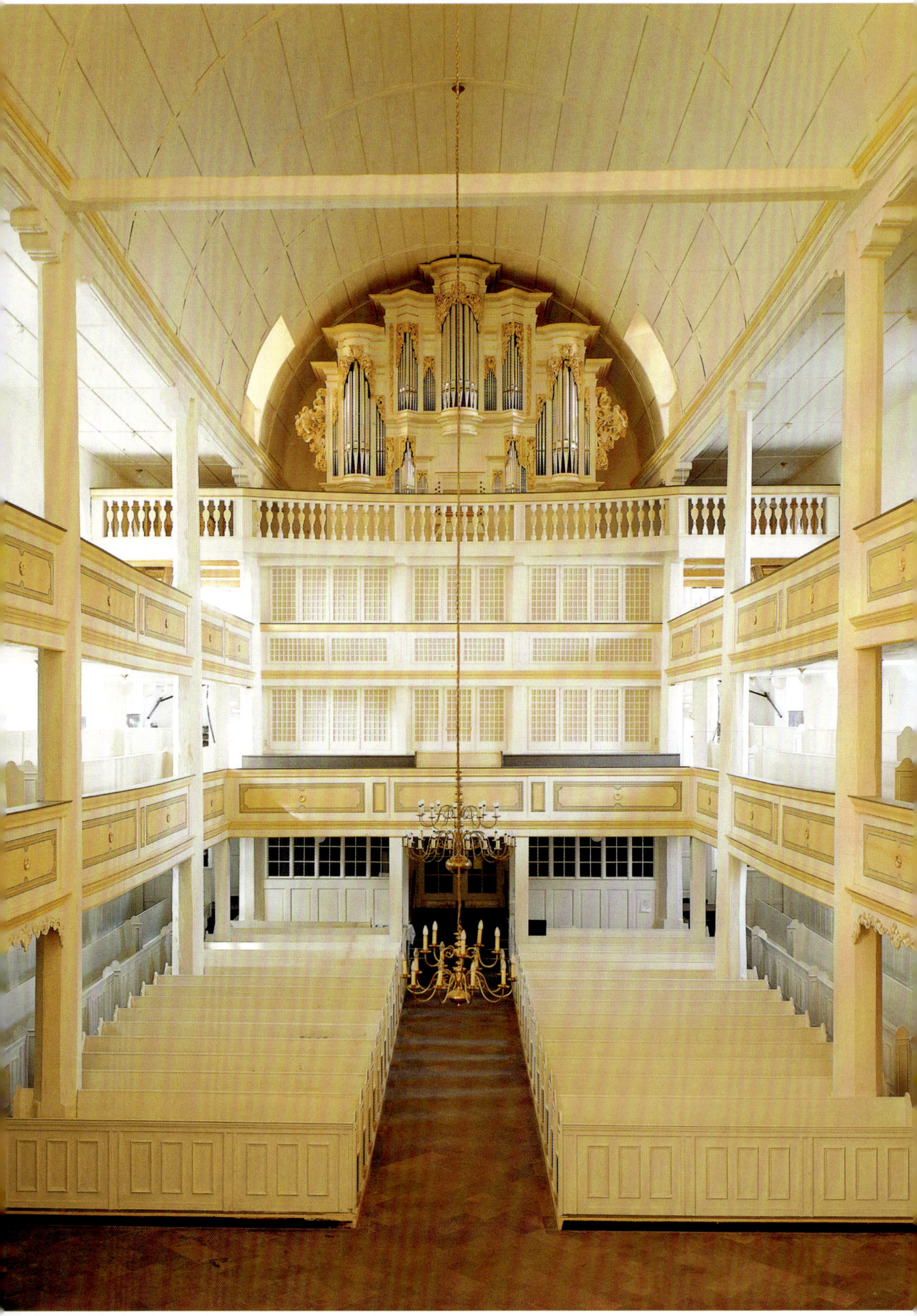

Bach's surviving organ at the west end of the New Church in Arnstadt, photographed recently by Constantin Beyer. There was space on either side up there for the choral singers to sit and stand. The church is now called Bachkirche.

ABOVE
A portrait of Georg Frideric Handel (1685–1759), painted in England around 1736 by Thomas Hudson.

RIGHT
A portrait of Georg Philipp Telemann (1681–1767); the artist is unknown.

The church in Dornheim, a few hundred yards east of Arnstadt, where Bach married his first wife, Maria Barbara, on 17 October 1707.

BELOW
The Wilhelmsburg palace in the centre of Weimar, and the nearby flat into which Bach and his wife moved in July 1708. Once again he was employed by Duke Wilhelm Ernst.

included playing in the Leipzig opera-house orchestra, and founding a *collegium musicum*, a group of fellow student musicians who began to perform public concerts in the local coffee-houses, as well as at academic ceremonies and to welcome visiting potentates; and much of the music they performed included orchestral works written by him. In August 1704, aged 23, he was appointed organist and director of music at the Neuekirche (New Church), one of Leipzig's four main churches, where he wrote and performed dozens of cantatas, probably with the help of his *collegium* colleagues.

Telemann left Leipzig in 1705, having been offered a post in the *Kapelle* of Count Erdmann von Promitz in Sorau (now Zary in Poland), where he married Amalie Louise Julianne Eberlin, the daughter of an affluent middle-class banker; but although he was fascinated by encountering much Polish folk-music in his travels around the count's vast estates in Upper Silesia, he stayed there only a year, moving to Eisenach in 1706 to become leader of the ducal orchestra. There he befriended Johann Bernhard Bach, who introduced him to his cousin Sebastian.

It was probably quite clear to Sebastian when they met that Telemann had all the capacities that he most admired in a musician and sought in himself. Telemann could compose in any style, whether traditionally contrapuntal or trendily modern with simple melodies. He could play virtually every instrument with abundant skill. He had immense energy and capacity for hard work, and confidence in his ability to provide employers and audiences with what pleased them. And he was evidently much liked by people he encountered in every class. What's more, he was extremely interested in maximising his income, and did so by taking on any additional tasks that were available, as well as organising the publication of his music. Before long, when he had moved to Frankfurt in 1712 as director of municipal music, he calculated that his annual income had risen to 1,600 gulden [£67,200], more than twice as much as Sebastian would ever earn in all the years ahead.

In the spring of 1709, Sebastian's boss, Kapellmeister Johann Samuel Drese, arranged a performance in Weimar of Telemann's Concerto in G

Major for two violins and orchestra, which took place in the Wilhelmsburg Palace, inspired by the visit in March of a very talented 21-year-old violinist called Johann Georg Pisendel, who was on his way to study at Leipzig. Pisendel was the son of a cantor in Cadolzburg, just west of Nuremberg, and had spent most of his childhood as a chorister, and then violinist, in the court chapel in neighbouring Ansbach. He was a brilliant player, and would later be recognised as the finest violinist in the whole of Germany. We do not know who the second violinist was in this performance in Weimar, but very possibly it was Telemann. In any event, Telemann and Pisendel began a friendship as close as Telemann's with Handel.

But the same was not true of Sebastian. Perhaps, despite the current happiness, he felt daunted by the energy and ambition of these two immensely able young men, and knew he lacked the confidence that would lead them to greater fame and fortune than he himself could achieve. He would certainly stay in touch with Telemann over the years, but emulating his determination and self-belief, let alone his ability to earn serious money, was another matter.

By the spring of 1710 Maria Barbara was pregnant again, and income remained a worry. Sebastian made several attempts to persuade Duke Wilhelm Ernst to increase his salary, but as yet with no success. On 22 November Maria Barbara gave birth to their second child, a son whom they named Wilhelm Friedemann after his two godfathers.[58] Wilhelm Ferdinand, Baron von Lyncker, was gentleman-in-waiting at the court, and Friedemann Meckbach was a lawyer in Mühlhausen, whose father, Conrad Meckbach, had been on the town council when Sebastian went to work there in 1707. The godmother was another Mühlhausen friend, Anna Dorothea Hagedorn, the daughter of Pastor Eilmar, who had commissioned his cantata *Aus der Tiefen rufe ich, Herr, zu dir*.

In March 1711 Sebastian improved his earnings by recruiting another young pupil, Philipp David Kräuter from Augsburg, who had been awarded a scholarship by his school. Sebastian sought an annual fee of

100 thalers for board and tuition, but the energetic student negotiated him down to 80 thalers [£3,840], for which he received as much as six hours of teaching a day, including composition, keyboard-playing and other instruments, and practical studies of the structure and mechanics of the organ. Kräuter stayed with him for two and a half years, and greatly benefited from doing so (almost immediately afterwards landing the post of cantor and music director at St Anne's Church in Augsburg). At last, in June, Wilhelm Ernst agreed to raise Sebastian's annual pay by a quarter to 200 fl [£8,400], as well as enlarging his allowances of wood and coal.

Sebastian and Maria Barbara now had two children, and the household contained the four of them, Maria Barbara's sister, and two earnest living-in students (the other being Johann Martin Schubart). This was the stable family life that Sebastian had always longed for, a vivid echo of how he remembered his early childhood. He persevered with his numerous organ compositions, his chorale arrangements for the 'Little Organ Book', his teaching* and his duties as chamber musician and court organist.

And then in February 1713 he received an exciting offer to compose a work to celebrate the birthday of Duke Christian of Saxe-Weißenfels, to be performed in Weißenfels, about 25 miles north-east of Weimar, on the road to Leipzig.[59] It was probably his landlord, the falsetto singer and dancer Adam Immanuel Weldig, who had just moved to Weißenfels, who suggested him for the job. Sebastian requested a libretto from his colleague the Weimar court poet Salomo Franck, and they decided – knowing that the duke shared their own employer's passion for hunting – to base it on a quartet of Greek and Roman mythological characters, led by Diana, the goddess of the hunt. The others are Endymion, the handsome young shepherd who was a grandson of Zeus; Pan, the god of shepherds; and Pales, the Roman guardian spirit of flocks. Franck's ideas for the plot were hardly consistent with ancient mythology, but the verses are lively

---

* Another family member, Johann Lorenz Bach (1695–1773), the son of one of Sebastian's first cousins, joined the household as a music student later in the summer of 1713.

and cheerful, and inspired Sebastian to construct a long, 15-movement cantata of recitatives, arias, duets and choruses.* Diana (soprano) begins (after her opening recitative) with *Jagen ist die Lust der Götter* ('Hunting is the delight of the gods'), accompanied by two horns and keyboard. The most striking movement is the ninth, Pales's aria, *Schafe können sicher weiden* ('Sheep may safely graze'), accompanied by two recorders, in which she lyrically applauds the happiness of a land well ruled. Here is Sebastian's first little masterpiece, harmonically quite simple, but very moving.

But this was not a happy time for Sebastian and Maria Barbara. The day after his return from Weißenfels, she gave birth to twins, whom they named Johann Christoph† and Maria Sophia. The boy died immediately, after an emergency baptism, and the girl two and a half weeks later, on 13 March. The ever-presence of death had returned to haunt Sebastian. Despite the apparent stability of his life in Weimar, the respect he was increasingly earning from his musical colleagues, the improved income, and his growing confidence as a composer, he must have felt a desperate surge of insecurity over the next few months, to which he responded in what had become his usual pattern: with an even greater devotion to work, and a spasm of desire to move to another place. Maria Barbara's recourse was different: to become pregnant again as soon as possible, which she did in July.

At the end of the year, an opportunity to move arose. In Halle, the town on the river Saale 50 miles north-east of Weimar where Handel had been born in the same year as Sebastian, the distinguished but controversial organist at the Church of Our Lady, Friedrich Wilhelm Zachow, had died in the summer of 1712, having occupied the post for 28 years. Towards the end of his life he had initiated the commissioning

---

* *Was mir behagt, ist nur die muntre Jagd,* BWV 208, often referred to as the Hunting Cantata.

† Sebastian had much improved his relations with his brother Johann Christoph several years earlier by writing a capriccio in his honour (see pages 42 and 53), and this was a further gesture of concession. Johann Christoph responded seven months later when his youngest son was born, christening him Johann Sebastian, and recruiting Sebastian as his godfather. But this boy too died within days of his birth.

of an enormous new organ in the church, with three manuals, pedal and 65 stops, for which the contract with the builder, Christoph Cuntzius, was not signed until several weeks after his death. In view of the highly ambitious scale of the project, and the huge investment involved – 6,300 thalers [over £300,000] – the church authorities in Halle were well aware that the appointment of a suitable replacement for Zachow was a tough assignment, requiring a top-class organist with the ability and experience to supervise the new organ's construction. They had already considered several possibilities, but Johann Sebastian Bach's reputation in the organ-building industry made him the ideal candidate, and in early December he was offered a generous fee to travel to Halle, lodging for three days at the Inn of the Golden Ring (where he ran up a surprisingly large bill for food, beer, brandy and tobacco),* and writing and performing a cantata.[60] By the 14th they had decided to offer him the job, and drawn up a detailed contract of employment.

Sebastian received two copies of the contract in Weimar in early January 1714. But by this time he was in two minds about the move. The main problem, as usual, was money. Although he had made clear to them that his pay would at least have to match the 200 thalers he was currently earning, the offer barely did so. It comprised an annual salary of 140 thalers, plus 24 thalers for lodging and 7 thalers 12 groschen for wood. In addition, there was 1 thaler on offer for each church composition, potentially producing an extra 50 thalers were he to write one work a week.

But the contract also spelled out some rather restrictive obligations, which caused him concern. For example, he had to undertake 'not to accept any secondary employment ... but to attend exclusively and industriously to his duties in this church'; and although he was 'free to seek other income, through teaching or otherwise, so long as he can do this without neglecting the said duties', he was seriously worried

---

* 3 thalers 22 groschen [£180]. The 18 groschen he spent on beer alone would have bought him 64 pints.

that there might be disputes about the meaning of 'otherwise'. But the most eccentric clause seemed to spell out precisely what notes he should play:

> To accompany attentively the regular chorales and those prescribed by the Minister, before and after the sermons in Sundays and feast days, as well as at Communion and at Vespers and on the eves of holidays, slowly and without unusual embellishment, in four or five parts, on the diapason, to change the other stops at each verse, also to use the fifth and the reeds, the stopped pipes, as well as syncopations and suspensions, in such manner that the congregation can take the organ as the basis of good harmony and unison tone, and thus sing devoutly and give praise and thanks to the Most High.[61]

This really did seem a bit excessive, particularly as it reminded him all too painfully of the rebuke he had received seven years before from the consistory in Arnstadt about his hymn accompaniments.* Did the Halle people know about this?

So he wrote what he hoped was a polite and respectful letter to church board member Augustus Becker, explaining that he could not yet sign the contract because (a) he had not yet been granted dismissal by the Weimar ducal authorities, and (b) he wanted to suggest some changes 'in respect of the *salarium* as well as of the duties'. He went on:

> As soon as we can agree upon the *station*, I shall appear at once in person and show by my signature that I am really willing to engage myself in Your Honour's service.[62]

But Becker and his colleagues, having felt that they had made unusually generous arrangements for Bach's candidature, and that he had more or

---

* See page 55.

less accepted the post while he was there, were furious, and wrote him a stiff letter saying that he had breached all the employment conventions and dealt with them unfairly. He was stung, realising that they probably assumed he had aimed to get their job offer so that he could improve his employment conditions in Weimar. He wrote back:

> That the most honoured Church Board is astonished at my declining the desired post of organist to which, as you think, I aspired, astonishes me not at all, since I see that they have given the matter so very little thought. You say I applied for the said post of organist, but I do not know of any such thing. This much I do know, that I presented myself and that the most honoured *collegium* applied to me; for I, after presenting myself, should immediately have taken my leave if the request and courteous invitation of Dr Heineccius had not compelled me to compose and to perform the piece you know of.
>
> Moreover, it is not to be assumed that one will go to a place where one's situation is worsened; but this I could not learn accurately in a fortnight or three weeks, since I am wholly of the opinion that even after many years one cannot rightly know one's livelihood in a place where one must count incidental fees as part of one's income, let alone in a fortnight; and that is more or less the reason I at first accepted and then, on request, in turn rejected the appointment. But it is by no means to be inferred from all these circumstances that I should have played such a trick upon the honoured Church Board in order to induce my most gracious master to increase my salary, since the latter already shows so much graciousness toward my service and art that I do not have to journey to Halle in order to have my salary increased.
>
> Accordingly I regret that the assurance of the honoured Church Board has thus had a somewhat uncertain outcome, and add the following: even if I had received just as good a salary in Halle as here, should I not then have been bound to prefer the prior service to the other one? You, as one learned in the law, can best judge of this and, if I may ask you to, can present this my justification to the honoured Church Board.[63]

It is hard not to sympathise with Mr Becker and his colleagues. Although they had several other able candidates for the post, they had made it abundantly clear to Mr Bach that he was their preference. They had lodged him in the town's most comfortable hotel at their expense, paid him 12 thalers [£576] for his audition cantata and travel expenses, and received his acceptance of the post before he returned to Weimar on 15 December. But then he had written them this distinctly unfair and contradictory letter, all the money was wasted, and they had to begin again. (In due course they had the decency to forgive him for misleading them, however, and recruited him two years later to test and approve the completed new organ.)

And it seems clear that, despite his denial, he did indeed use this event to put pressure on the Weimar ducal court to improve his position. At the beginning of March the court secretary announced that 'the former court organist Bach, at his most humble request,' had been granted the title of concertmaster. This was a new role in Weimar, and definitely a step up the ladder for Sebastian, although the authorities were careful to define his position as below that of the Vice Chapel Master, Johann Wilhelm Drese.[64] Sebastian's new tasks included taking charge of the instrumental players (but not the singers), and performing new compositions once a month in the chapel. He was now acting in practice as a chapel master, the players were obliged to attend his rehearsals in the palace church, and it was clear that, although Drese had not been demoted, the new arrangements were intended to increase Sebastian's influence on the court music in general and to improve its overall standards. He was also given the exhilarating task of composing a new cantata each month. And there was another salary increase, up from 200 to 250 thalers [£10,500].[65]

The Halle episode thus ended, despite the embarrassing correspondence with Augustus Becker, with several encouraging benefits. He had more power and influence in his workplace, a higher income, and a musical challenge – to adapt his compositional skills from the keyboard to the orchestra. He had of course already composed several cantatas, with reasonable success; but now he was in a position to concentrate on this genre, and to seek more approval from his employers by doing so. And finally, on 8 March, Maria Barbara gave birth to another son, christened Carl Philipp Emanuel. The gloom of the preceding year had receded, and Sebastian must have felt a new surge of optimism. Georg Philipp Telemann* travelled all the way from Frankfurt to be godfather to his son; the other godparents were his former landlord Adam Immanuel Weldig, and Catharina Dorothea Altmann, the wife of the court chamberlain at Arnstadt.[66] Sebastian immediately began to compose his first cantata under the new arrangement, to be performed on Palm Sunday.

Unusually, this fell on 25 March, the Feast of the Annunciation of the Virgin Mary, and so instead of basing it on the normal Gospel reading for the Sunday before Easter, he took the rather more cheerful line of celebrating the message to Mary that she was about to give birth to Jesus. *Himmelskönig, sei willkommen* ('Welcome, King of heaven', BWV 182) has eight movements, beginning with a charming sonata in G major for treble recorder and violin (possibly played by Sebastian), accompanied by mostly plucked strings and organ. Six of the movements are settings of verses whose author was probably his colleague the court poet Salomo Franck. The bright opening chorus is followed by a bass recitative setting of Psalm 40: 7–8: 'Then said I, Lo, I come: in the volume of the book it is written of me, I delight to do thy will, O my God: yea, thy law is within my heart', and a brief bass aria about the love of the son of God for mankind. The most moving aria is the next, accompanied by the recorder, in which the alto soloist urges all Christians to bow down before their saviour. The sixth movement is a chorale setting of a verse from a hymn written a

---

* Telemann's wife, Amalie Louise Juliane, whom he had married in Sorau, died in 1711 in childbirth. Desolated by his loss, he decided to leave Eisenach, and was soon appointed director of municipal music in the free imperial city of Frankfurt, where his career progressed dramatically.

century earlier by the Weimar cantor Melchior Vulpius (1570–1615); and the cantata finally ends with a lively chorus in G major about the gladness heaven will offer the faithful. Thus the newly appointed concertmaster pulled off a successful opening performance.

But another cantata had to be written, to be played on the third Sunday after Easter, only four weeks away. The words, probably again written by Franck, are clearly influenced by the day's Gospel reading,* in which Jesus explains to his disciples what he meant when he said, 'A little while, and ye shall not see me: and again, a little while, and ye shall see me.' This is his explanation: 'Verily, verily, I say unto you, That ye shall weep and lament, but the world shall rejoice: and ye shall be sorrowful, but your sorrow shall be turned into joy.' Franck's opening verse was

Weinen, Klagen, Sorgen, Zagen,	Weeping, wailing, worry, fear,
Angst und Not	anxiety and need
Sind der Christen Tränenbrot,	are the tearful bread of Christians
Die das Zeichen Jesu tragen.	who bear the sign of Jesus.

This inspired in Sebastian a truly profound musical expression of grief, set for the chorus in F minor and accompanied by organ and strings.† The intense emotion it expressed remained with him throughout his life, and he rearranged it many years later as the *Crucifixus etiam pro nobis* movement in his Mass in B Minor.

He was now increasingly conscious of the extraordinary effects he was capable of creating with his music, and how the expression of emotion was something he had underestimated in his scrupulously intellectual study of harmony, counterpoint and fugue. Since such powerful sentiments featured abundantly in the religious services to which he contributed, and since he felt such a profound sense of connection with so many of

---

* John 16: 16–22.

† BWV 12.

them, it became clear to him that the church cantata was an art form he could explore to its limits. Other composers, like Telemann and Handel, might regard chamber music or symphonies or concertos or operas as their appropriate *modus operandi*, or might treat music as primarily a form of human entertainment. But this was not for him. Music was capable of expressing the deepest feelings of humankind, not just joy and sorrow, but fear and love, humour, remorse, grief and oppression. Since cantatas are based on quotations from the Bible, with librettists' poems reflecting and pondering these quotations, these texts would be the inspiration for a huge variety of musical interpretations.

Another feature of the cantata that was intensely attractive was the dominating presence of hymn tunes. These were the songs of the people, the poor and lowly majority, and their expression in the chorales was a sign of the composer's sympathy with ordinary lives. Sebastian was not a revolutionary or a rebel, but he was increasingly drawn to the significance chorale settings had for ordinary listeners, and how oppressed they were – as was he – by the dominance of the aristocracy. His *Orgel-Büchlein*, which he was still working on, was another tribute to popular taste.

Over the next three and a half years he composed and performed at least 40 cantatas (of which, sadly, fewer than half survive).[67] Salomo Franck provided the libretti for many of them, but Sebastian also used texts by Erdmann Neumeister, a theologian and poet born near Weißenfels, and Georg Christian Lehms, the court poet at Darmstadt. Neumeister in particular had played an important part in developing ideas for the structure of this central element in Lutheran church music, the *Kirchen-Musik* that was played immediately after the reading of the Gospel lesson, modelling his texts on the libretti of Italian secular cantatas and operas, including recitatives and arias, and adding quotations from the Bible and verses from traditional hymns. These advances presumably struck Sebastian as highly appealing, providing the composer with new opportunities to express, and indeed dramatise, church teachings.

In August 1714, for the eleventh Sunday after Trinity, Sebastian performed a particularly striking cantata based on the Gospel reading, from Luke: 18, the parable of the Pharisee and the publican, with Jesus' lesson that 'everyone that exalteth himself shall be abased; and he that humbleth himself shall be exalted'. The libretto was by Lehms, published in Darmstadt a few years earlier as part of his collection of cantata poems entitled *Gottgefälliges Kirchen-Opffer*. The words are all about Sebastian's favourite subjects, distress, torment and misery, ending with a five-line verse about how penitence and confession of one's sins will lead to God's pardon and a happy heart. Sebastian's setting* is quite experimental. To emphasise the deeply personal feelings it expresses, it is set for a treble soloist alone, with no choir, and a small instrumental group comprising just an oboe, strings, bassoon and continuo. It begins with a long recitative, followed by a beautiful grief-laden aria in C minor. In the equally beautiful second aria, the wretched singer expresses his grief and deep repentance of his sins. The sixth movement, a chorale arrangement of a traditional hymn, is delightfully accompanied by a solo viola; and after another recitative the cantata ends with a bright gigue-like aria in B-flat major, to the words

| *Wie freudig ist mein Herz* | How happy is my heart |
| *Da Gott versöhnet ist ...* | That God is reconciled... |

For it was by no means only gloom and despondency that Sebastian found himself able to express. His cantata for the following Christmas Day, *Christen, ätzet diesen Tag* ('Christians, etch this day', BWV 63), has an immensely jolly opening chorus, followed by one of his most splendid, and longest, recitatives, *O selger Tag!* (O blessed day!); and it ends with a cheerful chorale in C major accompanied in its outer sections by trumpets.

On 11 May 1715 Maria Barbara gave birth to their sixth (and fourth surviving) child. They named him Johann Gottfried Bernhard, and

---

* *Mein Herz schwimmt im Blut* ('My heart swims in blood', BWV 199).

at his christening the next day they recruited three family-connected godparents: 39-year-old Johann Bernhard Bach, the Eisenach cousin who had introduced Sebastian to Telemann; Johann Andreas Schanert, the county registrar in Ohrdruf whom Sebastian had known in his teenage years there; and Maria Barbara's cousin Sophia Dorothea Emmerling, the wife of the court chef in Arnstadt.[68] A third Johann Bernhard Bach was there too: Sebastian's 16-year-old nephew, the son of Johann Christoph, who had recently joined the family as a music student, and made himself useful with music-copying. Sebastian's salary had been increased again in March, putting him at the same level as the kapellmeister, the elderly Johann Samuel Drese.[69] Little Bernhard was a new consolation and delight to his parents, who now had three sons and a daughter. But, as we shall see, a troubled life lay ahead for him.

A few months later, on 1 August, Duke Ernst August's half-brother Prince Johann Ernst, still a teenager – and a talented composer and musician whom Sebastian had taught and played chamber music with in the Red Castle – suddenly died. A six-month state mourning period ensued, during which no public or church music was allowed to be played; this released Sebastian from his tight cantata-composing schedule and allowed him to spend more time with his children, and to do more work on his *Orgel-Büchlein*. But he was back on cantatas by the new year, continually experimenting with new ideas for their structure and content.

None the less, 1716 was a bad year for the ducal employees in Weimar, as the feuds and disputes between the uncle and nephew grew more intense. Ernst August exacerbated the difficulties by claiming 16,000 florins [£672,000] from the treasury for a building project, which infuriated the austere Wilhelm Ernst, who immediately demanded 50,000 florins [£2,100,000] to enhance his collections, and reduced the Red Castle's allowance for candles. This drove Ernst August to submit a claim to the imperial court council, which infuriated his uncle, who began to ponder further ways of getting his own back.

In April Sebastian received his eagerly anticipated invitation to travel back to Halle to test the enormous new organ at the Church of Our Lady, and wrote an exceedingly sycophantic letter of acceptance.[70] He clearly still felt contrite about how he had treated them over the job offer two years earlier.

> Most noble, most highly honoured Sir!
>
> For the quite exceptional and most gracious confidence of your noble self and of all your noble *Collegium*, I am most deeply obliged; and as it is always my greatest *plaisir* to offer to Your Honour my most obedient service, I shall now be all the more zealous in waiting upon Your Honour at the appointed [time] and then to give satisfaction, so far as in me lies, in the desired examination. I beg you accordingly, without giving yourself too much trouble, to communicate this my decision to the honourable *Collegium*, and at the same time to convey to them my most obedient regards, and to assure them of my sense of respectful obligation for their very special confidence.
>
> Since, moreover, Your Honour has been good enough to take great pains on my behalf not only in the present instance but also heretofore, I acknowledge this with obedient thanks, and assure you that it shall ever be my greatest pleasure to call myself Your Honour's and my most especially highly honoured sir's most obedient servant,
>
> Joh. Seb. Bach, Concertmaster

The event was a very rewarding one, and definitely renewed his thoughts about moving once again to a new job. Two other organ experts recruited by the church board joined him in Halle. The first was Johann Kuhnau, a highly intellectual lawyer and composer who was organist and cantor at St Thomas's Church in Leipzig, and the other was Christian Friedrich Rolle, an organist in the ancient Saxon town of Quedlinburg. Sebastian performed a recital on 29 April, the first evening, and two days later the three experts drew up a detailed report, which criticised some important elements but largely approved of the new instrument.[71] On 3 May they all attended a formal dinner to celebrate the dedication of the organ, at which the menu included *boeuf à la mode*, pike, smoked ham, peas, potatoes, spinach and chicory, roast mutton, roast veal, pumpkin fritters, asparagus salad, lettuce, radishes, lemon rind and cherries.[72] Presumably there was also plenty to drink.

There was much in the way of self-respect and confidence to be gained by hobnobbing with people like Kuhnau and dining out with town councils. Similar events soon followed. In July he was asked, along with the Arnstadt organ builder Johann Anton Weiße, to test an organ in Erfurt (where his father Ambrosius had once been a town musician). When his boss the Weimar kapellmeister Johann Samuel Drese died in December, Sebastian was astounded when it became clear that Duke Wilhelm Ernst was not willing to appoint him as his successor. He was now even more determined to find himself a better job elsewhere. In March 1717 he was contacted by the court authorities in Gotha, where the kapellmeister, Christian Friedrich Witt, had fallen ill. Would he, they asked, undertake to perform the Easter Passion in the palace church? He was delighted to do so, particularly since he was paid 12 thalers [£578],* and when Witt died on 13 April there was a clear possibility that he might be headhunted to replace him. His reputation as an organist was now quite widespread around Thuringia, and even further afield. Sebastian at the age of 32 was becoming something of a local celebrity.

The previous year, on 24 January, before the mourning period for the death of young Prince Johann Ernst was over, his half-brother Duke Ernst August had married Princess Eleonore Wilhelmine of Anhalt-Cöthen, in a ceremony in the Nienburg Palace in Cöthen. Sebastian had performed at the wedding celebrations, and his skills were noticed by

---

* No evidence survives as to whether this Passion was composed by Bach, although some scholars believe he may have included some parts of it in the second version of his *St John Passion* in 1725.

Princess Eleonore's brother, Prince Leopold of Anhalt-Cöthen, who was himself an enthusiastic amateur musician. Now in the summer of 1717 the prince was seeking to employ a new kapellmeister, and Bach seemed the obvious candidate. Sebastian, no doubt feeling thoroughly underappreciated since his Weimar employers were not promoting him to succeed Drese, and sensing that the grass was greener in places like Halle, Erfurt, Gotha and Dresden, travelled north to Cöthen and immediately signed an agreement to accept the post.

Dresden, 100 miles east of Weimar, the capital of Saxony, and inhabited by the Elector Friedrich August, King Augustus II of Poland, was a spectacular city full of many medieval and baroque palaces and churches. The concertmaster at the court was the distinguished violinist, composer and dancing-master Jean Baptiste Volumier, who had trained in Paris in the 1680s and served as concertmaster to the Elector of Brandenburg in Berlin from 1692 to 1708. Volumier and his musical colleagues at the court had been somewhat taken aback when a distinguished French keyboard virtuoso called Louis Marchand, the organist at Versailles, had arrived in Dresden and performed before the electoral authorities, apparently in order to secure a post at the court. Augustus II employed a large number of performers, including a French choir of 20 singers, a Polish orchestra, 48 music staff, 60 ballet staff, and 27 actors; and they were all highly paid. In addition to Marchand's renowned playing skills, he had a particular advantage: Augustus II had converted to Catholicism in order to secure the kingdom of Poland – and Marchand was a Catholic.

Volumier came up with the idea of staging a keyboard competition between Marchand and the well-known Weimar organist Bach, and persuaded one of the state ministers, Count von Flemming, to allow the event to take place in his mansion. The king agreed to offer a 500-thaler prize for the winner. Sebastian knew Marchand's compositions (particularly his *Pièces de clavecin*), and was aware of his performing skills. The challenge was a real excitement. He wrote a polite letter to Marchand requesting his attendance, saying that he was ready to execute any improvisatory tasks his competitor might set him, and that he expected Marchand to do the same. Then he eagerly travelled to Dresden, imagining that with the support of his fellow Germans he would triumph.

Unfortunately, Marchand did not turn up. Sebastian performed in front of the large audience recruited by Volumier, and they are said to have enjoyed the concert. But Sebastian could have felt thoroughly annoyed and disappointed at the loss of the possible 500-thaler prize. The only comfort was that Volumier announced to the audience that Marchand, clearly terrified at the prospect of competing with their local hero, had fled from his hotel first thing that morning.*

And then when he came home to Weimar there was more trouble. When he signed up for the appointment in Cöthen, he had made the foolish mistake of not following the essential rule of seeking his employers' permission to move – a regulation he was well aware of in the light of his Halle experience. When he announced his wish to take up the Cöthen post, Duke Wilhelm Ernst was furious at this display of arrogance, and ordered him to be detained in the ducal court prison for a month.[73] He was eventually released on 2 December 1717, with notice that he had been unfavourably discharged by the Weimar court.†

---

* This story became a traditional, and much discussed, anecdote later in Bach's life, and is recounted in the obituary written by his son Carl Philipp Emanuel Bach. But there is no evidence that Marchand accepted the challenge, or that he left Dresden because of fear of it. See NBR 67, 306 and page 427.

† Because the Wilhelmsburg Palace burned down in 1774, it is not clear where Bach's imprisonment took place, but it was probably in the cellar. His post as court organist and chamber musician was taken over by his student Johann Martin Schubart. Kapellmeister Drese was succeeded by his son Johann Wilhelm Drese (1677–1745).

Chapter 6

DEATH IN CÖTHEN

(1717–22)

During his four weeks of incarceration in the extremely uncomfortable palace prison, Sebastian had time to reflect on the ruthless dominance of the aristocracy, and his own failures over the last few years to negotiate his way through the system and up the social ladder to a point where he could feel more secure. What could be more humiliating than ending up in jail?

He had been well aware over the last nine years that the Weimar court was unusually strife-ridden, inevitably involving their employees in the endless competition between the two dukes. Sebastian now realised that he had clearly antagonised the elder one, Wilhelm Ernst, by appearing to side with his nephew Ernst August. Apart from anything else, he had performed frequently in the Red Castle in violation of Wilhelm Ernst's ruling that performances there required his permission. This must explain why Wilhelm Ernst had clearly turned against him, regarding him as insubordinate and disloyal; and this must be why he had rejected the obvious possibility that on Johann Samuel Drese's death he should succeed Christian Friedrich Witt as the Weimar kapellmeister.

Sebastian was no doubt also aware that Ernst August had recently come up with a rather radical new idea: to appoint Georg Philipp Telemann, who was currently kapellmeister in Frankfurt, in overall charge of music at three of the

Thuringian courts – Eisenach, Weimar and Gotha. In due course Telemann, who was perfectly satisfied with his Frankfurt job, had refused the post and written to the duke strongly suggesting that Bach was ideally qualified to be the court director of music.[74] Sebastian had followed this up by making a formal written request for the job, in the same way that he had asked to be promoted to concertmaster; but he got no answer. It must have occurred to him now that perhaps all these events were part of the ducal strife. Ernst August must have been aware for more than a year that his uncle had turned against Bach. This was why he had taken him to Cöthen for his wedding in January 1716 – in order to persuade his future brother-in-law, Prince Leopold of Anhalt-Cöthen, to offer him a job. No doubt Ernst August's Telemann scheme was intended to prevent Wilhelm Ernst from appointing J. S. Drese's son Johann Wilhelm Drese (whom the musical fraternity in Weimar regarded as second-rate) as his father's successor – knowing as he did that Wilhelm Ernst would never agree to Bach's being given the post.

So perhaps Sebastian felt he should be grateful at least to the younger duke for having predicted the whole situation, and surreptitiously arranged his escape route. Perhaps these four weeks in prison were a small price to pay.*

And there was another consolation in the offing: a commission had arrived from Leipzig requesting Sebastian to examine a newly completed organ at the university church of St Paul. The rector of Leipzig University, Carl Otto Rechenberg, had probably been recommended him by Johann Kuhnau, the lawyer and cantor at St Thomas's Church with whom Sebastian had inspected the organ in Halle less than two years earlier. Two weeks after his release from the prison in Weimar on 2 December, he travelled to this major city for the first time. He was stunned by its size

---

* It is also possible, according to the composer and author Ernst Ludwig Gerber (1746–1819), whose father was a pupil of Bach's, that in the Weimar prison he began the composition of his 48 Preludes and Fugues. Gerber wrote: 'According to a certain tradition, he wrote his *Tempered Clavier* (consisting of fugues and preludes, some of them very intricate, in all the 24 keys) in a place where ennui, boredom and the absence of any kind of musical instrument forced him to resort to this pastime.'

(larger even than Dresden, the Saxon capital, where he'd been the previous month), its ancient history, its spacious parks, its broad lantern-lit streets, its flourishing linen, leather and book trades and – particularly – the famous university with its six colleges. Although music was not officially part of the curriculum (as it was at Oxford and Cambridge at this time), there were many keen music students, officially studying law – as Kuhnau had done. To be summoned as the official inspector of the university's main organ, just completed and installed in the chapel by Johann Scheibe, was a strong boost to his self-confidence after the Weimar humiliation.

He promptly wrote his report, addressing it to Dr Rechenberg, on 17 December, and was paid his 20-thaler [£840] fee the next day.[75] He pointed out some minor defects, which Scheibe had already agreed to rectify; and added a strong plea on Scheibe's behalf that he should be paid extra for adding more elements to the organ than had been listed in the original contract, including a wind chest in the *Brustwerck* (the main part of the organ), and the decorative gilding and sculptural additions. He reported that Scheibe would provide the university with a twelve-month guarantee, if they would agree to these reimbursements. And he also pointed out what an important influence the weather had on organs, recommending that part of the window behind the instrument be shielded by sheet iron or bricks, and that it could not be effectively tuned in the current wintry conditions. He signed his report 'Joh. Seb. Bach, Kapellmeister to the Prince of Anhalt-Cöthen, etc.'

But it could not escape his consciousness that this sophisticated, cultivated university, part of the cosmopolitan free imperial city of Leipzig run by its own town council, might be a more pleasurable and productive place for a musician to live and work, to make his fortune and reputation. He remembered his visits to Hamburg when he was a teenager, the affluence and respect that Johann Adam Reincken received there, the popularity of the opera house (where the career of his exact contemporary Georg Frideric Handel had begun to flourish before he moved to London in 1711), and the freedom enjoyed by citizens not controlled by ducal states. Leipzig and Hamburg – and indeed Handel – would remain in the front of his mind.

But for the moment, after the disastrous collapse of his employment in Weimar, he had no choice but to move to Cöthen. He, Maria Barbara and their four children (Catharina Dorothea had just celebrated her ninth birthday, Wilhelm Friedemann was seven, Carl Philip Emanuel nearly four, and Johann Gottfried Bernhard two and a half) travelled the 70 miles there from Weimar, arriving shortly before 29 December, accompanied as usual by Barbara's sister Friedelena and Sebastian's nephew and student Johann Bernhard. They moved to a flat in a house close to the main entrance to the royal palace where Prince Leopold had acceded to power 18 months before.

Cöthen (today spelled Köthen) had been the residence of the princes of Saxe-Cöthen since the division of the Anhalt region into five principalities in the 15th century. Prince Leopold's great-uncle, Prince Ludwig, had ruled from 1600 to 1650, and had built the magnificent palace in the old part of the town, surrounded by a wide moat crossed by three bridges, with broad and sumptuous gardens beyond them.[76] Leopold's father, Prince Emanuel Leberecht, like his predecessors, was a passionate Calvinist, a believer in the reformed Protestant tradition based on the theology of the Frenchman Jean Calvin (1509–64). One significant difference between Calvinism and conventional Lutheranism was the Calvinists' belief that music should be allowed only a very modest role in religious services, confined mostly to unaccompanied singing of psalms by the congregation. But despite his beliefs Prince Emanuel had married a Lutheran, Gisela van Rath, and with his approval in 1699 she had established in Cöthen a new church for her fellow Lutherans, St Agnus's (her own second name was Agnes). Prince Emanuel had died in 1704, when his son was only ten, so Princess Gisela became the regent of Cöthen for the next eleven years, until her son Leopold reached 21, and during this period she strongly supported the interests of the minority Lutheran population, building them a school, and founding a charity for the support of Lutheran girls and women of gentle birth.

During much of this period Prince Leopold and his mother lived apart. Between the ages of 13 and 16 he attended the *Ritter-Academie* in Berlin, and then took a grand tour in 1710, travelling to Holland, England, France and Italy. In the course of these travels he spent three months in Rome, and encountered the lively musical activities around Europe, the opera houses in Venice, Florence, Prague and The Hague, and developed his passion for art and literature. By the time he returned to Cöthen in his 20th year, in 1713, the prince had become an enthusiastic collector of music, and player of the violin, harpsichord and viola da gamba. But he was a Calvinist like his father, and music for him was a medium for entertainment and drama, not religion.

When Sebastian arrived four years later, he was well aware that Cöthen was not a place where he could continue his exploration of church music, and indeed the challenge was to turn his back on the obsession with organs, chorale settings and church cantatas that had filled his life so far, and focus on secular music, and performances to entertain the nobility. Perhaps even opera was in his mind. Prince Leopold had already established over the last few years a large and impressive array of court musicians, several of them recruited by his mother from Berlin, where in 1713 the King of Prussia had dismantled his court *Kapelle*. There were a total of 16, including four string players, two flautists, two trumpeters and a timpanist, all responsible to the newly appointed kapellmeister.[77] Sebastian liked them, and got on particularly well with the violinists Christian Ferdinand Abel and Joseph Speiß, in due course becoming godfather to their children.

The players apparently were required to perform in the palace at least once a week, with programmes of instrumental music, sonatas, concertos and solo pieces, and Sebastian immediately introduced regular rehearsals in his house – for which the court paid him a subsidy of 12 thalers [£576] a year.[78] And indeed money was now, for the first time in his life, less of a worry for Sebastian with his growing family. He had an annual salary of 400 thalers [£19,200], on top of more income from compositions, organ inspections and harpsichord repairs.[79] There was every motivation in this new environment to compose new music to demonstrate the skills of the talented instrumentalists Sebastian was in charge of, and to entertain the prince and his visitors. Maybe Cöthen was very remote, rustic, old-fashioned, with a small population. Maybe its dominant Calvinism meant that he couldn't pursue his thrilling compositions of religious works or his organ-playing skills. And none of his keyboard students had followed him to Cöthen – but no doubt he could recruit new ones. He was determined to take an optimistic view of this new post, working for a young prince who was extremely keen on music, and who was paying him quite generously.

In the spring of 1718, Maria Barbara was pregnant again. The prince, who had trouble with his lungs, had been advised by his physician to go to the newly fashionable health resort of Carlsbad, in north-western Bohemia,* and he took several of his musicians, including Sebastian and Joseph Speiß, there for three or four weeks in May and June. Carlsbad was a popular spa, visited by the affluent classes as much for social entertainment as for improving their health. Prince Leopold took his musicians so that they could perform entertaining concerts before the élite – and perhaps Leopold played too. The trip was highly enjoyable for them all, and Sebastian must have felt elevated by encountering these wealthy patrons of the arts. Carlsbad was like a summer festival.

On their return, more pleasant concerts followed in Cöthen, enlivened by visiting passing musicians. One was the bass singer J. G. Riemschneider – who later became an opera star, performed in three of Handel's operas in London, and ended up as cantor in Hamburg Cathedral. Another was the lutenist Johann Kropffgans. No programmes for these concerts survive, but we can speculate that the works Sebastian composed for his royal employer's pleasure included his marvellous Concerto in D minor for two violins and orchestra (BWV 1043); his solo violin and cello suites (BWV 1001–12); the Prelude in C minor for solo lute (BWV 999), no doubt performed by Kropffgans; a considerable number of keyboard works;

---

* Now Karlovy Vary in the Czech Republic.

and what he called the 'Six concertos with several instruments', which we know as the Brandenburg Concertos (BWV 1046–51). Certainly Leopold had become fond of his kapellmeister, and was thoroughly impressed by his playing ability, his lively compositions and the way he heightened the reputation of the court of Cöthen among smart circles around Germany.

So when on 15 November Maria Barbara gave birth to her seventh (and fifth surviving) child, he was christened Leopold Augustus – because the prince and his younger brother Prince Augustus had both agreed to be godfathers.[80] And that wasn't all: their sister the Duchess of Saxe-Weimar (Duke Ernst August's wife) was godmother, and two other distinguished members of the court were additional godparents, the privy counsellor Christoph Jost von Zanthier, and the wife of the marshal, Herr Gottlob von Nostiz. What an exciting moment, what an honour! Who could ask for grander godparents than these, or more opportunity for social climbing? The baptism took place in the Calvinist palace church on 17 November.

Three weeks later, Prince Leopold's birthday on 10 December was celebrated with the performance of two church cantatas written by Sebastian. The first, entitled *Lobet den Herrn, alle seine Heerscharen* (BWV Anh. I 5), was based on a text written by the well-known poet and professor of rhetoric at Halle University Christian Friedrich Hunold (whose pseudonym was Menantes). Hunold had already achieved acclaim as the librettist of several popular operas at Hamburg and Brunswick. The second was a serenata entitled *Der Himmel dacht auf Anhalts Ruhm und Glück* (BWV 66a).*

There was then another serenata, to celebrate New Year's Day in 1719: his secular cantata *Die Zeit, die Tag und Jahre macht* (BWV 134a). If you want musical evidence of how Sebastian felt about the unusually cheerful year he had just spent in the Cöthen court, with his new, energetic, musical, young royal employer, then BWV 134a provides it. Hunold wrote the text, which is all about praising and admiring the prince, his castle and

---

* Unfortunately, Bach's music for these cantatas, and four or five others he wrote over the next five years, is mostly lost.

the nobility of the house of Anhalt. Two characters (tenor and alto) represent Time and Divine Providence, and a chorus comes in at the end, representing the people and confirming that the prince and his family are blessed. It is not a great masterpiece, but there are some thoroughly jovial arias, which Sebastian would reuse in later compositions.

Some months earlier the prince had commissioned a new two-manual harpsichord from the renowned Prussian court instrument maker Michael Mietke, and in March 1719 Sebastian was charged to travel to Berlin to test the instrument, pay for it, and organise its delivery back to Cöthen, for which the court treasury advanced him 130 thalers [£6,240].[81] It was a productive journey, because while there* he met Margrave Christian Ludwig of Brandenburg, the youngest son of Frederick Wilhelm, Elector of Brandenburg, and impressed him with his keyboard skills. When Christian Ludwig's unrefined but powerful nephew Frederick Wilhelm I (the father of Frederick the Great) had assumed the throne in 1713, he allowed his uncle to remain living in the castle, where he employed his own group of musicians. This was the kind of contact Sebastian felt he might benefit from in the future.

The harpsichord, and Sebastian, were back in Cöthen by the middle of March 1719. Two months later, he heard that his famous contemporary Georg Frideric Handel – who was known everywhere to be prospering as a composer of bestselling operas and other works in London – was visiting the nearby town of his birth, Halle. Sebastian immediately sought, and was granted, permission to travel there by stage-coach. But when he got there Handel had just left. This was a bit depressing: was he to assume that the world's most famous – and possibly richest – composer was deliberately avoiding him? It would certainly stay in his mind that he might benefit from meeting this great contemporary Thuringian musician, if only to comprehend how his career had evolved with such huge success.

---

* Another plausible theory is that Bach met Brandenburg in Carlsbad in the previous year, 1718.

The domestic life of the Bach family, in their spacious flat close to the entrance to the royal palace, was another source of encouragement and pleasure for Sebastian. Catharina was now ten, Friedemann eight, and Emanuel five and a half; and all three were showing musical talent. He insisted they practise on the keyboard every day, taught them the elementary rules of notation, encouraged them to sight-read chorale tunes, and started writing simple keyboard pieces, such as his Six Little Preludes (BWV 933–8), to extend their ability (as he describes it on the opening page) 'to build a two- or three-part contrapuntal structure around a single distinctive motif'. In other words, it was not just playing skills he was urging them to work on, but improvisation and composition.

Even Johann Gottfried Bernard, at four and a half, was showing keen enthusiasm for playing and singing. Only the baby Leopold, godson of the prince, was too small to take part in the family's musical explorations. Sebastian no doubt felt proud that he had created this stable family environment, that the ancient family tradition of musical ability he had inherited from his father was clearly continuing, that he had four sons who would surely follow in their father's footsteps and become organists around Thuringia and perhaps beyond.

But then disaster struck again. On 28 September little Leopold Augustus, aged 10 months and 13 days, suddenly died. This was devastating, not least for Maria Barbara who had lost her twins only five years before. For Sebastian it was just more proof of the vulnerability of life on earth, how defenceless humans are to the random threats of the world we inhabit. In this life, there is really nothing we can rely on; only the life hereafter gives us hope. He felt even closer to Maria Barbara, and involved himself more intensely with his children. In January 1720 he began to compile a special present for his dear eldest son, Friedemann, who had just celebrated his tenth birthday: a new collection of keyboard pieces, preludes and trios in the simple keys of C major, D minor, F major and G minor (BWV 924, 926–30).[82] On its cover he wrote:

<blockquote>
Little Clavier Book
for
Wilhelm Friedemann Bach
begun in Cöthen
on 22 January in the year 1720
</blockquote>

Friedemann was touched, and kept it carefully, adding his own compositions on the later pages.

At the end of May it was time for Sebastian to join Prince Leopold and his fellow musicians for another trip to Carlsbad, and on this occasion the prince decided it should be a longer holiday, to last throughout June. They returned sometime in the second week of July, with no idea of the catastrophe that was about to afflict Sebastian. As he entered his house, his children told him that Maria Barbara had died a few days earlier, and had been buried on 7 July in the chapel grounds of Freidemann's Latin school. The entire school choir had sung at her funeral.[83]

This was perhaps the most devastating event in Sebastian's life so far, and of course it immediately recalled to him the death of his mother in 1694, and the disastrous effect it had had on his father and the rest of the family. The brief happy months of his time in Cöthen felt expunged. He started thinking of following the old patterns: moving once again to another place where the grass might be greener, or immediately finding himself another wife, as his father had done. But at least his children had one advantage over him and his siblings back then: that Maria Barbara's elder sister Friedelena was still with them. The whole family suffered intense grief for many months.

It may even have crossed his mind that his wife might have fallen victim to one of the terrible epidemics that had been assaulting Germany in recent decades. The bubonic Great Plague of Vienna had killed tens of thousands of the city's inhabitants in the 1680s, and another much larger outbreak, originating in the Ottoman Empire, had invaded eastern Europe, Saxony and Thuringia, hitting Dresden in 1680 and Halle and Erfurt two years later. That was how his cousin Johann Nicolaus had been orphaned. And then there was the smallpox epidemic that had attacked Ohrdruf in 1707, which fortunately his brother Christoph's family had survived.* Was his homeland corrupt and disease-ridden?

As for moving to escape, an opportunity arose quite soon when he heard that the organist at St Jacobi's Church in Hamburg had died in September.[84] Hamburg too brought back many memories – his several journeys there from Lüneburg in his teenage years, his encounters with the brilliant organist Johann Adam Reincken, his awareness that it was in Hamburg that Georg Frideric Handel had built up his career, and the energy and economic affluence of the music profession there. Perhaps Hamburg really was the place to seek greener grass. This time with the court's approval, Sebastian took the 200-mile journey by mail coach and arrived in Hamburg by the middle of November. On the 16th he gave a two-hour organ recital at St Catherine's Church, where Reincken – now in his nineties – was still the organist, and the audience included the Hamburg magistrate, and 'many other distinguished persons of the city'.†

There is some evidence that one work he performed that evening was his cantata *Ich hatte viel Bekümmernis in meinem Herzen* (BWV 21), which he had composed in Weimar several years before, in 1714.‡ This is a truly remarkable expression of profound grief, and we can only assume that he chose to include it because of its relevance to his own feelings. Just by reading the words of the first few movements we can see how accurately they express the anguish of a man who has just lost the wife he loved.

---

* See page 37, footnote.

† The event is described in Bach's obituary, written by his son Carl Philip Emanuel Bach in 1750. See *NBR*, p. 302.

‡ We have no knowledge of which other players participated in the performance.

2. Chorus
Ich hatte viel Bekümmernis
in meinem Herzen;
aber deine Tröstungen
erquicken meine Seele.

3. Arie
Seufzer, Tränen, Kummer, Not,
Ängstliches Sehnen, Furcht und Tot
Nagen mein beklemmtes Herz,
Ich empfinde Jammer, Schmerz.

4. Rezitatif (Tenor)
Wie hast du dich, mein Gott,
In meiner Not,
In meiner Furcht und Zagen
Denn ganz von mir gewandt?
Ach! Kennst du nicht dein Kind?
Ach! Hörst du nicht das Klagen

Von denen, die dir sind
Mit Blund und Treu verwandt?

Du varest meine Lust
Und bist mir grausam worden;
Ich suche dich an allen Orten,
Ich ruf und schrei dir nach, –
Allein mein Weh und Ach!
Scheint jetzt, als sei es dir
ganz unbewußt.

2. Chorus
I had great distress
in my heart;
but your consolations
comfort my soul.

3. Treble aria
Sighs, weeping, sorrow, distress,
Anxious yearning, fear and death
Harass my aching heart,
I feel affliction, pain.

4. Tenor recitative
Why have you then, my God,
In my need,
In my fear and trepidation,
Thus utterly forsaken me?
Ah! do you not know your child?
Ah! Do you not hear the
complaining
Of those who with you
Are connected with faith and
truth?

You were my joy
And have become cruel to me;
I search for you everywhere,
I call out and cry for you, –
Yet my pain and lamentation
Seem now entirely
unknown to you.

The verses, probably written by the Weimar poet Salomo Franck, were a perfect representation of how human tragedies can undermine religious belief. Sebastian's settings of them, as well the orchestral sinfonia which opens the work, with its exquisite oboe solo, express to powerful effect the emotions that grief incorporates, including anger and despair. Part two of the cantata attempts to alleviate some of the pain by expressing the comforts that God offers in the after-life, but musically these movements are noticeably less convincing.

Sebastian went on to display his organ skills by improvising for almost half an hour on the hymn tune *An Wasserflüssen Babylon* ('By the waters of Babylon').* Reincken was highly impressed by the performance, saying to him, 'I thought that this art was dead, but I see that in you it still lives.'† He invited Sebastian to stay, but there was a problem: Sebastian was understandably anxious not to repeat the error he had made in Arnstadt, when he had outstayed his absence as organist there – so he travelled back to Cöthen on the 23rd.

The cantor of St Jacobi, Joachim Gerstenbüttel, and the church committee had met two days earlier to discuss the arrangement of an audition for the eight applicants for the post of organist. The date was fixed for 28 July; Reincken and two other local musicians were appointed to join the cantor to assess the players; and there was a detailed discussion about whether or not the chosen organist should be expected to make a payment to the church. This was a regular issue in Hamburg (and elsewhere in Europe). Some jobs, particularly junior ones, were sold to the highest bidder, senior employees were not expected to pay, and the situation in between was unclear. The committee in this case specifically recorded the following decision:

---

* A version of this survives as BWV 653. The tune itself is included in the collection of Bach's harmonised chorales, published after his death.

† Quoted in C. P. E. Bach's obituary.

> There were many reasons not to introduce the sale of an organist's post, because it was part of the ministry of God; accordingly the choice should be free, and the capacity of the candidates should be more considered than the money. But if, after the selection had been made, the chosen candidate of his own free will wished to give a token of his gratitude, the latter could be accepted for the benefit of the Church and the Holy Sepulchre, entered in the books, and used again where it was needed.

When the audition took place as planned, three candidates had dropped out, but four others gave their best performances. The general view of those who heard them, clearly influenced by Reincken, was that none of them could compete with Bach, who was the ideal candidate. They wrote to him to say so, no doubt also explaining their policy about payments for the post. But by then Sebastian had lost his nerve, perhaps as usual influenced by his anxieties about money, and he wrote back requesting that his name be removed from the list. So instead they appointed Johann Joachim Heitmann, who showed his gratitude by paying the enormous sum of 4,000 marks [£64,000] to the church. Once again, Sebastian had failed to seize the opportunity to progress, like his contemporaries Handel and Telemann, to one of the major musical communities in Germany. But he could hardly have matched Heitmann's gift.

Back in Cöthen, Sebastian pursued another of his methods for dealing with life's miseries, devoting every moment of his time to work. He wrote more cantatas for the prince's birthday on 10 December and for New Year's Day,* more pieces for organ and keyboard, and more of the collection of preludes and fugues in all twelve keys, major and minor, which he intended to entitle *Das Wohltemperirte Clavier*. This concept – designing music in all the keys, including the remotest ones like F-sharp

---

* One of them survives in a rewritten version as BWV 184, *Erwünschtes Freudenlicht*. Its second movement is a delightful treble and alto duet, and the closing chorus is memorable too.

major and B-flat minor – was a direct result of Sebastian's exploration of tuning keyboard instruments in the manner described as well-tempered.

However passionate you are about music, tuning is a curiously abstruse subject, which may explain why tuners are often not musicians, and musicians are not tuners. The main problem dominating the world of music in the early 18th century was the attempt to resolve an issue dating back to ancient Greece, when Pythagoras, around 530 BC, dictated that harmony – like mathematics – was a symbol of the orderly nature of the world created by the gods. His experiments in measuring the vibrations of strings revealed that there did indeed appear to be inviolable mathematical relationships between different sounds.

The first thing Pythagoras discovered was that one note vibrates exactly half as much as its equivalent an octave higher, so the relationship between middle C and the C above it can be indicated as 1:2. It was also discovered that various other intervals, such as C to G one fifth above, C to F one fourth above, and C to E one third above, also corresponded with simple ratios (in these cases 2:3, 3:4 and 4:5 respectively).

As keyboard instruments came into use, people searched for tuning systems that would preserve as many as possible of these ratios in all keys. The problem was that if for example you tune a keyboard to preserve the ratio of 2:3 between all notes that lie a fifth apart in the C-major scale (so-called 'Pythagorean tuning'), the instrument sounds harsh and unpleasant in a key that makes a lot of use of C#, F# or G#.

In the centuries leading up to Bach's time many attempts were made by theorists to resolve this dilemma, such as with the 15th-century Spaniard Bartolomeo Ramos de Pareja's 'just intonation', and the 'temperament' (or *participata*) introduced by his Italian contemporary Franchinus Gaffurius. A hundred years later, 'mean-tone' temperament was widely used, involving very slightly shortening the fifth (2:3) gaps. Another solution was to introduce additional keys within the octave, so that, for example, C# and D♭ could be tuned differently.

But even in Sebastian's time musicians still tried to hang on, if they possibly could, to the fundamental assumption that sound, like numbers, was God's creation and contained God's messages. The distinguished Thuringian organist Andreas Werckmeister (1645–1706) wrote many influential treatises on the subject, based on the premise that music was an art 'prescribed by God himself for his service'; and in his book *Musicalische Temperatur* (the second edition of which was published in 1691) he proposed a tuning method that enabled all twelve keys to be played on keyboard instruments.

Sebastian's central idea, though, was probably less to do with tuning than with training, providing music students with an opportunity to familiarise themselves with reading and playing in the entire range of major and minor keys, so as not to be daunted by the more remote ones. Wilhelm Friedemann was his main student at the time,* and no doubt he was as fascinated as any student is by, for example, the notation of the E-flat minor prelude with six flats, and the following fugue in the same key with five sharps.

By March 1721 Sebastian also finished another project: the collection of six concertos which he had decided to donate to Christian Ludwig, the Margrave of Brandenburg, whom he had met on his trip to Berlin two years earlier to buy the harpsichord.[85] To accompany it he wrote a letter, in French, to the margrave:

> Your Royal Highness
>
> As I had a couple of years ago the pleasure of appearing before Your Royal Highness, by virtue of Your Highness's commands, and as I noticed then that Your Highness took some pleasure in the small talents that Heaven has given me for music, and as in taking leave of Your Royal Highness, Your Highness deigned to honour me with the command to send Your Highness some pieces of my composition: I have then in accordance with

---

* Sebastian's brother Johann Christoph died in February 1721, aged 49, and his son Johann Bernhard, who had been living as a student with Sebastian's family for six years, succeeded him as organist at St Michael's Church in Ohrdruf.

> Your Highness's most gracious orders taken the liberty of rendering my most humble duty to Your Royal Highness with the present concertos, which I have adapted to several instruments; begging Your Highness most humbly not to judge their imperfection with the rigour of the fine and delicate taste that the whole world knows Your Highness has for musical pieces; but rather to infer from them in benign consideration the profound respect and the most humble obedience that I try to show Your Highness therewith. For the rest, Sire, I beg Your Royal Highness very humbly to have the goodness to continue Your Highness's gracious favour toward me, and to be assured that nothing is so close to my heart as the wish that I may be employed on occasions more worthy of Your Royal Highness's service – I, who without an equal in zeal, am, Sire, Your Royal Highness's most humble and obedient servant
>
> Jean Sebastien Bach   Coethen, 24 March 1721

Evidently it was in his mind that Berlin might be another escape route, and one that would not involve any financial investment. Whether the unctuous style of the letter impressed or annoyed the margrave remains unclear, but despite the masterly quality of the Brandenburg Concertos nothing happened, and another two decades would pass before Sebastian visited Berlin again. In the meantime, knowing that he had wasted some very fine compositions, Sebastian reused quite a few of the movements in subsequent works.*

By June, a new young singer had joined the prince's group of musicians. Anna Magdalena Wülcken was born on 22 September 1701 in Zeitz, 20 miles south of Leipzig, the youngest daughter of a trumpeter named Johann Caspar Wülcken who now worked in the nearby town of Weißenfels.

---

* For example, the first movement of Concerto No. 1 appears as the opening Sinfonia in *Falsche Welt* (BWV 52, November 1726); and the third movement as the opening chorus of BWV 207 (December 1726). The Allegro third movement of Concerto No. 3 was adapted as the opening sinfonia of BWV 174 (June 1729). And the entire score of Concerto No. 4 was rearranged in the late 1730s for obbligato harpsichord, two recorders, and strings.

Magdalena's musical background was almost as impressive as the Bachs'. Both her grandfathers were professionals: her mother's father, Andreas Liebe, was an organist, and so was her brother Johann Siegmund Liebe (1670–1742). On the Wülcken side, trumpet-playing was the tradition: in addition to her father, three of her sisters married court trumpeters between 1710 and 1720, and her brother Johann Caspar Wülcken (1691–1766) was himself court trumpeter at Zerbst, near Cöthen. There is no proof that Bachs and Wülckens had encountered one another in Thuringia over the preceding years, but it would be nice to speculate that when Sebastian was composing cantatas in Weimar that required three or four trumpeters – such as *Christen, ätzet diesen Tag* (BWV 63) and *Der Himmel lacht* (BWV 31) – some of the Wülckens might have been involved in the performances.

In any event, one of Sebastian's duties as the Cöthen kapellmeister was to advise on the employment of singers and instrumentalists, and only eleven months after Maria Barbara's tragic death he persuaded Prince Leopold to engage this attractive 19-year-old singer as one of the court's chamber musicians. Her talents were immediately appreciated by the royal household, securing her a generous salary; and as far as we know she had every intention of continuing to work as a professional musician.

But to Sebastian, no doubt vividly remembering how his father Ambrosius had responded to his mother's death when he was nine, Anna Magdalena appeared the ideal new wife – attractive, energetic and highly musical. Admittedly she was 16 years younger than him, but wide age differences between couples were not uncommon, and it was particularly helpful that on 25 September, just after her 20th birthday, they were both invited to be godparents to the baby son of the prince's butler, Christian Hahn. Almost immediately afterwards they became engaged. It was an astonishing stroke of luck that this lovely young woman, who had lots of talent and was already earning a respectable living in the music profession, should have fallen for him, and be willing to sacrifice her independence by taking on a husband so much older than her, and his four children.

Their marriage took place on Wednesday 3 December.[86] They threw a big party, no doubt attended by all their local musical colleagues and their families, as well as Bach and Wülcken family members, and Sebastian bought 264 quart bottles of Rhine wine, at a cost of 84 thalers 16 groschen [£4,064],[87] to entertain the guests. This was the best way out of the misery of the last 18 months.

Magdalena was now stepmother to three boys and a girl who was only seven years younger than her. But with Sebastian's support she was determined to carry on with her public performances, and to their delight the prince offered her an annual salary of 200 thalers. That meant that the family's total income was now 600 thalers [£28,800], almost three times what it had been when Sebastian and Maria Barbara lived in Weimar. This suggests that for the first time in his life he felt really rather affluent – and he was about to feel more so.

There had been another family death that autumn: Martha Catharina Lämmerhirt, the widow of Sebastian's maternal uncle Tobias, and his daughter Catharina's godmother, had died on 10 September. Tobias and Martha had no children of their own, and in her will she divided her legacy among several relations, including Sebastian and his brother Jacob. However, the surviving Lämmerhirt heirs were rather offended by this, taking the view that Bachs had no right to their family money, and they embarked on legal proceedings to try to reverse the will. Sebastian was annoyed, and in March 1722 wrote a petition to the Erfurt town council:

> It is already known to Your Honours how I and my brother Joh. Jacob Bach (who is in the Royal Swedish service) come to be partial heirs in the Lemmerhirt [*sic*] estate. Since I now hear unofficially that the other honourable joint heirs are disposed to open a lawsuit concerning this estate, and since it would not suit either me or my absent brother, for I am not disposed to contest the Lemmerhirt will at law, but am

satisfied with what is bestowed and conferred upon me therein, on account of which I herewith for myself and *sub cautione rati* in the name of my brother wish to renounce and enter formal *protestation* against any legal proceedings, now therefore I have accordingly considered it necessary to notify Your Honours obediently of this fact, with the most humble request that you will graciously receive this my renunciation and protestation, and will kindly cause the *quotas* still due to me and my brother from the inheritance, from what already lies on deposit as well as from whatever may be deposited in the future, to be remitted, which high *faveur* I acknowledge with most obedient thanks, and remain therefore, Your Honours' most obedient servant

Joh. Seb. Bach.[88]

Fortunately for the Bachs, the Erfurt council agreed that there was nothing improper about Martha's will, the case was not pursued, and the legacies were duly paid out. Sebastian's share was a substantial 550 thalers [£26,400], almost as much as the family's annual income.

Magdalena was touched by – and perhaps a little envious of – Sebastian's Little Clavier Book for Friedemann, and soon in the new year she acquired a similar album and wrote on the front cover

Little Clavier Book
for
Anna Magdalena Bach
Anno 1722[89]

and Sebastian immediately began to write pieces into it. They include several of his harpsichord works that were later called French suites (BWV 812–16), minuets, an organ fantasia and a chorale prelude. They quite clearly were not designed to improve Magdalena's keyboard skills, but much more about declarations of the true love he felt for her. This young angel had taken on a difficult husband and his four troubled children, and he absolutely adored her for doing so.

He also continued to inscribe into Friedemann's book, including all but one of the twelve preludes from his *Well-Tempered Clavier* collection. In the course of this year he completed this extraordinary set of 24 keyboard compositions in major and minor keys in each of the twelve semitones, starting with C major and ending with B minor, and wrote a title page on which he described its purpose as 'for the use and benefit of enquiring young musicians and for the special diversion of those already well versed in this study'.[90] In other words, it was designed not only as an instruction manual for music students, but as a challenge to professional performers.

If he had followed the practice of his friend Georg Philipp Telemann, Sebastian could easily have arranged the publication of this remarkable work. At the cost of around 50 thalers [£2,400] a printed edition of a few hundred copies could have been placed on the market through music publishers in Leipzig, Hamburg or Frankfurt; and given that this manual subsequently became the most influential of all keyboard compositions over the next centuries he would certainly have made a substantial profit. It was not that he lacked the requisite initial financial outlay, given the Lämmerhirt inheritance and the sharp increase in family income. We can only assume once again that he lacked the confidence to pursue this option, and that he could not emulate Telemann's highly successful business treatments. The work remained, for the time being anyway, available only in the handwritten fair copy he had completed, and parts of it in Friedemann's Little Clavier Book.

Sebastian's and Magdalena's marriage in December 1721 was not the only important wedding that month in Cöthen. Eight days later (and the day after his birthday), Prince Leopold himself had married his 19-year-old cousin Princess Friederica Henrietta of Anhalt-Bernburg. Over the next few months it became apparent to Sebastian that her arrival on the scene was having some strange effect on his life and work as well as on his fellow musicians. She seemed a much less enthusiastic music-lover than her new husband, or perhaps there were financial constrictions in the court budget; but in any event it was clear that expenditure on music was being much reduced.* The number of music staff had decreased over the last few years and replacements had not been made, and the prince began to make clear that economising was now a court necessity.

Sebastian was reluctant to admit that he had played any part in this new situation, but he was of course aware that Magdalena's salary was twice as large as any of the other chamber musicians'. It was also the case that a new palace guard of 57 soldiers had been established, the new princess received an annual allowance of 2,500 thalers [£120,000], and other new expenses had been undertaken in recent months. In addition there was some evidence of disputes within the royal family about such issues as power-sharing and pensions. It was obvious that music had become a minor priority, whether or not Princess Friederica was part of the cause. This was very frustrating, and Sebastian felt newly motivated to begin looking for a job elsewhere. In June the news reached him of the death of Johann Kuhnau, the distinguished organist at St Thomas's Church in Leipzig, with whom Sebastian had co-operated over the organ inspection in Halle six years before, and again in Leipzig the following year. Perhaps this Leipzig post was really the kind of job he should be looking for, in a free imperial city (like Mühlhausen, only much bigger) run by elected town councillors rather than aristocrats.

In fact the Leipzig city council had already decided to offer the job to Georg Philipp Telemann, who had recently moved from Frankfurt to Hamburg as director of music and was already earning at least 1,000 gulden [£42,000] a year there. Telemann initially accepted the offer, but several weeks later, in the autumn of 1722, his Hamburg employers

---

* Nine years later, in 1730, Bach wrote about this in a letter to his childhood friend Georg Erdmann (see page 212).

offered him further financial advantages – including giving him the opportunity to direct the opera at the Goose Market, and appointing him leader of the *collegium musicum* – and by November he wrote to the council 'rather ungraciously to withdraw his acceptance'.[91]

So the Leipzig councillors had to start again.

Chapter 7

SCHOOLMASTER IN LEIPZIG

(1722–23)

Although Sebastian had recruited no new music students while he was working in Cöthen, he was certainly enjoying the process of training his own children, particularly in the skills of composition and keyboard-playing. He had already put a lot of effort into it, compiling a range of keyboard pieces specifically designed to lead these keen and talented youngsters up the musical ladder he had climbed himself. There were his Six Little Preludes,* and his collection of 30 two- and three-part 'inventions' and 'sinfonias', on the title page of which he wrote:

> *Aufrichtige Anleitung* ('Sincere Instruction') In which lovers of the keyboard, especially those who are keen to learn, are shown a clear method not only (1) of learning to play clearly in two parts, but also, after further progress, (2) of dealing correctly and well with three obbligato parts. At the same time, they are shown not only how to have good ideas but also how to develop them well. Above all, they are shown how to arrive at a singing style of playing, whilst also acquiring a strong foretaste of composition.†

---

* See page 113.

† BWV 772–86 and 787–801.

And of course there were his twelve preludes and fugues in *The Well-Tempered Clavier*, and his *Orgel-Büchlein* containing more than 40 hymn harmonisations, which were particularly useful for developing sight-reading skills. His own sight-reading ability had certainly been a source of considerable pride and self-confidence throughout his youth, making clear to him that young musicians should devote most of their early efforts to developing this capacity.*

He also had fond memories of his favourite pupils in Weimar – although he had heard the sad news that Johann Martin Schubart, who had succeeded him as court organist in Weimar in 1717, had died only four years later, aged 31, and his post had been taken over by his fellow pupil, Johann Caspar Vogler. Even sadder was the news that his brother Jacob, who was living in Stockholm as a member of the court orchestra, had died in April. On the brighter side, by the late summer of 1722 Magdalena was already pregnant. The first child of their marriage was born the following spring, and named Christiana Sophia Henrietta.

Looking back over his career in the last two decades, 37-year-old Sebastian could not feel he had been properly appreciated by the various employers, whether aristocrats or town councillors, to whom he had devoted himself. In Arnstadt there had been ceaseless rows both with his fellow musicians and with his employers. In Mühlhausen they had paid him a mere pittance, and failed to grasp his concept of 'a well-regulated church music'. In Weimar, Duke Wilhelm Ernst had turned viciously against him for no proper reason other than his own endless disputes with his nephew, and had sent him to prison. And now in Cöthen the prince – who had admittedly for some time appeared highly appreciative

---

* Johann Nikolaus Forkel, in his biography published in 1802, devotes an entire chapter to the subject of Bach's keyboard skills, including his 'facility in looking over scores and executing the substance of them at first sight on the keyboard'. Much of the information must have been provided by Bach's son C. P. E. Bach, who was also a highly skilled keyboard player.

of his performing and composing ability – had turned cold on him too. It was particularly frustrating to watch how Georg Philipp Telemann, whose talents were no greater than his, was always surging ahead in the world of music, and always being offered the best jobs.

So several factors inclined Sebastian to consider a move to Leipzig. First of all, the job was in a school, and so was associated with teaching, which was the one occupation he felt was really productive. Secondly, Leipzig was an important city with a large and fairly affluent population, and many foreign visitors, so it should be possible to increase his earnings as well as boost his reputation. Thirdly, it was the post Telemann had applied for, so – even though he had eventually rejected it – it must be worth having. And fourthly, after months in Cöthen with less and less to do, he really had no choice but to go for whatever job was on offer.

St Thomas's had an ancient history which offers some explanation for the rather peculiar roles of its cantor. In medieval times both the church and the school were under the control of Augustinian monks, and one of the school's main objects was to provide training for boys and young men to perform music in the church services, for which a gradually increasing number of scholarships – many of them contributed by the growing affluent middle classes – were available. When Leipzig adopted Lutheranism in the 16th century, control of the monastic foundation of St Thomas passed into the hands of the town council; but over the next century few other changes were made, and *Thomasschule* was still in effect a charity-based choir school, though it was officially known as a Latin school. Because of this history, staff appointments were the responsibility of the town council, rather than of the school's headmaster, Johann Heinrich Ernesti (1652–1729).

As things turned out, it was by no means an easy task to secure the post of director of music at St Thomas's School and choirmaster at the neighbouring St Thomas's Church. For one thing, the Leipzig councillors, clearly aggravated by the fact that their generous offer had been turned down by Telemann – and how long he had taken to make up his mind – prolonged the decision even more.[92] Kuhnau had died in June 1722, and Telemann was appointed in August; but his decision to decline was not announced until November. So the council met on the 23rd to discuss reassessing the five other candidates, plus two more who had applied since. But there was an immediate dispute among them about what qualifications and abilities they were looking for. Should the new appointee be a university-educated, trained teacher, or should he be a talented composer and promoter of contemporary music, who could advance Leipzig's reputation and compete with Hamburg, Dresden and Frankfurt?

The nine remaining contenders were all well qualified in both respects, although none had quite the energy and sparkle of Telemann. It is interesting to note how their career statuses compared with Sebastian's at this stage. Johann Friedrich Fasch (1688–1758), who had been educated at St Thomas's and read law at the university, was of course a familiar local figure, and already a prolific composer; and he had recently been appointed kapellmeister at the court of Anhalt-Zerbst. Christian Friedrich Rolle (1681–1751), whom we have already encountered when Sebastian reported on the new organ in Halle in 1716,* was a graduate of Halle University and a year earlier had taken the position of cantor at St John's Church in Magdeburg. George Lenck (1685–1744)† was cantor at Laucha an der Unstrut, near Naumburg. Georg Balthazar Schott (1686–1736), who had studied at Jena and Leipzig universities, was also familiar to the council because he was currently organist and music director at the New Church in Leipzig. Johann Martin Steindorff (1663–1744), cantor at St Mary's Cathedral in Zwickau, was much older than the other candidates (in his late fifties), and was therefore soon ruled out by the council and not auditioned. Andreas Christoph Duve (1676–1749), the son of a pastor in Brunswick, was currently cantor at St Martin's Church there. Georg Friedrich Kauffmann (1679–1735) was organist and music director at the Magdeburg court, and had already built his reputation as a composer. And

---

* See pages 94-5.

† Sometimes spelled Lembke.

finally there was Christoph Graupner (1683–1760), another former student at St Thomas's School and Leipzig University, kapellmeister at the court of Heße-Darmstadt, who had already done well in his early years composing operas in Hamburg, before moving to Darmstadt.

By 21 December, Duve had performed his audition in St Nicholas's Church and failed, Fasch had withdrawn on the grounds that he could not manage the teaching, and Lenck and Steindorff had been ruled out by the council. So that left Rolle, Kauffmann, Schott, Graupner and Bach. Graupner was already by then the clear favourite, and much impressed the local congregation with a performance of his Magnificat at the two churches of St Thomas and St Nicholas on Christmas Eve. His formal audition, in which he performed two of his cantatas, was fixed for 17 January; but by then most of the councillors, perhaps influenced by his Hamburg connections, were already convinced that he was the ideal candidate, and their only concern was whether his current employer, Count Ernst Ludwig of Darmstadt, would release him. Rolle and Bach were cited as suitable back-ups. Schott performed on 2 February.

In Cöthen, Sebastian prepared two cantatas* for his performance on 7 February, using texts probably supplied to him by the mayor, Gottfried Lange, and based on the Gospel readings of the day, from Luke: 18. Unfortunately, he did not feel very inspired, and although both cantatas are perfectly competent they are distinctly unmemorable. But they did get some brief press coverage, when the Hamburg *Relationscourier* published a report from Leipzig that the music was 'amply praised on that occasion by all knowledgeable persons'.[93]

By mid-February Graupner was still top of the list and the council finally offered him the job. But – to Graupner's own surprise – Count Ernst Ludwig turned out to be unwilling to lose him, and offered him an increased salary to persuade him to remain in Darmstadt. Rather more promptly than Telemann had done the previous year, he wrote to the council on 22 March declining the job.

---

* BWV 22 and 23.

They met again on 9 April, now more than ten months since Kuhnau's death. Three of the original ten candidates were still possibilities: the Leipzigian Schott, Kauffman from Magdeburg, and Bach from Cöthen. But there was little enthusiasm for any of them, and indeed one of the councillors is recorded as saying that 'since the best could not be obtained, mediocre ones would have to be accepted'.[94] One clear problem the committee faced was that none of the candidates appeared to be very enthusiastic about his schoolteaching obligations, which included Latin literature and grammar and the Lutheran catechism. As they had previously done with Telemann, the councillors agreed that whoever was elected would be allowed to employ a substitute for these tasks, as long as it was at his own expense. Among the remaining group of 'mediocre' musicians, Bach was offered the job first, accepted it verbally, and obtained a formal letter of release from Prince Leopold which was posted to the council on 13 April.* He returned to Leipzig a few days later, and signed a preliminary undertaking[95] which included the following points:

- I will conduct myself according to the school regulations ... and in particular I will instruct the boys admitted into the school not only in the regular classes established for that purpose, but also, without further compensation, in private singing lessons.
- I will faithfully attend to whatever else is incumbent upon me, and in addition – but not without the Council's knowledge and consent – in case someone should be needed to assist me in Latin language instruction, will ... compensate the said person out of my own pocket.

There was then another grander and more formal council meeting on 22 April at which Mayor Lange proposed Bach's appointment, indicating

---

* Although Prince Leopold, unlike Duke Wilhelm Ernst of Weimar, had no objection to Bach's dismissal, he retained him as honorary kapellmeister (*Kapellmeister von Hausa us*), which would require him to compose occasional music for events at the Cöthen court.

that his advantages were several: he 'excelled at the clavier'; he had teaching experience; and he had formally agreed 'to give not only public but also private instruction'. The councillors cast their votes in his favour, and finally, on 5 May, he was formally appointed and presented with a 14-point contract of employment. Several of these points would turn out to be of considerable significance, but it seems likely that Sebastian was by now so frustrated by the endless delays and obstacles that he signed it without debating them. It reads as follows:

1 I shall set the boys a shining example of an honest, retiring manner of life, serve the School industriously, and instruct the boys conscientiously;

2 Bring the music in both the principal churches of this town [St Thomas's and St Nicholas's] into good estate, to the best of my ability;

3 Show to the honourable and most wise Council all proper respect and obedience, and protect and further elsewhere as best I may its honour and reputation; likewise if a gentleman of the Council desires the boys for a musical occasion unhesitatingly provide him with the same, but otherwise never permit them to go out of town to funerals or weddings without the previous knowledge and consent of the Mayor and honourable directors of the School currently in office;

4 Give due obedience to the honourable inspectors and directors of the School in each and every instruction that the same shall issue in the name of the honourable and wise Council;

5 Not take any boys into the School who have not already laid a foundation in music, or are not at least suited to being instructed therein, nor do the same without the previous knowledge and consent of the honourable inspectors and directors;

6 So that the Churches may not have to be put to unnecessary expense, faithfully instruct the boys not only in vocal but also in instrumental music;

7 In order to preserve the good order in the Churches, so arrange the

music that it shall not last too long, and shall be of such a nature as not to make an operatic impression, but rather incite the listeners to devotion;

8 Provide the New Church with good scholars;

9 Treat the boys in a friendly manner and with caution, but, in case they do not wish to obey, chastise them with moderation or report them to the proper place;

10 Faithfully attend to the instruction in the School and whatever else it befits me to do;

11 And if I cannot undertake this myself, arrange that it be done by some other capable person without expense to the honourable and most wise Council or to the School;

12 Not go out of town without the permission of the honourable Mayor currently in office;

13 Always as far as possible walk with the boys at funerals, as is customary;

14 And shall not accept or wish to accept any office in the University without the consent of the honourable and learned Council.

Now therefore I do hereby undertake and bind myself faithfully to observe all of the said requirements, and on pain of losing my post not to act contrary to them, in witness whereof I have set my hand and seal to this agreement.

In general these undertakings were not dissimilar to those in employment contracts he had seen before, like the one he had signed in Arnstadt, and the one he had rejected in Halle. He knew he was responsible for the music in the two churches, as well as for teaching in the school. As for composition, it was a relief that clause 7 placed no restrictions on his style other than to proscribe 'an operatic impression'. He was aware too that whereas the school and the churches were controlled by the town council, the university was an independent institution responsible directly to the king in Dresden. The council explained that this was the reason for clause 14, preventing him from taking a formal university post without their permission; but like his predecessor Kuhnau he was expected to take responsibility for occasional services in the university church of St Paul's. These so-called 'old divine services' took place four times a year, at Easter, at the Lutheran Reformation Festival at the end of October,* at Christmas and on Whit Sunday – and the latter was only ten days away.

So he immediately put together a cantata† based on part of Jesus' reply to Judas in the Gospel reading for Whit Sunday, John 14: 23:

> If a man love me, he will keep my words: and my Father will love him, and we will come unto him, and make our abode with him.

He opened it by setting these words to a charming and lively treble and bass duet in C major, accompanied by two trumpets, strings, timpani and continuo. The rest of the cantata contains a striking treble recitative to words written by the Hamburg poet and theologian Erdmann Neumeister;‡ a rather more humdrum bass aria also in C major and also based on Neumeister's text; and a chorale setting of the first verse of Luther's famous hymn *Komm, heiliger Geist, Herre Gott*. This rather modest and brief cantata was the piece Sebastian first performed as the new St Thomas's School cantor, and his first connection with the university.

Another concern, as usual, was money. The basic salary paid by the council was a mere pittance: 21 thalers 21 groschen a quarter, making 87 thalers 12 groschen [£4,200] a year. But the housing he was offered was free, and he was assured that there would be substantial additional fees available for performances at weddings, christenings, funerals and other

---

* Martin Luther nailed his 95 theses on the church door at Wittenberg on 31 October 1517.

† BWV 59, *Wer mich liebet, der wird mein Wort halten*.

‡ See page 97.

special services, that he would receive regular payments from local charities, and that he would earn additional fees for maintaining and repairing the church organs, as well as a portion of the money received by his pupils' twice-weekly street singing as *Kurrende* (serenaders). Over the next few years, as we shall see, he did just about manage to keep his income up to the level he and Magdalena had earned in Cöthen, but it was a considerable effort. At least the title, *director chori musici*, was reasonably reputable.

The eight members of the Bach family moved in to their new flat at St Thomas's School on the afternoon of 22 May, having travelled there from Cöthen in two carriages, followed by four wagons containing their household goods. There were now five children: Catharina Dorothea aged 14, Friedemann (12), Emanuel (9), Bernhard who had just celebrated his eighth birthday, and the baby, Christiana Sophia Henrietta. Sebastian's sister-in-law Friedelena, now in her late forties, was with them too, and fortunately this newly renovated flat in the school building, on three floors, was considerably more spacious than anything they had enjoyed in Cöthen. The flat included an office for the cantor, containing instruments and the school's substantial music library, and here was where Sebastian would begin his immense range of compositions over the next few years. We can assume that many of the household possessions were similar to, or even inherited from, the crowded house in Eisenach where he spent his early childhood,* and that certainly quite a bit of the space was taken up with musical instruments. For example, we know that at the end of his life† he owned seven different kinds of harpsichords, three violins, three violas, two cellos and a double bass, as well as a viola da gamba, a lute and a little spinet.

Friedemann and Emanuel would shortly, on 16 June, be welcomed in to St Thomas's as school pupils.[96]

---

* See pages 16-17.

† As stated on page 304, they are listed in an inventory that came out in November 1750, which also includes his 119 thalers in cash (£5,712), the furniture, a range of books and much else (see *BachDokumente II*, no. 627).

Sebastian had already decided to devote a great deal of his time to composing new cantatas, to be performed every Sunday throughout the year, so that he could create and sustain the goal of a 'well-regulated church music' which he had mentioned in his letter to the Mühlhausen council when he left in 1708,* and which must have remained in his mind ever since. The next Sunday, 30 May, was only eight days away. The first cantata he produced,† on the first Sunday after Trinity at St Nicholas's Church, was a much more substantial work than the one he had performed two weeks earlier in St Paul's. It comprises 14 movements, seven to be performed before the sermon and seven after it. The text (probably provided by Gottfried Lange, the mayor who had assisted with his audition in February) was again based on the Gospel reading of the day, the parable of the rich man and Lazarus,‡ with its encouraging message that those who are meek and wretched in this life will, if they believe in God, inherit eternal bliss. The work includes a wide range of compositional elements that Sebastian would continue to explore in his cantatas over the next few years. It opens with a harmonically adventurous chorus, accompanied by oboe solo and strings, which changes half-way through to an elaborate fugue sung first by the four soloists and then by the choir. Three brief recitatives and two arias follow, and the first half ends with a short chorale with lively and joyful instrumental accompaniment.

After the pastor, Dr Salomon Deyling, had completed his sermon, the cantata reopened with a brief sinfonia based on the same hymn tune, with a trumpet solo. Then there are three more brief recitatives and two more arias, and the piece ends with a repetition of the chorale from the first half. The whole performance took about 30 minutes, and was reported to have gone down well with the congregation.[97]

---

* See pages 73-4.

† BWV 75, *Die Elenden sollen essen*.

‡ Luke 16: 19–31.

On the following day Sebastian was formally introduced to the school by the chairman of its board, Baumeister* Gottfried Conrad Lehmann, accompanied by the chief town clerk, Carl Friedrich Menser. It should have been a perfectly pleasant ritual, in which the school staff sat on one side of the upstairs auditorium (on the same floor as Sebastian's study) and the board members on the other, the town clerk announced Herr Bach's appointment, and the school choir sang a piece in the corridor outside before filing into the room. But Sebastian observed, perhaps for the first time, an example of the ceaseless tensions and petty disputes that were a constant pattern between the various councils and consistories that held responsibility for Leipzig's institutions.[98] It turned out that Dr Deyling (1677–1755), who – as well as being pastor of St Thomas's and professor of theology at the university – was superintendent of the St Nicholas's Church consistory and therefore Sebastian's boss, had declined to attend, and had 'delegated his duties' to the Reverend Christian Weiß, the pastor of St Thomas's and a school inspector. Weiß interrupted the ceremony by announcing that he had been instructed to represent the church consistory in Deyling's absence and to install the new cantor. Lehmann was furious, and pointed out that it was the town council's right to make the appointment, not the consistory's. Sebastian had already made a brief speech thanking the council for his appointment, and the event ended with another performance by the choir. But when Menser and Lehmann returned to the town hall and reported what had happened, Menser was ordered immediately to go and speak to Deyling about it. In due course, Deyling apologised, and the issue was closed; but Sebastian was now well aware that he had to be scrupulously careful not to offend either of these institutions.

He was also aware that his workload was substantially greater than it had been in Cöthen. On the first three days of the week he was in charge of Latin grammar classes from 7.00 to 8.00 a.m., and two singing lessons, at 9.00 a.m. and 12.00 p.m. He was also responsible for taking the pupils

---

* Master builder.

to early service on Friday morning. Thursday and Saturday were free, but had to be fully devoted to preparing for the Sunday services. These were pretty demanding, for several reasons. First, it turned out that, despite the agreement Sebastian had signed, he was in fact responsible for the Sunday music in four rather than two of the town's churches, not just St Thomas's and St Nicholas's but also the New Church in the north-west Ransche quarter and St Peter's in the southern Peter's quarter – and of course also for the quarterly old services in the university church of St Paul's, on the eastern bank, as well as for music to celebrate events such as the town council elections in August each year. For these tasks the 50-odd resident students were divided into four choirs of around twelve boys each, with a prefect in charge. Choir One, containing the best singers, performed the cantatas alternately in the two main churches, accompanied by instrument players from the town music company. Choir Two sang unaccompanied in whichever church had no cantata that Sunday. Choir Three sang in the New Church, and Choir Four was confined to singing hymns in St Peter's. So an essential task every week, probably on Saturday, was to train and rehearse all the choirs, particularly the first two, and the prefects in charge of them.

As for the non-musical teaching Sebastian had undertaken, it was pretty clear that he could not find time for it, and so he decided – with the approval of Mayor Lange – to take advantage of clause 11 in his employment contract, and make a private agreement with his colleague Carl Friedrich Pezold to pass the Latin grammar teaching over to him, and pay him an annual 50 thalers [£2,400] for doing it.

When Sebastian had time to look around and appreciate the qualities that his new residential town provided, its structure and architecture were certainly uplifting. The old walled town was quite small – the tradition was that you could walk around the entire circuit in only 8,954 paces, about five miles – but lately some pleasant suburbs had been constructed beyond the walls, with fine parks and lime, yew and mulberry trees planted everywhere. The narrow streets in the centre were lined with hundreds of lamps, which made walking around at night much more agreeable, and in the last few years many of the rich local families had built themselves grand baroque stately homes in these streets, transforming the town's atmosphere.

There was also a strong sense of economic and commercial vitality. The discovery and mining of silver and tin in the Orr mountains south of the city at the end of the 15th century had brought great prosperity to the town. For several centuries there had been much active national and international trading in Leipzig, and regular week-long trade fairs had been operating three times a year since the mid-15th century, attracting thousands of exhibitors and visitors, often boosting by more than a third the existing population of around 32,000. Local traders included some 20 book printers and publishers, and a range of manufacturers of gold, silver, silk, velvet, wool, cotton and linen, over 100 wholesale dealers and several hundred retail shops.*

A vivid description of Leipzig written by the German historian and teacher Johann Georg Keysler (1683–1743) who travelled there in 1730 tells us that the citizens were civil and polite, the buildings elegant, and the surrounding gardens 'make it appear superior to many capital cities'.[99] He was particularly impressed by the Magistrates' Library in the centre, freely open to the public on Wednesday and Saturday afternoons, containing 25,000 books, including many 15th-century versions of the Bible, and a Latin version written in 1273. It was also a museum, with striking

---

* Lady Mary Wortley Montagu, visiting Leipzig in November 1716, wrote in a letter to her sister that it was 'a town very considerable for its trade', and described her shopping there. A few decades later, another British visitor to the city wrote, 'Trade is the soul of Leipzig. Considering that it is an inland place, and without the advantage even of a navigable river, the greatness of its commerce is very surprising; but it is owing to its fairs, of which they have three very considerable ones every year.' (Joseph Marshall, *Travels through Holland, Flanders, Germany, Denmark, Sweden, Lapland, Russia, the Ukraine and Poland, in the Years 1768, 1769, and 1770*, London 1772.)

collections of ancient swords, urns, antiques, medals, fossils, minerals, an Egyptian mummy, four huge globes made in Venice, and several fine paintings including portraits of Luther and his wife.

The St Thomas's School building where the Bachs lived stood in the south-western quarter of the old town, looking out across the wall over the Bösen park. Keysler describes it as 'very large', with 'a fine orangery; and in a pavilion, adorned with some paintings, is to be seen a numerous collection of curiosities in the animal and botanic kingdoms. In an enclosure within the garden are kept some small white stags of a different species from the common deer, as appears by their horns.' A few hundred yards away from the school stood Pleißen Castle, a strong citadel inhabited by the city's military governor, who represented the Saxon electoral court, and his troops. Beyond the castle, on the south side, was St Peter's Church. The town hall stood in the spacious central Market Square, and a few hundred yards to the east were St Nicholas's Church, St Paul's and the university.

The entrance to the apartment was through a grand door in the southern end of the building. On the ground floor were an entrance hall, one living room and one bedroom, and below them a cellar housing storage, washing facilities, pantry and lavatory. On the first floor was the main sitting room, with two windows looking out over the square (with the church on the left) and another looking south; next to it the main bedroom where Sebastian and Magdalena slept; and Sebastian's office with access to the school library and classrooms. On the floors above, including two attics, were more bedrooms for Friedelena and the children.

But there was a darker side to the town. About 20 years earlier the town council, motivated to handle standard urban problems such as poverty and crime, had organised the construction of a massive building in northern Leipzig, just inside the wall on Brühl Street, to provide housing for the poor and orphans as well as a penitentiary for criminals and an insane asylum.[100] George House currently had about 200 inmates, of whom nearly half were wretched orphaned children, and a staff of about 20. Despite the dramatic recent advances in international trade in Leipzig, and improvements in the general economy, almost as much as 50 per cent of the town's inhabitants were 'close to or in an actual state of poverty, a proportion which grew throughout the century'.[101] It was all too clear to Sebastian that, unless he could make achievements similar to those of his contemporaries Telemann and Handel, he stood alarmingly close to this kind of disaster. For two reasons he was particularly conscious of this negative side of city life, first because one of his few friends, Johann Ernst Kregel – who would soon become godfather to a Bach child* – had been the first town councillor to take on the management of George House; and secondly because in April that year, 1724, a major investigation into George House's management was launched by the governing mayor, Adrian Steger (who had been involved in the council meeting that formally approved Sebastian's appointment in April the previous year).[102] Avoiding poverty and finding means to improve his income were clear priorities.

Furthermore, writing and performing a new cantata every week was no easy task. First of all, there had to be a libretto that was appropriate for whatever Sunday service was coming up, and although there were existing cantata texts to borrow from, there were certainly not enough. Sebastian had copies in his library of Erdmann Neumeister's *Geistliche Poesien* and Georg Christian Lehms's texts,† and was aware of other clergymen who wrote cantata libretti, such as Johann Michael Heineccius (1674–1722) whom he had met in Halle. Salomo Franck, the court poet in Weimar, had provided him with the words for almost all his church cantatas in the Weimar period, and most of his secular ones came from the late Halle poet Christian Friedrich Hunold (1681–1721). Now in Leipzig there seemed to be no easy solutions to this problem. But for the first few weeks at least he could draw on his existing works, the cantatas he had written in Weimar and Cöthen.

---

* Ernestus Andreas, who died on 1 November 1727 a few days after his birth (see page 195).

† See page 97.

Once he had composed a movement, the parts had to be written out and distributed to the players and singers, so that they had some time to practise. Fortunately, Magdalena (although by the summer she was already pregnant again) could help here, with her meticulous copying skills. The music had to be ready by Saturday, when they got together for rehearsals.

Sebastian wrote his first new cantata in June, for performance on the 20th. He used a text from Neumeister's *Geistliche Poesien* based on Christ's statement in his Sermon on the Mount that 'all things whatsoever ye would that men should do to you, do ye even so to them'.* The overall message, attacking the human shortcomings of hypocrisy, slander and discrimination, appealed strongly to Sebastian, and inspired an attractive opening alto aria, the words of which can be translated thus:

> A clear intention of German faith and goodness makes us beautiful before God and mankind. The Christian's hard work and trading throughout his life would make him stand on this footing.

The aria, accompanied by lively strings and basso continuo in 3/4 time in F major, is followed by a long and mostly simple recitative in which the tenor elaborates on this theme:

> Honesty is one of the gifts of God. The fact that in our time so few men have it is because we do not ask God for it. We are naturally evil. If we want to be worthy, then this must be governed by God's spirit, and guided along the path of virtue. If you seek God as your friend, you must not inflict duplicity, deceit and cunning on your neighbours. A Christian should endeavour to be like a dove, and live without falsehood. Love your neighbour as yourself.

---

* Matthew 7: 12. This was the fourth Sunday after Trinity, when the Gospel reading (Luke 6: 36–42) is Christ's similar exhortation to good works, beginning 'Be ye therefore merciful, as your Father also is merciful'. The cantata is BWV 24, *Ein ungefärbt Gemüte*.

The next movement is a splendid chorus in G major, to the words of Jesus from St Matthew's Gospel, accompanied by trumpet and strings, in which the soloists enter one by one in the central passage; and it ends in G major. There follows a second recitative, this time sung by the bass, in which the message is a reflection on its predecessor:

> Hypocrisy is created by the devil. If you adopt it, you wear his livery. Do Christians covet this? God forfend. Honesty is rare. The wicked often appear in the guise of angels, with the wolf concealed within sheep's clothing. What could be worse? Slander, abuse and discrimination are everywhere. Dear God, protect me.

The tenor then sings an aria in A minor, accompanied by two oboes d'amore and bassoon, conveying the message that 'loyalty and truth must be your purpose; speak openly as your heart feels; and kindness and virtue make us like God and his angels'. The cantata ends with a soothing chorale setting of the first verse of Johann Heermann's 1630 hymn *O Gott, du frommer Gott*, enlivened with obbligato string accompaniment.

The six movements were performed immediately after the Gospel reading, and took less than 20 minutes. Then the congregation sang a hymn, and the sermon followed. Later, during communion, they performed a second, slightly shorter, cantata, one of Sebastian's Weimar compositions.* The procedure in the Leipzig churches, on certain Sundays anyway, required that the communion be accompanied by music; Sebastian had previously provided this by performing some of his longer existing cantatas which are divided in two halves.†

Ein ungefärbt Gemüte is no masterpiece, but it is a standard example of the kind of work he was now committed to producing at least once a week – and indeed sometimes more often because of special services

---

* BWV 185, with text by Salomo Franck.

† Such as BWV 75, 76 and 21, performed on 30 May, 6 June and 13 June 1723.

like the Feast of John the Baptist, which occurred on Thursday 24 June, and the Feast of the Visitation of the Virgin Mary, on Friday 2 July, or the town council election on 30 August. By the end of the year he had written or revised at least 25 cantatas, or as many as 200 movements – in other words, more than one movement a day, an extraordinary level of productivity. Most of them are not particularly memorable, but they were most efficiently composed to exploit the skills of his students and instrumentalists, thoroughly fulfilled his professional obligations, and in his view represented an important step in modernising the town's church music.

Compared with the range of cantatas he composed in Cöthen and Weimar, they also contained features of a much more sophisticated kind which would greatly influence his future compositions. He became fascinated with the ways in which pitch, harmony and rhythm could represent and echo the meaning of the words. Instrumental combinations, and the use of less common instruments such as recorders, slide trumpets and oboes d'amore, could also create a special atmosphere appropriate to the biblical readings of the day, or indeed, in the case of weddings or town council celebrations, all sorts of suitable emotions. And a notable number of movements from these cantatas were reused in his later works.

The one performed on 1 August, *Schauet doch und sehet, ob irgend ein Schmerz sei wie mein Schmerz* (BWV 46), is a revealing example. It opens with a chorus setting of the harrowing words from Jeremiah 1: 12:

> Behold, and see if there be any sorrow like unto my sorrow, which is done unto me, wherewith the Lord hath afflicted me in the day of his fierce anger.

In a powerful expression of human grief, the chorus opens in D minor with two treble recorders accompanied by the strings, in a truly haunting 67-bar section with extraordinary harmonic complexity. Sebastian knew this was a masterpiece, and nine years later, in 1733, he rearranged it as the central part of his Missa in B minor,* written to impress the Elector of Saxony after disputes with the Leipzig town council: the music turned out to be perfectly adaptable to the words from the Latin litany *Qui tollis peccata mundi, miserere nobis* ('Thou that takest away the sins of the world, have mercy upon us').

The chorus is followed by an equally emotional tenor recitative, also accompanied by the treble recorders. There is no record of who wrote these poetic words, so we can speculate that Sebastian did so himself; and whether he did or not, we can sense all too clearly from the musical setting how he felt about them:

So klage, du zerstörte Gottesstadt, du armer Stein- und Aschenhaufen! Laß ganze Bäche Tränen laufen, weil dich betroffen hat ein unersetzlicher Verlust der allerhöchsten Huld, so du entbehren mußt durch deine Schuld. Du wurdest wie Gomorra zugerichtet, wiewohl nicht gar vernichtet. O besser wärest du in Grund verstört, als daß man Christi Feind jetzt in dir lästern hört. Du achtest Jesu Tränen nicht, so achte nun des Eifers Wasserwogen, die du selbst über dich gezogen, da Gott, nach viel Geduld, den Stab zum Urteil bricht.

Then cry aloud, O fallen town of God, you wretched heap of stone and ashes! Let whole streams of tears be flowing, for you have been struck by an irreplaceable loss of that most precious grace, the loss of which you must bear through your own fault. You were, like Gomorrah, castigated, even if not annihilated. O, better if you were razed to the ground than that the enemy of Christ should now slander you. You need not the tears of Jesus, yet need now the waves of passion which you call upon yourself; for God, who is so patient, strikes the rod of judgement.

---

* This subsequently, towards the end of his life, became the opening section of the Mass in B Minor, BWV 232.

The recorders also play a touching part in the other movements, including the penultimate aria for alto, and the beautiful closing chorale, taken from a 17th-century hymn by Johann Matthäus Meyfart, expressing human relief that the wrath of God has been averted by the death of Jesus.

Indeed, most of the cantatas he wrote in the second half of 1723 are full of adventurous experiments in musical ways of conveying the religious messages of the relevant Sunday, as well as means of improving and dramatising the conventional cantata structure. For his chorale settings he chose hymn tunes, which often had significant historical associations for him, and applied the *stile antico* or motet style to their arrangement. He developed the *da capo* structure in his arias, by elaborating the repetition of the opening section. He hugely expanded his fugal skills in many of the choruses, such as the opening movements in BWV 105 (*Herr, gehe nicht ins Gericht mit deinem Knecht*, on 25 July), BWV 69a (*Lobe den Herrn, meine Seele*, on 15 August) and BWV 25 (*Es ist nichts Gesundes an meinem Leibe*, on 29 August). And above all he became increasingly entranced by his ability to 'word-paint', to represent through the music the verbal messages of the text. Here is one example: in the alto aria that is the third movement of BWV 136 (*Erforsche mich, Gott, und erfahre mein Herz* on 18 July), the text describes the arrival of the day of judgement, and the terror that will be inflicted on hypocrites. The word *erzittern* (tremble) inspires a melisma, where the single word is represented by a long range of notes. And then the wrath of God which follows involves an abrupt change of tempo. The chorale that ends BWV 105 (see above) is another example: the choir sings the simple hymn in harmony, but the accompanying strings represent the gradual calming of the Christian's conscience. They start with semiquavers for the first five and a half bars, followed by triplet quavers for another five and a half bars, then quavers, then triplet crotchets; and when the choir falls silent the chorale ends with two quiet bars of crotchets. Thus the listener is gradually drawn from deep anxiety to peaceful reconciliation.

Many of these advancements reached a new level of subtlety on 17 October with the cantata for the 21st Sunday after Trinity, BWV 109 (*Ich glaube, liebe Herr, hilf meinem Unglauben*), based on a quotation from Mark 9: 24: 'Lord, I believe; help thou mine unbelief.' The agonising struggle for faith in God was a new source of inspiration for Sebastian, and in the cantata he employed a range of musical devices to express it, of which perhaps the most memorable is the brilliant orchestral accompaniment of the final chorale, a verse from one of Lutheran Germany's most popular and familiar hymns, Lazarus Spengler's *Durch Adams Fall* (1524). The tenor aria, too, reaches a new level of beauty, no doubt inspired by the opening words *Wie zweifelhaftig ist mein Hoffen*, meaning 'How full of doubt is my hope'. Unquestionably, Sebastian was now regularly motivated by the dark side of the human mind – and indeed his own – to provide a deeply emotional musical expression of it.

On 14 November, for example, the Gospel reading from Matthew 24, was Jesus' response to his disciples' question 'what shall be the sign of thy coming, and the end of the world?' Jesus' harrowing reply includes the clear statement that non-believers are destined for dreadful destruction. For Sebastian's opening tenor aria* he (or possibly his anonymous librettist) wrote the following five-line gruesome text:

Es reißet euch ein schrecklich Ende,	A terrible end awaits you,
Ihr sündlichen Verächter, hin.	you sinful enemies.
Der sünden Maß ist voll gemessen,	Your degree of sin is fully measured,
Doch euer ganz verstockter Sinn	but your thoroughly stubborn minds
Hat seines Richters ganz vergessen.	have quite forgotten your judge.

His setting in D minor is distressingly severe, full of melismas, harmonic travels, swirling demisemiquavers and sudden stops, a brilliantly dramatic musical expression of God's anger.

---

* In cantata BWV 90.

Rather less successful was the next week's much longer eleven-movement cantata,* which also dealt with the coming of the last judgement, possibly because most of the music had been written several years earlier in Weimar. It is thoroughly skilful and competent, but lacking the emotional power Sebastian was increasingly finding ways to articulate.

As Christmas approached, his work schedule became even more intense. In the village of Störmthal, a mile or two south of Leipzig, a new organ had been installed in the church and a cantata was required at the beginning of November for its consecration service. Sebastian was fortunately able to draw on a long secular cantata he had written in Cöthen (BWV 194a), and he devoted a lot of time to adapting it for the event, producing a twelve-movement work† in two halves that lasted nearly 40 minutes – an example of devotion to duty and hard work, but with no serious inspiration. Nor was the cantata for Christmas Day,‡ another that he had originally written in Weimar, a masterpiece – although it does contain a long and quite striking alto recitative. Closely observant listeners may have begun to conclude that the composer was not very good at expressing cheerful celebrations, and felt more at home amid gloom and despondency.

But Sebastian had been working on a piece that with any luck would refute this assumption, also to be performed on Christmas Day. His Magnificat,§ based on the song of the Virgin Mary from Luke 1: 46–55, was unquestionably his most impressive and moving vocal composition so far, conveying an intense feeling of joy and optimism appropriate at Christmas.

His setting of these Latin words followed in several ways a long tradition of Magnificats of which he was well aware, including ones by composers such as Vivaldi, Albinoni and his contemporary Telemann. Each verse would

---

* *Wachet! betet! betet! wachet!* (Watch, pray, pray, watch), BWV 70, performed on 21 November.

† BWV 194, *Höchsterwünschtes Freudenfest* ('Most wonderful celebration').

‡ BWV 63, *Christen, ätzet diesen tag* ('Christians, etch this day').

§ BWV 243a.

be the source of an individual movement, ending with the *Gloria Patri*; and in addition he followed the Lutheran tradition of inserting *laudes*, hymns in Latin and German, which expanded on the Christmas story. This would make 16 movements in all (12 numbered verses and four *laudes*, indicated by letters, A-D), but he also wanted to make sure that the overall piece was not too long, so they are all quite brief compared with those of his cantatas. The text inspired the following arrangements:

1 Magnificat anima me Dominum,
   My soul doth magnify the Lord,
   5-voice chorus, 3 trumpets, timpani, 2 oboes, strings, bassoon, organ.
   3 minutes

2 Et exsultavit spiritus meus in Deo salutari meo.
   And my spirit hath rejoiced in God my Saviour.
   Treble solo, strings, organ.
   2¼ minutes

A Vom Himmel hoch, da komm ich her, Ich bring euch gute neue Mär;
   Der guten Mär bring ich so viel; Davon ich singen und sagen will.
   From the high heavens I come here. I bring you good news. The good news is so abundant that I must sing and speak of it.
   Unaccompanied 4-part chorus.
   1½ minutes

3 Quia respexit humilitatem ancillae suae; ecce enim ex hoc beatam me dicent
   For he hath regarded the low estate of his handmaiden: for, behold, from henceforth [all generations] shall call me blessed.
   Treble solo, oboe, bassoon, organ
   2½ minutes

HARMONY AND DISCORD

4   ... omnes generationes

...all generations

5-voice chorus, 2 oboes, strings, bassoon, organ.

1½ minutes

5   Quia fecit mihi magna qui potens est, et sanctum nomen eius.

For he that is mighty hath done to me great things; and holy is his name.

Bass solo, cello, double bass, organ.

2 minutes

B   Freut euch und jubiliert; Zu Bethlehem gefunden wird.

Das herzeliebe Jesulein, Das soll euer Freud und Wonne sein.

Rejoice and be merry; in Bethlehem was found the most dear baby Jesus, to be our comfort and joy.

5-part choir, cello, double bass, organ.

1¼ minutes

6   Et misericordia a progenie in progenies timentibus eum.

And his mercy is on them that fear him from generation to generation.

Alto and tenor duet, strings, organ.

3½ minutes

7   Fecit potentiam in brachio suo, dispersit superbos mente cordis sui.

He hath showed strength with his arm; he hath scattered the proud in the imagination of their hearts.

5-voice choir, 3 trumpets, timpani, 2 oboes, strings, bassoon, organ.

2 minutes

C   Gloria in excelsis Deo! Et in terra pax hominibus, bona voluntatis.

Glory be to God in the highest, and on earth peace, good will towards men. (Luke 2: 14)

5-voice choir, 2 oboes, strings, bassoon, organ.

1 minute

8   Deposuit potentes de sede et exaltavit humiles.

He hath put down the mighty from their seats, and exalted them of low degree.

Tenor solo, strings, organ.

2 minutes

9   Esurientes implevit bonis et divites dimisit inanes.

He hath filled the hungry with good things, and the rich he hath sent empty away.

Alto solo, 2 recorders, cello, organ.

3 minutes

D   Virga Jesse floruit, Emanuel noster Apparuit; Induit carnem hominis, fit puer delectabilis; Alleluja.

Jesse's rod did flourish. Our Saviour has appeared clad in the flesh of men as the most lovable son; Alleluia.

Treble and bass duet, cello, double bass, organ.

3 minutes

10   Suscepit Israel puerum suum recordatus misericordia suae.

He hath holpen his servant Israel, in remembrance of his mercy;

2 trebles and alto trio, trumpet, strings.

1½ minutes

11   Sicut locutus est ad Patres nostros, Abraham et semini eius in saecula.

As he spake to our fathers, to Abraham, and to his seed for ever.

5-voice choir, cello, double bass, organ.

2 minutes

12   Gloria Patri et Filio et Spiritui Sancto! Sicut erat in principio et nunc et semper et in saecula saeculorum. Amen.

Glory be to the Father, and to the Son, and to the Holy Ghost. As it was in the beginning, is now, and ever shall be, world without end. Amen.

5-voice choir, 3 trumpets, timpani, 2 oboes, strings, bassoon, organ.

2 minutes

So the whole piece could be performed in little more than half an hour; but it creates a powerful overall effect on its audience which outstrips that of any of the preceding cantatas. In the light of our new familiarity with how particular groups of words stimulate Sebastian to create musical expressions of them, we can cast our eyes over the text and predict which sections will inspire his most creative and emotional responses. 'And my spirit hath rejoiced in God my Saviour' is certainly an unusually charming if brief treble aria, pleasantly accompanied by the strings. More striking is the next verse, with its reference to poverty and God's respect for deprived human beings; and Sebastian creates an intensely dramatic effect by leading it straight into the following chorus about 'all generations'. Equally moving is the expression of the words 'And his mercy is on them that fear him from generation to generation', sung by the alto and tenor, and the following fugal chorus, with its trumpets and orchestra, and the sudden silence at the end succeeded by a sombre concluding Adagio. The words 'He hath put down the mighty from their seats' are also inspirational, providing a lively tenor aria accompanied by the strings.

But the high moment comes next, and its motivation is self-explanatory: at the heart of Mary's song are the words 'He hath filled the hungry with good things: and the rich he hath sent empty away'. The exquisite alto aria is the only movement in the whole Magnificat accompanied by the treble recorders, which give it a uniquely gentle beauty; and *dimisit inanes* ('sent empty away') is movingly expressed by the sudden ending on a single note.

The Magnificat ends with three more brief and cheerful movements, and the congregation in St Thomas's Church on the evening of Christmas Day were no doubt moved by the entire work. Sebastian must now have felt that he had crossed a new line in his composition, and began to consider tackling a much more ambitious project: the creation of a Passion in time for performance on Good Friday the coming April.

Traditional Passions had been performed in Lutheran churches at Easter since the 16th century, and had gradually developed into more complex compositions, in which the narrative was elaborated with chorales and Italian-style operatic genres such as arias, reflecting and commenting on the Gospel narrative. The St Matthew and St John Passions attributed to Luther's contemporary Johann Walter (1496–1570) remained the most popular, but dramatic oratorio Passions began to appear in the second half of the 17th century, of which the three by Heinrich Schütz (1585–1672) are perhaps the most famous. Sebastian was well aware of the genre, and indeed performed his contemporary Reinhard Keiser's *St Mark Passion* in Weimar in 1713, adding to it a few movements which he composed himself. His Leipzig predecessor Johann Kuhnau had also written a *St Mark Passion*, and had performed it at St Thomas's Church only a year before his death in 1722. So although Leipzig was well known for its conservative attitudes to church services, the oratorio Passion was now accepted as a regular Easter event. Various librettos existed, and Sebastian had a copy of B. H. Brockes's *Der für die Sünde der Welt gemarterte und sterbende Jesus* which would provide a suitable text on which to base his composition. He had three months in which to compose and rehearse his *St John Passion*.

Chapter 8

THE HEIGHTS OF COMPOSITION

(1724–26)

The pursuit of weekly new cantatas was clearly going to become even tougher in 1724, if only because Sebastian was gradually running out of previous compositions that could be re-performed or adapted. One advantage in tackling the Passion composition in the spring was that during the 40 days of Lent no choral music was required in the churches, which meant that only 15 or so cantatas were needed after Christmas. Another way of dealing with the pressure was to simplify their structure, for example by including several simply accompanied chorales.* But even though Sebastian made the most of these advantages, he must have been determined that all the works should maintain the standards he had set himself in 1723, and every now and then he felt inspired to produce something memorable. BWV 64 on 27 December, for instance, contains a beautiful soprano aria, about how worldliness will vanish in a cloud of smoke but the love of Jesus is eternal. And more achievements were to come.

On New Year's Day the cantata was an outstandingly festive work entitled *Singet dem Herrn ein neues Lied* ('Sing unto the Lord a new song'),† from Psalm 149: 1. The following day, the piece‡ was almost embarrassingly simple, opening with a plain chorale, and none of the nine movements – of which two others

---

* For example, in BWV 40, performed on 26 December, BWV 64 (27 December) and BWV 153 (2 January) there are three chorales among the eight or nine movements.

† BWV 190.

‡ BWV 153, performed on 2 January.

are plain chorales – lasted more than a minute or two. The tenor aria, though brief, is a dramatic expression of *Stürmt* (storm), there is a fairly attractive alto aria, and the work ends uniquely with all three verses of a hymn. Four days later, for Epiphany on Thursday 6 January, the cantata* was lavishly orchestrated with two horns, two treble recorders, two oboes d'amore plus the usual strings; both the opening chorus and the tenor aria convey a cheerful, dance-like atmosphere. And then the following Sunday, 9 January, came *Mein liebster Jesus ist verloren*,† which has an appropriately lamenting opening tenor aria to these words, which Sebastian had originally composed in Weimar. On 16 January too the performance was a revival, of cantata BWV 155, composed in 1716.

But as proof that his intense work programme would not suppress his newly developed compositional abilities, at the end of January Sebastian came up with two brilliant new pieces. The cantata for the third Sunday after Epiphany, *Herr, wie du willt, so schicks mit mir*,‡ opens with an exceptionally inventive structure. A beautiful orchestral passage played by two oboes, strings and horn turns out to be the introduction to the opening verse of a famous hymn by Kaspar Bienemann sung by the chorus. But it is more than that; the chorale is interrupted three times, with the same orchestral accompaniment, by passionate recitatives from the tenor, bass and soprano, commenting on Bienemann's verse. This hugely dramatic composition is about the horror of death, and indeed the torments of life, and the movement opens and closes with the repeated statement by the choir that belief in God is the only solution: *Herr, wie du willt* ('Lord, as thou wilt').

There follows a pleasant tenor aria with oboe accompaniment, expressing the struggle between confidence and disbelief, a brief bass recitative and a very moving bass aria, *Herr, so du willt* ('Lord, if thou wilt'), in which the singer begs for God's intervention to appease his anguish;

---

* BWV 65.

† 'My dearest Jesus is lost', BWV 154.

‡ BWV 73.

and the cantata ends with a simple chorale from another 16th-century hymn, expressing the ever-presence of God.

And as if that was not enough, the following Sunday's cantata* opens with one of the most beautiful and moving arias Sebastian ever composed. The Gospel reading for the fourth Sunday after Epiphany tells the strange story of how Jesus was on board a ship with his disciples: 'And, behold, there arose a great tempest in the sea, insomuch that the ship was covered with the waves: but he was asleep.' The aria ponders on these words:

Jesu schläft, was soll ich hoffen?	Jesus sleeps, what hope do I have?
Seh' ich nicht	Do I not see,
Mit erblaßtem Angesicht	With an ashen countenance,
Schon des Todes Abgrund offen?	The abyss of death open before me?

Setting it in E minor with a pair of treble recorders – which he now frequently used for the most emotional occasions – Sebastian composed a song in which the word 'sleeps' is expressed in a single low note (B) which the alto soloist holds for two and a half bars while the instruments play 21 notes. Death too is expressed in a long-held note. The effect is profound. There are other fine elements in this cantata, including a tenor aria with dramatic demisemiquavers representing the tempest, and sudden adagios in the evocation of faithful Christians reaching the shore. It ends with a verse from the exquisite hymn *Jesu, meine Freude* by Johann Franck. Sebastian's standards were rising every week.†

---

* *Jesu schläft, was soll ich hoffen*, BWV 81.

† Three more new cantatas were performed in February, BWV 83, 144 and 181. The text of the latter, entitled *Leichgesinnter Flattergeister* and based on the Gospel reading for that Sunday, Luke 8: 4–15, the parable of the sower, is believed by some scholars to have been written by Bach himself, and is an exceptionally dramatic interpretation of Jesus' message that only people on 'the good ground' will benefit from the word of God. The musical setting, on the other hand, is less memorable.

At the end of February, as he was reaching the completion of the *St John Passion*, Magdalena, now aged 22, gave birth to her second child, a boy whom they named Gottfried Heinrich after his two godfathers – the Leipzig mayor, Herr Gottfried Lange, and a lawyer called Heinrich Graff. His godmother was Frau Ernesti, the wife of the headmaster of St Thomas's School. Gottfried Heinrich was Sebastian's ninth child so far; four of the nine had already died. The ever-presence of death was never far from his mind, but it was encouraging that this baby boy appeared to be thoroughly healthy. Friedemann and Emanuel were getting on well in the school, and had been joined by their younger brother Johann Gottfried Bernhard. Catharina Dorothea, now 15, was at home to help manage the household, along with her aunt Friedelena Margaretha. Domestic life was pleasant, and the family frequently got together to sing and play music.

Sebastian's reputation was now blossoming, not just because of the enhanced standards of his cantata compositions but because the performing abilities of several of his numerous music students had improved so noticeably. They had now been benefiting for seven months from his intense and inspiring music classes, which took place four days a week and represented nearly a fifth of the school's entire education. Music was a compulsory subject for all the students, about 150 in total, and clearly Sebastian could not focus personally on all of them; we can assume that he concentrated his attention on the few who showed unusual musical talent and interest.* Virtually all the students sang every Sunday in one of the four churches, but presumably only a few played instruments or sang solos. He encouraged these individuals to exploit their abilities in the whole musical range, including sight-reading, playing several string, wind and keyboard instruments, singing (which involves breathing skills and voice control) and composition.

But Sebastian was not wholly or even principally dependent on his school pupils for the performance of cantatas in the churches; his main source of performers was the small group of professional members of the

---

* See Christoph Wolff, page 248.

town music company, which comprised four town pipers (*Stadt Pfeiferei*) and at least three beer fiddlers, all of whom could play several instruments*; and in addition some of their sons and students. And he could also recruit students from the university, of whom several in due course became professional musicians. One of these was Johann Adolph Scheibe (1708–76), the son of the organ builder Johann Scheibe whose instrument Sebastian had inspected six years before.† Johann Adolph, who had been educated at St Nicholas's School and had just joined the university to read law, was later described by Sebastian, in a testimonial designed to assist his career, as 'thoroughly at home not only on the clavier and violin but also in composition'.[103] We will hear more of him 14 years later. Most of these undergraduates too could play several instruments, including violins, cellos, flutes, recorders and keyboards. Although we do not know who specifically played which parts in the 30 or so cantatas performed up until then in Leipzig, it is interesting to note that most of them included strings, oboes and basso continuo (involving the organ and/or harpsichord); 14 included two or three trumpets; four involved one, two or three recorders; and occasional additions included a horn (probably played by Gottfried Reiche, the senior town piper), a viola da gamba, a bassoon, a cornett, several trombones, and timpani. So the total orchestra usually numbered ten or twelve players, accompanying a choir of twelve or fourteen singers.

The two churches where these works were performed every Sunday, St Thomas's next to the school, and St Nicholas's in the east of the city, were both grand and spacious churches with a central and two side aisles. St Nicholas's, the city's main church, was founded around 1165 and substantially extended 300 years later into the Gothic architectural style. The large organ was mounted on the wall at the west end of the south aisle, and fairly close to it in the centre was a modest choir loft where around 25 singers and players sat and performed behind the congregation

---

* They included two trumpeters, two violinists, two oboists and a bassoonist.

† See page 107.

and facing the altar. St Thomas's Church too had a large organ, recently restored by Johann Adolph Scheibe's father, at the west end of the nave, with rather more spacious galleries around it for the performers. There was also a second, smaller, organ on the arch half-way down the nave, with a modest choral loft next to it. Since the participants had more room, and were closer together – and possibly because the acoustics were clearer – Sebastian definitely preferred performing the more complex cantatas in St Thomas's.

So naturally it was there that he planned the first performance of the most substantial work he had composed so far (BWV 245). In March, having just passed his 38th birthday, he organised the printing of the *St John Passion* booklet, providing the text and announcing its performance at St Thomas's Church on Good Friday, 7 April.

But unfortunately he had ignored the fact that the town council had, three years before, imposed a strict rule that Passion performances should take place alternately every year in the two churches, and that the previous year's had been in St Thomas's. As he should have kept in mind after signing his contract with the council in May the year before,* the third clause stated all too clearly that obedience to his employers was a fundamental undertaking. They might have ignored this matter, except that St Nicholas's superintendent, Dr Johann August Höltzel,† made a formal complaint to the council, and they had no choice but to order Sebastian to move the performance to St Nicholas's. He apologised, and told them that he had chosen St Thomas's because there was more space there, and the harpsichord at St Nicholas's needed repairing. The council agreed to pay for the repairs and for a leaflet announcing the move to St Nicholas's, and also to arrange for more space to be available in the choir loft. So the dispute was resolved. But Sebastian,

---

* See page 135.

† Or was he the city councillor? See 'The Rise of the Poor, Weak, and Wicked: Poor Care, Punishment, Religion, and Patriarchy in Leipzig, 1700–1730', by Tanya Kevorkian.

recalling the row the previous year between Lehmann and Deyling at his introduction to the school,* no doubt felt a growing irritation at the way the different authorities to whom he was connected – the town council, the head schoolteachers and the church superintendents – were affecting his career. And more disputes were to come.

No record survives of how the *St John Passion* was received by the congregation in St Nicholas's on 7 April, but this intensely expressive work, based on the Gospel text combined with hymn verses and poetic words providing the arias and choruses, must have moved the audience and impressed the council.† There are some beautiful and dramatic arias, such as *Ach, mein Sinn* ('Ah, my emotion'), and *Es ist vollbracht* ('It is fulfilled'), accompanied by the viola da gamba. And perhaps the most profound moment comes at the end, with the final chorus, *Ruht wohl* ('Rest well') in C minor, followed by the stupendous chorale ending with the words *Ich will dich preisen ewiglich!* ('I will praise thee for evermore'). Once again the words inspired the truly emotional music.

Sebastian must have been at least satisfied, if not considerably inspired, by this new musical category, which involved much more drama than did cantatas, let alone the rest of his compositions so far. He may even have pondered again whether he should get involved, as had his famous contemporaries Handel and Telemann, in the world of opera; but Leipzig was alas not the place to do so, since its opera house had closed down three years earlier and was now being used as a prison. Certainly more Passions could come up in the future, once he had completed his three-year-long cantata stretch.

But for now it was back to cantatas. Those needed for Easter were revivals or rearrangements of his Weimar and Cöthen works, as were

---

* See page 140.

† Indeed he re-performed it the following year, on 30 March 1725, with some important changes.

several more performed in April and May. The 7 May cantata,* on the other hand, shows some inspiration, with its connection with the words of Jesus in St John's Gospel, speaking to his disciples before he was arrested by the chief priests and Pharisees, particularly the verse 'But now I go my way to him that sent me; and none of you asketh me, Whither goest thou?'† The alto aria is particularly striking, with its message that good fortune is all too unreliable, since what human beings believe in the morning can change so drastically by the same evening (based on *Ecclesiasticus* 18: 26). Sebastian was again beginning to question his own fate. Two weeks later, on 21 May, another cantata was inspired by the same section of the Gospel, where Jesus says, 'They shall put you out of the synagogues: yea, the time cometh, that whosoever killeth you will think that he doeth God service.'‡ The first two movements, based on these words, are followed by a rather beautiful alto aria, the five-line verse of which perhaps Sebastian wrote himself:

Christen müssen auf der Erden	Christians on earth must be
Christi wahre Jünger sein.	true disciples of Christ.
Auf sie warten alle Stunden,	Every hour they expect,
Bis sie selig überwunden,	until heaven delivers them,
Marter, Bann und schwere Pein.	torture, banishment and bitter pain.

And the final chorale is one of the inspiring hymns he had included in the *St John Passion* six weeks earlier.

For the Whit Sunday performance on 28 May at the university church of St Paul's – a fixture Sebastian was anxious to retain because he was paid the somewhat generous fee of 12 gulden [£500] – he merely replayed the

---

* *Wo gehest du hin?*, BWV 166.

† John 16: 5.

‡ *Sie werden euch in den Bann tun*, BWV 44, where the first two movements are based on John 16: 2.

cantata of the previous year, BWV 59.* But on 11 June he came up with another truly remarkable work, based on a 16-verse hymn written by the famous poet Johann Rist in 1642, entitled *O Ewigkeit, du Donnerwort* ('O eternity, you thunderous word').† Two of its eleven movements, though not often performed in this century, can be regarded as masterpieces. Rist's third verse is almost a perfect statement of Sebastian's own feelings about life and death, and inspired an astonishing tenor aria, accompanied by strings and continuo in C minor, expressing the utter terror of eternal damnation. In Rist's verse the singer addresses eternity, saying 'you terrify me', 'flames that burn for ever are like no fire ever witnessed', and 'my mind is directed to hell'. The theme is expressed by the opening tune played by the cello, by long-held notes expressing *Ewigkeit*, and dramatic semiquavers for the burning flames. And if that agonisingly beautiful piece were not enough, there is another aria, the sixth movement, that is even more extraordinary, beginning with the words *O Mensch, errette deine Seele* ('O man, save your soul'). This is in D minor, also with strings and continuo, and one of its remarkable elements is perpetual hemiola: the triple bars virtually all sound duple. The structure too is very unusual, with the words – apart from the opening line – never repeated, and following the form A–A'–B'–B. As Albert Schweitzer wrote in his biography of Bach in 1905, 'Nowhere else in music has the painful writhing of a body been so realistically depicted.'[104] The cantata as a whole, set in two parts and taking nearly half an hour to perform, contains many other unusual features, and is one of the most dramatic he had so far composed. Through the past months Sebastian had increasingly developed the unique capacity to express in music his own complex personal emotions.

Competent cantatas continued to emerge every Sunday through the summer, despite a brief distraction when he and Magdalena were called to visit Cöthen to perform before Prince Leopold and his wife (for

---

* See page 137.

† BWV 20.

which they were paid the massive fee of 60 thalen [£2,880]). One cantata, performed on 20 August, is particularly memorable because of its unusual and rather operatic qualities – *Herr Jesu Christ, du höchstes Gut* (BWV 113), based on a 16th-century hymn by Bartholomäus Ringwalt. And there is an unusually long and masterly alto aria in the 3 September cantata,* gently accompanied by muted violins and pizzicato strings, also based on the text and tune of a 16th-century hymn. Sebastian continued to compose at least one cantata movement every single day as the months passed, every now and then achieving comparably unique signs of his genius. Not all of these masterpieces were now influenced by miserable concepts such as death or eternal damnation, and indeed occasionally they refer at least to resignation and even sometimes to happiness. For example, the opening chorus of the 22 October cantata, *Scmücke dich, o liebe Seele* ('Adorn yourself, dear soul'), is truly and calmly beautiful,† accompanied by two treble recorders as well as the usual oboes and strings. Even more exquisite is *Mache dich, mein Geist, bereit* ('Prepare yourself, my spirit'), with its opening choral fantasia, and its two wonderful arias.‡ But the gloom does not depart.

Three moderately competent cantatas came out for Christmas 1724, of which *Ich freue mich in dir* ('I rejoice in you')§ is the most cheerful, containing an exceptional treble aria in B minor, accompanied by strings with a solo violin. On Christmas Day there was also a remarkable Sanctus mass;¶ and another masterpiece, the highly dramatic nine-movement cantata

---

* *Allein zu dir, Herr Jesu Christ*, BWV 33/3, starting with the words '*Wie furchstam wankten meine Schritte*' ('How fearfully my footsteps faltered').

† BWV 180. The author Nicholas Anderson understandably describes it as 'one of Bach's most translucently textured chorale fantasias', creating 'a sound-picture of intimacy and enchantment' (*J. S. Bach*, ed. Malcolm Boyd, p. 440).

‡ BWV 115. The masterly second movement, an alto aria, contains many subtle elements, accompanied by oboe d'amore, strings and continuo.

§ BWV 133.

¶ This was included in the Mass in B Minor (BWV 232), compiled by Bach towards the end of his life, in 1748.

entitled *Ich hab in Gottes Herz und Sinn mein Herz und Sinn ergeben* ('I have surrendered my heart and mind to God's heart and mind', BWV 92), was first performed at the end of January. Sebastian was now at the very peak of his compositional genius, full of confidence, writing marvellous music every day, constantly introducing dramatic new sounds and harmonies, and fully and deeply exploiting the capacities and talents of his singers and players. The finest church cantatas he composed and performed in Leipzig over the next two years may be said to comprise the following:

Date	BWV	Title and notes
2 February 1725	125	*Mit Fried und Freud ich fahr dahin* ('In peace and joy I depart'). Mostly about death, with the prospect that life hereafter is preferable, this cantata starts with a very beautiful hymn-based chorus, accompanied by full orchestra and a solo flute.
11 February 1725	127	*Herr Jesu Christ, wahr' Mensch und Gott* ('Lord Jesus Christ, true man and God'). Also about death, this too opens with a lovely hymn-based chorus; but the finest part is the soprano aria, in which pizzicato recorders symbolise funeral bells.
2 April 1725	6	*Bleib bei uns, denn es will Abend werden* ('Abide with us as evening falls'). Another fine opening chorus; and the fifth movement, the tenor aria, is a masterpiece and one of the clearest expressions of Bach's religious belief.
22 April 1725	103	*Ihr werdet weinen und heulen, aber die Welt wird sich freuen* ('Ye shall weep and lament, but the world shall rejoice'). The libretto was written by Bach's 30-year-old neighbour,

Date	BWV	Title and notes
		the female poet Christiane Mariane von Ziegler,[105] but the most striking movement is the opening chorus, inspired by Jesus' words about his death and resurrection (John 16: 20), with its sudden introduction of a bass soloist singing 'ye shall be sorrowful'.
13 May 1725	183	*Sie werden euch in den Bann tun* ('They will put you under a ban'). Even more focused on death, this contains a moving tenor aria saying, 'I don't fear the horror of death … for Jesus' protective arm will cover me' (but the music portrays fear). The whole cantata is masterly, but rarely performed because, apart from the brief ending chorale, there are no choruses, and the instruments are unusual, including two oboes d'amore, two oboes da caccia and a cello piccolo. The text is also by von Ziegler.
21 May 1725	68	*Also hat Gott die Welt geliebt* ('God so loved the world'). This superb cantata contains the famous song 'My heart ever faithful', as well as other fine and unusual elements Again the text is by von Ziegler.
4 July 1725	36c	*Schwingt freudig euch empor* ('Soar joyfully aloft'). A secular cantata composed to celebrate a university don's birthday. Bach so approved of this set of eight movements that he reused it at least four times, the first being the following year for the birthday of

Date	BWV	Title and notes
		Princess Charlotte in Cöthen (see page 180 below).
25 December 1725	110	*Unser Mund sei voll Lachens* ('May our mouths be full of laughter'). A splendid musical representation of the happiness of Christmas.
27 December 1725	151	*Süßer Trost, mein Jesus kömmt* ('Sweet comfort, my Jesus comes'). Inspired by the late Darmstadt poet Georg Christian Lehms (1684–1717), whose texts Bach had used back in Weimar, this cantata opens with a truly wonderful treble aria, dominated by a beautiful flute solo. More Lehms libretti were to come.
13 January 1726	32	*Liebster Jesu, mein verlangen* ('Beloved Jesus, my desire'). This too opens with an exceptionally beautiful treble aria, based on text by Lehms, followed by five good movements.
12 May 1726	146	*Wir müssen durch viel Trübsal in das Reich Gottes eingehen* ('We must through much tribulation enter into the kingdom of God'). This opens with a stunning organ concerto movement and a beautiful chorus (both later reused as the first two movements in one of the famous harpsichord concertos, BWV 1052). The text is from St Paul's statement in Acts 14: 22). No doubt 'much tribulation' (the German word *Trübsal* is normally translated as 'grief') was the inspiration.

Date	BWV	Title and notes
28 July 1726	170	*Vergnügte Ruh, beliebte Seelenlust* ('Pleasing rest, beloved inner joy'). One of the more unusual cantatas, involving no choir, only an alto soloist and much organ accompaniment, and two exceptional arias. The text, again, was from Lehms.
11 August 1726	45	*Es ist dir gesagt, Mensch, was gut ist* ('He hath shewed thee, O man, what is good'). The best parts include a splendid opening fugal chorus, based on Micah 6: 8, followed by a tenor recitative and wonderfully dramatic aria.
25 August 1726	102	*Herr, deine Augen sehen nach dem Glauben* ('O Lord, are not thine eyes upon the truth?') A very fine opening chorus, based on words from Jeremiah 5: 3.
29 September 1726	19	*Es erhub sich ein Streit* ('A great strike arose'). The high point is the fifth movement, an exquisite tenor aria, *Bleibt, ihr Engel, bleibt bei mir* ('Stay, ye angels, stay by me').
20 October 1726	169	*Gott soll allein mein Herze haben* ('God alone shall have my heart'). Among several striking features, including obbligato organ passages, this cantata contains the alto aria masterpiece *Stirb in mir* ('Die in me'). Death continues to be the overwhelming influence. The fine opening organ-based sinfonia was reused some twelve years later as the opening movement in the E-major harpsichord concerto (BWV 1053).

Date	BWV	Title and notes
3 November 1726	49	*Ich geh und suche mit Verlangen* ('I go and seek with longing'). A fine organ-based sinfonia, followed by an aria and recitative dialogue between Jesus (bass) and the soul (treble), with no choir. The sinfonia was also reused in the E-major harpsichord concerto, as the third movement.
17 November 1726	55	*Ich armer Mensch, ich Sünderknecht* ('I, wretched man, I, slave of sin'). It is hard not to imagine that the opening tenor aria, one of the most passionate he had composed so far, is anything other than a personal statement. In G minor, it is stunningly accompanied by flute, oboe d'amore, two violins and continuo.
2 February 1727	82	*Ich habe genug* ('I have had enough'). This remains one of the most famous of all the cantatas, and its message too is extraordinarily personal, set for a bass soloist. Bach was well aware of its significance, and later adapted it for further performances, including for a treble soloist.

Other exciting events in 1725 included a second visit to Weißenfels at the end of February, at the request of Duke Christian. This was where Sebastian had performed his 'hunting cantata' twelve years before, to celebrate the local duke's birthday, and now he had been invited to do it again. He composed a new cantata for the event, and then reused it at Easter (with the text changed).* He also made some significant changes

---

* BWV 249, the Easter Oratorio, performed on 1 April.

for performance of the *St John Passion* (BWV 245) on Good Friday, 30 March. Around this time Magdalena gave birth to his tenth (and her third) child, Christian Gottlieb,* who was baptised on 14 April. His seven surviving children were now Catharina aged 17, Friedemann aged 14, Emanuel aged eleven, Johann Gottfried Bernhard aged nine, Christiana aged three, Gottfried Heinrich aged one, and Christian.

And more secular cantatas were to come, of which the most striking† was performed on 3 August to celebrate the name-day of a philosophy don at the university, August Friedrich Müller (1684–1761). Based on a text provided by the local poet Picander (Christian Friedrich Henrici, 1700–64),‡ it is a dramatic and quite long work with 15 movements, accompanied by the largest orchestra Sebastian had ever compounded: three trumpets, timpani, two horns, two flutes, two oboes (one doubling as oboe d'amore), strings including viola da gamba and viola d'amore, and continuo. It was probably performed in the open air close to Müller's house in Katharinenstraße near the university, and would have entertained the partygoers for up to 45 minutes.

But in the late summer of 1725 another dispute with the authorities, based as usual mainly on the issue of money, was about to infuriate Sebastian, making him once again feel that his extremely hard work, his utter devotion to church music, and his intense concentration on teaching the talented young students (presumably one by one or in small groups) were being totally ignored by his employers.

The musician Johann Gottlieb Görner (1697–1778) had been educated at St Thomas's School, and attended Leipzig University until 1716. Since graduating he had already attained a range of musical posts in the city – first as organist at St Paul's until 1721, then as music director there (a post

---

* Possibly he was named Christian in honour of the Weißenfels duke, although one of his godfathers, Christian Wilhelm Ludwig, a local Leipzig singer, had the same name.

† BWV 205, *Zerreißet, zersprenget, zertrümmert die Gruft*.

‡ Picander probably also wrote the libretto for BWV 36c, performed in the previous month, July (see page 168).

he still held), and currently as organist at St Nicholas's Church. Görner was a passionate Leipziger, and would indeed live there for the rest of his long life, as organist at St Thomas's and director of one of the town's *collegium musicum* ensembles. Because one of his main tasks was running the regular Sunday services at St Paul's, and he felt that as a university graduate he had a close connection to it, he found it irritating that four times a year he had to give way to allow Bach to perform what was called the *Alt-Gottesdienst* (old divine service), at Christmas, at Easter, on Whit Sunday and at the Reformation Festival. No doubt noting that Bach had merely repeated an existing cantata on 28 May, he managed to persuade the university authorities that this situation could be resolved by Bach's removal. So he was delighted to find that for the next old service, at the end of October, he had been formally appointed sole music director at the university church.

Sebastian's first step in protest was to complain to the university, on the grounds that when he had been appointed director of music at St Thomas's the post had specifically included being in charge of the *Alt-Gottesdienst* four times a year, for which he was entitled to be paid 12 gulden [£500]. Understandably, he argued that they had no right to deprive him of this essential income. Their response was to offer a compensation: Görner would continue to be in charge of the church music, both old and new, but they would none the less pay Bach half the fee, 6 gulden. He was furious, and refused to accept it. On Friday 14 September he wrote a letter to the Elector and Duke of Saxony, Friedrich August I, in Dresden,* explaining in full detail how the university had deprived him of his entitlement, and asking him to intercede. Sebastian's main point was that 'the withdrawal of the salary, which, in fact, always belonged to the old service even before the new was instituted, is deeply disturbing and slighting to me'. But he went further, and suggested

---

* See page 102. August the Strong, as he was known throughout Europe, had already lived a remarkable life, inheriting Saxony from his elder brother in 1694, and being elected King of Poland in 1697 after he had converted to Catholicism. He was renowned for his love of fine arts and architecture, and although less interested in music was also an opera fan.

'to Your Royal Majesty and Serene Electoral Highness that Your Majesty may graciously command that the Worshipful University at Leipzig shall leave the arrangement as it was formerly, and assign to me the directorship of the new service in addition to the directorship of the old, and particularly the full salary for the old service and the incidental fees accruing from both'. In other words, he was actually suggesting that Görner should be sacked, or at least limited to his post as organist at St Nicholas's.

Friedrich August responded fairly promptly, asking the university to submit a report explaining its own views on the subject, which it did by October. Sebastian then wrote to him again on 3 November, saying 'my most humble and obedient request goes forth to Your Royal Majesty and Serene Electoral Highness that you will communicate to me a copy of the said report in this matter, and be graciously pleased to wait, and defer Your Majesty's determination until I have made the most necessary comments upon it'. In due course he received the university's report, and was not surprised to find that they had no intention of conceding. The essence of their case was set out in seven points: first, that Bach was wrong to suggest that the precentorship of the old and new services had ever officially been connected with St Thomas's; secondly, that Bach was wrongly claiming that he had not been paid for the services he had performed so far at St Paul's, since his appointment in 1723, and their accounts showed that he had been paid 13 thalers and 10 groschen [£634]; thirdly, that in any event he had frequently not attended the services, sending a choir prefect to run them instead; fourthly, that there was no case for appointing the cantor of St Thomas's to direct music in the university church, since he was already in charge of church music in the rest of the town; fifthly, that the fee paid to Görner for the new service, 12 gulden, was in no way connected to the old service fee; sixthly, that there were a lot of problems with the town church music, involving the school pupils and the town music company (*Stadt-Pfeiffer* etc.), and the university therefore had every reason to have its church services independently managed by its own cantor; and finally, a further statement that Görner's fee was newly instituted when he was appointed in charge of the new service, and had no connection with the direction of the old service.

But Sebastian was not giving up. On 31 December he wrote a third, very long, letter to Friedrich August, in which he thanked him for his having been sent a copy of the university's report, summarised their seven points, and went on to say that 'these exceptions taken by the university will not stand and are easily disposed of'. In a long-worded style he set out his argument against each of the seven points as follows:[105]

1. As to the connection of the new service with the old, I did not say that the connection was a necessary one, only that the direction of the latter had formerly been combined with the former; and it was not for me to enquire as to the power and liberty of joining or separating them; that can be settled in the proper place. On the contrary, I accept that the direction of the old service, according to previous custom, is granted and vouchsafed to me in the university's report. But, if this were so, the direction of the music at the degree ceremonies, and other solemn university events at St Paul's, including the fee for the same, ought not to be withheld from me, since all this, at any rate as regards the music, was in direct connection with the old service, according to custom before the new service was instituted.

2. I am not in the least surprised that the university can refer to a profitable fee of 13 thalers 10 groschen which I ought to have received from them, and to contradict me by denying that I have done the work for nothing until now, since the fee is something separate and apart from the salary of 12 gulden [£500], and this gratuity does not include the salary. Actually, however, my complaint concerns not the fee but the salary of 12 gulden, which was always customary and belonged to the old service, but which has hitherto been withheld from me. Indeed, as may be seen from the rector's accounts put forward by the university,

even this fee, which ought to have amounted to 13 thalers 10 groschen, has not once been paid in full, but instead I have been paid by the two beadles, as they will be able to testify on oath, not more than 16 groschen 6 pfennige [£32.96] every quarter, instead of the 20 groschen 6 pfennige [£40.96] in the rector's accounts, and at the three high feast days, as well as at the Feast of the Reformation, each time not more than 1 thaler [£48], instead of 2 thalers 12 groschen [£120], making a total of only 6 thalers 18 groschen [£324] instead of 13 thalers 10 groschen [£634] in the year. Nor did my predecessors, Schelle and Kuhnau (as the affidavits executed by their widows, herewith as exhibits A and B will show), receive a larger sum for the quarterly and festival music, and yet in the extract from the rector's accounts concerning them a much higher amount is set down.

3. The fact that I have frequently not attended the services in person, and that the record of 25 October 1725 shows as much, is of no importance; for just as the month and date show that the record was made only after I had complained to the university, while before that time nothing had been registered against me, so it will be found that such absence has not occurred more than once or twice, and this for legitimate reasons, since I was travelling on necessity, and in particular on one occasion had something to attend to in Dresden.* Moreover, the prefects are assigned to the said quarterly music, so that my predecessors, Schelle and Kuhnau, never conducted these in person, but the singing of the motets was arranged and directed by the prefects.

4. Still less can there be any merit in the urging of the university that it is not possible for the music in the churches on both sides to be taken care of by one person; for according to this a reference to the organist

---

* He was reported in a Hamburg newspaper to have travelled to Dresden on 19 September 1725 to perform two organ recitals in the church of St Sophia, and to have been 'very well received by the local virtuosos at the court and in the city since he is greatly admired by all of them for this musical adroitness and art' (*NBR* 118).

of St Nicholas's, Görner, will be found even more important, and the direction of the music in both churches even less possible for him, since the organist not only has to wait for the end of the concerted music before and after the sermon at the same time in St Nicholas's and in St Paul's but also must play the organ right through to the very last hymn, whereas the cantor can leave after he has attended to the concerted music and need not be present for the hymns to the end of the service; and thus the late Kuhnau in his time attended to both quite well without prejudice or confusion; and in the church, where no formal music is to be provided, common music can be directed perfectly well by the vicars and prefects.

5. Now, particularly as concerns the disputed 12 gulden [£500], the university will never be able to assert with reason that they gave these 12 gulden to my predecessor Kuhnau for the direction of the music as a new, added gratuity. The state of the case is that these 12 gulden have been from time immemorial the salary for providing the music for the old service, and my predecessor, to avoid the disadvantageous consequences to be feared from a separation of the directorships, directed the music for the new service for nothing, and never demanded a penny for it, nor did he ever rejoice in any alleged new gratuity if 12 gulden. Indeed, receipts for these 12 gulden were regularly signed not only by Kuhnau but by Schelle and even before that, before anybody had ever thought of the new services. And as the affidavits of the widows Schelle and Kuhnau, exhibits A and B, clearly state that the 12 gulden were always the salary for the arranging of the music for the old service, accordingly the university cannot escape making public the above-mentioned receipts.

6. Similarly, the question of whether there was a good relation with the students in the direction of the new service, and they did not wish to lend the cantor their aid for nothing, cannot prejudice the salary attached to the music for the old service; for as there is no desire

either to concede or to deny this, and it is well known that students who are lovers of music are always ready and willing to assist, I, for my part, have never had any unpleasantness with the students; they are wont to assist me in both vocal and instrumental music without hesitation, and to this hour gratis and without payment.

7. Moreover, if the music director of the new service should remain for the time being, so far as Görner is concerned, in status quo, and although no one desires to cast doubt on the fact that for this new arrangement a new salary could be granted, yet the salary of 12 gulden hitherto assigned to him is not at all a newly instituted item, or intended as something new for this new directorship, but on the contrary the same was withdrawn from the musical directorship of the old service and only later, while the cantorate of St Thomas's was vacant, when Görner was appointed to the new directorship, assigned to this new directorship.

His letter does not end there. He went on to argue that, since the university had already offered him 6 gulden as a compensation for his removal from the old service, 'they certainly would not have done this had they not been convinced that the matter rests on sound foundation'; and that 'this alteration seems to me all the harder when they choose to ignore all salary whatever, and to deprive me of it altogether'. And he set out in detail the financial losses he had already suffered: the university should have paid him, over the two and three-quarter years since he began his activities in St Paul's on Whit Sunday in 1723, total fees of 36 thalers 18 groschen 6 pfennige [1,548.96], of which he had actually received only 18 thalers 13 groschen 6 pfennige [£890.96], as well as the 12 gulden annual salary, which over the period should have been 33 gulden [£1,386]. His letter ends:

Therefore my most submissive prayer is presented to your Royal Majesty and Serene Electoral Highness, most graciously to command the university not only to leave the arrangements as they were, and to assign to me in the future the full salary of 12 gulden for the old service, with the incidental fees for the degree ceremonies and other formal events formerly attached to it, but also to pay me the outstanding fee of 18 thalers 5 groschen and the remaining regular salary of 33 gulden, and to make good all the expenses I have had in this respect; or, in case the university should not be convinced by what has hitherto been adduced, to disclose the receipts given by Schelle and Kuhnau both for the special fees and for the regular salary. This great favour I will recognise with humblest thanks all my life, and remain your Royal Majesty's and your Serene Electoral Highness's most humble and obedient Johann Sebastian Bach.

Exactly three weeks later, on 21 January 1726, Friedrich August announced his decision in the form of a brief and polite letter to the university committee, explaining it thus:

Since We now see that the musical directorship of the old service is an old affair and has no relation to the new service, accordingly we let the matter rest at that, and, since you have also offered to leave the directorship to him, as regards the old service, and to pay him regularly the fees intended for the same, acquiesce therein and, not unjustly, in the special arrangements you have made concerning the new service. And thus Our desire is that you will make good your offer but, for the rest, in the circumstances, reject the request of the said cantor. This is Our will.

So despite his immense efforts to force the university to upgrade his status and improve his income, Sebastian had totally failed, and had no choice but to continue in charge of the St Paul's old service four times a year, for which he was paid the same modest salary and fees that his predecessors had received over the last 50 years.* Here was more devastating proof

---

*   Johann Schelle was cantor at St Thomas's from 1677 to 1701, succeeded by Johann Kuhnau, who died in 1722.

that his employers did not appreciate him, let alone reward him for the huge efforts he had made to fulfil and indeed increase his professional obligations. It was also a sharp reminder of how he had been treated by Duke Wilhelm Ernst in Weimar, and how Prince Leopold had withdrawn his support in Cöthen. One small compensation was the fact that he remained honorary kapellmeister at Cöthen, and was paid 30 thalers [£1,440] when he and Magdalena travelled there again in December to perform at the birthdays of Prince Leopold and Princess Charlotte.*

Other recompenses lay in a range of things: the increasing appreciation of his skills and talents among many professional musicians, the fine range of young men he had taught who were becoming professionals, his exceptional ability to work hard and create a range of music, and the deeply touching affection of his wife. Five months later, on 5 April 1726, Magdalena gave birth to her fourth child, baptised Elisabeth Juliana Friderica.

---

* The cantata performed for Princess Charlotte was BWV 36a, *Steigt freudig in die Luft* ('Rise joyfully into the air'), based on its predecessor BWV 36c (see page 168).

Chapter 9

SURVIVING DISASTERS

(1726–29)

Although Sebastian had frequently tried to deny to himself that he had suffered a traumatic and damaging childhood – four of his siblings and cousins dying before he was eight, and both his parents gone within ten months when he was only nine – there was no doubt that these memories had had a profound effect on his life so far. Death was perpetual: three of his children had died in Weimar and Cöthen, and his lovely first wife had died six years ago. And now there was more: in June 1726 Christiana Sophia Henrietta, his and Magdalena's first child, died at the age of three, only two months after the birth of her sister Elisabeth. Christiana was buried on 1 July. This recurrent devastation was an inescapable factor in Sebastian's life. His mind was now constantly in the past, and in July it struck him that the only person in his childhood who had represented any level of consistency and loyalty was his friend Georg Erdmann, with whom he had taken the long 200-mile walk from Ohrdruf to Lüneburg back in 1699.

Georg Erdmann's life and career had developed far more dramatically and successfully than Sebastian's. Some time after leaving St Michael's School, in 1708 he enrolled at Jena University to study law, and in 1714 he joined the Russian army in Riga, the Latvian city that four years earlier had been surrendered to the Russians by Sweden. Erdmann was in the service of Prince Anikita Ivanovich Repnin (1668–1726), one of the

Russian generals in the Great Northern War against Sweden. In 1718 Erdmann was appointed Russian diplomat in the Polish city of Danzig on the Baltic Sea, and legal adviser to the imperial Russian court.*

Sebastian had learned that Erdmann was currently at Gotha, the town close to where he had been born in 1682, and where he was temporarily sorting out some family issues. On 28 July Sebastian wrote the following grovelling letter, and had it taken to Gotha:

> Dear noble and most honoured Sir, and (if still permissible) esteemed brother.
>
> On this favourable occasion it is my obligation to enquire about your excellency's well-being, and sincerely wish its lasting continuation. The brief oral message from the bearer of these lines gave me such pleasure that I have the burning desire to receive more extensive details regarding the recent circumstances duly becoming to your merits. I therefore am emboldened to submit to your excellency to what extent my curiosity may be gratified. If accordingly you will be disposed towards remembering a devoted erstwhile school colleague and travel companion, and comply with his humble request, grateful indebtedness will oblige your honour's humble servant,
>
> Joh. Sebast. Bach.[107]

Gotha, nearly 100 miles south-west of Leipzig, was too far away for Sebastian to be able to travel there, but in due course he received a friendly postal reply, in which Erdmann asked how Bach's career had developed over the last 20 years. This was a small compensation in these miserable times, and Erdmann remained in his mind.

The only way to cope with depression was to focus even more intensely on work, and the main task now was to pursue the teaching of his music

---

* Peter the Great died in 1725, and was succeeded by several descendants who died young, causing trouble in the Russian state. Georg Erdmann died on 12 October 1736, during the reign of Anna Ivanovna.

students, many of whom were beginning to show talent. Over the next few years, dozens of them became professional musicians, many of them organists, and often attained their first posts with the help of a testimonial provided by their teacher. For example, in July Sebastian wrote the following for the benefit of a young organist named Jacob Ernst Hübner:

> Since by special request the bearer of this, Mr Jacob Ernst Hübner from Löbau, has asked the undersigned to provide him with written testimony regarding his proficiency in music, especially on the keyboard, I do not wish to decline such a just request but fairly state that he is in good command of the fundaments (those particularly required) for the organist's service. The examples of proof that he has given me were fully satisfactory. In his possible future advancement no doubt he will, with further work at the organ, show his ability to new advantage and demonstrate the present testimony to represent nothing but the truth. Written at Leipzig, 20 July 1726.
>
> Johann Sebastian Bach
> Princely Anhalt-Cöthen Kapellmeister,
> also Direct. Chori Musici at Leipzig,
> and Cantor at St Thomas's.[108]

Hübner was soon appointed organist at Waldenburg, south of Leipzig. It must have been increasingly clear to Sebastian that the only people who really seemed to appreciate him were the young men who had taken part in his music lessons and church performances, and that his teaching abilities were having a profound impact on the music profession throughout Thuringia.

This did provide some inspiration, and using one of the local printers Sebastian decided for the first time to publish a keyboard work, based on some similar publications brought out several decades earlier by his predecessor Johann Kuhnau, entitled 'Keyboard Practice' (*Clavier-Übung*).

He chose a seven-movement piece in B-flat major (probably composed some time in the past), which he entitled Partita 1,* and on the title page he wrote that it contained 'preludes, allemandes, courantes, sarabandes, gigues, minuets, and other galanteries', and was 'composed for music-lovers to refresh their spirits'.[109] It is a charming piece, not very easy to play, which most piano players still learn today. The booklet came out in the autumn of 1726, and evidently a lot of copies were sold or acquired by his students. It seemed a good idea to produce more, and over the next four years he arranged the publication of six other partitas.†

But in addition to the weekly cantata compositions, he had been working on another highly ambitious and complex project, a new Passion, this time based on St Matthew's Gospel. He had already made contact with the young local poet Christian Friedrich Henrici, who had provided him with libretti for several church and secular cantatas since 1724. Henrici had recently published them in a collection of his poems, under the pseudonym Picander, which he dedicated to Count Franz Anton Sporck, the famous Bohemian patron of opera and the arts. Henrici had agreed to provide a *St Matthew Passion* libretto, and over many months Sebastian had been working on what would become the greatest composition of his entire life. He probably aimed to finish it by Easter 1725, but because it was not complete that year he re-performed the *St John Passion*. Nor was it finished the following year, no doubt because of the stressful rows with the university. But now it was reaching completion, and the plan was to perform it in St Thomas's on Good Friday, 11 April 1727.[110]

---

* BWV 825. He dedicated it to Prince Leopold's young son Emanuel Ludwig.

† Partitas BWV 826 and 827 came out in 1727, BWV 828 in 1728, and BWV 829 and 830 in 1730. The six partitas were reissued together in 1731. Three more collections of keyboard pieces were published later: *Clavier-Übung II*, containing BWV 971 (the Italian Concerto) and BWV 831 (Overture in the French Style), in 1735; *Clavier-Übung III*, mainly containing church organ music, in 1739; and *Clavier-Übung IV*, containing the *Goldberg Variations* (BWV 988), in 1741.

Henrici was born in Stolpen, near Dresden, in 1700 and had read law at Wittenberg University before arriving in Leipzig in 1721. His first few years there, when he wrote erotic poems and satirical verses, were somewhat impoverished, but this year he had become employed by the post office. By 1736 he was promoted to a senior job there, and later, in the 1740s, he became a well-paid assessment and liquor tax collector, retaining the post until his death in 1764. Over the next 20 years his writing provided the libretti for at least 30 of Sebastian's compositions, including twelve secular cantatas.

The *St Matthew Passion* of course remains one of Bach's most famous and popular compositions, and readers will be familiar with it. But it is irresistible, in the light of the previous pages' account of his hundreds of church cantatas, to offer an explanation of how the Passion compares with Sebastian's vast range of previous religious works. Perhaps the first point to make is that the textual inspiration, which so often influenced his creation of exceptional movements in the cantatas, did not really reside in Picander's poetry. Indeed, most German critics since the 19th century have agreed with the view, expressed by Bach's first major biographer Philipp Spitta, that Picander was no more than a competent poet, and even that 'his talent was less than mediocre'.[111] The real influence was clearly the fact that St Matthew's account of Jesus' arrest and crucifixion is infinitely more dramatic and vivid than any others in the New Testament, and Sebastian was determined from the start to express the full text, unaltered and unabbreviated, in the most appropriately emotional music he could devise.

Because there was more space in St Thomas's Church, including the small swallow's-nest organ loft half-way down the nave, he was able to set up two four-part choir groups, plus a third soprano group (the ripieno), and have them accompanied by two separate orchestras. The ripieno trebles, presumably, were located in the swallow's nest, next to the little organ there. Unlike in today's performances, the soloists were simply members of one of the two main choirs.

The Passion opens with a profoundly moving chorus in E minor (movement 1), accompanied by the full orchestra, and sung by both choirs plus the ripieno. It was clearly inspired by Picander's seven-line poem, which is brilliantly linked, both musically and verbally, to the hymn sung by the ripieno trebles.

Poem
Kommt, ihr Töchter, helft mir klagen, — Come, daughters, help me mourn;
Sehet – Wen? – den Bräutigam, — Look – at whom? – the bridegroom,
Seht ihn – Wie? – als wie ein Lamm! — Look at him – how? – like a lamb!
Sehet – Was? – seht die Geduld, — Look – at what? – look at his patience,
Seht – Wohin? – auf unsre Schuld; — Look – where? – at our guilt;
Sehet ihn aus Lieb und Huld — Look at him, with love and grace,
Holz zum Kreuze selber tragen! — Carrying wood for the cross himself!

Hymn
O Lamm Gottes, unschuldig — O lamb of God, innocently
Am Stamm des Kreuzes geschlachtet, — Slaughtered on the branch of the cross,

Allzeit erfunden geduldig, — Always found patient,
Wiewohl du warest verachtet. — Although you were despised.
All Sünd hast du getragen, — You have borne all sin,
Sonst müßten wir verzagen. — Otherwise we would have to despair.

Erbarm dich unser, o Jesu! — Have mercy on us, O Jesus!

The drama then opens with the tenor evangelist, in recitative form, singing the words of St Matthew 26: 1–2, followed by a simple four-part chorale commenting on this passage, sung by both choirs (movements 2–3). The Gospel narrative continues, with one (or both) of the choirs intervening every now and then to represent the chief priests and scribes, the disciples, and other groups of people. And then one of Picander's verses, usually in the form of an arioso followed by an aria, is sung by one of the soloists offering a reflective and moving comment on the narrative. The arias, and their preceding preludes (named recitatives in the score), represent personal, individual reflections on the drama, whereas the chorales, based mostly on familiar hymn tunes and set in simple harmonies, tend to convey the modest but intense views of the congregation as a whole.

The first aria comes after the story of how Jesus, in the house of Simon the leper, defends the woman who poured her precious ointment on his head (6–8). His disciples (sung by choir 1) had criticised her for doing so, saying that the ointment could have been given to the poor. Jesus's part is sung by a bass soloist in choir 1, and in all his recitatives he is accompanied by the strings, comprising a subtle contrast with the evangelist's narrative,* and indeed with all the other characters in the story. The following alto aria (10), *Buß und Reu* ('Grief for sin'), is another superb musical expression of misery. Then the disciple Judas Iscariot is offered 30 silver pieces to betray Jesus to the chief priests (11); there follows another beautiful aria, *Blute nur, du liebes Herz!* (12).†

We have now reached Matthew 26: 17, whereafter on Jesus' instructions the disciples arrange to eat the Passover supper at a house in Jerusalem. As he sits down with them in the evening (15), Jesus says (accompanied by strings), 'Verily I say unto you, that one of you shall betray me.' The

---

* Picander's libretto in the entire Passion comprises a total of 28 poems.

† The words, translated in English since the 19th century as 'Break in grief, thou loving heart; for a child whom thou didst nourish, yea, a friend whom thou didst cherish, gathers wicked foes around thee, and doth like a serpent wound thee', are actually rather more dramatic. A truer translation would be: 'Just bleed, you dear heart! Oh, a child whom you raised, who sucked at your breast, threatens to murder his guardian, as he turns into a snake.'

disciples are horrified, 'exceeding sorrowful, and began every one of them to say unto him, Lord, is it I?' In the five bars in which choir 1 sings these words, the word 'Lord' is repeated eleven times, the twelfth disciple being omitted. A chorale (16) intervenes, both choirs, representing the congregation, singing 'It is I', before the completion in recitative form of Jesus' dedication of his flesh and blood in the form of bread and wine (17). A more cheerful soprano aria (19) in G major follows.

Jesus and his disciples then go out into the Mount of Olives, where he tells Peter 'that this night, before the cock crow, thou shalt deny me thrice'. One striking element in this section is that there are two chorales (21 and 23), before and after this recitative account, which are both based on the same hymn (the tune of which was written by Hans Leo Haßler in 1601).* Clearly this hymn, which occurs three more times in the Passion – and most strikingly after Jesus 'yielded up the ghost' – was a powerful indication of the congregation's faithful consistency. It is followed by their moving to a place called Gethsemane, where Jesus feels his heaviest sorrow, 'even unto death'. Here is another inspiration for Bach (as death has frequently provided in the existing cantatas): first, a unique recitative for a tenor of choir 1 (25), who is interrupted by chorale lines sung by choir 2 ('O Saviour, why must all this ill befall thee?'); and then a rapturous aria in C minor (26) in which the tenor and the choir combine to resolve to find rest in Jesus from the torments of the consciousness of sin.†

The next few verses cover the account of Christ's agony in the garden, interrupted by a bass recitative and aria (28–9), and another chorale (31), until, in recitative 32, Jesus is betrayed by Judas and is finally arrested. This is another major compositional inspiration. Aria 33 begins in a tender harmony played by wind and string instruments, and two voices in choir 1 in duet, gently singing *So ist mein Jesus nun gefanken* ('Behold, my

---

* The hymn is familiar to Anglican churchgoers: number 111 in *Hymns Ancient and Modern*, 'O sacred Head, surrounded by crown of piercing thorn'.

† See Spitta, Vol. 2, p. 555.

Saviour now is taken'), shockingly interrupted by choir 2, who loudly sing 'Loose him, leave him, bind him not!' And as if that were not enough, both choirs burst out with a long forte section, calling upon God to hurl lightning and thunder down on 'the treacherous betrayer' and his accomplices, and portraying the most dramatic moment in the Passion so far. The first half concludes with another brief recitative, ending with 'Then all the disciples forsook him and fled' (Matthew 27: 56), followed by a simple hymnal chorale.*

The next stage in the service was the priest's sermon, after which the Passion reopens with another deeply moving piece (36), combining the alto soloist from choir 1, singing *Ach, nun ist mein Jesus hin* ('Ah, now is my Jesus gone'), with choir 2 singing the words of the Song of Solomon 6: 1, 'Whither is thy beloved gone, O thou fairest among women?' And then the plot proceeds: Jesus is taken to the palace of Caiaphas, where the council seek to find 'false witnesses against Jesus, to put him to death'. After another chorale (38), two false witnesses (alto and tenor from choir 2) briefly sing their accusational duet, but Jesus holds his peace. A tenor recitative and then an aria in A minor follow, the latter remarkably accompanied by the viola da gamba, a passionate seven-stringed cello-like instrument which Sebastian had already used in several of his previous compositions, including the sixth Brandenburg Concerto.† The aria, simple but harmonically subtle, conveys Picander's poetic concept of endurance in the face of human liars and cheats. And the drama continues, with the high priest renting his clothes with anger when Jesus has said to him, 'Hereafter shall ye see the Son of man sitting on the right hand of power, and coming in the clouds of heaven.' The council, represented by both choirs, sing 'He

---

* In a later performance, on Good Friday 30 March 1736, this chorale was replaced by one of the choruses from the *St John Passion*, 'O Mensch, bewein dein Sünde groß', which adds considerable effect to the closure of Part 1.

† BWV 1051. See page 121. Other cantatas featuring the viola da gamba include BWV 106 ('Actus Tragicus'), 152, 76 and 205.

is guilty of death', and after physically assaulting Jesus they sing 'Prophesy unto us, thou Christ, who is he that smote thee?'. The scene ends (44) with a repetition of the hymn tune in chorale 16, with the words *Wer hat dich so geschlagen?* ('Who has struck you so?').

Throughout this horrific condemnation of Jesus in the high priest's palace, Simon Peter was sitting unnoticed among the servants outside in the court, in order to 'see the end'. The drama now focuses on him. In the next recitative, two maids (soprano and alto) accuse him of being associated with Jesus of Nazareth; both times he denies it. Then a chorus (choir 2) makes the third accusation and, after his third denial, 'immediately the cock crew'. The musical setting of how 'he went out, and wept bitterly' is magical. It is immediately followed by one of the most beautiful and subtly complex arias of all time (47), introduced by the solo violin in B minor, and sung by the alto soloist from choir 1: *Erbarme dich, mein Gott* ('Have mercy, Lord, on me'). The section ends with another simple chorale in A major (48), accompanied by flute, oboe, strings and organ.

The next turn in the story is a brief account of how Judas Iscariot felt deep repentance for his betrayal, tried to return the money he had been paid, was denied by the chief priests and elders, and hanged himself. In a short duet, two bass soloists (priests 1 and 2) sing the words of Matthew 27: 6: 'It is not lawful for to put them into the treasury, because it is the price of blood.' This inspires another fine aria (51), also introduced by the solo violin: *Gebt mir meinen Jesum wieder* ('Give, O give me back my Saviour'), in G major, after which in due course the evangelist introduces the audience to Jerusalem's Roman governor, Pontius Pilate (choir 1 bass). The governor's first question to Jesus is 'Art thou the King of the Jews?', to which Jesus replies 'Thou sayest'.

As the crucifixion draws nearer, the music's intensity increases, but most impressively the general pattern remains as stable as it has been since the beginning. After the evangelist's statement that 'the governor marvelled greatly', a now familiar chorale is sung again for the third time, indicating congregational stability. Then Pilate raises the issue of releasing one of the prisoners, either Barabbas or Jesus; his wife briefly intervenes; he ignores her statement that her dream has persuaded her that Jesus is 'a just person'; and he formally asks the people which of the two should be released. The single fortissimo chord sung by both choirs, 'Barabbas', is extraordinarily powerful and enough to shake any audience; it is followed by an equally powerful eight-bar choral fugue, 'Let him be crucified', starting in A minor with the basses of both choirs, and ending in B major, the dominant of the E-minor key in which the subsequent chorale is sung.* A gentle soprano recitative and aria intervene (57–8), before the double choir repeats the fugal 'Let him be crucified', a tone higher and even more aggressively. After Pilate has sung 'I am innocent of the blood of this just person', all the people embark on the most aggressive chorus, singing 'His blood be on us, and on our children'.†

A fine, and harmonically complex, choir 2 alto recitative and aria intervene (60–61), before Jesus is dragged by the Roman soldiers to the common hall, stripped of his clothes, forced to wear a plaited crown of thorns, and humiliated in numerous other ways. The fourth version of the Haßler chorale (63) is some compensation to the audience. The next aria (66), sung by a bass, and the second to be accompanied by a viola da gamba, is appropriately moving, with the words *Komm, süßes Kreuz* ('Come, healing cross'). And then Jesus is crucified, a thief on either side of him. Two dramatic choruses follow as he is reviled by the passing public, the chief priests, scribes and elders (Matthew 27: 39–43). Then there is the penultimate recitative, *Ach Golgotha* (69) and its fine sequel, sung by an alto soloist from choir 1 with gentle comments from choir 2.

The final drama is as subtly composed as any preceding part of the Passion: Jesus' cry to God (*Eli, Eli, lama sabachthani?*), its misinterpretation by the public ('This man calleth for Elias'), his assault with a sponge filled with vinegar, and his last cry before he yielded up the ghost. In A minor the succeeding chorale is the fifth and final repetition of the Haßler hymn

---

* Another repetition, this time of the first chorale in the Passion, third movement.

† It should not be assumed that this was an anti-Semitic expression; there was, and had been for many decades, a substantial and respected Jewish community in Leipzig.

(72).* After a dramatic recitative by the evangelist, describing how 'the veil of the temple was rent in twain', 'the earth did quake', and the graves of many of the dead were opened up, the simple but exquisite expression is sung in A flat by both choirs: 'Truly this was the Son of God'.

The last recitative (74), a bass solo accompanied by softened strings, is a wonderful representation of the peace and calm that evening naturally brings, however tormented the day has been, inspiring one of Sebastian's finest musical constructions. The last aria (bass from choir 1) is followed by the evangelist's account of how Joseph of Arimathea laid Jesus' body in his tomb, with Mary Magdalene and Mary the mother of James and Joses sitting nearby. Then both choirs sing the words of the chief priests, remembering that Jesus 'that deceiver said, while he was yet alive, After three days I will rise again', powerfully moving from E flat through several keys to D major. The end of Matthew 27 is now reached. Four soloists from choir 1, with choir 2, sing a brief and beautiful choral farewell to Jesus; and then the last chorus (with both choirs) begins and ends in C minor. So we reach the finale of the longest and most complex work Sebastian had yet composed – and ever would – and perhaps the greatest musical composition in the whole of human history.

******

But nothing went really right for Sebastian, despite the immense hard work he had put in for several years in Leipzig, and the intense involvement in music teaching that had enabled a range of his pupils to perform not only this masterpiece, but the hundreds of subtle and clever cantatas he had produced since his appointment four years earlier. Depression was now a continual –

---

* In some modern performances of this chorale, it is sung *a capella* (unaccompanied), even though Bach orchestrated it with flute, oboe, strings, continuo and organ. Philipp Spitta reported in his biography (Vol. 2, p. 550) that this 'error' had become 'an almost universal custom' in the 19th century, of which he strongly disapproved.

although not constant – feature of his life, and the only way he could conceive survival was to continue concentrating on hard work and on his beautiful young wife, and to think as little as possible about promotions and higher earnings.

A few more cantatas were composed in the summer, including one commissioned to celebrate the name-day of Elector Friedrich August I on 12 August, and reused with changed words (probably by Picander) three weeks later for the annual installation of the city council.[112] Considering that neither the Elector nor the council had provided support or indicated appreciation of Bach's exceptional abilities, it is a competent work. But a much more inspiring event for Sebastian came the following month, with the announcement of the death of Friedrich August's estranged wife, Electress Christiane Eberhardine.[113] Christiane had for many years been a highly popular aristocrat in Saxony, mainly because back in 1697, after only four years of marriage to Friedrich August, she had powerfully protested against his decision to convert to Catholicism in order to become King of Poland, and separated from him, moving to live in Pretzsch Castle, 35 miles north of Leipzig. Despite the break-up she retained her royal status, and it was at Pretzsch that she had brought up their son, in the Lutheran faith.* Upon her death a four-month period of state mourning was officially announced.

The Leipzig memorial service, planned to take place on 17 October in the university church of St Paul's, was organised by a group of upper-class students led by Hans Carl von Kirchbach, who commissioned one of his teachers, the young poet Johann Christoph Gottsched (1700–66),† to write the libretto. Sebastian received the text at the beginning of the month and immediately began work on it – but unfortunately Johann Gottlieb Görner, the church's musical director, was once again

---

* After her death, his father sent him to Italy, where he too became a Catholic; and he subsequently succeeded his father, becoming King August III of Poland.

† Three years later, Gottsched was appointed professor of poetry at Leipzig University. He later became professor of logic and metaphysics there, and was recognised as one of the most important literary figures of his generation.

infuriated that Bach was taking over music in his church, and launched another complaint with the university authorities, specifically objecting to Kirchbach's having commissioned Bach instead of him. They attempted to arrange a compromise, asking Kirchbach to apologise to Görner, and Bach to sign a document swearing that this was an unprecedented event, and 'that I am never to make any claim to the directorship of the music in St Paul's, much less contract with anyone for music for such solemnities or otherwise without the consent and permission of the university'.[114] But Sebastian, incensed and reminded again that none of the officials seemed to appreciate him, refused to sign the document, and they were forced to follow another compromise by paying Görner a generous compensation of 12 thalers [£576]. So Kirchbach's plan was allowed to go ahead.

The score was completed by the 15th, only two days before the funeral,* so there was not much time to rehearse the eleven movements; none the less the performance went well, and was approved by the town officials and professors of the university, as well as all the other grand and highly-ranked attendees. The first half, comprising seven movements, begins with a stunning chorus in B minor accompanied by the string and wind orchestra, with Sebastian unusually conducting it at the harpsichord. Gottsched's inspirational words begin by addressing the deceased lady, *Laß, Fürstin* ('Let, Princess'). The following movements are equally beautiful: a touching soprano recitative and aria, another exquisite recitative beginning with the words *Der Glocken bebendes Getön* ('The trembling sound of the bell') with the bell represented by 'pizzicato' flutes, a superb alto aria, a third recitative and a poignantly simple accompaniment to the chorus which ends the first half.

There was then a sombre funeral oration delivered by Kirchbach, before the shorter second half, comprising three more movements, ends with a masterly chorus, *Doch, Königen! du stribest nicht* ('But, Queen, you do not die'), also in B minor.[115] Although the whole work consists of only eleven

---

* The date, 15 October, is written at the end of the autograph score in Bach's handwriting. The work is known as the *Trauer Ode* ('Mourning Ode'), BWV 198.

movements and takes only about 25 minutes to perform, it is almost as staggeringly emotional as the *St Matthew Passion* first performed six months earlier. The tragedy of death, once again, was the profound inspiration.

And yet more death was to come. Magdalena had been pregnant again when the Passion was performed in April, and only ten days after the funeral she gave birth to her third son, named Ernestus Andreas at his baptism on 30 October. But the following day he died. Sebastian had every reason to feel increasingly convinced that life in this world was a perpetual nightmare, and that only the life hereafter was any possible compensation. On the other hand, composing music had for many years been his lifeline to survival. The discipline and hard work had suppressed much of his depression, and the creation of beauty was a source of pride and had retained his vigour and ingenuity. But even that was now threatened. Having created more than 200 church and secular cantatas, as well as hundreds of other compositions, he must have been beginning to wonder whether this intense productivity had brought him or his family any benefits, let alone survival.

Inescapable was the memory of the deaths around him throughout his life: two brothers and a sister in his childhood, his mother and father when he was nine in 1694–5, Maria Sophia and Johann Christoph in 1713, Leopold Augustus in 1719, his dear wife Maria Barbara in 1720, his brother Jacob in 1722, and two more of his children in the last two years. But at least he had seven surviving children, who must have brought him joy: Catharina was now 18, and an indispensable housekeeper; Friedemann (16), Emanuel (13) and Bernhard (12) were all doing well in St Thomas's School, and in the flat were little Heinrich (3), Christian (2) and Lieschen (1). Despite the abrupt death of Ernestus Andreas in October, Magdalena was pregnant again in February 1728.

In January Sebastian made another brief visit to Cöthen at the request of Prince Leopold, to perform at the New Year festivities. That month the state mourning of Christiane Eberhardine ended, and regular cantata performances were again required each Sunday in Leipzig; but

Sebastian no longer felt obliged, let alone inspired, to persist with weekly compositions, so with occasional exceptions existing ones were reused. But he did manage to produce one in February, at Picander's request, for the memorial service of a distinguished lawyer, J. C. von Ponickau, who had died the previous October. Its memorable and subtly complex opening movement is a tenor and bass duet accompanied by flute, oboe, violin and continuo, based on the words of Genesis 32: 26: 'I will not let thee go, except thou bless me.'* Death again was the inspiration.

Towards the end of the summer, another ridiculous and trivial dispute erupted with the authorities. This time, it was a formal complaint from the sub-deacon of St Nicholas's church, the Reverend Gottlieb Gaudlitz, addressed to the town council, that the cantor was refusing to comply with the priest's choice of hymns to be sung in the evening service. Dr Deyling, the superintendent, was asked to resolve this by informing the cantor 'that when the ministers who are preaching cause it to be announced that particular hymns are to be sung before or after the sermon, he shall be governed accordingly and have the same sung'.[116] Once again Sebastian decided to fight his case for choosing the hymns, on the grounds that it was traditionally the cantor's right to do so, and Gaudlitz was attempting to bring in an innovation. On 20 September he wrote a long and formal letter to the council, ending 'with the humble request that you will protect me in respect to the old practices concerning the hymns and their ordering'. It would appear that for once he won his argument, even if it did not improve his relations with the sub-deacon.[117]

But as now happened so frequently in Sebastian's life, tragedy struck again the following day. His little son Christian Gottlieb died on 21 September, aged three and a half. It was less than a year since Magdalena's fifth child had died at birth. More than half of Sebastian's 13 children had now died in their childhoods. Perhaps it was a tiny compensation that Magdalena was about to give birth again – and it was a new daughter. Regina Johanna was

---

* BWV 157, *Ich laße dich nicht, du segnest mich denn.*

baptised on 10 October, and her three godparents were all the siblings of Magdalena: her two sisters, Katharina Meissner and Johanna Krebs, and her brother, Johann Caspar Wülcken, who was a court trumpeter in Zeitz, a few miles south of Leipzig. But the celebration of Regina's birth was thoroughly overshadowed by the death of Christian.

If you want to get a sense of how Sebastian actually felt in this disastrous time, there is a magical source. He wrote a cantata that week, for performance on the 21st Sunday after Trinity,* using a libretto provided by Picander. It is no masterpiece, but it is an extraordinary expression of the complexities that the pain and misery of this life inflict on the mind. It opens with a dramatic sinfonia with the orchestra and the organ,† which is simply an expression of fury. This is followed by a beautiful tenor aria, based on Picander's six-line poem starting *Ich habe meine Zuversicht/Auf den getreuen Gott gericht* ('I have my confidence assigned to the faithful God'). The main part conveys Sebastian's newly assured belief in the life hereafter, but in the second section drama re-enters with the words *Wenn alles bricht, wenn alles fällt* ('If everything breaks, if everything fails'), using broken chords and intense harmonic changes. And the next movement is also very unusual, an exceptionally long recitative, accompanied by harpsichord and cello, inspired by its opening words *'in den allergrößten Nöten'* ('the very worst of trouble'). The work ends with an alto aria, another brief but quite dramatic recitative, and a simple four-part chorale.

This miserable year ended with two more deaths. His former employer Prince Leopold, whom he had visited in January for the New Year festivities in Cöthen, died on 19 November. This meant that Sebastian no longer had the respectable post of kapellmeister to the Prince of Anhalt-Cöthen. Some compensation occurred in March 1729, when he, Magdalena and Friedrich attended the prince's funeral service and he was paid the massive fee of 230

---

* BWV 188, *Ich habe meine Zuversicht*.

† This movement was later, around 1738, adjusted for use in one of the now famous harpsichord concertos, BWV 1052.

thalers [£11,040] for his composition of a funeral cantata (largely based on the *St Matthew Passion*),* and to cover the costs of staying several days there.

And then his 51-year-old sister, Marie Salome Wiegand, died at Christmas, and was buried on 27 December.

---

* BWV 244a, *Klagt, Kinder, klagt es aller Welt*.

Chapter 10

PROFESSIONAL CRISIS

(1729–30)

Although Sebastian had suffered so many unwelcome responses from his employers over these recent months, and despite the seemingly incessant family deaths, he managed to hold on to his self-confidence and his ability to concentrate on hard work and complex projects. At the beginning of 1729 some compensations were offered, reminding him that at least among his fellow musicians he was respected – and even regarded as famous for his organ-playing skills.

The first was that Duke Christian of Saxe-Weißenfels happened to visit Leipzig to attend the New Year's Fair in January, and Sebastian took advantage of this by composing a celebratory cantata performed in his honour on the 12th.* The duke was clearly interested in sophisticated music, had known Bach for 16 years and had employed him for celebrations several times in the past. Realising that Bach had lost his post as kapellmeister at the court of Cöthen, the duke offered him another invitation to Weißenfels to perform at the celebration of his birthday on 23 February. Sebastian was there, with his wife, for several days; and in due course he was appointed the duke's honorary kapellmeister.

Another uplifting event came in February, when Sebastian's eldest son matriculated at Leipzig University, to study law. Friedemann's 18th birthday

---

* BWV 210a, *O angenehme Melodie*. Bach later adapted it as a wedding cantata, *O holder Tag, erwünschte Zeit* (BWV 210), which is the only version that has survived (see page 286).

had been celebrated in November, and he had left St Thomas's School at the end of the year. This was a crucial step up the social ladder, and few family members had attended university before. Friedemann was distinctly talented musically, and a skilled keyboard and violin player. There seemed every prospect that this gifted young man, to whom Sebastian had assigned a great deal of music teaching during his childhood, would achieve real success in this role (although of course musicians were by no means as classy as lawyers). But Sebastian was less aware that Friedemann suffered from a sense of incompetence derived from his father that would undermine his career.

Since Sebastian's depression had chipped away at his commitment to massive cantata compositions and productions, he evidently realised that the only solution was to focus on some other form of work, and an appropriate opportunity happened to arise at just the right moment. One of the two *collegium musicum* orchestras in Leipzig, which had been founded in 1701 by Georg Philipp Telemann,* was regularly performing every Friday evening in winter in Gottfried Zimmermann's grand coffee-house in Katharinenstraße, just a few streets away from St Thomas's, and in summer every Wednesday in the coffee-garden behind the building. Until now it had been run by Georg Balthasar Schott, the organist and music director of St Nicholas's Church who had been one of the eight unsuccessful contenders for Sebastian's job in 1723.† But now Schott had been appointed cantor in the ducal town of Gotha, near Eisenach where Sebastian was born. His successor as St Nicholas's organist, Carl Gotthelf Gerlach (1704–61), was entitled to take over the running of the *collegium musicum* orchestra, but he agreed to concede the job to Sebastian, no doubt grateful for the organ teaching he had given him in recent years.

So this was a great opportunity to perform cheerful and popular music, particularly during the spring and autumn trade fairs when large numbers

---

* See page 87.

† See page 132.

of foreigners attended and they performed twice a week.* There were several other coffee-houses around the town, and one of them, Richter's in Schellhafer Hall, also hosted regular secular concerts twice a week, conducted by Johann Gottlieb Görner.

One major work he probably composed for the *collegium musicum* was the somewhat operatic secular cantata called 'The competition between Phoebus and Pan',† based on text by Picander. It has 15 movements, and lasts nearly an hour. Picander's plot line is based, at least in part, on the story in Ovid's *Metamorphoses*‡ of how in ancient Greece Phoebus Apollo, the son of Zeus and the god of music, competed musically with Pan. Apollo had created the lyre, and Pan had found a flute thrown away by Athena. His challenge to Apollo was to prove that the flute made sweeter music than the lyre. By far the most sophisticated and moving movement, and also by far the longest, is Phoebus Apollo's aria, expressing how much he loves the beautiful boy Hyacinthus. The only drawback is that it was accompanied by a flute, which was not Apollo's instrument. So perhaps Sebastian had not read Ovid!

And in April, the *St Matthew Passion* was performed again on Good Friday in St Thomas's Church. Of course Sebastian was still music teacher at St Thomas's School, and derived some confidence from the fact that a lot of his students (including his eldest son) were now graduating and going to university or becoming professional musicians. But things were not going well at the school, certainly from his point of view. Increasingly few of the new pupils had any musical ability, making it harder to maintain the tough task of performing cantatas and other music in the four town churches every Sunday. It also seemed that Carl Friedrich Pezold, who

---

* No records survive of the programmes performed, but it can be assumed that Sebastian introduced during the first few years much of his existing orchestral, chamber and keyboard music composed in the past, as well as his copies of works by, for example, Albinoni, Handel, Vivaldi, Telemann, Lully and Couperin.

† BWV 201, *Geschwinde, ihr wirbelnden Winde*.

‡ Books 6 and 11.

had undertaken Sebastian's non-music teaching,* was not doing a decent job with it. In general, the school's standards had been dropping in recent years, probably partly because the headmaster, Ernesti, was now in his seventies. In May, Sebastian interviewed 24 young boys seeking residential appointment at the school, assessing their musical capacities; only 14 passed his test.[118] The school's board chairman, Dr C. L. Stieglitz, reported to the town council[119] that Mr Bach had pointed out that this was likely to cause a serious problem with the Sunday services in the town's churches, since a total of 44 boys was needed, and most of the existing students had recently graduated and left St Thomas's. This attitude, involving much greater efforts to recruit musically talented boys to the school, was apparently not going down well with the town council, and it became increasingly annoying to realise that they had virtually no intention of supporting the enormous contributions Sebastian had made to church performances over the last six years. Clearly more disputes with his employers were to be expected.

Towards the end of June, Sebastian heard that the world-famous composer Georg Frideric Handel, who had been permanently in London since 1712, was currently revisiting his native town, Halle. It was irresistible to make another attempt to meet him. The last time, ten years earlier, Sebastian had toiled all the way there to find that Handel had already left. This time, since Sebastian was currently suffering from an abnormally high temperature, he persuaded his son Friedemann to make the journey, and to offer Handel an invitation to Leipzig. Despite his illness, it was terribly exciting to conceive social contact with this brilliant musician, several of whose works he had made copies of.†

Handel's career had blossomed dramatically over the last 18 years. Queen Anne towards the end of her life had patronised him, and

---

* See page 141.

† Philipp Spitta, in his 19th-century biography of Bach, reported (Vol. 2, p. 11) that copies in Bach's handwriting existed of Handel's *Brockes Passion*, one of his Concerti Grossi, and a solo cantata.

awarded him a £200 annual pension. Her successor after her death in 1714 was George I, Elector of Hanover, whose love of music ensured his admiration of Handel's genius, and he confirmed and doubled the pension. During the last ten years Handel had composed and performed a wide range of operas for presentation mainly at the Haymarket Theatre in London, many of them with huge success.

But this was not Sebastian's lucky day. Friedemann came back to say that Handel regretted that he was unable to attend, since he was obliged to return to Britain. Moreover, there was no evidence that he was aware of Bach's compositions.

And then there were more deaths. Friedelena, Maria Barbara's elder sister, who had been living with Sebastian's family and looking after the children for more than 20 years, died on 28 July, and was buried two days later. She was 53. Two and a half months later, on 16 October, the venerable but elderly headmaster of St Thomas's, Johann Heinrich Ernesti, died, and Sebastian was motivated to compose a brief but beautiful double-choir motet for his funeral in St Paul's.* What inspired him, apart from his respect for the scholarly and kind-hearted man with whom he had worked for six years, was reading St Paul's epistle to the Romans, particularly the lines about the works of the flesh and of the spirit: 'to be carnally minded is death; but to be spiritually minded is life and peace'. The two verses he chose to set to music were these, from Romans: 8:

> 26. Likewise the Spirit also helpeth our infirmities: for we know not what we should pray for as we ought: but the Spirit itself maketh intercession for us with groanings which cannot be uttered.
> 27. And he that searcheth the hearts knoweth what is the mind of the Spirit, because he maketh intercession for the saints according to the will of God.

---

* BWV 226, *Der Geist hilft unser Schwachheit auf*. In modern performances, it ends with a four-part chorale, *Du heilige Brunst*, but scholars believe this was not part of the motet but may have been sung later in the funeral.

The new year brought another family tragedy: Magdalena's seventh child, baptised on 1 January 1730 as Christiana Benedicta, died just three days later. This was the fourth calamity Magdalena and Sebastian had experienced since moving to Leipzig, and it was hardly possible for either of them to avoid thinking that catastrophes were a family feature. And more were to come. The only way they could cope was to keep on trying, with the belief that 'to be spiritually minded is life and peace', and that their devotion to music would entitle them and their children to a life hereafter. Magdalena was pregnant again later in the year.

Meanwhile, the general view in Leipzig was that standards in St Thomas's School had declined dramatically over the last few years, and the town council felt under considerable pressure to find and appoint a new headmaster who could undertake substantial improvements. It took them several months to do so, and the council's unanimous choice was the highly sophisticated and literate Johann Matthias Gesner, whom Sebastian had known some years before when (from 1715 to 1729) he was a teacher and librarian at the gymnasium school in Weimar. Gesner had recently been appointed headmaster at the gymnasium in Ansbach, in south-east Germany (near the town of Roth, where he was born in April 1691), but the council persuaded him to resign on the grounds that moving to Leipzig would significantly improve his status. He was appointed on 8 June 1730, and agreed to take up the post in September.

But more signs appeared that council members were displeased with the performance of the school's music teacher, including a recorded statement by one member that they might 'fare better in this appointment than in that of the cantor',[120] no doubt influenced by Sebastian's requests that they should hire more musicians and recruit more talented students, and also by Pezold's failure to handle the non-music teaching. And further complaints about him were noted in the minutes of the council meeting at the beginning of August:

The St Thomas School had many times been the subject of deliberation, and the plans and projects were at hand, but they would need to be investigated further. In which connection it should be remembered that when the cantor came hither he received a dispensation concerning the teaching; Mr Pezold attended the functions poorly enough; the third and fourth classes were the nursery for the whole school, and accordingly a competent person must be placed in charge of them; the cantor might take care of one of the lowest classes; he did not conduct himself as he should (without the foreknowledge of the chief magistrate he sent a choir student to the country, who left without obtaining leave), for which he must be reproached and admonished; at present it must be considered whether the said classes should not be provided with a different person; Mr Kriegel was said to be a good man, and a decision would have to be made about it.[121]

Several comments by specific council members on this statement were also recorded, including one by the former mayor, Gottfried Lange,* saying, 'Everything was true that had been mentioned against the cantor, and he could be admonished and the place filled with Mr Kriegel'; another saying, 'Not only did the cantor do nothing, but he was not even willing to give an explanation of that fact; he did not hold the singing class, and there were other complaints in addition; a change would be necessary, a break would have to come some time, and he would acquiesce in the making of other arrangements'; and a third saying, 'the cantor was incorrigible'. In other words, they all agreed with the decision that the cantor's income should be restricted. Three weeks later, the mayor reported that he had spoken to Bach, 'but he shows little inclination to work, and the question is whether the class ought not to be given to Mr Krügel instead of Petzold [*sic*], without additional salary'. The council then decided that 'arrangements to that effect are to be made'.

---

* See page 133.

Sebastian had decided to defend his position by drafting a detailed memorandum about the school's whole music position, which he would submit to the council as soon as possible. It was dated 23 August, and presumably reached the councillors by the end of the month. It is headed 'Short, but indispensable sketch of what constitutes well-appointed church music; with certain impartial reflections on the decline of the same'. This is what he wrote:

> Well-appointed church music requires vocalists and instrumentalists. The vocalists in this town consist of the pupils of St Thomas's School, being of four sorts: trebles, altos, tenors and basses. If the choir are to perform church pieces properly and as is fitting, the vocalists must in turn be divided into two sorts, namely soloists and choristers.
>
> The soloists are normally four in number; sometimes also five, six, seven or even eight; that is, if one wishes to perform music for two choirs. The choristers, too, must be at least eight, two for each part.
>
> The instrumentalists are also divided into various sorts, as violinists, oboists, flautists, trumpeters and drummers. N.B. The violinists also include those who play the viola, the violoncello and the violone.
>
> The number of resident students in St Thomas's School is 55.* These 55 are divided into four choirs, for the four churches in which they must partly perform music with instruments, partly sing motets, and partly sing chorales. In three of the churches, i.e. St Thomas's, St Nicholas's and the New Church, the pupils must all be musical. St Peter's receives the residue, those, that is to say, who do not understand music and can only barely sing a chorale.
>
> Every musical choir should contain at least three trebles, three altos, three tenors and as many basses, so that even if one happens to fall ill (as very often happens, particularly at this time of year, as the prescriptions

---

* This of course does not include the much larger number of non-residential pupils, including Sebastian's own sons. It is also notable that the number listed at the end of Sebastian's paper adds up to 54, not 55.

sent by the school physician to the dispensary must show), a motet may be sung with at least two voices per part. (N.B. How much better it would be if the group were so arranged that four singers could be available for each part, each choir thus consisting of 16 persons.)

Thus the number of those who must understand music comes to 36 persons in all.

The instrumental music consists of the following parts: two, or even three, for the violin 1; two or three for the violin 2; two for the viola 1; two for the viola 2; two for the violoncello; one for the violone; two or, if the piece requires, three for the oboe; one, or even two, for the bassoon; three for the trumpet; one for the drum; total 18 persons at least for the instrumental music. N.B. If it happens that the church piece is composed with flutes also (whether they are recorders or transverse flutes), as very often happens for variety's sake, at least two more persons are needed, making altogether 20 instrumentalists.

The number of persons appointed to play the church music is eight, four town pipers, three professional fiddlers, and one associate. Modesty forbids my speaking truly of their quality and musical knowledge. However, it ought to be considered that they are partly inefficient and partly not in such good practice as they should be. This is the list of them: Mr Reiche for the 1st trumpet; Mr Genssmar [*sic*] for the 2nd trumpet; vacant for the 3rd trumpet; vacant for the kettledrums; Mr Rother for the 1st violin; Mr Beyer for the 2nd violin; vacant for the viola; vacant for the violoncello; vacant for the violone; Mr Gleditsch for the 1st oboe; Mr Kornagel for the 2nd oboe; vacant for the 3rd oboe or taille; the associate for the bassoon. Thus there are lacking the following most necessary players, partly to reinforce certain voices, and partly to supply indispensable ones, to wit: two first violins; two second violins; two to play the viola; two violoncellos; one violonist; two for the flutes.

The lack that shows itself here has had to be made good hitherto partly by the university students but mostly by the school pupils. The students used to be very willing to do this in the hope that in time they might derive some advantage from it, or perhaps be favoured with a salary or fee (as was formerly the custom). But since this has not occurred, but on the contrary the few slight benefices formerly devoted to the choir have been successively withdrawn, the willingness of the students has likewise disappeared, for who will labour in vain, or give his service for nothing? Be it furthermore remembered that, as the 2nd violin usually, and the viola, violoncello and violone always (in the absence of more capable performers) have had to be played by students, it is easy to estimate how much the choir have been deprived of in consequence. This refers only to Sunday. But I should mention the music for festivals (on which days I must supply both the principal churches with music), the lack of necessary players will show even more clearly, particularly since I must give up to the other choir all those pupils who play one instrument or another, and must get along without their assistance.

Moreover, it must not pass unnoticed that the fact that so many poorly equipped boys, and boys not at all talented for music, have been accepted to date has necessarily caused the music to decline and deteriorate. For it is easy to understand that a boy who knows nothing about music, and who cannot even sing a second, can have no natural musical talent, and consequently can never be of any use in the musical service. And even those who bring some elementary knowledge to school with them are not ready to be used immediately, as is required. For time will not allow their being duly trained for a year, or until they are skilled enough to be of use, but as soon as they are admitted they are placed in the various choirs, and they must at least be sure of time and pitch to be of any use in the service. Now, as every year some of those who have done something in music leave the school, and their places are filled by others, many of whom are not yet ready to be used or have no ability whatsoever, it is easy to understand that the choirs must decline.

And it is notorious that my honoured predecessors, Messrs Schell [*sic*] and Kuhnau, already had to rely on the help of the university students when they wished to produce a complete and well-sounding music which, indeed, they were enabled to this extent to do, that not only several vocalists – a bass, a tenor, and even an alto – as also instrumentalists, particularly two violinists, were favoured with separate stipends from a certain noble and learned councillor, and thus encouraged to strengthen the church music. Now, however, that the state of music is quite different from what it was, since our artistry has increased very much, and the taste marvellously changed, and accordingly the former style of music no longer seems to please our ears, considerable help is therefore all the more necessary to choose and appoint such musicians as may be able to satisfy the present musical taste, and to undertake the new kinds of music, and thus be in a position to do justice to the composer and his works. Now the few benefices, which should have been increased rather than diminished, have been withdrawn entirely from the choir. It is, anyhow, somewhat strange that German musicians are expected to be capable of performing at once and extempore all kinds of music, whether Italian or French, English or Polish, just as may be done, say, by those virtuosi for whom the music is written and who have studied it for a long time beforehand, or even know it almost by heart, and who besides have such high salaries that their work and diligence is well rewarded; while, on the other hand, these are not taken into consideration, but they are left to take care of themselves, so that many a one, for worry about his bread, cannot think of improving – let alone distinguishing – himself. To illustrate this statement with an example, we need only go to Dresden and see how the musicians there are paid by the king. It cannot fail, since the musicians are relieved of all concern for their living, free from chagrin and obliged each to master but a single instrument; it must be admirable and delightful to hear. The conclusion is easy to draw: that in ceasing to receive the perquisites I am deprived of the power to bring the music into a better condition.

Finally, I find it necessary to append the enumeration of the present students, to indicate the musical proficiency of each, and thus to leave it to more mature consideration whether in these circumstances the music can continue to be maintained, or whether its still greater decline is to be feared.

It is, however, desirable to divide the whole group into three classes. The really efficient boys are the following: Pezold, Lange, Stoll (prefects). Frick, Krause, Kittler, Pohlreüter, Stein, Burckhard, Siegler, Nitzer, Reichhard, Krebs major and minor, Schönemann, Heder and Dietel. The names of the motet singers, who must first have training in order to be used eventually for part-singing, are as follows: Jänigke, Ludewig major and minor, Meißner, Neücke major and minor, Hillmeyer, Steidel, Hesse, Haupt, Suppius, Segnitz, Thieme, Keller, Röder, Ossan, Berger, Lösch, Hauptmann and Sachse. Those of the last class are not musical at all, and their names are: Bauer, Gross, Eberhard, Braune, Seyman, Tietze, Hebenstreit, Wintzer, Össer, Leppert, Haussius, Feller, Crell, Zeymer, Guffer, Eichel and Zwicker. Total: 17 usable, 20 not yet usable, and 17 unfit.

Joh. Seb. Bach, Director Musices[122]

This so-called short, but surprisingly detailed, handwritten statement provides a very clear account of Sebastian's view of his role in Leipzig, and of the ever increasing problems he had encountered – but had tried to suppress – since his arrival seven years earlier. The initial point was that his purpose as cantor was to improve musical performance in the churches, and the hundreds of cantatas he had already composed were clearly a major step towards doing so. The trouble was that virtually every week there was a shortage of competent singers and players, and because the council's policy in recruiting pupils placed no emphasis on musical talent, there had been no improvement. And money, as usual, was also a factor: his predecessors, Johann Schelle (whose name he misspelled) and Johann Kuhnau, had succeeded in employing university students to perform regularly by getting the council to pay them modest fees. But this was no longer happening, and so that advantage too was declining. The third point was that several of the town pipers and fiddlers were pretty incompetent too, not least because they were elderly.

But the trouble with Sebastian's laborious statement was that it offered no response to the council's own concerns, which were not about the increasingly complex church music styles that required more participants and more payment. Their point was about the school staff, and the decline in general educational levels. So in effect Sebastian's statement was ignored, and his relations with his employers did not improve.

As modern readers, we can fully understand the contradictory views described and elaborated on both sides of this dispute. The council was absolutely justified in seeking to remedy the growing general educational decline in St Thomas's School, which inevitably involved examining the behaviour and attitudes of its crucial teachers. There was no denial that part of this major problem was distinctly related to the cantor's unusual character. The fact that Sebastian's 1723 supporter and advocate, Gottfried Lange, fully agreed with the council's criticisms makes it clear beyond doubt that Sebastian was not performing his role as schoolteacher at all well. On the other hand, his detailed description of the chaos surrounding the school's traditional performance in the grand Leipzig churches – particularly the gross shortage both of singers and players and of finances to employ more of them – is also persuasive. It was to be hoped that the town council's decision to appoint the music-loving Johann Matthias Gesner as the new headmaster would lead to a resolution of this serious problem.

As for Sebastian's own view at the time, he clearly hoped that Gesner, who was due to arrive in September, would improve both his position and the situation in general. But he also began to think about finding a new post elsewhere, even though he was now in his mid-forties.

If we want to understand his frame of mind regarding these painful issues, we should listen to a cantata he composed for performance on the 15th Sunday after Trinity, and performed on 17 September, just after Gesner took up the office of headmaster. *Jauchzet Gott in allen Landen!** is a very unusual

---

* 'Praise God in every land!' (BWV 51). This superb four-movement cantata seems to be rarely performed in modern times.

work, involving no choir, and only a single treble soloist. The accompaniment features a highly dramatic obbligato trumpet in the opening aria, with strings and continuo, and it is difficult and intricate both to play and to sing, surely revealing to the congregation – particularly members of the town council – how fascinating church music now could be. The following recitative is also exceptional, inspired by the words *Wir beten zu dem Tempel an, da Gottes Ehre wohnet, da dessen Treu, so täglich neu, mit lauter Segen lohnet. Wir preisen, was er an uns hat getan. Muß gleich der schwache Mund von seinen Wundern lallen, so kann ein schlechtes Lob ihm dennoch wohlgefallen* ('We pray at your temple, where God's honour dwells, where his faithfulness, daily renewed, is rewarded with pure bliss. We praise what He has done for us. Even though our weak mouth must gape before His wonders, our meagre praise is still bringing pleasure to Him'). And the piece ends with a splendid chorale, the hymn tune sung by the treble being surrounded by lively string-orchestral accompaniment, and ending with a beautiful and complex Alleluia. This is a clear statement that musical talent has a great deal to offer, that additions to the standard performance are really valuable, and that praise to God is the only solution to weak misery.

And another revelation survives. A few weeks later, on 28 October, Sebastian wrote another, this time much longer and more informative, letter to Georg Erdmann in Danzig, where for twelve years he had held the post of Russia's diplomatic representative, and legal adviser to the Russian court:

> Most honoured Sir.
>
> Your honour will forgive an old and faithful servant for taking the liberty of troubling you with this. Nearly four years have now elapsed since Your Honour favoured me with a kind reply to the letter I sent you. Since you then, as I recall, graciously requested that I should give you some news of my vicissitudes in life, I hereby proceed to obey you. You know the course of my life from my youth until the change that led me to Cöthen as kapellmeister. There lived there a gracious Prince, who both loved and understood music, and I expected there to spend my life and end my

days. As it turned out, however, his Serene Highness married a Princess of Berenburg, and then it appeared that the musical interests of the said Prince had become somewhat lukewarm, while at the same time the new Princess seemed to be unmusical; and it pleased God that I should be called to be director musices and cantor at the St Thomas School here. At first it did not altogether please me to become a cantor from having been a kapellmeister, and for this reason I postponed my decision for three months; but this position was described to me in such favourable terms that finally (and especially as my sons seemed inclined to study here) I risked myself in the name of the Most High and made the journey to Leipzig, took my examination, and then made the move. Here, following God's will, I remain to this day. But since now I find (1) that this appointment is by no means so remunerative as it was described to me; (2) that many fees incidental to it have been withdrawn; (3) that the town is very expensive to live in; and (4) that the authorities are odd, and little interested in music, with the result that I live under almost constant vexation, jealousy and harassment, I feel compelled to seek, with God's assistance, my fortune elsewhere. If Your Honour should know of, or be able to find, a suitable appointment in your town for your old and faithful servant, I humbly request you to give me the benefit of your favourable recommendation. Nothing shall be wanting on my part to give satisfaction and justify your favourable recommendation and intercession. My present position secures me about 700 thalers [£33,600], and when there are rather more deaths than usual the fees increase in proportion; but if the air is healthy they fall accordingly, as last year, when I lost over 100 thalers [£4,800] of the usual funeral fees. In Thuringia I could live better on 400 thalers [£19,200] than I can here with twice that amount, because of the excessive cost of living. I must now make some small mention of my domestic circumstances. I am now married for the second time, my late first wife having died in Cöthen. Of my first marriage three sons and a daughter are living, whom Your Honour will graciously remember having seen in Weimar. Of my second marriage, one son and two daughters are living. My eldest son is a law student, and of the other two one is in the first and the other in the second class, and my eldest daughter is still unmarried. The children of my second marriage are still young; the eldest is a boy aged six. But they are all born musicians, and I can assure you that I can already form a vocal and instrumental ensemble from my family, particularly as my present wife sings a very pleasing soprano, and my eldest daughter can also join in not too badly. I should almost overstep the bounds of courtesy by troubling Your Honour any further, so I hasten to conclude with most devoted respects, and remain Your Honour's lifelong and most obedient and humble servant,

Leipzig, 28 October 1730　　　　　　　　　　　　Joh: Sebast: Bach[123]

Clearly what Sebastian thought might positively influence his childhood friend were mainly his and his family's musical skills and performance, and also money, which were two crucial factors in their teenage years. Perhaps he made no reference to his approach to schoolteaching, or to the vast range of his existing compositions, because neither of these activities would be his preference for a new post in Danzig. What he evidently hoped for was to become an admired and famous performer and conductor, even if this involved travelling further from Thuringia than he had ever been before. Whether or not Erdmann replied is unknown, but even if he did there was no suggestion of a suitable role Sebastian could take on in Danzig, and it became clear to him over the next few months that he would probably remain in Leipzig for the rest of his life.

In these less than auspicious circumstances it is remarkable that Sebastian composed another masterpiece in the autumn of 1730, and that its inspiration was the three simple verses written by Martin Rinckart for Johann Crüger's famous hymn *Nun danket alle Gott*, dated 1648.* It

---

*　Hymn 379 in *Hymns Ancient and Modern*, where the text was translated by Catherine Winkworth (1827–78), beginning 'Now thank we all our God'. The cantata is BWV 192.

The palace church in Weimar, where the organ was incredibly high above the ground. The painting is by Christian Richter, c.1660.

Prince Leopold of Anhalt-Cöthen (1694–1728), who employed Bach from 1717 for five years. The portraitist is unknown.

BELOW
The central market square in Leipzig, engraved by Johann Georg Schreiber in 1712. The building in the centre is the Altes Rathaus.

St Thomas's Church in Leipzig, engraved by G. Bodenehr.

An exterior view of St Thomas's Church in Leipzig today.

LEIPZIG IN 1722, *painted by Amy Shuckburgh.*

A: *Pleißen Castle;*
B: *Bösen Park;*
C: *St Thomas's School;*
D: *St Thomas's Church;*
E: *St Peter's Church;*
F: *the Altes Rathaus;*
G: *the New Church;*
H: *Katharinenstraße, site of Zimmermann's coffee-house;*
I: *St John's Church;*
J: *St Paul's Church;*
K: *Leipzig University;*
L: *St Nicholas's Church;*
M: *St Nicholas's School;*
N: *Brühlstraße, site of George House.*

13

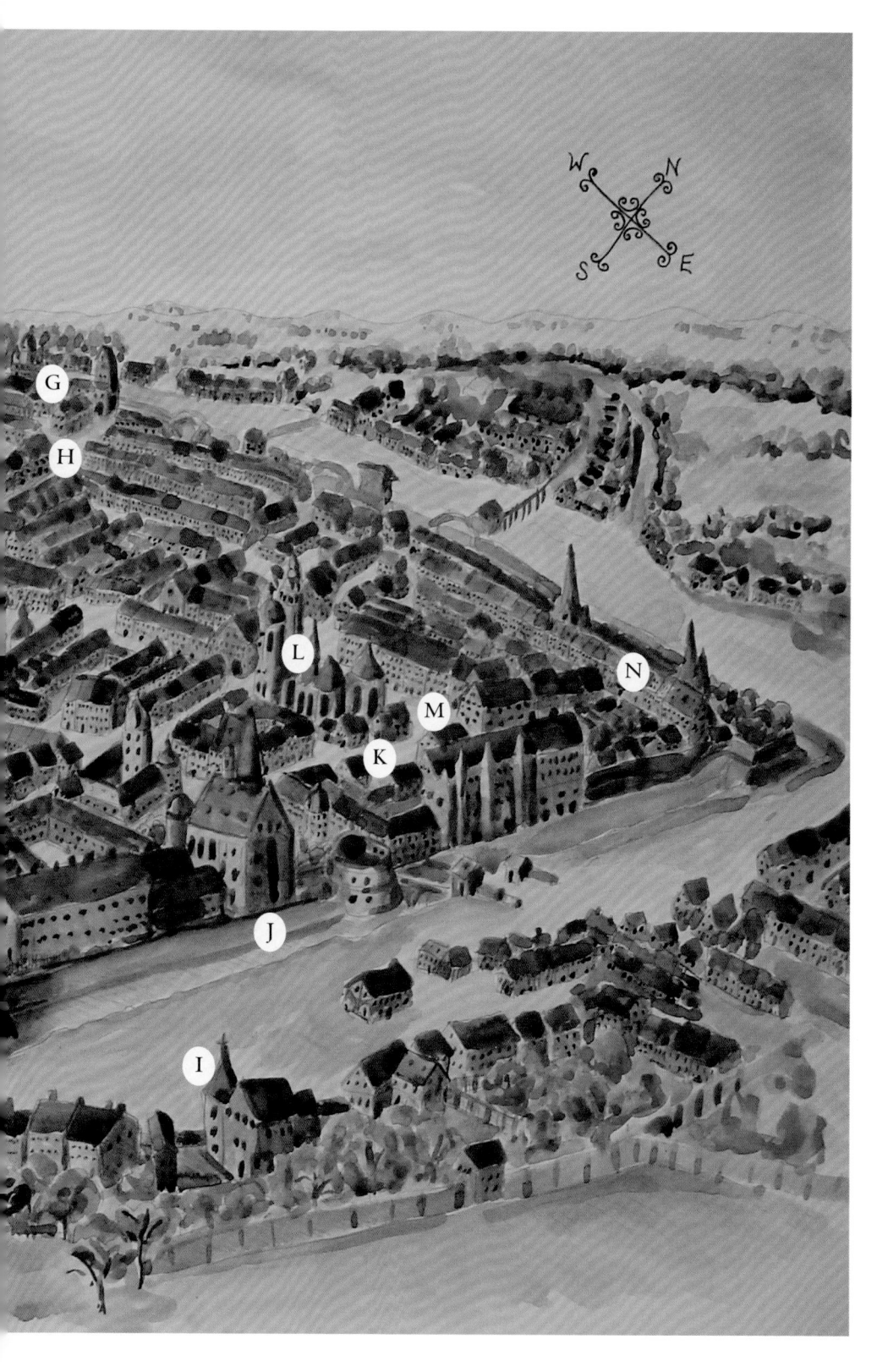

St Nicholas's Church in Leipzig today.

LEFT
Johann August Ernesti (1707–81), the headmaster of St Thomas's School from 1734 to 1759, painted by Anton Graff.

OPPOSITE, ABOVE
Zimmermann's coffee-house in Leipzig, where Bach regularly performed the collegium musicum *for several years from 1729. It was engraved by Johann Georg Schreiber in 1712.*

OPPOSITE, RIGHT
St John's Church, outside the town, where Bach was buried in July 1750.

Ein Theil der Cather Straſse.
1. Das Hohmännische 2. Örtelische
3. Schacherische Haus.
1
2
3

50
Die S. Iohannes Kirch mitt dem Kirchhoff und Gotts Acker,
vor dem Grimmiſchen Thor zu LEIPZIG.
1
1. Die S. Iohannes Kirch.
2. Der Kirchhoff.
3. Pforte oder Eingang.
4. Die Todten Capellen.
5. Eingang in den Neuen Gotts Acker.
6. Die Voor Statt.
7. Anstoss des Pfar Hausser.
8. Das Zucht Haus.
Ioh. Stridbeck Iun. del. G.B. exc.
Cum Priv. Sac. Cæs. Majest.

The only existing authorised portrait of Bach, first painted in 1746 by Elias Gottlob Haußmann (1695–1774), and copied by him two years later. This is the original version.

comprises only three movements, one for each verse, and opens with a splendid chorus in G major accompanied by two flutes, two oboes, strings and continuo, in which the hymn tune is eventually — from bar 41 — sung by the sopranos, after an extended fugal comment on the text by the three lower voices. The second movement, in D major, is a beautiful soprano and bass duet, and it is followed by a more compact choral fantasia, back in G major, in which the hymn tune is more dominant. The work is a clear statement that Sebastian is still unwaveringly determined to maintain his compositional skills, to ignore the critical attitudes of his employers, and to express his strengthening belief in the life hereafter.

Chapter 11

RESUSCITATION

(1730–34)

Johann Matthias Gesner's arrival as headmaster of St Thomas's heralded a considerable improvement in the status of the school's cantor, because Gesner's appreciation of musical skills was much more sophisticated than his predecessor's. Eight years later, after he had moved to Göttingen University as professor of philology, Gesner wrote a brief account in Latin of 'my colleague at the Leipzig St Thomas School' in which 'the accomplishments of our Bach' are described as remarkable. He particularly mentions Sebastian's keyboard and organ-playing skills, and his exceptional ability as a conductor:

> ... singing with one voice and playing his own parts, but watching over everything and bringing back to the rhythm and the beat, out of thirty or even forty musicians, the one with a nod, another by tapping with his foot, the third with a warning finger, giving the right note to one with the top of his voice, to another from the bottom, and to a third from the middle of it – all alone, in the midst of the greatest din made by all the participants, and, although he is executing the most difficult parts himself, noticing at once whenever and wherever a mistake occurs, holding everyone together, taking precautions everywhere, and repairing any unsteadiness, full of rhythm in every part of his body – this one man taking in all these harmonies with his keen ear and emitting with his voice alone the tone of all the voices.[124]

Gesner was not the only person to write notes about Sebastian's skills. As early as 1717, towards the end of his time in Weimar, the prolific music journalist Johann Mattheson had commented on his organ-playing ability and said that 'one must esteem the man highly'.* And several other lavish praises of his keyboard dexterity have survived, mainly written by people in the world of music.[125]

Another exciting project Gesner undertook soon after assuming his post was to organise the reconstruction of the school building. Some alterations and improvements had been made in previous years to Sebastian's flat and other parts of the house, but the building was still regarded as too cramped for the number of teachers and boys, and Gesner's plan was to add two storeys to it, raising it from three to five floors, plus three attics. The building work was to begin in April 1731, and the Bach family, along with the other residents, would have to move out for more than a year. The current family comprised ten Bachs, including eight children. Catharina was 22, Friedemann (20) was reading law at the university, Emanuel (17) and Bernhard (15) were pupils at the school, and Heinrich (7) appeared to be suffering from some kind of learning disability and was being given private tutoring. Then there were Elisabeth Juliana Frederica, who had just celebrated her fifth birthday, and Regina Johanna, who would be three in October. Magdalena was pregnant again, and in March 1731 gave birth to a new daughter, baptised Christiana Dorothea (no doubt partly in memory of Christiana Benedicta who had died just after birth the year before). It was arranged that in June they should move into the house of Dr Christoph Donndorf, a law professor, in Hainstraße, only a street away from St Thomas's.

Three weeks after Dorothea was born, and just before they moved out of the school building, Sebastian produced a brilliant new cantata which vividly displays his determination to survive the past tragedies. *Der Herr ist mein getreuer Hirt* ('The Lord is my true shepherd', BWV 112) was performed in St Nicholas's Church on 8 April, based on the Gospel reading for the second

---

* See page 4.

Sunday after Easter,* which begins, 'Jesus said, I am the good shepherd: the good shepherd giveth his life for the sheep.' All five movements are based on the words of a familiar 16th-century hymn by Wolfgang Meuslin, and the tune by Nikolaus Decius (1522); but they are subtly and beautifully composed, scored with two horns and two oboes d'amore in addition to the usual strings. The most beautiful is the fourth, a soprano and tenor duet which begins with the inspirational words *Du bereitest für mir einen Tisch vor mein' Feinden allenthalben* ('You prepare for me a table before my enemies who stand around me'). Listening to it, you would find it hard not to imagine that this statement of belief and optimism is being expressed specifically by Sebastian and Magdalena; and that the subsequent simple chorale which ends the cantata is a display of support for them by the musical community.

The Bachs benefited from several improvements and enlargements to their apartment on the southern side of the school building,† including an extended and heated room on the second floor and a new bedroom there, and another new bedroom in one of the attics. These alterations organised by the headmaster were an encouragement for Sebastian in the face of such a series of crises with his employers, and made him believe that he need no longer 'feel compelled to seek, with God's assistance, my fortune elsewhere', as he had written in his long letter to Georg Erdmann. We can also get a sense of the Bachs' daily life at home by looking again at the inventory mentioned in the footnote on page 138, which listed all his possessions. They included two pairs of candlesticks, nine cups, several coffee- and teapots, two sugar bowls, two or three snuffboxes for smoking, twelve knives, forks and spoons, two golden rings, 24 plates and two copper kettles. The

---

* It should be added that for Easter 1731 Bach had composed a third Passion, BWV 247, much of the music of which has not survived. None the less, several reconstructions of it have been published and performed in the last century, based on the surviving libretto by Picander and evidence that much of the music was derived from previous compositions.

† See page 143.

furniture comprised seven wooden bedsteads, six tables, 18 leather chairs, a writing desk, a wardrobe and two chests of drawers.

It would be interesting to know what food they ate and drank there – and throughout Sebastian's life – but there is little evidence apart from the fact that Thuringia has always been the region of boiled dumplings, cakes and sautéed sausages, and that the local produce included cauliflower, cabbage, broad beans, onions and cucumbers, as well as wheat, turnips, sugar beet and small, tasty loaves of bread. The cooking was presumably supervised by his sister-in-law Friedelena until she died in 1729, and thereafter by his daughter Catharina.

And another reinforcement of his self-esteem was the new role he had acquired as director of the *collegium musicum* founded 20 years earlier by Telemann. Attendance at Zimmermann's coffee-house was free – presumably because, before and after the concert, the audience would come to buy the food and drink in the restaurant. And the performances regularly drew up to 150 listeners in the large hall in the centre of the building – and on warm days in the back garden – three days a week. The ensemble consisted of 50 or 60 players and singers, most of them members of the university; and one of the greatest advantages to Sebastian over recent months was that many of them were now willing to join his Sunday cantata performances, settling the constant problem he had expressed in his memorandum to the town council in August 1730 about the shortage of competent school musicians. (Zimmermann's fine building was destroyed in World War II.)

This popular and secular weekly event was a new and much needed encouragement to Sebastian to develop a wider range of compositions, including more secular cantatas and more orchestral pieces. Although rather few reports survive of what was actually performed at these popular concerts, it is clear that he composed a number of surviving works around this time, of which a typical example is the orchestral suite in D major (BWV 1068) for three trumpets, two oboes, timpani, strings and basso continuo. It is a highly competent and jolly work, and contains one exceptional movement which was revived by the German violinist August Wilhelmj in 1871 under the title 'Air on the G String', and has remained famous ever since.

There are several other striking pieces that were almost certainly produced around this time for the coffee-house concerts, including the simple and beautiful three-movement sonata in E-flat major for flute and harpsichord (BWV 1031), with its memorable Siciliano second movement. We do not know who performed it, but it seems very likely that Sebastian was keen to display his keyboard skills; and this might also explain the appearance at that time of at least two concertos for three harpsichords and strings (BWV 1063 and BWV 1064), played perhaps by him and his two eldest sons. The latter, and particularly its second Adagio movement, is especially poignant. Another equally impressive concerto he now produced, this time for four solo harpsichords (BWV 1065), is based on Vivaldi's Concerto for Four Violins (Op. 3, No. 10). It turns out that most of these concertos were derived from his own previous compositions for solo instruments such as violin or oboe, probably written in Weimar or Cöthen; but now for the first time in musical history the keyboard is the solo instrument. It is a major achievement.

As for the weekly church services, Sebastian was now relying on re-performing his huge existing collection of cantata compositions, sometimes making minor (or even major) changes to them, and composing a new one only once every few months. As the installation of the new town council approached in August, he felt inspired again to write something that would express his determination to survive tragedy. This cantata* starts with a splendid sinfonia in D major, featuring three trumpets, two oboes, strings and continuo, but completely dominated by the organ – which was clearly played by Sebastian himself, demonstrating his dramatic skills. This is followed by an equally memorable chorus based

---

* BWV 29, *Wit danken dir, Gott, wir danken dir*. The sinfonia is based on the opening movement of Bach's unaccompanied violin Partita in E Major (BWV 1006), probably also composed in Cöthen.

on the opening verse of Psalm 75: 'Unto thee, O God, do we give thanks, unto thee do we give thanks: for that thy name is near thy wondrous works declare.'* There are then five impressive movements, and it ends with a fine chorale also accompanied by the trumpets. The whole piece is a clear statement to the town council that he has no intention of withdrawing himself from his commitment to the city of Leipzig.

Given the reference to Dresden in his long August 1730 memorandum to the council, it was also rather encouraging that he received another invitation to travel there for a week in September to perform some organ recitals in St Sophia's Church.† Although he had made a clear decision to hold on to his Leipzig post, he continued to be rankled from time to time by his awareness of the affluent music professionals employed in Dresden, and the royal family's clear appreciation of high-class music. Extending his connection with that city was a definite possibility, both by his visits there and by his *collegium musicum* performances. His eldest son Friedemann would shortly graduate from university, and might conceivably find his first job there.

In October Emanuel, who was now 17, joined his brother at the university. At the end of November, sadly, Magdalena's father Johann Caspar Wülcken died in Weißenfels at the age of 69.

The *St John Passion* was performed again at Easter in 1732, and two weeks later the Bachs moved back in to their now spacious St Thomas's apartment. Magdalena was pregnant again, and on 21 June she gave birth to her ninth child, a boy, who two days later was baptised Johann Christoph Friedrich. Naturally Sebastian had asked his recent landlord, the law professor Dr Christoph Donndorf in whose house they had lived for a year, to be his godfather. The baby boy appeared healthy at his birth, and for the first time for ages it looked as if a child of Magdalena's would survive. Sebastian was

---

* Bach later reworked this movement as 'Gratias agimus tibi', and it is part of the Mass in B Minor.

† See page 176. His previous performance there was in September 1725.

again inspired to produce an unusual and revealing cantata, which allows us to surmise his contrasting emotions at this time. The beautiful opening chorus of *Ich ruf zu dir, Herr Jesu Christ* ('I call on you, Lord Jesus Christ')* is in G minor, accompanied by two oboes, solo violin and the usual strings. The complex instrumentation, as in many other cantatas, is based on a simple hymn tune sung by the trebles. The other movements comprise alto, treble and tenor arias, all three of which convey a deeply personal sense of how the hymn's words inspire his creations: for example, 'give me hope' in the first; 'I shall never be mocked again' in the second, and 'help me defend myself when misfortune comes upon me' in the third. The cantata ends with a simple but harmonically subtle chorale, with the words *Ich lieg im Streit und widerstreb; hilf, o Herr Christ, dem Schwachen!* ('I lie in dispute and I resist; help me, O Lord Christ, in my weakness'). Another cantata composed that month, BWV 9, contains an equally revealing tenor aria stirred by the hymn words *in solcher Not uns keine Hand behilflich sein* ('in such distress no hand could help us'). It was almost as if he expected more distress at any moment.

And he would have been right. Their little daughter Christiana Dorothea, aged one and a half, died at the end of August. Magdalena had now lost five of her nine children since 1726, and Sebastian eight of his 16. Catharina was now 23 (and not married), Friedemann at 21 would soon be graduating from the university, Emanuel was 20, Bernhard 17, Heinrich 8, Elisabeth 6, Regina Johanna 3 and Friedrich 9 months old. Meanwhile Magdalena was pregnant again, with her tenth child expected in November.

Two months before, on 1 February, the Elector of Saxony and King of Poland, Augustus the Strong, had died in Warsaw, and a six-month state mourning period had been announced. This meant that the Leipzig churches were music-free, which allowed Sebastian to contemplate expanding his compositions and performances, and to help Friedemann find himself a job as musician somewhere not too far away. Dresden was the main target – and amazingly within a few months, in June,

---

* BWV 177.

Friedemann had been appointed organist at the city's St Sophia's Church, where Sebastian had several times performed in the past on the splendid Silbermann organ. It was certainly a considerable encouragement to find that his eldest son could now enter the world of professional musicians, and not in some remote village but in the capital city of Saxony.

Moreover, in April, the new elector, Friedrich August II, had made a two-day visit to Leipzig for a special mourning reception arranged by the town council, followed by a service in St Nicholas's Church. This was a further motivation for Sebastian to extend his connections with Dresden, and given the Lutheran and Catholic links there it occurred to him to compose a piece that could be shared by them all: a Latin mass. After the traumas and miseries of recent months he was now again inspired to create a masterpiece, comprising twelve movements covering the Kyrie and Gloria which represent the Missa Brevis.* He set it for a five-part choir (two trebles, alto, tenor and bass), four soloists, and a string orchestra with trumpets and timpani, plus two flutes, two oboes and two bassoons. Some of the movements were skilfully derived from previous cantata compositions,† thoroughly sustaining the idea that the vast range of works he had composed in the past could be reused in many different ways. The work as a whole would take nearly an hour to perform, and in July Friedemann arranged that the first performance should take place in his new church, St Sophia's, at the southern end of Sophienstraße.‡ Sebastian felt he might obtain court approval if he dedicated the piece to the Elector, and the title wrapper was inscribed with the words: 'To His Royal Majesty and Electoral Highness of Saxony, demonstrated with the enclosed Mass – for 21 [voices], 3 violins, 2 sopranos, alto, tenor, bass, 3 trumpets, 1 hunting horn, 2 transverse flutes, 2 oboes, 2 bassoons, violoncello,

---

* These are the first two sections of Bach's Mass in B Minor, BWV 232, which he completed towards the end of his life.

† For example, the second movement of BWV 29 (see page 221), and the opening movement of BWV 46 (see page 147).

‡ The church was destroyed by allied bombers at the end of World War II.

and continuo – his most humble devotion, the author, J. S. Bach.'[126] So while in Dresden on 17 July, in the usual grovelling style he wrote the following letter:

> My Most Gracious Lord, Most Serene Elector, Most Gracious Lord!
> To Your Royal Highness I submit in deepest devotion the present small work of that science which I have achieved in *musique*, with the most wholly submissive prayer that Your Highness will look upon it with most gracious eyes, according to Your Highness's world-famous clemency and not according to the poor *composition*; and thus deign to take me under your most mighty protection. For some years, and up to the present moment, I have had the directorship of the music in the two principal churches in Leipzig, but have innocently had to suffer one injury or another, and on occasion also a diminution of the fees accruing to me in this office; but these injuries would disappear altogether if Your Royal Highness would grant me the favour of conferring upon me the title of Your Highness's court kapellmeister and would let your high command for the issuing of such document go forth to the proper place. Such most gracious fulfilment of my most humble prayer will bind me to unending devotion, and I offer myself in most indebted obedience to show at all times, upon Your Royal Highness's most gracious desire, my untiring zeal in the composition of music for the church as well as for the orchestra, and to devote my entire forces to the service of Your Highness, remaining in unceasing fidelity Your Royal Highness's most humble and most obedient servant,
>
> Johann Sebastian Bach[127]

His hope was that the court officials with whom he had recently become acquainted would pass his petition directly to Friedrich August II, and that remembering Bach's remarkable skills and fine *collegium musicum* performances the Elector would speedily grant him the post of court kapellmeister. But there was no response. Once again he must have felt that no one in the upper classes seemed to appreciate his expertise and hard work, let alone the exceptional qualities of his compositions.

Money, as usual, was one of the principal reasons he still felt greatly in need of further support from the aristocracy. The school staff – and particularly the cantor – were very dependent for their income on the standard fees due for any use of the church for weddings, christenings, funerals and memorial services.* Another infuriating refusal to pay came in August, when a local businessman named Johann Friedrich Eitelwein had arranged his marriage in the village church of Plaußig, just five miles north of Leipzig. In Eitelwein's view it was outrageous to be charged fees in the city when he attended a service elsewhere, and so he had ignored the invoice. Sebastian wrote two formal and detailed letters of complaint to the town council and the consistory, and had them signed by the school's headmaster, Gesner, and the organist at St Nicholas's, Johann Schneider. By November, the consistory had instructed the council to 'notify Eitelwein to pay the usual fees most promptly, failing which he must be held to it by appropriate means'. So eventually Sebastian got his fee of 6 thalers [£288].

In the meantime, another opportunity had arisen to flatter the Dresden royal family when he was commissioned to produce a work to celebrate the eleventh birthday of the Elector's son, Friedrich Christian, to be performed by the *collegium musicum* on 5 September.† Picander produced an elaborate and operatic text based on the famous classical story known as 'Hercules at the Crossroads', in which Hercules in his youth is confronted by two women, one representing pleasure and the other virtue. The story (written by Cicero around 60 BC) tells us that 'when Hercules came to the age of puberty and thus entered upon the road of life, he was much tortured by his desires, and withdrew to a solitary place where he meditated upon the two paths that seemed open to him: that of *voluptas* [pleasure], and that of virtue'. Many artists since medieval times

---

* See pages 137-8.

† BWV 213.

had painted splendid portraits of Hercules and the two attractive ladies representing pleasure and virtue, most of them indicating that although he eventually chose Virtue he sensed some regret that he would miss out on the more beautiful and less clothed Pleasure.

Picander's text involves additional characters: a chorus representing the Muses; Mercury (or Hermes), the god of the crossroads; and Echo, the nymph of the trees and springs. The opening chorus is exceptional, accompanied by two corni da caccia, two oboes and strings; and it is immediately followed by a surprise: Hercules, the most popular male hero in classical mythology, is sung by an alto – perhaps to signify the fact that he was very young, and might represent eleven-year-old Prince Friedrich. In his brief opening recitative, he asks the crossroads, *Und wo? Wo ist die rechte Bahn?* ('And where? Where is the right way?'). The third movement is by far the most beautiful in the whole work, Pleasure's aria, sung by a soprano, beginning with the words *Schlafe, mein Liebster* ('Sleep, my darling'), no doubt inspired by the concept that pleasure may actually supersede virtue. But it doesn't. The following movements are competent enough, including Virtue's tenor aria, an alto and tenor duet in which Hercules and Virtue sing *Ich bin deine* ('I am yours') and *Du bist meine* ('You are mine'), and a fine but quite brief closing chorus involving the Muses and Mercury (bass), addressed to the prince.

On 5 November, Magdalena gave birth to her tenth child, a boy whom they baptised Johann August Abraham; but he died the next day. And then just a few months later, on 25 April 1733, their four-and-a-half-year-old daughter Regina Johanna also died. Since her and Sebastian's marriage twelve years earlier, seven of her ten had died. And despite all the physical intimacies that Sebastian had been engaged in throughout his life, he now had only seven surviving children. But he and Magdalena were not deterred from continuing to enlarge their family; indeed, within the next twelve months or so she was pregnant again for the eleventh time.

For an impression of how Sebastian was now feeling about the calamities and frustrations that had affected his life, particularly over the last few years, another work composed in November and performed on 8 December provides a vivid sense of how to aim at resuscitation. It was commissioned to celebrate Electress Maria Josepha's birthday, and is a secular cantata entitled *Tonet, ihr Pauken! Erschallet, Trompeten!* ('Sound, you drums! Ring out, trumpets!).* Although most of Sebastian's secular choral compositions are based on libretti written by professionals such as Picander, there is a strong impression that he wrote these nine verses himself – not least because of their frequent references to music, to avoiding the effects of depression, and to the pride of having talented sons – not to mention the Muses.† The lines clearly represent a consistent affirmation that music-playing is a powerful source of self-confidence, that nature represents optimism, and that the Muses – who were themselves divine singers – encourage the aristocracy to settle quarrels and become dear to their subjects. And there is more: references to poetry, to the composition and performance of new songs, and how this music, with the queen's help, can penetrate into 'the wide circle of the earth'. It is hard to imagine that anyone other than Sebastian could have written these words.

1. Chorus

Tönet, ihr Pauken! Erschallet, Trompeten!	Sound, you drums! Ring out, trumpets!
Klingende Saiten, erfüllet die Luft!	Resonant strings, fill the air!
Singet itzt Lieder, ihr muntren Poeten,	Sing your songs now, you lively poets,

---

* BWV 214, performed on 8 December 1733.

† Albert Schweitzer, whose biography of Bach was first published in 1905, wrote, 'The text must be by Bach himself, since no author's name is given in the programme book printed by Breitkopf. The original imprint of the text is in the Royal Library at Dresden, showing that the programme books were sent to the Court' (Vol. 2, p. 284). No subsequent academic research has proved otherwise, although contemporary scholarly biographers, such as Christoph Wolff, continue to state that the librettist is 'unknown'.

Königin lebe! wird fröhlich geruft.

Long live the Queen! This is our joyful shout.

Königin lebe! dies wünschet der Sachse,

Long live the Queen! This is the wish of Saxony,

Königin lebe und blühe und wachse!

Long live the Queen and may she thrive and prosper!

2. Tenor recitative
Heut ist der Tag
Wo jeder sich erfreuen mag.
Dies ist der frohe Glanz
Der Königin Geburtsfests-Stunden,

Today is the day
when everyone may rejoice.
This is the joyful splendour
of the time of the Queen's birthday,

Die Polen, Sachsen und uns ganz

which means for Poles, Saxons and all of us

In größter Lust und Glück erfunden.

the greatest pleasure and delight.

Mein Ölbaum
Kriegt so Saft als fetten Raum.

My olive tree
has both sap and luxuriant growth.

Er zeigt noch keine falben Blätter;
Mich schreckt kein Sturm, Blitz,

As yet it shows no yellow leaves;
I am scared by no storm, lightning,

trübe Wolken, düstres Wetter.

dismal clouds, gloomy weather.

3. Treble aria
Blast die wohlgegriffnen Flöten,
Dass Feind, Lilien, Mond erröten,

Blow the firmly-held flutes,
so that the enemy, lilies and the moon may blush,

Schallt mit jauchzendem Gesang!
Tönt mit eurem Waffenklang!

ring out with exultant song!
Let the clash of your weapons sound!

Dieses Fest erfordert Freuden,	This festival demands joys
Die so Geist als Sinnen weiden.	that feed both spirit and mind.

4. Treble recitative

Mein knallendes Metall	My exploding metal
Der in der Luft erbebenden Kartaunen,	as the heavy canon makes the air shudder,
Der frohe Schall;	the joyful noise;
Das angenehme Schauen;	the pleasing sight;
Die Lust, die Sachsen itzt empfindt,	the delight that Saxons now feel,
Rührt vieler Menschen Sinnen.	move the minds of many men.
Mein schimmerndes Gewehr	My glimmering weapons
Nebst meiner Söhne gleichen Schritten	with my sons' measured march
Und ihre heldenmäßge Sitten	and their heroic ways
Vermehren immer mehr und mehr	increase ever more and more
Des heutgen Tages süße Freude.	the sweet joy of today.

5. Alto aria

Fromme Musen! meine Glieder!	Devoted Muses! My companions!
Singt nicht längst bekannte Lieder!	Do not sing songs that have been long known!
Dieser Tag sei eure Lust!	Let this day be your delight!
Füllt mit Freuden eure Brust!	Fill your hearts with joy!
Werft so Kiel als Schriften nieder	Throw down both quill and writings
Und erfreut euch dreimal wieder!	and rejoice with triple joy!

6. Alto aria

Unsre Königin im Lande,	Our country's Queen,
Die der Himmel zu uns sandte,	whom heaven sent to us,

HARMONY AND DISCORD

Ist der Musen Trost und Schutz.
is the Muses' comfort and protection.

Meine Pierinnen wissen,
Die in Ehrfurcht ihren Saum noch küssen,
Vor ihr stetes Wohlergehn
Dank und Pflicht und Ton stets zu erhöhn.
This is known by my Pierides*
who in reverence kiss her hem,
for her continual prosperity
constantly to increase their gratitude and duty and song.

Ja, sie wünschen, dass ihr Leben
Möge lange Lust uns geben.
Indeed they wish that her life
may long give us delight.

7. Bass aria
Kron und Preis gekrönter Damen,
Crown and praise of crowned ladies,

Königin! mit deinem Namen
Füll ich diesen Kreis der Welt.
Was der Tugend stets gefällt
Und was nur Heldinnen haben,
Sein dir angeborne Gaben.
Queen! with your name
I shall fill the whole world.
What is always pleasing to virtue
and what only heroines have
are your gifts from birth.

8. Bass recitative
So dringe in das weite Erdenrund
Then throughout the wide circle of the earth

Mein von der Königin erfüllter Mund!
may my voice, full of the Queen, penetrate.

Ihr Ruhm soll bis zum Axen
Her fame should grow right up to the axis

Des schön gestirnten Himmels wachsen,
of heaven with its beautiful stars;

Die Königin der Sachsen und der Polen
may the Queen of the Saxons and Poles

---

* The nine Muses.

Sei stets des Himmels Schutz empfohlen.	be entrusted to heaven's constant protection.
So stärkt durch sie der Pol	Then through her heaven's pole strengthens
So vieler Untertanen längst erwünschtes Wohl.	the prosperity desired for a long time by so many of her subjects.
So soll die Königin noch lange bei uns hier verweilen	Thus may the queen for a long time tarry here among us
Und spät, ach! spät zum Sternen eilen.	and late, ah! late hasten to the stars.

9. Chorus

Blühet, ihr Linden in Sachsen, wie Zedern!	Blossom, you linden trees in Saxony, like cedars!
Schallet mit Waffen und Wagen und Rädern!	Resound with weapons, wagons and wheels!
Singet, ihr Musen, mit völligem Klang!	Sing, you Muses, with full sound!
Fröhliche Stunden, ihr freudigen Zeiten!	Joyful hours, you happy times!
Gönnt uns noch öfters die güldenen Freuden:	Grant us more golden joys still more often:
Königin, lebe, ja lebe noch lang!	Queen, may you live, yes may you live long!

The first verse, as usual accompanied by full orchestra and choir, is a musical masterpiece. It begins, as the text requires, with the *Pauken*, the timpani, followed by three trumpets, two flutes, two oboes and the strings. The next seven movements are either recitatives or arias sung purportedly by four Greek and Roman gods: Eirene, daughter of Zeus and the goddess of peace (tenor), Bellona, Roman goddess of war (soprano), Pallas, the goddess Athena (alto), and Fama, the voice of the people (bass). It ends with a short but almost as fine chorus in which Eirene, Bellona and Pallas are joined by the choir, and the trumpets and timpani.

Over the following months Sebastian composed several more secular cantatas, some of which do not appear to have survived. For example, for the coronation of Friedrich August II as King Augustus III of Poland, celebrated in Leipzig on 19 February 1734, Sebastian produced a revised version of the fine work he had composed back in 1725 for the university philosopher A. F. Müller.* The text (entitled *Blast Lärmen, ihr Feinde! Verstärket die Macht*, BWV 205a) does still exist, although its writer is unknown. Maybe it was Picander, or it might have been Sebastian himself. But a cantata that does survive, also involving the Elector whose accession to the throne was celebrated again in October, is *Preise dein Glücke, gesegnetes Sachsen* ('Praise your good fortune, blessed Saxony', BWV 215), comprising nine movements and lasting more than half an hour. The opening chorus is much the most striking movement, with its eulogistic words about Saxon welfare and security.† Since the Elector and his wife attended its performance in Leipzig on 5 October, there was further hope that they might respond to his application to be appointed court kapellmeister. And another advantage was that ten days later the council paid him a generous fee of 50 thalers [£2,400] 'for the provision of the music recently offered to His Royal Majesty'.[128] There were certainly major financial advantages to be gained from accepting town council commissions of this sort.

What now became increasingly clear was that he had a huge range of compositions that could be adapted for any purpose, and the adaptations‡ were often almost as complex and challenging as producing new works. One major idea he began to explore was of an Oratorio consisting of several cantatas to be

---

* See page 172.

† Several years later, this piece was adapted to be included in the Mass in B Minor (BWV 232), with the words 'Osanna in excelsis'.

‡ Described by scholarly Bach experts as 'parodies'. This seems a curious word to use, since its standard meanings include 'burlesque or satirical imitation', 'travesty' and 'an imitation so poor as to seem a deliberate mockery of the original'. In many Bach compositions, his adaptations of previous works are even finer than their originals.

performed over the Christmas season. Over the next few months he produced an extremely remarkable six-part *Weinachts-Oratorium* (Christmas Oratorio, BWV 248), to be performed over Christmas and New Year, much of it consisting of new versions of previous works – particularly from the recent secular cantatas composed in the last year or two, such as the opening chorus and all the arias in 'Hercules at the Crossroads' (BWV 213), most of the movements from *Tönet, ihr Pauken!* (BWV 214), and one of the arias in *Preise dein Glücke* (BWV 215). The plan was to replace the standard performance of cantatas over the Christmas period. The first three sections were performed in the St Nicholas and St Thomas churches on 25, 26 and 27 December, Part 4 on 1 January for the Feast of the Circumcision, Part 5 for the first Sunday of 1735 (2 January), and the final sixth part on 6 January for the Feast of the Epiphany.

The work is almost as ambitious a composition as the great Passions that Sebastian had written back in the 1720s, and the six parts together take more than two and a half hours to perform. In some respects he conceived the Oratorio as a similar construction, involving three textual sources: the Bible text, chorales, and specially-written verses commenting on the story. But one concern which strongly affected its creation was the fact that the biblical accounts of Jesus' birth are much briefer than those of his death, and are largely confined to Luke: 2 and twelve verses in Matthew. So much more comment and thought was required to extend the work to the scale he had in mind. No doubt Picander played an important part in developing the texts, but it is pretty clear (particularly since Picander never published the text along with all his other libretti) that Sebastian himself also developed much of them.

The composition performed on Christmas Day opens in D major with the masterly first chorus (1) from the *Tönet, ihr Pauken!* cantata (BWV 214). The words, with their musical reference, have a Bach-like element which enables the piece to be reproduced with only very few, tiny alterations to the notes:

Jauchzet, frohlocket, auf, preiset die Tage,	Celebrate, rejoice, rise up and praise the days,

Rühmet, was heute der Höchste getan!	laud what the All Highest has done today!
Lasset das Zagen, verbannet die Klage,	Abandon despair, banish lamentation,
Stimmet voll Jauchzen und Fröhlichkeit an!	strike up a song full of joy and cheerfulness!
Dienet dem Höchsten mit herrlichen Chören,	Serve the All Highest with glorious choirs!
Laßt uns den Namen des Herrschers verehren!	Let us worship the name of the Lord!

The story then begins with a long tenor recitative (2), in which the evangelist sings words from the first six verses of Luke: 2, immediately followed by an invented insertion in which the alto soloist sings a second recitative (3), and an aria (4) taken from the 'Hercules at the Crossroads' cantata, BWV 213/9. There then follows a chorale (5) based on Sebastian's favourite hymn tune, written by Hans Leo Haßler in 1601, which he used five times in the *St Matthew Passion*,* and would produce again, with dramatic orchestral accompaniment, as the final movement of this Oratorio. The evangelist's recitative announcing that Mary wrapped Jesus in swaddling clothes and laid him in a manger (6) is followed by an unusual combination of a chorale sung by trebles only, interspersed with recitative comments by the bass soloist, underlining the text of the hymn (7). The bass follows with another aria (8), this one adapted from *Tonet, ihr Pauken!* (BWV 214/11), and then the Christmas Day performance ends with a splendid orchestral accompanied chorale, *Ach mein herzliebes Jesulein* ('Ah, little Jesus, my heart's love').

This is the general pattern of the subsequent five movements, although there are still several surprises to come. Part 2, for instance, opens with a uniquely beautiful sinfonia (10), strongly conveying the atmosphere of the shepherds abiding in the fields, and the angel of the Lord who stood by them

---

* See page 188. It also appears in at least three other cantatas, BWV 161, 135, and 159.

and made them sore afraid – the story of which is then sung in recitatives. The two arias in this part (15 and 19), like those in the first, are adapted from the two secular cantatas BWV 214 and 213, the latter being that masterpiece that is Pleasure's aria. In this version, to combine with the other movements, the key is lowered to G major and the aria is sung by the alto soloist; but the harmonisation is unaltered and even the text is surprisingly close:

BWV 213

Schlafe, mein Liebster und pflege der Ruh, folge der Lockung entbranter Gedanken! Schmecke die Lust der lüsternen Brust, und erkenne keine Schranken. (Sleep, my beloved and take your rest, follow the lure of inflamed thoughts! Taste the desire of a lustful breast, and allow no limitations.)

BWV 248

Schlafe, mein Liebster, geneißer der Ruh, wache nach diesem vor aller Gedeihen! Labe die Brust, empfinde die Lust, wo wir unser Herz erfreuen! (Sleep, my beloved, enjoy your rest, watch over the felicity of all! Refresh the breast, feel the desire where we gladden our hearts.)

Part 3 opens with a fine but brief chorus (24) adapted from the final movement of BWV 214, and contains a treble and bass duet (29) derived from BWV 213, and another beautiful alto aria (31), accompanied by solo violin, which Sebastian probably composed that year rather than adapted.

Part 4 was performed on New Year's Day, to celebrate the Feast of the Circumcision, and opens with the exceptional chorus (36) that is the starting-point of 'Hercules at the Crossroads' (BWV 213/1). Here, the words are altered slightly more (no doubt by Picander), but remain closely connected:

BWV 213

Laßt uns sorgen, laßt uns wachen über unsern Göttersohn. Unser Thron wird auf Erden herrlich und verkläret werden, unser Thron wird aus ihm ein Wunder machen. (Let us take care, let us watch over our divine son. Our throne will be glorious and transfigured on earth, our throne will make a marvel of him.)

BWV 248

Fallt mit Danken, fallt mit Loben vor des Höchsten Gnadenthron! Gottes Sohn will der Erden Heiland und Erlöser werden. Gottes Sohn dämpft der Feinde Wut und Toben. (Fall down with thanks, fall down with praise before the Most High's throne of grace! The Son of God will be the saviour and redeemer of the world. The Son of God suppresses the rage and fury of the enemy.)

Among its striking elements are the wide range of orchestral accompaniment, and the long-held notes: the basses sing F from bar 26 to bar 38, and this is repeated when the tenors sing C in bars 64 to 69, the trebles sing C in bars 174 to 180, and finally the altos sing F in bars 210 to 216. And this chorus is followed, after the evangelist's announcement of Jesus' circumcision, with another very unusual movement (38): it begins with the bass soloist singing a recitative in praise of Jesus, then suddenly being joined by the treble for a brief duet, before he ends with what we might assume is the composer's personal statement – performed in complex harmony – about his own emotions, particularly with regard to distress, discomfort and death:

Auch in dem Sterben sollst du mir das Allerliebste sein; in Not, Gefahr und Ungemach seh ich dir sehnlichst nach. Was jagte mir zuletzt der Tod für Grauen ein? Mein Jesus! Wenn ich sterbe, so weiß ich, das ich nicht vertrieben. Dein Name steht in mir geschrieben, der hat des Todes Furcht vertrieben. (Even in death, Thou shalt be dearest of all to me; in distress, danger and discomfort, I longingly look to Thee. What was that horrifying death that struck into me recently? My Jesus, when I die I know that I will not perish. Thy name, which has conquered the fear of death, is inscribed within me.)

Given the catastrophes Sebastian had endured over the last few years, and the clear evidence that he was determined to survive them and draw on his religious belief as a means of doing so, it is hardly surprising that he felt entitled to insert a personal statement into this great and complex work.

The next treble aria (39) comes from 'Hercules at the Crossroads' (BWV 213/5), and is followed by another brief treble and bass duet (40). Then there is another (tenor) aria derived from BWV 213, and the piece ends with a rather splendidly intricate chorale accompanied by the brass, horns and the rest of the orchestra.

Part 5 was performed the following day, the first Sunday of the new year (1735), and opens with a chorus (43) Sebastian also seems to have composed rather than adapted. The biblical text is now from Matthew: 2, involving the story of the wise men from the east, and King Herod's fears that the new-born king will usurp his rule. The first aria (47), derived from the cantata *Preise dein Glücke* (BWV 215/7), contains another text almost certainly written by Sebastian himself. The original version was for treble soloist, but it has now been adapted for bass in F-sharp minor, and the words are a clear extension of the recitative in Part 4:

> *Erleucht auch meine finstre Sinnen, erleuchte mein Herze durch der Strahlen klaren Schein! Dein Wort soll mir die hellste Kerze in allen meinen Werken sein; dies lässet die Seele nichts Böses beginnen.* (Enlighten, too, my dark thoughts, illuminate my heart through the rays of Thy clear brilliance! Thy word shall be the brightest candle for me in all my doings; it shall prevent my soul embarking upon evil.)

The simple orchestration and the unusual key make it exceptionally expressive, and listeners aware of Sebastian's troubled life would find it hard to deny its clandestine message.

The final part, performed on 6 January for the Feast of the Epiphany, opens in D major with a more cheerful chorus. One subsequent dramatic moment is the tenor recitative's introduction to Herod (bass), who instructs the wise men to find Jesus, so that 'I may come and worship him also' (Matthew 2: 8); it is immediately followed by a treble recitative calling him *du Falscher* ('you forger'). The most moving part is the final chorale, based on the Hans Leo Haßler hymn tune, with astoundingly elaborate orchestration.*

1734 was thus another busy year, in which he determinedly recovered his self-confidence and self-belief, and composed a range of works of which he could feel thoroughly proud. Indeed there is evidence that there were more compositions than mentioned so far, including an unusually moving nine-movement church cantata entitled *In allen mein Taten* (BWV 97) which appears to have been performed on 25 July. It is based entirely on a nine-verse hymn text attributed to Paul Fleming in 1642, and the hymn tune, which he used twice in the *St Matthew Passion* (chorales 16 and 44), is engrained in the beautiful opening chorus, and again in the ending chorale. There are some other enjoyable movements, but the finest is an alto aria, making clear that Sebastian was inspired by the verse that reads 'Though I be late retiring, arise early in the morning, lie still or go forth, in weakness and in bondage, with every blow about me, yet His word comforts me.'†

---

* The Victorian composer and musician Sir George Macfarren (1813–87) correctly described it as 'a song of triumph, to which end it is embroidered with interludes and counterpoint of exulting brightness, including the flourish of trumpets and drums, and passages that best bring out the tone of all the other instruments; and it peals from amid this din of joy, as would thunder peal through the turmoil of the elements, were thunder the voice of gladness instead of destruction'.

† *Leg ich mich späte nieder,*
　Erwache frühe wieder,
　Lieg oder ziehe fort,
　In Schwachheit und in Banden,
　Und was mir stößt zuhanden,

Another work probably composed this year is the so-called Coffee Cantata (BWV 211), a semi-operatic piece for performance in Zimmermann's coffee-house in Katharinenstraße, based on a poem by Picander, all about a daughter's addiction to coffee and her father's anger and anxiety about it. And in October he composed another *dramma per musica* (secular cantata BWV 206) for Frederick August II's birthday, although it was not actually performed then, because when the royal couple announced their visit to Leipzig he had replaced it with *Preise dein Glücke, gesegnetes Sachsen* (BWV 215). But it was to be hoped that the council would pay him the 50 thaler [£2,400] fee for a later performance.*

In September, Emanuel had left Leipzig University and moved to Frankfurt an der Oder, east of Berlin on the Polish border, where he continued to study law and also taught keyboard-playing. But another blow occurred in the autumn, when Johann Matthias Gesner announced his resignation as headmaster of St Thomas's, in order to travel west to Göttingen University, where he had been appointed professor of philology. This was a sad loss, because Matthias had been a genuine friend over the past four years, and indeed his wife, Elisabeth Charitas (1695–1761), had taken on the role of godmother to Johann August Abraham, the baby who had died in November the previous year. Interestingly, the baby's godfathers included the school's young assistant headmaster, Johann August Ernesti (1707–81), who had studied theology at the university until 1730. On 21 November Ernesti, aged 29, was formally appointed to the senior post and became Sebastian's boss.

So tröstet mich sein Wort.

* It was indeed performed two years later, in Zimmermann's coffee-house on 7 October 1736, to celebrate Elector Friedrich August II's birthday.

Chapter 12

LOOKING BACK

(1734–37)

As Sebastian's 50th birthday approached, he must have been increasingly convinced that even if his employers failed to comprehend or appreciate his creativity he should never be ashamed of his achievements or the remarkable talents that he had inherited from his ancestors. For some time he had been compiling a family tree dating back nearly 120 years, beginning with his great-great-grandfather, Vitus Bach, who had died in 1619. Some interesting facts about the family's history made it clear to him that his Bach ancestors presented a unique musical talent which had developed over several generations.

Vitus* had apparently been born in Hungary, where he was a baker, and around 1560 he had been forced to leave the country because of his Lutheran religion, moving to Germany and settling in the little village of Wechmar, a few miles south of Gotha. There he had established a successful bakery business, and had brought up at least two sons, the elder of whom was named Johannes Bach (known as Hans). Vitus had apparently so much enjoyed music that when he went to work at the mill he took his cither with him and played it while grinding the corn. This clearly inspired his sons. Hans began his working career in the baking

---

* Later described as 'simple old Veit' by Carl Philipp Emanuel Bach, when he added further details to the genealogy.

trade, but was taken on as an apprentice with the Gotha wind players – though in 1619 he returned to Wechmar and took over his father's business, married an innkeeper's daughter called Anna Schmied, with whom he had three sons. The younger of Vitus's sons, later identified as Caspar, in the meantime became a carpet maker, and he too had three sons who learned music.

Sebastian was able to identify some 25 male Bachs descended from Vitus before his own birth in 1685, of whom at least 18 became professional musicians. Nine of them were instrumentalists, playing viola da gambas, violins and oboes; seven were organists; and at least three became successful composers. And now there were even more, about 30 current Bachs, many of whom were musicians living and working in Thuringia or Saxony. Inspired by this extraordinary family tradition, Sebastian had begun to compile a genealogy with all the details he could find,[129] many of them obtained from the young relatives who had attended St Thomas's or the university over the last twelve years, including Johann Elias (b. 1705), the grandson of his uncle Georg Christoph Bach (1642–97), and his nephew Johann Heinrich (1707–83), the fourth son of his late brother Christoph. Remarkably, Sebastian could identify as many as 14 current professional Bach musicians,* plus his own eldest sons Friedemann and Emanuel, now at university in Frankfurt an der Oder. And in a few months' time, 20-year-

---

* Johann Bernhard Bach (1676–1749), organist in Eisenach; Johann Christoph Bach, (1685–1740), town music director in Erfurt; Johann Ernst Bach (1683–1740), first cousin, organist in Arnstadt; Johann Nikolaus Bach (1669–1753), organist in Jena; Johann Günther Bach (1703–56), tenor and schoolteacher in Erfurt; Johann Friedrich Bach (1706–43), schoolteacher in Andisleben, north of Erfurt; Johann Egidius Bach (1709–46), schoolteacher in Großenmunra; Johann Lorenz Bach (1695–1773), former student, organist in Lahm; Johann Elias Bach (1705–55), cantor at Schweinfurt; Tobias Friedrich Bach (1695–1768), nephew, cantor at Udestädt, near Erfurt; Johann Bernhard Bach (1700–43), nephew and former student, organist in Ohrdruf; Johann Christoph Bach (1702–56), nephew, choirmaster and schoolteacher in Ohrdruf; Johann Heinrich Bach (1707–83), nephew and former student, cantor at Öhringen, near Heilbronn; and Johann Andreas Bach (1713–79), nephew, oboist in Prince of Gotha's army.

old Bernhard too would join the community, as organist in Mühlhausen. The total number of 53 Bachs he listed in his genealogy had almost all remained in Thuringia or moved to neighbouring Saxony and Franconia. Nine of them had lived and worked in Erfurt, seven in Arnstadt, and five in Eisenach where Sebastian was born. Only three had moved abroad, including his brother Jacob who had died in Stockholm in 1722, and his cousin Johann Michael, also born in 1685, about whom all he could write was that he 'learned the art of organ-building, but travelled to northern countries and never returned, so there is no information available about him'. He must have found it a considerable comfort to recognise that it was a long family tradition to remain in the centre of Germany and to be devoted to the creation and performance of music, even if Telemann and Handel had done otherwise. It was also interesting that though Bachs had worked in 24 local towns in the last 150 years, only one (he himself) had been in Cöthen and Leipzig, and only one (Friedemann) in Dresden. Perhaps this was an indication that their standards were rising, and that his sons were already heading towards further achievements.

In January 1735 he had to compose another cantata* to cover the fourth Sunday after Epiphany, where the Gospel reading was (and still is) the story of Jesus preaching to his disciples that through belief in God they could survive their fears of natural storms and devils (Matthew 8: 23–34). Three of the five movements are based on a Martin Luther hymn paraphrasing the text of Psalm 124, which covers the same subject. But much the most striking of the five movements is the second, a treble aria in B-flat major, accompanied by a horn and strings, based on words Sebastian might well have written himself:

> *Unsre Stärke heißt zu schwach, unserm Feind zu widerstehen. Stünd uns nicht der Höchste bei, würd uns ihre Tyrannei bald bis an das Leben gehen.* (Our strength is said to be too weak to defy our enemy. If God did not stand by us, their tyranny would surely threaten our very existence.)

---

* *Wär Gott nicht mit uns dieser Zeit* (BWV 14).

The power and complexity of this piece convey not just the incomparable advantages of religious belief, but how strong bravura music can reveal the terrible fear of wrathful enemies.

So although he had decided that his church-service requirements could now mostly be fulfilled by the large range of cantatas he had composed in the past, composition remained his obsession. In the spring he produced his second *Clavier-Übung*,* containing two remarkable harpsichord works, the Italian Concerto (BWV 971) and the Overture in the French Style (BWV 831), and had it published by Christoph Weigel Junior in Nuremberg. His aim was to follow the example of his predecessor Johann Kuhnau, whose two *Clavier-Übung* collections, in major and minor keys, had been published in 1689 and 1692.

In May Sebastian undertook a third, shorter but more beautiful, oratorio, this time for Ascension Day on the 19th (BWV 11). As was the case with his much longer six-part Christmas Oratorio,† several of the eleven movements were adapted from previous works, including the radiant opening chorus in D major accompanied by trumpets and drums. By far the most moving is an alto aria (movement 4) which was also probably derived from a previous cantata, and which he would again redesign in simpler form for the Mass in B Minor.‡ There is as usual no evidence as to who wrote the text, but again because the harmony and accompaniment are so poignant and pitiful we may be tempted to believe he himself wrote the words about the loss of a loved one:

Ach, bleibe doch, mein liebstes Leben,	Ah, stay yet, my dearest life,
Ach, fliehe nicht so bald von mir!	Ah, do not forsake me so soon!
Dein Abschied und dein frühes Scheiden	Your farewell and your early departure

---

* See page 183.

† See pages 233–9. The first oratorio, produced for Easter 1725 (BWV 249), was also mainly based on a previous composition.

‡ The penultimate alto solo movement, Agnus Dei.

> *Bringt mir das allergrößte Leiden.* cause me the greatest suffering.
> *Ach ja, so bleibe doch noch hier;* Ah yes, stay yet awhile,
> *Sonst werd ich ganz von* or I shall be overwhelmed
> *Schmerz umgeben.* with grief.

And it is followed later, in movement 8, by a brief but very unusual alto recitative which more or less repeats the same message:

> *Ach ja! So komme bald zurück: tilg einst mein trauriges Gebärden, sonst word mir jeder Augenblick verhaßt und Jahren ähnlich werden.* (Ah yes, then come back soon: remove once and for all my sorrowful bearing, otherwise every moment will be abhorrent to me and seem like years.)

Even if no friends or neighbours could recognise these passionate personal statements about his tragedies and his concepts of surviving them, it must have been at least some private comfort to express them musically in such an intense and appropriate form.

Around this time Sebastian learned that the Marienkirche organist in Mühlhausen, Johann Gottfried Hetzehenn, who had been a colleague of his back in 1707–08, had recently died, and that no appointment had yet been made to replace him. This seemed like a real opportunity for his keyboard-skilled son Bernhard to secure an important post in one of the major towns in Thuringia; and so on 2 May Sebastian wrote a formal letter to the town council reminding them that he had once been an organist in the town, and requesting that Bernhard should be auditioned. His request was granted, and in June he and Bernhard took the long 200-mile journey there. During the following week Sebastian undertook a full test of the church's organ, for which he made no charge, and then Bernhard performed his audition on it. On 16 June the council formally agreed to his appointment. This gave Sebastian increasing confidence that his sons would continue in the long Bach family tradition of dominating the music world. A secular cantata performed on 3 August for the celebration of Friedrich August II's name-day (BWV 207a), based with minor changes on one he had composed nine years earlier for the appointment of a professor at the university (BWV 207), conveys this boost in confidence. His three sons by Maria Barbara were doing really well, Friedemann as an organist in Dresden, Emanuel studying and teaching at Frankfurt an der Oder, and now Bernhard in Mühlhausen. And on 5 September Magdalena gave birth to her tenth child, baptised on the 7th as Johann Christian, with Herr Johann August Ernesti, the school's new headmaster, as his godfather.* The family now living in St Thomas's School had decreased to six, comprising Sebastian aged 50, Magdalena about to celebrate her 34th birthday, Heinrich aged eleven, Lieschen aged nine, Friederich aged three, and the new baby boy known as Christel.

New ranges of compositions proceeded dramatically over the next few months, including smaller works for individual instruments played by his students – for example, the flute sonatas BWV 1030, 1032 and 1033, of which the first remains the most popular nearly three centuries later, particularly with its long opening Andante in B minor. But by far the most time-consuming and complex venture was Sebastian's agreement to co-operate with Georg Christian Schemelli to compile a massive collection of hymn tunes to be published under the title *Musikalisches Gesangbuch* ('Musical Songbook'). It contains a total of 954, printed on nearly 700 pages (thus even larger than the standard edition of *Hymns Ancient and Modern*, first published in 1861), covering a large range of standard Lutheran hymns from the 16th and 17th centuries, together with a number of sacred songs that had developed more recently. Schemelli was music manager in the nearby ancient town of Zeitz, and had been commissioned to produce the collection by his town council. A preface written by the local vicar, Friedrich Schultze (1690–1766), mentions that a number of the hymn tunes

---

* Ernesti had also been godfather to Johann August Abraham, who had died the day after his birth (see page 227).

'were in part composed anew' by Bach and 'in part improved by him in the thoroughbass', so it is quite clear that Sebastian played an important part in compiling and arranging much of the contents – even though only two of the tunes, entitled *Vergiß mein nicht* ('Forget me not', BWV 504 and 505), are actually assigned to him in the printed book which was published in 1736 by the Leipzig publisher Bernhard Christoph Breitkopf.*

Schultze's preface also suggested that revised and cheaper editions of the book were planned to appear later; but the fact that they were never published indicates that the book's sales failed to reach the level the Zeitz council hoped for. So Sebastian probably felt convinced that music publishing was not a profitable activity. He would continue with his *Clavier-Übung* plans, the next of which would involve a large number of organ chorales; but he did not expect to make money out of it.

This time, his scheme was to include a much wider and larger range of pieces, many of which he had no doubt improvised and composed on organs over the last decades. The main piece is a fine Prelude and Fugue in E-flat major (BWV 552); and then there are dozens of chorale preludes and duets. The two previous *Clavier-Übung* collections were aimed at ordinary keyboard-playing, on the harpsichord or clavichord; but this new one was a representation of his greatest skill, and the pieces comprised a wide variety of styles, to give organists a sense of the huge range of performing abilities – with both hands and feet (*manualiter* and *pedaliter*) – for which organ-playing could provide. It was designed not just for his numerous local students, but for the thousands of practising organists around the country.†

---

* Over recent decades there has been much scholarly dispute about which of the 954 hymns Bach composed and which he re-harmonised, but it is generally accepted that he did a great deal of both. Sadly, one tradition that he composed the popular British Christmas carol 'O little one sweet' has been disproved; it is now attributed to the Prussian composer Valentin Thilo (1607–62).

† The book was finally published privately by Bach in 1739 in time for the Leipzig Easter fair. No evidence survives regarding the number of copies printed or sold.

A third performance of the *St Matthew Passion* (BWV 244) took place in St Thomas's Church on Good Friday, 30 March, for which Sebastian made one significant change, removing the simple chorale that ended the first part and replacing it with a splendid chorus taken from the *St John Passion*,* with the words *O Mensch, bewein dein Sünde groß* ('O man, lament thy great sin'). He now very clearly saw the whole work as the finest of all his thousands of compositions, and planned to create a newly-handwritten script of it to ensure that this 'great Passion' (as Magdalena is recorded as describing it)[130] would last long into the future.

But his self-confidence and optimism had always been undermined by trivial issues with his employers and neighbours, and in the summer a typical new setback emerged regarding his employment status. Perhaps the initial irritation was the fact that the new headmaster who had replaced Gesner (with whom Sebastian had got on quite well) was the ridiculously youthful Johann August Ernesti, the former deputy head, who was now aged 29, only 18 months older than Sebastian's daughter Catharina.

The problem arose in June 1736, when Sebastian's senior prefect, Gottfried Theodor Krause, was found guilty of over-chastising and possibly assaulting a junior pupil, and sentenced to be beaten by the headmaster. The prospect frightened G. T. Krause so much that he ran away from Leipzig and never reappeared, so Sebastian had no choice but to replace him promptly with prefect number two, Johann Gottlieb Krause (no relation), to protect the weekly cantata performances in St Thomas's and St Nicholas's churches. J. G. Krause handled the role for several weeks, managing choir rehearsals and conducting when Mr Bach was playing; but then Sebastian changed his mind and decided that another student, named Samuel Küttler, should replace Krause as first prefect. On 10 July he told Küttler to visit the headmaster, tell him that this was Mr Bach's requirement, and request his approval.

Headmaster Ernesti's response was perfectly reasonable: he would approve Küttler's appointment provided he had been properly tested to

---

* See page 163.

ensure his musical ability; he added only the comment that he felt the two prefects should have been properly tested back in June, so that they would not now be required to change positions. Küttler reported this to Sebastian.

But then things got worse. Later that day J. G. Krause knocked on the headmaster's door and asked for his help. Krause felt tremendously hurt that he was being sacked by Mr Bach, and told Mr Ernesti he felt he was being 'dismissed for no fault of his own'. It suddenly became clear to the headmaster that the school's music master was not acting properly by randomly sacking an earnest young student from such a crucial position, and that his duty as headmaster was to take control of the matter. So he instructed Krause to return to Mr Bach and inform him politely 'that I should be very pleased if he could remain in his post'. Ernesti later heard that Krause tried unsuccessfully several times to talk to his music teacher, then eventually begged Mr Bach to explain why he was being dismissed – to which he received the reply that it was because of the headmaster. Sebastian had very unwisely told him that the reason he was being dismissed was that when the headmaster had suspended Gottfried Theodor Krause back in June and replaced him with Johann Gottlieb Krause, this was a breach of the fundamental rule that prefects were appointed by the music teacher.

When Krause reported these facts to Ernesti, he had little choice but to accept that his senior position in the school was being challenged by the cantor. So inevitably his next step was to report the details to the chairman of the school's board, Dr Christian Ludwig Stieglitz, which he did on 12 July. Stieglitz, who had been supportive of Sebastian's concerns about the school's music standards in 1729,* none the less agreed with Ernesti that this was not an appropriate reason to de-promote Krause, that Mr Bach should not have allowed this matter to become known among the school pupils, and that therefore J. G. Krause should remain in the role of first prefect. On the same day, Ernesti spoke directly to Sebastian, who admitted that he had been influenced by his senior colleague's sacking of Gottfried

---

* See page 202.

Theodor Krause and replacing him with Johann Gottlieb, to which Ernesti pointed out that it was not sacking but suspension; and that if Sebastian would not agree to retaining J. G. Krause he should consult the board chairman before taking any further steps. Sebastian nodded and left.

But the following Sunday, 15 July, at St Nicholas's Church, Ernesti noticed that Krause was not in the choir – so it seemed that Sebastian had sacked him anyway. He thought for a moment that he should go straight up to the choir gallery and order Krause to be reinstated, but (as he wrote later in his report to the council) 'I wished to spare his dignity before the student group, with whom currently his authority is inadequate'. So instead he wrote a formal letter to Sebastian, 'in which I pointed out to him how greatly he had transgressed by taking upon himself such a change ... in order to revenge himself for what he considered an infringement of his rights, so that now even the innocent must suffer; and although I could at once reinstate the dismissed prefect, I would prefer, in order to prevent the impairment of his authority, to see him reinstate him himself, for in that way we should both be satisfied'.

Sebastian was now in serious trouble again, and for a while he pondered whether to submit totally to the headmaster or to struggle on and protect his self-belief. His first step, on 17 July, was to talk to the deputy head, and ask him to visit Ernesti and tell him that he would reinstate Krause at the next choir lesson. But then he changed his mind and continued with Küttler, and when Ernesti sent him a reminder he replied saying apologetically that he was away elsewhere for two weeks, and would handle the matter as soon as he returned.

For several weeks the matter remained unresolved. But on Saturday 11 August Ernesti felt he had no choice but to take it up again, not only because Bach had lied to him several times, but in order to protect the reputation of the earnest student Krause. Ernesti vividly remembered that two years earlier, when Gesner was still headmaster, Krause had been in great trouble having acquired excessive debts, and after the staff had ordered him to make major changes to reduce them, he had done so and dramatically improved his school status. So that day Ernesti wrote Bach another letter, pointing out that it appeared he had no intention of fulfilling his promise to reinstate Krause, and giving him notice that if he did not immediately do so the headmaster, 'by authority of the order I previously received from the Director [Dr Stieglitz]', would do so himself on Sunday morning.

Sebastian had by now decided to fight his case, and for his status as manager of virtually all the town's music; and so on 12 August he wrote a formal letter to the mayor, Johann Gottfried Winckler, in which he pointed out that the council's St Thomas's School regulations specifically stated that the school's cantor had the right to appoint prefects, on the grounds that they should have musical abilities to enable them to manage the choirs, and that:

> the present headmaster, Herr Johann August Ernesti, has, as a new departure, sought to effect the replacement of the prefect of the first choir without my previous knowledge and consent, and accordingly has recently appointed Krause, previously prefect of the second choir, to be prefect of the first choir. He has further refused to withdraw the appointment despite all the protests that I, in perfect good will, have made to him.

He ended the letter with a simple request that the council resolve the dispute and instruct Mr Ernesti to restore Mr Bach's right to appoint the new head prefect.[131] He also forwarded a message to Ernesti informing him that he had sent the letter. For some reason, his assumption was that the headmaster would immediately withdraw Krause and allow him to make his own choice. But he was wrong. Ernesti immediately turned up at the school (when Sebastian was not present), publicly ordered the two prefects to return to their previous posts, and announced that if anyone other than Krause took on the first prefect's duties he would be disobeying the headmaster and would receive 'severe punishment'. He also instructed Krause to report this to Mr Bach.

As soon as Sebastian heard about this, he became determined to continue the fight with Ernesti, and to quash the supremacy that this young schoolmaster was attempting to exert. Back in St Nicholas's Church, he ordered Küttler to come with him to St Thomas's, and there he told Krause to go back to St Nicholas's. Also that morning he visited Dr Salomon Deyling,* the pastor and superintendent of St Thomas's Church consistory, in the hope that this highly sophisticated 59-year-old gentleman, who was also professor of theology at the university, would unequivocally agree that Ernesti's attempts to dominate the music community were ridiculous and should be suppressed. Alas, Deyling would make no immediate decision; but he was not hostile. There was also a brief encounter with Ernesti, but Sebastian avoided making any concessions.

After lunch, the two prefects again turned up at the wrong churches, presumably having been ordered to do so by the headmaster. So again in St Thomas's Sebastian told Krause to leave the choir loft, and replaced him with another student. Later that evening, at the school dinner table, he ejected Küttler for having obeyed Ernesti.

On Monday Sebastian wrote another formal letter to the town council:

> Although I informed you yesterday regarding the encroachments that the headmaster, Mr Ernesti, has with the greatest impropriety made, through the replacement of the prefect, upon the functions entrusted to me as musical director and cantor of St Thomas's School, and although I have thus already most humbly entreated your most gracious protection, yet I find myself obliged once more to let you know that, although I had informed Mr Ernesti that I had already delivered my complaint in this matter to you, and was awaiting your authoritative decision, he nevertheless, disregarding his duty to show respect to the town council, yesterday made bold again to inform all the students that no one was to dare, on pain of expulsion and beating, to take the place of Krause, the boy mentioned in

---

* See page 140.

my most humble report of yesterday, who is incapable of choral direction (but whom he wishes to enforce on me as prefect of the first choir), either in the chanting or in directing the usual motet. As a result, at yesterday afternoon's service at St Nicholas's Church, to my great shame and public humiliation, there was not a single pupil willing to take over the chanting, let alone the direction of the motet, for fear of the threatened penalty. The service would indeed have been seriously upset if a former St Thomas's School pupil, Johann Ludwig Krebs, had not at my request taken over the post in place of one of the current students. Since, as stated in my previous message, it is not according to the school's regulations the right of the headmaster to replace prefects, and since the headmaster has greatly transgressed his rules and caused deep injury to me in the discharge of my office, and sought to weaken and even destroy the authority I must have over the students with regard to the church and other music (which authority was entrusted to me when I was appointed by the town council); and if since such irresponsible conduct continues there is a threat that the services may be disturbed and the church music fall into the most serious decay, and the school as well, my earnest entreaty is that the council should promptly instruct the headmaster to cease disturbing me in the discharge of my office, to stop ordering students to disobey me by threatening them with dire punishments, and thereby to ensure that the school and choirs should be improved and not deteriorated. In the hope of receiving your gracious protection in my office, I remain with most obedient respect, your wholly obedient

Leipzig, 13 August 1736   Johann Sebastian Bach[132]

Having delivered this letter to the town hall,* Sebastian no doubt felt rather more confident that his case was fair and his chances of being supported by the counsellors were high. There was no immediate

---

* This medieval building (the Altes Rathaus) still exists, on the east side of the market square, and is now a museum containing much interesting information about Leipzig's history.

response, so he prepared a third document, setting out in more detail the intricate reasons Ernesti's actions were so improper. He headed it 'The full and true account concerning the student Krause, whom the headmaster wishes to force upon me as first prefect'. He began his report by explaining that last year Krause had earned a damaging reputation in the school because of his huge debts of over 20 thalers [£960], and the staff's decision was then to give him a three-month period to change his way of living; he would be expelled if he failed to do so. Remarkably, the report went on, the headmaster evidently liked Krause, and later asked Sebastian to appoint him prefect; and when Sebastian replied that he was totally unsuited to such a post, Ernesti insisted that he should do it all the same in order to help Krause reduce his debts, that doing so would protect the school's reputation, and that Krause would graduate and leave the school fairly soon anyway. Sebastian then wrote:

> Accordingly, because I wished to favour the headmaster, I appointed Krause the post of prefect in the New Church, where the students only sing motets and chorales and have nothing to do with more complex musical performance, since the latter is managed by the organist. I bore in mind that he would remain in the school for only one more year, and there was no reason to suppose that he would be required to conduct the second choir, let alone the first.
>
> But later, the 1st prefect, named Maximilian Nagel, at the last New Year's church performance, complained that because of a weak constitution he would be unable to continue in his role, so I was obliged to make immediate changes, promoting the 2nd prefect to 1st, and inevitably the much discussed Krause to the 2nd. But since he made various mistakes, as the assistant headmaster reported to me, and when these mistakes were investigated the blame for them was placed by the other students solely and entirely on the prefect, who beat the time wrongly; and since I also recently carried out a test of his conducting

skills, and found that he seriously failed it, being unable accurately to beat the two principal kinds of time – i.e. even or four-quarter, and uneven or three-quarter – but made an even measure of three-quarters, and *vice versa* (as all the students can testify), I was convinced that he was incompetent, and therefore there was no possibility of appointing him 1st prefect, particularly since the works performed by the first choir, mostly composed by myself, are incomparably harder and more complex than those sung by the second choir, and require the appointment only of students capable of performing them. Although there is other evidence of Krause's incapacity, it is my belief that the reasons hereby fully explained are sufficient to prove that my complaint presented to you is justified, and requires a prompt and speedy remedy.[133]

Having now provided the council with three very thorough and carefully-written explanations of the reasons he regarded Ernesti's efforts to promote Krause as totally improper, Sebastian felt even more convinced that these outrageous attempts to undermine his status as the city's choral music director and school cantor would be thoroughly suppressed by the town council, and that they might even consider sacking and replacing the headmaster.

But in fact the councillors were finding the whole dispute extremely confusing, since they were clearly aware that Ernesti was a thoroughly honest and hard-working schoolteacher, who had fully earned his promotion to headmaster two years earlier. Their first step was to consult him, showing him Bach's letters, and asking for a full account of the reasons a staff member was making these dramatic public complaints. Two days later, on 17 August, Ernesti wrote an extremely long and detailed description of the events leading up to Bach's protests and his improper treatment of the school pupils, written in a highly persuasive and kindly style.[134] It included a number of convincing explanations, and a shocking range of accusations that Bach was not telling the truth.

To begin with, he pointed out that Bach's first letter wrongly stated that, under the school's rules, the cantor had the sole right to appoint prefects; in fact, they required consent from both the headmaster and the school director. Secondly, it was not the case that the headmaster had appointed Krause in June; Bach had done so, and Ernesti had agreed with the appointment because Krause had already acted competently as fourth, third and second prefect.

Ernesti's account went on to reveal that several times over the past five weeks Bach had given false information to his pupils and colleagues about the whole situation. For example, on 10 July Bach had told Krause that he was sacked from the first-prefect position because the headmaster had appointed him – which was not the case; the truth was that in June Ernesti had told Krause 'that he should *for the time being* fill the post of 1st prefect'. Then on 12 July Bach had admitted directly to the headmaster that he had demoted Krause 'because of the encroachment of his rights by the headmaster', to which Ernesti had pointed out that suspension was not dismissal, that the empty post had to be filled, and that he and the school director, Stieglitz, forbade him to dismiss Krause. But Bach had done so on the following Sunday, 15 July, which prompted Ernesti to send him a letter saying that he had 'greatly transgressed', and that although the headmaster could immediately reinstate Krause he would prefer, in order not to undermine Bach's authority, that he reinstate him himself.

And then on 17 July Bach had sent a message to Ernesti via the school's deputy head, saying all right, he would reappoint Krause. But he did not do so. Ernesti then sent him a reminder, to which he replied that he was away from Leipzig for two weeks (until about the end of the month), but would resolve the issue on his return. Nothing happened at the beginning of August, so on Saturday the 11th Ernesti sent him a third reminder, saying that if he did not immediately reinstate Krause the headmaster would do so himself on Sunday, as instructed by Stieglitz. There was no reply. Ernesti made clear that in these circumstances he had no choice but to announce to the school on Sunday (as Bach had reported in his second letter) that Krause and Küttler should return to their previous posts as first and second prefects, and that if anyone other than Krause took the first post he would be disobeying the headmaster and director, and would be seriously punished.

He went on to explain that, as a result of this announcement on Sunday morning, Bach 'ran at once to the superintendent' (Salomon Deyling), hoping to receive his support. Deyling's response (as he reported to Ernesti later in the day) was rational: that he would consult the headmaster and director, and reach a decision in due course. But Bach pretended otherwise, returned to St Nicholas's church to order Küttler to come with him to St Thomas's, and there fired Krause. When Ernesti spoke later to Deyling, he confirmed that he had given Bach no decision, and agreed that the prefects should remain in their positions until Stieglitz returned to Leipzig and reached a final conclusion. 'I acquainted the cantor with this decision, but received the answer that he would not budge on this matter, no matter what the cost.'

And then there was another revelation that Bach was not telling the truth. In his second letter, on 13 August,* he had written that on the previous day he had replaced Krause with the university student Johann Ludwig Krebs – but this was not true. In fact he had appointed a school pupil named Claus, and after the service Claus had apologised to the headmaster for having accepted the position. And that evening, Bach had dismissed Küttler from the school dinner table for having obeyed the headmaster.

Ernesti's very long letter concluded with two more points. The first was to reiterate that he had not appointed Krause without Bach's knowledge and consent, that he was not attempting to take over prefect appointments, and that he was merely following the school rules that as headmaster he should concur with the appointments. Bach was undermining these rules, first by asserting that the headmaster did not have the right to reinstate a prefect, even with Stieglitz's approval; secondly by attempting to remove a prefect 'simply to spite the headmaster'; and

---

* See pages 252-3.

thirdly by promising to reinstate him (thereby conceding that the boy was not incompetent) but failing to do so. So the council must dismiss Bach's complaint, reprimand him for his disobedience and insubordination, and order him to follow the school rules and attend to his duties more industriously. And Ernesti's final point was to suggest that the disastrous event that had led to Gottfried Theodor Krause's ascendance in June was Bach's fault too, since he had failed to accompany the first choir to a recent wedding service, thereby enabling Krause to commit the misdeed for which his punishment had been ordered.

The council studied this extensive report with considerable care, but it was not easy to reach a conclusion about what steps to take to resolve such a complex dispute between two competent and intelligent schoolteachers. One thing they decided not to do, at least at this stage, was to inform Bach of the accusations against him. And two days later, on the 19th, they received yet another letter from him:

> There will still be present to your most gracious memory, your magnificences and you, most noble sirs, what I felt compelled to report to your honours concerning the disorders that were caused eight days ago during the public divine service by the actions of the headmaster of the St Thomas School here, Mr Ernesti. Since the same thing took place today, both in the morning and in the afternoon, and, to avoid a great commotion in the church and a *turbatio sacrorum*, I had to make up my mind to conduct the motet myself and to have the intonation taken care of by a university student, and the situation is becoming worse and worse, so that without the most vigorous intervention on the part of you, my high patrons, I should hardly be able to maintain my position with the students entrusted to me, and accordingly should be blameless if further and perhaps irreparable disorders should result from it; now, therefore, I have been able to avoid calling this in proper fashion to the attention of your magnificences and you, most noble sirs, with the

most humble request that your honours will deign to put a prompt stop to these activities on behalf of the headmaster and, by hastening the principal decision I have prayed for, will, in accordance with your honours' well-known zeal for the good of the community, prevent the results otherwise to be feared, such as further public annoyance in the church, disorder in the school, and reduction of the authority with the students that is necessary to my office and other evil consequences. I remain, your magnificences and most noble sirs, your obedient

Leipzig, 19 August 1736　　　　　　　　　　　　Johann Sebastian Bach[135]

Sebastian was increasingly determined not to acquiesce to the ridiculously youthful headmaster, and was very reluctant to accept that Ernesti was acting logically and reasonably, or that he had made any attempt to protect the cantor's status. Indeed, further ideas were occurring to him as to how the battle might continue. One possibility might even be to obtain the support of the Dresden royal family, and he also began to consider making a further petition to receive the title of court kapellmeister. By 27 September he had decided to do so, and wrote a new letter reminding them of his application in July 1733.*

In the meantime, the council had made a further request to Ernesti to explain the details of Bach's case, and these troublesome conflicts that had continued in the school for several months. They showed him all four letters they had received from Bach, and on 13 September Ernesti provided them with another carefully-written statement, headed 'Memorandum', in which he made several new points. He began by stating that Bach's account concerning the incompetence of the student J. G. Krause was both incomplete and untruthful. Mr Bach was making these claims because he thought he would lose his right to pass judgements on students. The fact was that if a boy was unsuited to the post of first prefect, 'then he is most certainly unequal to the other posts as well', because all four prefects had

---

* See pages 224-5.

the same duties, including conducting the motets in church, beginning the hymns, and conducting a choir at the New Year's performances in people's homes. The only difference was that the first prefect did the latter at Michaelmas as well, and conducted the choir at wedding ceremonies. But the second prefect conducted the orchestral music of the second choir on feast days, which the first prefect did not do. Mr Bach argued that the pieces performed by the first choir were more intricate, but the fact was that he conducted them himself. The former first prefect, Maximilian Nagel, had never done anything except play the violin.

So why did Mr Bach now insist that the first prefect should conduct the complex pieces? In the past, when he was away, they had been conducted by the New Church organists, Georg Balthasar Schott (who had left for Gotha in 1729) and Carl Gotthelf Gerlach – as the latter would confirm if required.

And if Krause really was incompetent, as Mr Bach claimed, why had he not demoted him for that reason (with the headmaster's approval), instead of stating to the students that it was because of the headmaster's involvement? Furthermore, if it was the case that he had found Krause problematic as a conductor in December and January (and not in the six years he was in his singing class), he should not have appointed him prefect in the first place. And the test he had given Krause on 19 July was 'a trap': the headmaster had later questioned several students about what happened, and they had revealed that Krause made one single slip, which he instantly corrected. Clearly Mr Bach had wanted him to make an error, so it was hardly surprising that he did.

Moreover, Mr Bach's claim that the headmaster had asked him to appoint Krause as a prefect was completely untrue. What had actually happened was that the two of them were riding home from Magister Abraham Kriegel's wedding on 6 November 1736, and Mr Bach asked Mr Ernesti if Krause should become fourth prefect (not third, as Mr Bach had written in his third letter to the council). What was making him hesitate was that Krause had been 'a disreputable dog', with which Mr Ernesti agreed – that two years earlier he had had debts of 20 thalers [£960] (of which 12 thalers were for a suit of clothes), 'as I had found noted by Mr Gesner in the account book'. Since Gesner had decided to pardon him because of his notable talents, and since the debts were now largely paid off, he probably should become a prefect. Mr Bach had replied, 'Oh, I suppose he is competent enough!' So thereafter he had become in succession third, second and first prefect, 'and I can testify on my honour that I never received any complaint about him'. The headmaster signed his second account 'Magister Jo. Aug. Ernesti' and dated it 13 September 1736.[136]

The council found this whole range of complaints between the two schoolteachers extremely difficult to resolve, particularly as they were fully aware that, since both were highly skilled and competent teachers, it would be no solution to sack either of them. In the meantime, Sebastian had no choice but to carry on with the existing prefects, doubtless extremely annoyed at the headmaster's intervention and at the council's failure to reach a final decision in his favour. And then another upsetting issue arose, when his son Bernhard complained that he was unhappy in the post of organist in Mühlhausen (where he had been since June 1735), partly because he was poorly paid and was acquiring debts.

Perhaps pondering on his own youth, Sebastian came up with another promising possibility, for the news had just reached him that the organist at the Lower Church in Sangerhausen, a few miles west of Leipzig, had just died. At the end of October he wrote a polite letter to Johann Friedrich Klemm, a Sangerhausen town councillor,* asking whether a 'person very close to me' could be considered for the post, and what the salary would be.[137] Once again he got a fully encouraging reply, indicating that since Bach's approval of professional musicians was highly respected throughout Thuringia it was very likely that his recommendation would be accepted. Mr Klemm's reply included a statement that the Sangerhausen council had not yet decided what the salary would be, but he would let

---

* He had known Klemm's father back in 1702, when he himself had applied unsuccessfully for the post of organist at the main Sangerhausen church (see page 43).

him know shortly when they had. As usual money was the crucial factor, and since no second letter from Mr Klemm appeared for more than two weeks, on 18 November Sebastian wrote to him again, this time an even more flattering and respectful message, in which he revealed that the 'person very close to me' was one of his sons. He also wrote:

> And who knows whether a divine decree is not here at work, by virtue of which your most noble council is now better in a position, by choosing one of my children, to keep the promise made to my humble self almost 30 years ago,* in the conferring of the post of organist then vacant, since at that time a candidate was sent to you by the highest authority of the land, as a result of which, although at that time, under the regime of the burgomaster Vollrath, all the votes were cast for my humble self, I was nevertheless, for the aforementioned reason, not able to have the good fortune of emerging with success. Your honour will please not take it unkindly that I disclose my fate at that time on this occasion; only the fact that the first entrée of my written correspondence found such gracious ingress brings the thought to me that perhaps divine providence is taking a hand here.[138]

Not long after, Bernhard was indeed appointed organist there, which was a great relief.

But the St Thomas's School dispute was not over, and in the same month Sebastian wrote his fifth appeal, this time addressed to the town consistory, in which he summarised the crisis, stated that 'not only have I been very much injured and disturbed in the fulfilment of my office by this undertaking of the headmaster's but also the respect that the students owe me has been withdrawn, and I have thus been deprived of my rightful standing with them', and begged the consistory to intervene, uphold his status and instruct the headmaster to refrain from appointing prefects without his knowledge and consent.[139]

But that same week an even more encouraging dispatch came from

---

* It was in fact 34 years before, in July 1702.

the royal court in Dresden, a certificate confirming his appointment as composer to the king's court band, initialled by Elector Friedrich Augustus II, signed by the prime minister A. R. von Brühl, and sent to him by Count Hermann Carl von Keyserlingk, whose daughter was a music student of Friedemann's in Dresden.[140] At last, after the application he had made nearly three and a half years before, Sebastian had achieved the royal connection to which he had for so long felt entitled. A few days later he travelled again to Dresden, and on 1 December he performed a long and exciting organ recital there, which was reported in the local press. Encouraged, he decided not to post the letter to the Leipzig consistory.

But eventually, in February 1737, the town council issued a formal decree in response to Mr Ernesti's detailed reports. The document began by saying that the council had learned 'with displeasure' that there were misunderstandings between members of the school staff regarding the appointment of the senior prefect, given that St Thomas's School's rules and regulations were clearly stated, as follows: first, that the cantor had to accept the eight boys for each of the four choirs with the consent of the headmaster, and to choose the prefect for each choir with the approval of the school director. And if the first prefect turned out to be incompetent for any reason, he should be automatically replaced by the second. Secondly, neither the headmaster nor the cantor, nor any other individual teacher, had the right to exclude a student. If a prefect was to be excluded, he could be replaced only by another regular student. Moreover, it was improper that prefects should be punished in public, attracting disrespect from the students they had supervised – let alone that they should ever be subjected to public whipping. Furthermore, teachers should always be present at public and wedding services, in order to avoid the kind of excesses of which Gottfried Theodor Krause had been found guilty. The council's final statement declared that Johann Gottlieb Krause should remain as first prefect until he graduated from the school this coming Easter; and that the school rules should be 'precisely adhered to', particularly in the case of any disagreements.

Although clearly the council members were criticising the headmaster for some of the events of the last eight months, it was frustrating for Sebastian to find that they were not supporting his repeated claims that Mr Ernesti's interventions had undermined the school music classes and the regular church performances, as well as the crucial status of the school cantor. Increasingly confident that with his new royal connections the battle would end in his favour, he rewrote the letter to the Leipzig consistory, signed it as 'Composer of the Court Kapelle of His Royal Majesty in Poland, and director of choral music in this place', and dated it 12 February 1737.[141] The next day, the consistory informed both Dr Deyling and the town council that they had received Bach's latest complaint about the headmaster, and requested that, in order to avoid further disturbances at church services, the council should reach a decision without further delay.

But once again they found it very difficult to reach a decision, and for several more months the issue remained unresolved, even though Krause had graduated from the school and joined Leipzig University in May. The fact was that the majority of town councillors felt that, despite the evident capabilities of both Ernesti and Bach, the issue was an absurd one and should simply die out over time. There was no doubt that Ernesti had responded excellently to the requirements of the school as a whole, but that Bach too, despite his unsociable characteristics,* had contributed much to Leipzig's musical reputation (particularly with the weekly concerts in Zimmerman's coffee-house) and over the past 14 years had skilfully trained a number of students to become professional musicians.

In fact Sebastian had recently, in March, resigned as conductor of the *collegium musicum*, and passed the mantle to his former student Carl Gotthelf

---

* There is no absolute proof that Bach was unsociable, but the impression derives from several facts, such as a shortage of long-term friendships, the surviving letters and press reviews, the numerous disputes, the absence of social evidence, and the events shortly after his death.

Gerlach (1704–61), who had been appointed organist of the New Church in 1729.* This was probably for several reasons: that he wanted to devote as much time as possible to his new post as royal composer, that the interminable disputes in the churches had caused him much public injury and disturbance (as he had said in his letter to the consistory in February), and that he felt he might become increasingly unpopular in the Leipzig community. But fighting on had, through most of his life, been his method of coping with adversity, and in the summer he decided to resume yet again the dispute with Ernesti, writing another complaint to the consistory:

> Your magnificences and you, most noble, also most reverend and most distinguished sirs, will most graciously deign to recall that I, on the date of 12 February this year, complained about the headmaster of the St Thomas School, Magister Johann August Ernesti, concerning the hindrance offered me in the discharge of my duties and concerning the injunction laid upon the students not to obey me and the resultant humiliation to me, and how I most humbly sought your honours' protection and aid.
>
> Since that time a noble and honourable council has sent me a decree, of which a copy is attached as exhibit A; but on the one hand it does not give me satisfaction in respect to the humiliation to which I was subjected by the said headmaster, and on the other it does me, indeed, great harm. For in the first place I have been very greatly injured in my dignity by the threat to the students publicly made by the headmaster, in open church services, and in the presence of all the students of the highest class, of expulsion and forfeiture of his bond for any student who should be tempted to obey my orders, for which reason I request, not without reason, the restoration of my honour.
>
> And, in the second place, the said decree of the council is based upon a set of school regulations promulgated in 1723, about which the facts are as follows: they differ in many respects from the old school regulations,

---

* Bach resumed the post in October 1739, and continued in it until around 1741.

and to my great disadvantage in the discharge of my office as well as in the fees accruing to me, but they have therefore never been acknowledged as valid; and indeed, when it was suggested that they be published, the blessed late headmaster Ernesti* opposed this step on the ground that they must first of all be sent to the most worshipful consistory, and the decision of the latter concerning them must be awaited. Since their ratification has, to my knowledge, never taken place I can accordingly not be governed by these new and to me unfavourable school regulations, particularly since they would greatly diminish the fees accruing to me, and the decision must still be based upon the old school regulations; therefore, the said decree of the council, which is based on the new regulations, cannot dispose of the matter. And particularly that part cannot be maintained according to which I should not have the power to suspend or even expel a boy from any office in the choirs once given to him …;† for cases arise in which a change must be made on the spot and no lengthy investigation can be undertaken into such trivial disciplinary and school matters, while in every elementary school the power to make such changes in matters concerning music is given to the cantor, since it would be impossible to control the boys or to do justice to one's office if they knew that there was nothing once could do to them.

I have accordingly thought it necessary to bring these matters to the attention of your magnificences, most reverend, most noble, and most distinguished sirs, and my most humble petition herewith once again goes forth to you:

To uphold me in preserving the necessary dignity in the discharge of my office; to forbid the headmaster Ernesti any and all unwarranted encroachments; also to take the necessary steps to see that my honour before the students, which has been violated as a result of the said

---

* Johann Heinrich Ernesti, who had been headmaster of St Thomas's School since 1684, died in October 1729.

† A few words in the surviving letter are missing here.

headmaster's conduct, shall be restored; and to protect me against the new school regulations, to the extent that they injure me and prevent me from discharging the duties of my office.

For the assistance shown me in this matter I shall always remain, with due respect, your magnificences and most reverend, most noble, and most distinguished sirs, your obedient

Leipzig, 21 August 1737   Johann Sebastian Bach[142]

Within a few days, the consistory informed Mr Deyling and the town council about Bach's letter, and requested that they produce a solution within two weeks. But again they felt unable to do so, and on 4 October their decision was 'to let the matter rest for a while yet'.

Sebastian felt humiliated by both bodies' failure to support – despite his hard work and commitment to Leipzig performance and musical education – the credible and detailed complaints he had sent them six times over the past year. There was now only one possible course of action: to take advantage of his connection with the royal family. So on 18 October he wrote a formal but very carefully constructed letter to Elector Friedrich August, first expressing his grateful appreciation of the appointment as court composer, and going on to request his support over 'my present afflictions'. He meticulously outlined the dispute, and enclosed copies of his complaints to the council and consistory, as well as the council's decree issued on 6 February. The letter ends:

I therefore entreat Your Royal Majesty in humblest submission most graciously to order: (1) that the council here should uphold me without injury in my rightful request in respect to the appointment of the choral prefect and to protect me in the exercise of that right; and (2) that the consistory here should oblige the headmaster Ernesti to apologise for the abuse to which he has submitted me, and also, if Your Majesty please, to instruct Dr Deyling to exhort the whole student body that all the school boys are to show me the customary respect and obedience that are due to me.[143]

Two months later, Friedrich August's court issued a decree, addressed to the Leipzig consistory and signed by two of the Elector's staff.[144] It stated that 'our court composer, Johann Sebastian Bach, has complained to us about the headmaster of St Thomas's School' for appointing a musically incompetent prefect without his approval, and when Mr Bach was compelled to replace the prefect, the headmaster 'not only opposed his purpose but also, to his great injury and humiliation, forbade all the boys, in general assembly and on pain of whipping, to give their obedience in the arrangements the cantor had made'. The decree then simply stated that 'we therefore desire herewith that you shall take such measures, in response to this complaint, as you shall see fit'. In other words, the Elector had made no decision, and was clearly unwilling to become personally involved.

On 5 February 1738 the consistory again informed Dr Deyling and the council that they should produce a final report within a fortnight, and again they failed to do so. Once again Sebastian had lost another of his long campaigns.

Chapter 13

FAME AND TRIUMPH

(1737–40)

Not everything in 1737 was a disaster for Sebastian, now in his 53rd year. His three eldest sons were all following his professional advice, Friedemann in Dresden, Emanuel in Frankfurt and Bernhard in Sangerhausen; Gottfried Heinrich, privately educated in the flat, was showing keyboard and compositional talent at the age of 13;* and the three other youngsters – Lieschen (eleven), Friederich (five) and Christel (two) were being pleasantly brought up by Magdalena. And indeed she was again pregnant, for the twelfth time in 15 years. Furthermore, they were joined this year by Johann Elias Bach, the 32-year-old son of one of Sebastian's cousins,† who took on the role of Sebastian's secretary and teacher of the young children, as well as studying theology at the university. Domestic life in the comfortable, spacious rooms provided reassurance in the face of the endless disputes with the school and town authorities.

We can deduce this by listening to a remarkable secular cantata that Sebastian composed for performance in September.‡ It was commissioned to celebrate the appointment of an important minister in the Dresden cabinet, Johann

---

* It is indeed likely that he composed the six-verse song *So oft ich meine Tobacks-Pfeife mit gutem Knaster angefült* ('Each time I take my pipe and fill it with good tobacco', BWV 515), which he copied in to his mother's clavier book.

† Johann Valentin Bach (1669–1720), son of Johann Ambrosius Bach's younger brother.

‡ *Angenehmes Wiederau*, BWV 30a, performed on 28 September 1737.

Christian von Hennicke, who had been donated a peerage in 1728, and this year a grand fief property a few miles south of Leipzig named Wiederau, near Pegau. Picander wrote a splendid poetic text praising the place and its owner, with narratives from four characters: fate, happiness, time, and the local river Elster. The most inspiring was the opening chorus, *Angenehmes Wiederau, freue dich in deinen Auen!* ('Charming Wiederau, take pleasure in your meadows!'), a lovely tune with splendid accompaniment by trumpets and drums; and several of the arias and recitatives are also truly original and lively. Clearly what motivated Sebastian to write it was pride in his new connection with the aristocracy. But he was also well aware that this exceptionally successful composition could be transferred to the church, which inspired him to commission a new text (probably also by Picander), which was performed a year or two later (*Freue dich, erlöste Schar*, BWV 30).

Magdalena gave birth in October to her seventh (and second surviving) daughter, who was baptised on 30 October as Johanna Carolina; one of her godmothers was Picander's wife, Johanna Elisabeth Henrici.

A number of journalists and music specialists in Leipzig and other towns had in recent years quite frequently written about Mr Bach the outstanding musician,* particularly commenting on his remarkable organ and other keyboard skills, and sometimes his compositions. The distinguished music specialist Johann Mattheson (1681–1764) had written about him several times, from as early as 1717 when he was working in Weimar. But now there was a new music journalist, Sebastian's former student Johann Adolph Scheibe (1708–76),† who was working in Hamburg and with the support of Telemann had just founded a fortnightly journal entitled *Critische Musikus*. His first printed reference to Sebastian was an article on the exceptional quality of contemporary German keyboard music, in which he wrote:

---

* See page 218.

† See page 161.

In some types of clavier pieces there is a clear distinction between the German style and others. In foreigners we find that neither the structure, nor the ornamentation, nor the working out of these pieces is so perfect as in the Germans. For they know how to exploit this instrument with the greatest strength and according to its true nature better than all other nations. The two great men among the Germans, Mr Bach and Mr Handel, illustrate this most strikingly.[145]

But in May he wrote another piece involving Bach in the form of a humorous letter purportedly written by a foreign musician, which conveyed not just praise but jokesome disapproval:

Finally, Mr ----- is the most eminent of the musicians in -----. He is an extraordinary artist on the clavier and on the organ, and he has until now met only one person with whom he can dispute his distinction.* I have heard this great man play on various occasions. One is amazed at his skill, and one can hardly comprehend how it is possible for him to achieve such agility, with his fingers and with his feet, in the crossings, extensions, and extreme jumps that he manages, without mixing in a single wrong note, or misplacing his body by any violent movement.

This great man would be the admiration of whole nations if he had more comfort, if he did not take away the natural element in his pieces by giving them a bombastic and confused style, and if he did not darken their beauty by an excess of artifice. Because he judges according to his own fingers, his pieces are therefore extremely difficult to play; for he demands that singers and instrumentalists should be able to execute with their voices and instruments whatever he can play on the clavier. But this is impossible. All ornaments, every little embellishment, and everything that one understands as part of the method of performance, he expresses with actual notes, and this not only takes away from his

---

*   Probably a reference to Handel.

pieces the beauty of harmony, but also makes the melody indistinct throughout. All voices must work together with each other and be of equal difficulty, and one recognises among them no principal voice. In short, he is in music what formerly Mr von Lohenstein was in poetry. Bombast has led both of them from the natural to the artificial, and from the sublime to the obscure; and one admires in both the onerous labour and an exceptional effort, which, however, is vainly employed because it conflicts with nature.[146]

There is no evidence that Sebastian read this when it was published, but evidently before long one of his Leipzig acquaintances, a rhetor at the university named Johann Abraham Birnbaum (1702–48), drew his attention to it and recommended that a counter-criticism be written to defend his reputation. Birnbaum suggested that one possible reason for Scheibe's printing these ruthful criticisms was his resentment that back in 1729, when he had applied for the post of organist at St Thomas's Church, Bach had been one of the judges who had appointed Johann Gottlieb Görner instead. But Sebastian recalled that he had written a lavish testimonial for Scheibe in April 1731, saying 'that he is thoroughly at home not only on the clavier and violin but also in composition, and accordingly I do not doubt that he will be in a position adequately to attend whatever office God may assign to him'.[147] Scheibe's article was not wholly critical, either, so it seemed he was not an enemy.

On the other hand, it was also clearly an advantage in the music profession to obtain printed comments in the national and local press, whether or not they were all favourable, so in due course Sebastian agreed to assist Birnbaum in preparing what would eventually, on 8 January 1738, be published under the title 'Impartial Comments on a Questionable Passage in the Sixth Number of *Der Critische Musicus*'.[148] It is a long article, elegant and sophisticated in style, and voicing unquestionably by far the greatest praise of Bach ever published hitherto. To begin with, Birnbaum made the following points:

in the music profession critics and journalists rarely had the ability to make true assessments; the praise (in the first paragraph) was incomplete, and the blame (in the second paragraph) was groundless; calling Mr Bach a 'musician' (*Musikant*) was improper: he was in fact a great composer, a master of music, and a unique virtuoso on the organ and clavier; and there was only one Bach in the world, and no one could equal him.

Tackling Scheibe's specific criticisms in the second paragraph, he then argued that the following accusations were all absurd: 'lack of amenity' given Bach's brilliant handling of consonances and dissonances; 'turgid and confused style' given that in his church compositions, overtures, concertos and other musical works there were decorations always appropriate to the principal ideas he had wished to develop, and any confusion in performances was the fault of the players and not the composer; 'excess of art which darkens the beauty of his works' given that it was impossible that the greatest art should darken the beauty of a thing; 'very difficult to play' given that, although it might be true, it was so only for those unwilling to train their fingers to fluent motion and correct fingering; and 'ornaments and grace notes written out' given that players and singers often placed them wrongly, damaging the composer's reputation. As for 'no singer can be recognised as the principal voice', it was utter nonsense. The article ended with the statement that 'I, together with all other true admirers of the great Bach, wish the author in the future more salutary thoughts and, after the completion of his musical journeys, the happy beginning of a new life that may be free of all unnecessary desire to find fault'.

So now not only was Sebastian the Dresden court composer, but also he had become nationally, and even internationally, known as one of the world's greatest musicians. This was a huge encouragement in the face of all the disputes he had faced and fought in Leipzig for years. Increasingly, articles about him began to appear in the press.

But Adolph Scheibe, who had known Bach very well in his Leipzig years, was not at all impressed by the Birnbaum article, and promptly wrote a devastating attack, stating that 'it smacks too strongly of the partiality and injustice of its author and that the latter has revealed in it only too clearly how little he knows the true basis of music, and its real beauty'. He described it as containing 'disorderly statements' defending 'one of the greatest musicians of our time'. Indeed, Mr Bach, 'this famous man, has been more injured than exalted by this flattering essay in praise of him'. And he also argued that one of the most ridiculous elements was the claim that the word *Musikant* ('musician') was improper. The piece appeared in his *Critische Musicus* magazine in February.[149] And to prove his full understanding of Bach's exceptional qualities, he also published a few months later a scholarly account of the great virtues of the Italian Concerto (BWV 971) which Sebastian had produced in his second *Clavier-Übung* in 1735:

> I must briefly mention that concertos are also written for one instrument alone, without any accompaniment by others – especially clavier concertos or lute concertos. In such pieces the basic structure is kept the same as in concertos for many instruments. The bass and the middle voices, which are added now and then to fill out the texture, must represent the subordinate parts. And those passages that above all form the essence of the concerto must be most clearly differentiated from the rest. This can very well be done if, after the principal idea of a fast or slow movement is concluded with a cadence, new and distinct ideas enter and these in turn give way to the principal idea in varying keys. By such means, a piece of this sort for one instrument becomes quite similar to one for many instruments. There are some quite good concertos of this kind, particularly for clavier. But pre-eminent among published musical works is a clavier concerto of which the author is the famous Bach in Leipzig, and which is in the key of F major. Since his piece is arranged in the best possible fashion for this kind of work, I believe that it will doubtless be familiar to all great composers and experienced clavier players, as well as to amateurs of the clavier and music in general. Who is there who will not admit at once

that this clavier concerto is to be regarded as a perfect model of a well-designed solo concerto? But at the present time we shall be able to name as yet very few or practically no concertos of such excellent qualities and such well-designed execution. It would take as great a master of music as Mr Bach, who has almost alone taken possession of the clavier, and with whom we can certainly defy foreign nations, to provide us with such a piece in this form of composition – a piece that deserves emulation by all our great composers and that will be imitated all in vain by foreigners.[150]

None the less, Sebastian's supporters continued to dispute with Scheibe, particularly another of his former students, Lorenz Christoph Mizler von Kolof (1711–78), who had graduated from the university in 1734 and recently become a teacher there, and two years later began to publish a book series entitled *Neu eröffnete musikalische Bibliothek* ('Newly opened musical library'). He too wrote an attack on Scheibe's statements, involving the use of the word *Musikant*, and the suggestion that Bach's music was too complex. But Scheibe himself was doing increasingly well in the music profession, and by 1740 he had left Hamburg and been appointed kapellmeister to the Danish court in Copenhagen, where he continued to compose masses, cantatas, chamber music and keyboard works. And although several Bach supporters were infuriated by his journalism, Sebastian himself must have felt a certain sense of pride that this talented former student, despite certain setbacks in his youth, had achieved so much.

By now, he had rejoined the *collegium musicum*,* and had started composing a range of new orchestral works, partly for performance in Zimmerman's coffee-house and partly for the Dresden orchestra. A striking example is the orchestral suite in B minor (BWV 1067), dominated by a solo transverse flute accompanied by the strings, with seven movements of which the most impressive are the Rondeau (second), the Bourrée

---

* See page 265.

(fourth) and the Badinerie (seventh). Equally striking are the harpsichord concertos he compiled from previous compositions, many from violin or oboe concertos that he had probably produced back in Cöthen or even in Weimar, and some from cantatas written in the 1720s. Perhaps the most remarkable is the concerto in D minor (BWV 1052), in which the keyboard part – no doubt played by Sebastian himself in the coffee-house – is strikingly complex and emotional.* The most moving element in the E major concerto (BWV 1053) is neither the first nor the third movement, both derived from cantatas composed in 1726,† but the Siciliano second movement, which vividly expresses pain and agony in a simple string accompaniment to the harpsichord's exploration of harmony. Most of the others, particularly BWV 1054 derived from the violin concerto BWV 1043 in D minor, BWV 1058 derived from the violin concerto BWV 1041 in A minor, and BWV 1054 derived from the violin concerto BWV 1042 in E major, are equally sophisticated, demonstrating the composer's impressive playing skills. Increasingly, Sebastian evidently felt his huge range of past compositions were a masterly showcase of his talents, and although revising them in different keys for different performances took almost as much time and effort as composing new ones, he became increasingly interested in re-examining his mass of stored manuscripts to produce new works.

Within the Bach family, there were positive as well as the usual negative signs. Emanuel had just moved from Frankfurt to Berlin, where he was appointed harpsichordist to the Crown Prince Frederick of Prussia (who became King Friedrich II of Prussia, known to us as Frederick the Great, in 1740). Friedemann seemed to be doing well in Dresden, where Sebastian visited him in May 1738. But the same month it emerged that Bernhard had suddenly vanished from Sangerhausen, apparently having again run up much debt and failed to pay his bills. Sebastian read this

---

* The opening Allegro movement is derived from a cantata produced around 1726, BWV 146, and the closing Allegro is from BWV 188, *Ich habe meine Zuversicht* (see page 197).

† See pages 169–171.

dreadful news in a letter from Mr Klemm, the town councillor who had appointed Bernhard nearly two years earlier. Immediately after his return from Dresden, Sebastian wrote him a long reply:

> Your honour will not take it amiss that absence has prevented me from replying before now to your esteemed letter, since I returned only two days ago from Dresden. However, with what pain and sorrow I compose this reply your honour can judge for yourself as the loving and caring father of your own offspring. I have not laid eyes on my unfortunately misguided son since last year, when I had the privilege of enjoying your honour's many kindnesses. You will also recall that at that time I not only paid his board, but also the Mühlhausen account (which probably brought about his departure from that town), and also left a few ducats behind to settle some debts, in the hope that he would now take up a different *genus vitae*. But now I learn, with the deepest dismay, that he once more borrowed here and there, has not mended his ways in the slightest, but on the contrary has absconded without giving me the least indication of his whereabouts.
>
> What more can I say or do? Since no admonition, or even any loving care and *assistance*, will suffice any longer, I must bear my cross with patience and leave my unruly son to God's mercy, not doubting that He will hear my sorrowful prayers and finally, according to His Holy Will, that he will learn to acknowledge that conversion can come only from Divine Goodness.
>
> Since I have now opened my heart to your honour, I have every confidence that you will not impute the bad conduct of my child to me, but will recognise that a devoted father, whose children are dear to him, will do everything he can to help to promote their welfare. It was this that made me recommend my son when you had the *vacance*, in the hope that the more civilised life in Sangerhausen and the eminent patrons there would equally move him to behave differently, and on this account I again express my

most dutiful thanks to your honour as author of his advancement. Nor do I doubt that your honour will try to persuade your noble council to postpone the threatened change until it can be learned where he is keeping himself (God being my omniscient witness that I have not seen him since last year), so that we may learn what he has decided to do: to remain and alter his ways, or to seek his fortune elsewhere. I would not have your noble council inconvenienced, but I would request only such patience until he should turn up, or until it can be discovered where he has gone.

Since also various *creditores* have been in contact with me, and I can hardly agree to pay these claims without my son's oral or written admission of them (which is my legal entitlement), I beseech your honour to be so good as to make enquiries as to his whereabouts, and then you need only give me definite information so that a final effort may be made to discover if, with God's help, his impenitent heart can be won over, and he can be made to see his mistakes. Since hitherto he was fortunate enough to lodge with your honour, please let me know at the same time whether he took with him the little furniture he has, or what still remains of it. Awaiting a prompt reply, and wishing you a happier holiday than I shall have, I remain, with most humble respects to your wife, your honour's most devoted servant'

Leipzig, 24 May 1738   Joh. Seb. Bach[151]

The loss of another son was no surprise to Sebastian, since he had already lost five over the past 25 years; but it was particularly disturbing that Bernhard's problems appeared to be primarily about money, an issue that had affected the family for so long. Mrs Klemm had written him a second letter about Bernhard's debts, to which he replied:

Dear Madam,

You will not take it unkindly that I cannot accede to the suggestion in your letter regarding the statement of claims sent to me, because in the first place, before I make a decision, I need to be shown my (alas misguided) son's acknowledgements in his own handwriting; and secondly I must know if he has not yet returned home, in order to take appropriate steps. He has not been with me since my journey to Sangerhausen last year, as I can give assurance with God and my family as my witnesses. If you, Madam, can learn where he is staying, and provide me with such definite information, I would not only acknowledge it with all thanks, but take pains to reimburse you. Awaiting a most prompt reply, I remain your most devoted servant,

Leipzig, 26 May 1738   Joh. Seb. Bach[152]

It was not that Sebastian himself was currently short of money, because on 5 May he had been paid 50 thalers [£2,400] by the university for a performance of a secular cantata* he had composed to celebrate the forthcoming marriage of Elector Friedrich August's sister, Princess Maria Amalia, to King Carl IV of Sicily.

But many months went by before Sebastian learned that Bernhard had actually moved not very far away, to the town of Jena, south-west of Leipzig, where his distant cousin Johann Nikolaus Bach (1669–1753) had for many years held the post of town and university organist. Nikolaus, now 69, was the eldest son of Johann Christoph Bach (1642–1703), the beloved organist at Eisenach with whom Sebastian had spent crucial times in his childhood learning about the organ.† The dreadful realisation was that, despite his perfectly competent musical abilities, Bernhard must have been terrified of his father and had run away to find an alternative. Even family relationships, on which Sebastian had been so dependent all his life, were proving to be far from reliable. But as it turned out, running away did Bernhard no good. In January 1739 he matriculated at

---

* Entitled *Willkommen! Ihr herrschenden Götter der Erden!* ('Welcome! You ruling God of the world!'). The text of this *dramma per musica* survives, but the music does not.

† See page 22.

Jena University to study law, but only four months later, on 27 May, he died of acute fever, the tenth of Sebastian's lost children. Sebastian must have begun to wonder whether he himself was the cause of all these torments, and whether despite all his efforts his children were unhappy. Friedemann was not that far away, in Dresden; but maybe Emanuel had gone much further, to Frankfurt an der Oder and now Berlin, in order to distance himself from his father as Bernhard had done.

There had been another brief row with the council in March, not dissimilar to the one way back in 1724,* about his plan to perform a Passion on Good Friday without obtaining their permission; and when the clerk complained to him Sebastian's reply was that, since he earned no benefit, he didn't care.[153]

The presence of Elias in the household over the past months had considerably uplifted the family, because he was a charming and sociable man who was willing to do an immense amount of work to help his cousins, as well as pursuing his university studies. In the summer of 1739, for instance, he had encouraged Friedemann to spend several weeks in Leipzig, along with two of his remarkable Dresden colleagues, the outstanding lute player Silvius Leopold Weiß (1686–1750) and his student Johann Kropffgans, and they had performed some beautiful works on several evenings in the St Thomas's School building, no doubt in the presence of many friends. Quite possibly Sebastian was inspired by their presence to compose some of his lute suites, such as BWV 997 and 998. And he was still working on his third *Clavier-Übung*, which was finally published at the end of September and contained a wide range of organ pieces, and a second collection of keyboard preludes and fugues in every key from C major to B minor.† He had also produced four rather splendid Latin Masses (BWV 233–6) based mainly on movements from his previous

---

* See page 162.

† *The Well-Tempered Clavier*, popularly known in the modern world as '48 Preludes and Fugues', was never printed in Bach's lifetime, but many copies were owned by his pupils. The first printed version was published by the Leipzig company Hoffmeister & Kühnel in 1801.

cantatas composed in the 1720s, and may well have felt that the pieces were more moving and appropriate to the traditional Kyrie and Gloria. All four of them contain three choruses and three arias, and still remain considerably more popular than the cantatas from which they were derived.

He took several journeys this year, some with Magdalena and some involving the traditional organ examinations and recitals, of which the best remembered was on 7 September in the ancient town of Altenburg. The new Trost organ in the late-Gothic castle church there (which still survives) enabled Sebastian to give a rousing and memorable performance of the Credo hymn (*Wir glauben all an einen Gott*) starting in D minor and rising to E-flat minor for verse two, then to E minor for verse three. In November they also spent a week in Weißenfels, Magdalena's former home-town 35 miles south-west of Leipzig, probably to perform in the castle privately before the duke, Johann Adolf II.

But music composition and adaptation continued to be Sebastian's main obsession, and the works that he now produced convey a sense of his feeling prey to incessant disputations and relentless family deaths. Already mentioned since 1737 are the masterly two versions of *Angenehmes Wiederau* and *Freue dich* (BWV 30a and 30), the beautiful suite for flute, strings and basso continuo (BWV 1067), the nine harpsichord concertos (BWV 1052–60), and the lute suites (BWV 995 and 997). But there is much else dating from this period, including a collection of long and quite impressive organ chorale pieces revised and re-copied from his previous Weimar compositions (BWV 651–68), and another much more moving lute piece (BWV 998) in three movements, Prelude, Fugue and Allegro, all of which seem to convey how to endure a troubled life.

He also compiled three sonatas for viola da gamba and keyboard, presumably to be performed by some of his gamba-playing students such as Carl Friedrich Abel (1723–87), and again based on previous compositions. By far the most moving and significant is the one in G major (BWV 1027) – a revised version of the sonata for two flutes and continuo (BWV 1039) that he had composed a few years earlier. All four movements express

Sebastian's complex range of emotions, starting with a subtle opening Adagio in G major which ends with a suggestion that pains and troubles must be endured with the prospect of a better future. This is followed by a lively and charming Allegro, also in G major, communicating a brighter and more optimistic view of life. There then follows a truly beautiful, quite brief slow movement in E minor, conveying the multifarious elements of pain and loss; and the work ends with another vigorous but equally intricate expression, again in G Major, of survival and optimism. Although Sebastian adjusted this four-part trio sonata to several instrumental settings, the most convincing for modern listeners is BWV 1039. A number of other flute sonatas existed in his collection of compositions,* but none is so moving as this one.

Also in 1740, in his 30th year, Sebastian's former student and supporter L. C. Mizler von Kolof published another brief Bach story mentioning the publication of Part III of the *Clavier-Übung*, about which he stated that 'the author has here given new proof that in this field of composition he is more practised and more fortunate than many others. No one will surpass him in it, and few will be able to imitate him. This work is a powerful refutation of those who have made bold to criticise the composition of the court composer.' Whether Scheibe would now shut up about Bach's defects remained unclear, but Sebastian still had plenty to reflect on in terms of how he had been undermined, not just by the losses of his parents, wife and children, but by the ridiculously critical and unmusical attitudes of his employers and the Leipzig authorities.

---

* BWV 1030, 1031 1032, 1033, 1034, 1035, 1038, and 1044. There is also, of course, the 5th Brandenburg Concerto, BWV 1050, composed nearly 20 years before.

Chapter 14

TOWARDS THE END

(1741–50)

Although ageing inevitably comprised patterns of ceaseless reflection on the past, regrets, social hostility and other factors, Sebastian continued to believe in his abilities and skills, and in his capacity to invoke true talent among his numerous students and other music-lovers. Another project that strongly appealed to him was to compile a fourth *Clavier-Übung*, this time focused on the keyboard, containing a wide range of variations on an aria. The opening theme is a simple one in G major that any player could handle, but the variations become more and more complex, powerfully testing the abilities and skills of the player. Over several months he composed a total of 30 variations, increasingly diverse in style but all related to the simple original theme; every third variation was a canon, two of them in G minor. By far the most moving and intricate piece in the whole set – though not a canon – is number 25 in G minor, which takes longer than all the others to play, and fully conveys the complexity of the composer's emotions. The work ends with a repetition of the simple opening aria.

Clavier-Übung IV was published in Nuremberg* in the autumn of 1741, and a copy was sent to Count von Keyserlingk† because, suffering from

---

* See page 244.

† See page 263.

insomnia, he had requested some keyboard pieces that could be played to him late at night by his 14-year-old employee Johann Gottlieb Goldberg. And so eventually the work became known as the *Goldberg Variations*.* Sebastian's own printed copy (which was rediscovered in 1974) contains a wide range of additional canons, which he was finding an increasingly fascinating and demanding compositional subject.

In the late spring, Magdalena was pregnant again, for the 13th time. In July, Sebastian travelled to Berlin, intending to spend several weeks with Emanuel and possibly to have the honour of meeting his royal employer, King Frederick II. He found it a much more encouraging city than Leipzig, and almost considered moving permanently to the Prussian state. But early in August another crisis arose: Johann Elias Bach wrote to say that Magdalena was suffering a serious illness, her pulse 'throbbing violently', and that Sebastian should return as soon as possible. He promptly wrote back that he would indeed rapidly return, and then received another letter from Elias reporting that her health had worsened over the last fortnight, and strongly implying that she might shortly die. Was he about to lose his second wife, yet another in the relentless progression of family deaths he had encountered since childhood? By mid-August he had returned to Leipzig, and fortunately in due course Magdalena recovered. In February 1742 she gave birth to her eleventh and Sebastian's 20th child, a daughter baptised on the 22nd as Regina Susanna.

Travelling now became more difficult, since once again there were seven children living in the St Thomas's building: in addition to the new baby, there were Catharina Dorothea, now 33, the troubled Gottfried Heinrich (18), Lieschen (15), Friederich (9), Christel (5) and Johanna Carolina (3). Increasingly Sebastian's primary occupation was to re-examine his huge range of past compositions, and to seek inspiration for new works.

His principal project over the next few years was fuelled by his obsession with fugues and canons, as a revelation of the charms and complexities of

---

* BWV 988.

contrapuntal music demonstrated on the organ or harpsichord. He probably did not intend the works to be performed, but merely to provide music students with a comprehensive view of this style's potential range. Indeed, his possible intention in due course was to have the collection published, maybe as a fifth *Clavier-Übung*, under the name *Die Kunst der Fuge* ('The Art of Fugue').*

It starts with this simple theme in D minor:

The first four pieces are fairly simple and straightforward four-part fugues based on the theme, and the movements become increasingly complex, involving counter-fugues, inversions, diminutions and augmentations, as well as the insertion of new themes including his own self-signature, BACH (in German music, the note Bb is called B, and B natural is called H):

Most notably, D minor dominates all of the highly varied pieces, showing how music can convey both great sadness and also a huge range of musical skills, demonstrating the subtleties and complexities offered by contrapuntalism for those who study and understand it. Clearly this music was not meant for performance, merely as a demonstration of compositional skills, but if you listen to it, in whatever form (instrumental, orchestral or keyboard), you connect with the composer's frame of mind, his suffering of tragedies and his efforts to cope with and survive them.†

Other surviving clues to Sebastian's frame of mind in 1742 include several cantatas composed this year. For example, in the spring he was commissioned to write a wedding cantata (the bride and groom are

---

* BWV 1080.

† Although Bach composed some 20 pieces in this work, it was never completed, and printed only after his death by his son Emanuel.

unknown), which he based on one of his previous compositions, BWV 210a.* The striking element is in the text – of which the author is also unknown – which strongly connects Sebastian's three cardinal subjects: music, love and death. In the ten movements, the most remarkable words are in the second recitative (movement 5):

So glaubt man denn, daß due Musik verführe und gar nicht mit der Liebe harmoniere? On nein! Wer wollte denn nicht ihren Wert betrachten, auf den so hohe Gönner achten? Gewiß, die gütige Natur zieht uns von ihr auf eine höhre Spur. Sie ist der Liebe gleich, ein großes Himmelskind, nur, daß sie nicht, als wie die Liebe, blind. Sie schleicht in alle Herzen ein und kann bei Hoh' und Niedern sein. Sie lockt den Sinn zum Himmel hin und kann verliebten Seelen des Höchsten Ruhm erzählen. Ja, heißt die Liebe sonst weit stärker als der Tod, wer leugnet? Die Musik stärkt uns in Todes Not. O wundervolles Spiel! Dich, dich verehrt man viel. Doch was erklingt dort vor ein Klagelied, das den geschwinden Ton beliebter Saiten flieht?

Do we really believe that music leads us astray, and does not harmonise with love? Oh no! Whoever would not consider its true worth, a worth that such exalted patrons value? Certainly, kind nature draws us from it to a higher plane. It is like love, a great child of heaven, except that it is not so blind as love. It steals into all hearts, be it high or low. It draws our thoughts to heaven, and can tell loving souls of the glory of the Highest. Yes, who would deny that love is yet more powerful than death? Music comforts in the hour of death. O wondrous art! You, you are much honoured! But what a lament rings forth, and drives away the nimble-fingered sound of popular strings?

It is hard to believe that anyone but Sebastian himself could have written these words, even though there is no proof that he did. The cantata ends with a quite charming soprano aria expressing the optimism and joy of marriage.

---

* See page 199.

Another commission was to celebrate the town council's installation in August; this – also based on several previous works – was the cantata *Gott, man lobet dich in der Stille zu Zion* ('Praise waiteth for thee, O God, in Sion').* Much the most beautiful movement is the fourth, a soprano aria accompanied by solo violin, strings and basso continuo. And in the same month an even more striking piece was produced in honour of the district captain of Leipzig, Carl Heinrich von Dieskau, who had become lord of the manor at the nearby north-western village of Kleinzschocher. Based on a libretto written by Picander, it comprises no fewer than 24 movements, including an opening sinfonia, 21 brief arias and recitatives, and two major arias, accompanied by harpsichord, strings, lute, flute and horn. Picander's text involving two lower-class rural characters (soprano and bass) is full of humour, prompting Sebastian to construct an unusually jokey musical expression throughout the 30-minute work, ending with a memorable chorus based on this popular tune:

Wir gehn nun wo der Tu-del-sack, der Tudel-tudel -tudel -tudel -tudel -tudel-sack in uns – rer Schenke brummt.

We're going to the tavern, – the tavern tavern tavern tavern tavern tavern tavern where the merry bagpipes drone.

This so-called *Cantate burlesque*, entitled *Mer hahn en neue Oberkeet* ('We have a new régime') and now well-known as 'The Peasant Cantata',† is probably the last secular piece Sebastian created; and indeed he had by now largely resigned from the *collegium musicum* and much reduced his duties and obligations. In the autumn his young cousin Johann Elias Bach moved out, having been appointed tutor at the school in Zöschau, a village on the

---

* BWV 120. The opening aria is based on the words of Psalm 65, verse 1.

† BWV 212.

road to Dresden; and on 7 November Elias wrote him a lavish thank-you letter speaking of 'your highly cherished household' and 'my most highly cherished cousins, mother and daughter, as well as sons'.[154] Although he was still father to five young children, Sebastian must have increasingly been feeling his age and finding himself less energetic. Over the next few years he continued in the role of school cantor, avoiding further disputes with Ernesti and the town council, although he must have been well aware that despite his huge contributions to music teaching, composition, concerts and organ standards,* he remained unpopular among many of the senior figures in the town and university. It surely seemed, since so many of his former music students and colleagues still greatly admired him, that there was a huge gap between music-lovers and the rest. And yet even that was not certain, for he could not forget the interminable disputes based on Scheibe's article about him in 1737. Indeed in 1745, after eight years of it, Scheibe – who had moved to Copenhagen as musical director to King Christian VI of Denmark (1699–1746) – reprinted Birnbaum's writing in his magazine, with a huge range of footnote commentaries; although clearly this was more of an attack on Birnbaum than on Bach.†

In 1744, three years after Sebastian had visited him in Berlin, his son Emanuel married Johanna Maria Dannemann, the 20-year-old daughter of a wine merchant; this strongly suggested that Sebastian should soon pay another visit. But this year also saw an alarming event: King Frederick of Prussia's expansionist determination to embark on another war against the Habsburg province of Silesia caused panic in Saxony – not least because the Elector, who was also King August III of Poland, was understandably hostile to Frederick's policies. The result was that Prussian troops invaded Leipzig on 30 November 1745, and remained

---

* There are records that he tested organs at St John's Church in December 1743, at Zschortau, north of Leipzig, in August 1746, at Naumburg, to the west, in September 1746, and at St Thomas's Church in November 1747.

† Birnbaum died in August 1748.

there for a full year. The Bachs' two royal supporters were evidently at war with each other. So even though Sebastian learned that his first grandson, named Johann August, had been born in November 1745, he no doubt felt unable to make the journey.

As the months passed, Sebastian gradually withdrew from the challenges and competitions he had embarked on throughout his life. It was not that his talent had weakened, nor that his sense of responsibility as school cantor and church musician had declined. On the contrary, he continued to train and assist the four choral prefects, to provide private lessons to talented students and his children, and to conduct the main Sunday services in St Thomas's and St Nicholas's. But his days of composing, particularly cantatas and orchestral works, were largely over. One advantage, from which he obtained increasing self-confidence, was that he could spend more time at home with his wife and the four young children, Friederich, Christel, Johanna Carolina and Regina Susanna.

One notable event in 1746 was Friedemann's resignation from his post as organist in Dresden and subsequent move to Halle (Handel's birth town), where he was appointed organist in the medieval Liebfrauenkirche (Church of Our Lady), the post Sebastian had applied for and declined back in 1714.* It appeared that Friedemann had been appointed without going through the standard trial performance, no doubt through his father's influence. And another encouraging boost came when the highly successful artist Elias Gottlob Haußmann (1695–1774) – who was the town's official portraitist and subsequently appointed to the Saxon court – undertook this year to paint a formal portrait of Sebastian, using the style he applied to all his portraits of official figures in Leipzig and elsewhere. Posing for the artist involved a number of sittings over several weeks, in which Sebastian wore his formal clothes, placed his wig on his head, and held in his right hand a symbol of his compositional skills: the manuscript of a brief but sophisticated *Canon triplex à 6 Voc* ('Triple canon for six

---

* See page 90.

voices', BWV 1076), signed at the bottom 'J. S. Bach'. Although there was no symbol of his teaching and performing abilities, and Haußmann seemed to portray the eyesight problems Sebastian was beginning to encounter, the result none the less seemed highly appropriate, conveying his lifelong dedication to work and his eminent distinction.*

But two rather depressing events also took place this year: Magdalena's mother, Margarethe Elisabeth, died in Weißenfels in her eighties in March; and another publication appeared about the endless Scheibe criticism, summarised by Christoph Gottlieb Schröter (1699–1782) in an article published in Lorenz Christoph Mizler's journal *Musikalische Bibliothek*.† Mizler (1711–78), who was currently working as a physician in Erfurt, had in 1738 formed an organisation called the Corresponding Society of Musical Sciences which so far contained twelve highly distinguished members, including Telemann and Handel, as well as Schröter. Although Schröter's article was fully supportive of both Birnbaum and Bach, it was not pleasant to see Scheibe continually attacked. So when Mizler invited Sebastian to join the society, for a time he remained reluctant.

However, things improved in 1747. Since the Prussian army had left Leipzig the previous Christmas, and the hostility between Saxony and Prussia was much reduced, Sebastian could at last visit Emanuel in Potsdam, near Berlin, and for the first time meet his wife and two-year-old son. Friedemann had apparently come from Halle to Leipzig to celebrate his father's 62nd birthday on 21 March, and they agreed to make the journey together by coach in little more than a month's time.

The voyage to Potsdam was evidently long and uncomfortable, over winding roads and through the hills and forests, and it probably took them at least two or three days before they arrived in the late afternoon on

---

* The portrait hung for many years in St Thomas's School, and now survives in the Altes Rathaus in the central town square. A very similar copy painted by Haußmann two years later in 1748 is now privately owned by the musician William H. Scheide, who lives in Princeton, New Jersey, USA.

† See page 275.

Sunday 7 May. In the royal household every evening there was a chamber-music performance, which naturally involved the king's harpsichordist, Emanuel. Just before the concert began, Emanuel told his boss that his father, the Leipzig music director, had just arrived, to which King Frederick immediately responded by ordering that the 'old Bach' be asked immediately to come to the palace. The concert was postponed, Emanuel rushed over to his flat to summon his father, and a few minutes later Sebastian finally entered the building and encountered the Prussian monarch.

King Frederick had secretly in his childhood studied music and learned to compose and to play the keyboard and the flute, and by now he was well aware of the complexities of the German music profession; and he was evidently aware too of the compositional and keyboard-playing skills of Johann Sebastian Bach. Since he had recently acquired several new fortepianos constructed by the instrumentalist Gottfried Silbermann (with whom Sebastian had attended the organ inspection in Naumburg the previous year), his immediate suggestion was that they walk around the palace and that Bach play and improvise on each of the instruments. They were followed by dozens of other musicians, including Friedemann and Emanuel. After a while (according to Friedemann's account many years later),* Sebastian asked the king 'to give him a subject for a fugue, in order to execute it immediately without any preparation'. This is what King Frederick played – hardly a simple melody, but rather a dramatic challenge to the apparently renowned composer:

Sebastian, however, despite his long journey and advancing age, was fully up to the challenge, and for several minutes improvised a

---

* An account provided by Friedemann to Johann Nikolaus Forkel for his biography of Bach, first published in 1802.

remarkable and complex three-part fugue based on this theme, stunning all the listeners.

The following day he was summoned again by the king, this time to perform on the organ in the city's main church, the Holy Ghost; and again he impressed the public – and within a few days a brief account of his visit appeared in the local Berlin newspaper, including the statement that 'Herr Bach found the theme propounded to him so exceedingly beautiful that he intends to set it down on paper as a regular fugue and have it engraved on copper'.[155] Despite the pressures of these close royal encounters, Sebastian must have determined to write a new set of compositions based on the theme which he could dedicate to the king, not least to assist Emanuel's career.

Within a few days, he was back in Leipzig and working non-stop on what he would entitle *Musikalisches Opfer* ('Musical Offering', BWV 1079), comprising no fewer than 16 movements. The first two are impressive three-part and six-part fugues based on the 'royal theme'; then come ten canons of different styles, some very brief and some more complex, all playable by instruments or keyboards. In addition, and by far the most impressive piece in the work, is a four-movement trio sonata for flute, violin and continuo, which has little connection to the king's theme but strongly expressive of the composer's emotions.

The pieces were completed within the next six weeks, and at considerable expense Sebastian arranged their engraving by the Schübler company in Zella, and had the text – comprising a noble letter addressed to the king – printed by Breitkopf in Leipzig. A hundred copies of the 'Musical Offering' were formally published at the beginning of July. Apart from the special edition he posted to King Frederick (he never received a reply), he handed copies to a number of friends and students, and also managed to sell some, at a price of 1 thaler [£48], providing a modest profit.

Another significant event had taken place the previous month. In June, Lorenz Christoph Mizler revisited Leipzig and succeeded in persuading Sebastian (no doubt with the Potsdam event in mind) to join the Corresponding Society of Musical Sciences of which he was secretary; Sebastian became the club's 13th member. All members were required to pay an annual subscription of two thalers [£96], to communicate with their fellow members, and (until they were aged 65) to provide the secretary with an annual scientific or musical contribution that could be published in the *Musikalische Bibliothek*. Mizler had several other expectations, including the provision of an oil-portrait of each member, which encouraged Sebastian to commission Haußmann's second version of his portrait, completed in 1748. His contribution that year, naturally, was a copy of the 'Musical Offering'; and later he also provided a copy of the brief canon depicted in his portrait, and various other works including the set of five canonic variations on the Christmas hymn for organ (BWV 769).

Sebastian's ability to produce so rapidly such an impressive work as the 'Musical Offering' re-motivated him to create other works, and the one he fully concentrated on this year was inspired by the realisation that some of his finest choral works had been based on the Latin Kyrie and Gloria texts. One incentive, since his huge range of cantatas were almost all connected to specific Sundays and could be performed only once a year, was that a complete *missa tota* work could be used any time, particularly on celebratory days like Christmas, Easter and Ascension. And the full Latin text was itself an inspiration. He had created several traditional short masses in the past, mostly in the 1730s, and over the years had performed a number of others by composers such as Durante, Bassani, Palestrina and Scarlatti. But the one that most encouraged this new project was the superb piece he had produced for the Dresden elector, Friedrich August II, back in 1733.* So those twelve Kyrie and Gloria movements for two trebles, alto, tenor and bass were the starting-point.

The work opens with a uniquely gentle four-bar choral statement in B minor, *Kyrie eleison* ('Lord, have mercy upon us'), followed by the beautiful fugal chorus accompanied by flutes, oboes d'amore, bassoon, strings and continuo. The following *Christe eleison* is a duet sung by the two treble soloists,

---

* See page 222.

accompanied by two solo violins and continuo in D major, and *Kyrie eleison* is then repeated by the choir in a new, brief and subtle fugal theme. The tremendous *Gloria in excelsis Deo* follows, with three trumpets symbolising the holy trinity. Then a sharply contrasting tone emerges with the *Laudamus te* ('We praise thee'), in which the treble soloist is accompanied by a quiet and beautiful solo violin, followed by the fugal *Gratius agimus tibi*, and the treble and tenor duet *Domine Deus* accompanied by muted strings, flute and 'pizzicato' bass. This breaks suddenly into the haunting chorale *Qui tollis peccata mundi* ('Thou that takest away the sins of the world') in the original key of B minor, representing the theological heart of the work. Three more movements bring the first section to its end: the exquisite alto aria *Qui sedes ad dexteram Patris*, a bass solo accompanied by the corno da caccia (horn), and the brisk choral *Cum Sancto Spiritu* ending in D major. This is the completion of the existing *Missa Brevis* provided to Friedrich August II.

The creation of the second section, based on the words of the Nicene Creed dating from the fourth century AD, was highly symbolic for Sebastian. These words, affirming the fundamental Christian belief, form the central part of all holy communion services, and it was essential that he create a musical indication of his own faith. The section starts in D major, the same key as the close of the first. This nine-movement second section has its own cohesive format, with *Crucifixus* at the centre (derived from the opening chorus of a cantata composed in Weimar way back in 1714),* and two movements on either side, representing Christ's incarnation, crucifixion and resurrection. The sixth movement, *Et resurrexit*, features a very striking dominance, on three occasions, by the bass singers, particularly with the words *Et iterum venturus est cum gloria judicare vivos et mortuos* ('And he shall come again with glory to judge both the quick and the dead'). This trinity of pieces at the centre is flanked by two beautiful solos, the treble and alto duet *Et in unum Dominum*, and the bass aria *Et in Spiritum Sanctum*. The section begins and ends with pairs of

---

* See page 96.

choruses, closing with the dramatic Vivace *Et expecto*. Perhaps the most striking moment in the entire work lies at the centre of this section, when *Crucifixus* moves on to *Et resurrexit*.

Section three, the Sanctus, is derived from the mass Sebastian composed for Christmas Day in 1724,* but it needed some alterations and revisions to correspond to these new settings. In this version it is a glorious D-major chorus for six-part choir, accompanied by three trombones, three oboes, timpani, bassoon, strings and continuo. The piece changes half-way through to 3/8 time, with a flowing fugue to the words *Pleni sunt coeli et terra gloria ejus* ('Heaven and earth are full of thy glory').

The fourth and final section comprises five pieces, all derived from earlier compositions, but in their structure here they achieve a magnificent conclusion to the whole mass. The splendid *Osanna*, with which the section opens, is repeated after the tenor aria *Benedictus*, and was derived from two earlier cantatas composed in the 1730s. The brief and exquisite *Agnus dei*, for alto solo, had also appeared twice before, in a wedding cantata in 1725, and (in a more complex form) in the Ascension Oratorio in 1735.† *Benedictus* and *Agnus dei* are together perhaps the most personal elements in the entire mass. And the *Dona nobis pacem* in D major, which repeats the setting of *Gratias agimus tibi* in the opening section, brings this profoundly moving work to a close. Sebastian had created, from many of his previous compositions, another masterpiece, comparable and possibly even superior to the *St Matthew Passion* composed 20 years before.‡

But opportunities to perform it in Leipzig or elsewhere – such as church restorations in Dresden or Berlin – seemed not to arise, and were that to continue the only step he could take was, rather than have it printed at huge expense, to make sure the carefully-written manuscript

---

* See page 166.

† See page 244.

‡ The Mass in B Minor, BWV 232.

survived (Emanuel many years later described it as 'the great Catholic mass') as a work in which he felt great pride and confidence.*

One of Sebastian's many talented music pupils had recently become very close to the family. Johann Christoph Altnickol (1720–59) had begun studying theology at Leipzig University in spring 1744, had immediately joined the student group, and was showing increasing talent as a bass singer, violinist and cellist; and on graduation he decided to enter the music profession. On his 28th birthday, 1 January 1748, Sebastian wrote him a lavish testimonial stating that 'not only did he act for four years diligently as assistant for our *Chorus Musicus*, but he also has shown, in addition to his vocal performance, such outstanding work on various instruments as one could desire from an accomplished musician. A number of fine church compositions of his have found no less ample approval in our town.' This immediately enabled Altnickol to obtain the post of organist and schoolteacher at a town in Silesia; but because he had fallen in love with Sebastian's daughter Lieschen (now 22), he begged her father to try and find him another appointment nearer by. So on 24 July Sebastian contacted the town council in Naumburg, where he had handled an organ test two years earlier, and strongly recommended Altnickol for the post of organist there. In due course he was granted the appointment, living only a few miles west of Leipzig. He and Lieschen were married in St Thomas's Church on 20 January 1749. (Sadly, Altnickol died ten years later.) The same church, on Good Friday in April, was the venue for the fourth performance of the 25-year-old *St John Passion* (BWV 245).

Although the long disputes with his headmaster Ernesti, and with his former student Scheibe's critical press article, had calmed down several years before, they were none the less vivid in Sebastian's mind, and in May 1749 a published article sent to him by another of his former students, Johann Friedrich Doles (1715–97), infuriated him by recalling those frightful

---

* Present-day scholars believe that its first complete performance appears not to have occurred until 1859, more than a century later, in Leipzig, performed by the Riedel-Verein.

battles. Doles had been the school music teacher in Frieberg (not far from Dresden) since 1744, and after a recent school performance of one of his choral compositions the headmaster, Johann Gottlieb Biedermann, had published a pamphlet entitled *De vita musica* ('Of musical life') in which he jokingly criticised the world of music and strongly argued that the subject had much too high a position in school education. This reminded Sebastian of the reasons Ernesti had endlessly argued against his right to appoint the prefects for his four choirs; and this in turn stimulated him to re-embark on the long fight to preserve this national tradition. So, as a member of Mizler's Corresponding Society of Musical Sciences, he contacted his fellow member Christoph Gottlieb Schröter, who had written the Scheibe summary back in 1746, and commissioned him to review and invalidate Biedermann's ridiculous publication. Schröter undertook the commission, agreeing that the article was absurdly critical of musicians in general, and that it clearly revealed the headmaster's 'unfriendly attitude to the innocent art of music'. Sebastian's idea, presumably, was that if Schröter wrote a convincing review it would be published in Mizler's *Musikalische Bibliothek* magazine. Indeed, by December 1749 a draft had been prepared and Sebastian wrote to another of his former students, Georg Friedrich Einicke (1710–70), now a music teacher in the western town of Frankenhausen, saying that 'Schröter's criticism is well written, and to my taste, and it will soon make its appearance in print'. And he added the sarcastic comment that, if the campaign continued successfully, he had no doubt that Biedermann's dirty ears would be cleaned out, and 'become more fit to listening to music'.

But in fact, the more Sebastian studied Schröter's piece, the more intensely he felt that it was far too polite in view of Biedermann's ludicrous attack on the world of music. So he started to make dramatic alterations to the article, strengthening as far as he could the cases in favour of music teaching as a crucial element in school education. He then sent a printed version of his revisions to Einicke, who passed it on to Schröter. Unfortunately, this caused the dispute to rage up to the level of the previous ones, because Schröter was himself infuriated, responding to Einicke that Bach's 'violent changes made in my criticism offend me deeply', that no reader familiar with his style of writing could possibly believe that the revised version had been written by him, and that he should inform Bach of this. Einicke had no choice but to pass these comments on to Sebastian, who then realised that once again he had made a foolish blunder in relation to his fellow musicians. So on 26 May 1750 he wrote back to Einicke, saying, 'To Mr Schröter please extend my compliments until such time as I am able to write, since I wish to disclaim the blame for the changes to his criticism, as they are not at all my fault; on the contrary, they are entirely the fault of the man who took care of the publication.'

This untruth recalls the incessant comments he made in defence of Ernesti's attacks – and once again, once Einicke had passed it on to Schröter, the result was disastrous. On 5 June Schröter wrote to Einicke:

> The music director Bach remains at fault, no matter how he twists and turns, now or in the future. But he can put a good and prompt end to this dispute if he will, first, openly acknowledge that he is the author of the piece; secondly, expose the fact that headmaster Biedermann's principal purpose, despite his title, was not at all directed to the praise of music and its kindred arts, and that the two and a half sheets of 'Flowers in praise of music' represent only a torn covering through which his unfriendly attitude towards the innocent art of music is clearly to be seen; and thirdly, at the same time the unknown author of the article, who is claimed to be 'honest', must be challenged to identify himself. Indeed, such an action on the part of a music director would do Mr Bach unusual honour, give our Mr Mattheson an unexpected and well-merited pleasure, and contribute to the further growth of the noble art of music. This well-intended proposal is made, with the request that it is to be transmitted with most obedient compliments to Leipzig, by C. G. Schröter.[156]

Einicke promptly passed this message on to Sebastian by post.

But Sebastian had become unwell. Occasional illnesses, particularly affecting his vision (possibly owing to hypoglycemia), had already started in the spring of 1749, with the dreadful result that the town council immediately started considering who should replace him when he died. Indeed in June one of the potential candidates, Johann Gottlob Harrer (1703–55) – recommended by his Dresden employer Count Heinrich von Brühl (1700–63) – was actually given a formal audition by the council,[157] which undermined Sebastian with the impression that the council were longing to get rid of him. Although he was of course aware that ageing was impairing his physical health, when the council election service took place on Monday 25 August he decided to perform one of the most powerful works he had ever composed for this annual event, the cantata entitled *Wir denken dir, Gott*, first produced in 1731,* with its splendid organ part in the opening sinfonia, in the hope that this would demonstrate that his organ-playing abilities had by no means declined. Whatever view the town councillors took after this performance, at least there appeared to be no further candidate auditions implying that he would soon to be gone.

Alas, by the spring of 1750 his eyesight was continuing to decline. Perhaps fortunately, a distinguished English oculist and eye surgeon named John Taylor (1703–72) – who had treated King George II, the Pope, and several aristocratic families throughout Europe – had travelled to Leipzig to give a university lecture on his subject, arriving on 28 March. Clearly this was the ideal doctor to treat Sebastian's failing eyesight, and two or three days later Taylor gave him an elaborate cataract treatment with the result that (as a journal in Berlin reported on 4 April) 'he has recovered the full sharpness of his sight, an unspeakable piece of good fortune that many thousands of people will be very far from begrudging this famous composer, and for which they cannot sufficiently thank Dr Taylor'.[158] The doctor also treated two other Leipzig men, named Koppen and Meyer, and because several

---

* BWV 29. See page 221.

other inhabitants called for his help, he postponed his intended departure to Berlin for several days. As it happened, Sebastian's eyesight began to decline again, and on 6 April, the day before his departure, Dr Taylor performed a second operation on him.

For a little while longer, thereby, Sebastian was able to cope with his heavy school and town responsibilities, particularly with the assistance of his senior pupils; but in May problems arose again, not so much to do with his eyesight but swelling and stomach pain. Indeed, that month the university medical faculty reported that Koppen and Meyer's operations had been fairly successful, but Mr Bach was 'suffering from bouts of inflammation and the like'. Around 20 July, he suffered a stroke and intense fever, and was attended by two senior town physicians. It was evident now that his life was about to end. On 22 July, the archdeacon of St Thomas's Church, Christoph Wolle, attended him in his bedroom and administered the sacrament. Six days later, on Tuesday 28 July, he died peacefully at around 8.20 in the evening.

Three days later, on Friday 31 July, the funeral took place at St John's Church, attached to St John's Hospital outside the town walls, and Sebastian was buried there, in his 66th year.

Epilogue

Bach had achieved a great deal in his life through the first half of the 18th century, including the huge range of compositions which remained in the hands of the family and fellow musicians throughout eastern Germany, his connections with royal families and aristocrats, and the tutoring of a large number of players who continued to perform his works and dominate the music profession. But it seems pretty clear from the surviving evidence that he had never become an international superstar, as it were, and that he was by no means as popular a figure as some of his contemporaries such as Handel and Telemann. Even his burial in the grounds of St John's Church did not include a grand gravestone indicating exactly where his body was laid,* and there appears not to have been a later memorial service. His job as cantor was promptly filled, under the town council proceedings, by Johann Gottlob Harrer in early October, and council records reveal that according to the account of the chief magistrate, Dr Christian Ludwig Stieglitz, in the course of trials for the post, 'Mr Bach had been a great musician, it is true, but not

---

* For many decades after his death, it was apparently assumed that he was buried a few yards south of St John's Church, and 144 years later, on 22 October 1894, his bones were claimed to have been discovered and were re-buried inside the church under the altar. The church was destroyed in World War II (in 1943), but the tomb survived; and in 1950 the remains were again transferred, this time to the chancel in St Thomas's Church. In recent times, scientists interested in the history of diseases have sought to test the remains using DNA analysis in order to determine his illnesses; but the St Thomas's Church authorities have refused them access, which suggests a fear that the church's grand chancel does not, after all, contain him. See page xii.

a schoolteacher, so that a person must be sought to fill his place as cantor of the St Thomas School who would be skilful in both capacities; he believed that both could be found in Mr Harrer, who had stated that he was master of both the Latin and the Greek languages, and had promised to accept willingly his subordinate place; therefore he wished to give him his vote for the post of cantor of the St Thomas School.'[159]

Furthermore, there do not appear to have been many press announcements of Bach's death, or obituaries. A brief death notice appeared in a Berlin newspaper on 6 August, stating that:

> last Tuesday, that is, the 28th instant, the well-known musician Mr Joh. Seb. Bach, royal Polish and electoral Saxon court composer, kapellmeister of the princely court of Saxe-Weißenfels and of Anhalt-Cöthen, choral director and cantor at the St Thomas School here, in the 66th year of his life, from the unhappy consequences of the very unsuccessful eye operation by a well-known English oculist. The loss of this unusually able man is greatly mourned by all true connoisseurs of music.[160]

The only proper obituary, published four years later by Lorenz Mizler in his magazine *Musikalische Bibliothek*, was written by Emanuel with the help of Sebastian's former student Johann Friedrich Agricola (1720–74).[161] This is a thoroughly revealing, though brief, account of the life of Johann Sebastian Bach as understood by his second-eldest son, then aged 50. Indeed, it is the only detailed document about Bach that has ever or will ever authentically portray what really happened in those 65 years.

Emanuel wrote it towards the end of 1750 and sent it to Mizler in March 1751. Interestingly – and perhaps the same is true of many obituaries – it contains quite a range of errors, no doubt first because of children's unawareness of their parents' early years, and secondly to promote the family reputation. For example, it opens with the statement that 'Johann Sebastian Bach belongs to a family that seems to have received a love and aptitude for music as a gift of nature to all its members in common. So much is certain, that Veit Bach, the founder of the family, and all his descendants, even to the seventh present generation, have been devoted to music, and all save perhaps a very few have made it their profession.' In fact, Sebastian's family tree makes it perfectly clear that while a large proportion of family members were professional musicians, 25 per cent were not.

The obituary goes on to explain why virtually all the Bach musicians stayed in Thuringia, on the grounds that they loved the land, its local rulers and their fellow countrymen. This of course was not the case with Sebastian's sons, all of whom travelled far more widely around Europe to further their careers.* Another small but interesting error comes next, in the description of Sebastian's being orphaned at the age of nine and moving to live with his grown-up brother Johann Christoph. Emanuel states that Christoph died shortly after the dreadful row over Sebastian's secret copy of his brother's music manuscript. In fact, Christoph lived much longer, dying in 1721 aged 50.

As it proceeds, the obituary's details not surprisingly become more accurate, and the longest paragraph is devoted to the Marchand story.† There is a bit more about Weimar, and surprisingly little about Leipzig – no doubt Emanuel was all too aware that his father had fallen out with so many of this grand town's officials and employers. After a brief description of his ageing and death, Emanuel adds a list of his father's compositions, (a) the few that were printed, and (b) 'the unpublished works of the late Bach [which] were approximately as follows' – with several more errors. For example, there is absolutely no evidence that Sebastian created 'Five full annual cycles [*Jahrgänge*] of church pieces, for all the Sundays and holidays'; indeed, it is pretty clear, as we have seen (Chapter 8), that the maximum span was three years. Emanuel also mentions 'Many oratorios … Magnificats', and 'Five Passions', when it is almost certainly the case that there were only three, *St Mark*, *St John* and *St Matthew*.

---

* See page 243.

† See page 102-3.

There is then a succinct account of Sebastian's two marriages, including the deaths of Emanuel's mother, and the deaths of 11 of his 19 brothers and sisters. This is followed by three interesting and extended paragraphs describing Sebastian's exceptional musical abilities: his range of compositions, amazing performance skills, and unique hearing. Indeed, he is described as 'the greatest organist and clavier player that we have ever had'.

From the ensuing decades a number of comments and strong approvals of his compositions and other talents have survived, mostly articulated by people in the music profession; so he was not forgotten. But his prime legacy was in the continued – and continuing – use of his keyboard works, particularly the 48 Preludes and Fugues (*The Well-Tempered Clavier*), in music teaching. Their eventual publication at the beginning of the 19th century, by Hoffmeister & Kühnel in Leipzig, led to the appearance of Forkel's biography (first published in 1802, and in English in 1820),[162] on which all subsequent accounts of Bach's life have been based.

The surviving evidence also suggests that family affairs continued to be troublesome – a reminder of the problems Bach experienced in his orphaned youth. To start with, despite the several months in 1750 when he was aware that death was approaching, he wrote no will to ensure the security of his wife and younger children. As a result, within a mere two weeks of his death Magdalena was forced to make a financial application to the town council, and another in October to the university.[163] His estate and possessions were examined during the following months,[164] and despite the wide range of musical instruments he owned (seven harpsichords, three violins, three violas, two cellos, a double bass, a viola da gamba, a lute and a spinet), as well as his substantial book library and many other objects, the total value amounted to a mere 1,159 thalers [£55,632], of which Magdalena was entitled to only one-third. She died in poverty less than ten years later, on 27 February 1760, aged 58.

The rest of his possessions were dispersed among his children, and in particular most of the vast range of handwritten music ended up with his two eldest sons, Friedemann and Emanuel. Friedemann fell into employment and financial difficulties in the 1760s, and is believed to have sold a great deal; but Emanuel was far more protective of his inheritance, so that most of what has survived derives from him.

But the reason Bach became world-famous in the 19th century is strongly associated with the performance in Berlin of the *St Matthew Passion* by Mendelssohn in 1829. Felix Mendelssohn-Bartholdy, who was born in Hamburg in 1809 and had already become an internationally renowned pianist and composer, was a member of Carl Friedrich Zelter's Berlin *Singakademie*, and it was there that he encountered the Passion and decided to arrange a public performance of it. Zelter (1758–1832), who had been acquainted with Friedemann and Emanuel Bach (both of whom had died in the 1780s), had acquired copies of a considerable range of their father's works, including concertos, cantatas, motets and the Mass in B Minor. Zelter suggested that the Passion was inappropriate for public performance, but Mendelssohn's belief in it was unwavering, based as it was on a strong family tradition: two of his grandparents had studied music with one of J. S. Bach's pupils, J. P. Kirnberger, who had promoted and preserved much of Bach's music throughout the 18th century.

Mendelssohn's performance of the *St Matthew Passion* in Berlin took place in the *Singakademie* on 11 March 1829 (with several parts omitted), on what was believed to be the centenary of its first production. Several more performances took place in other cities, and over the next ten years the work became more and more famous. So, increasingly, musicians throughout Germany sought to rediscover the works of this lost genius, and in due course the *St John Passion*, the Mass in B Minor and a number of cantatas were included in the concert repertoire. Gradually, Bach was becoming internationally renowned. Two or three more events are worth mentioning: in 1850 (seven years after the creation of the Handel Society in London) the *Bach-Gesellschaft* (Bach Society) was formed in Leipzig, with the principal aim of producing a complete collection of Bach's works; in 1874

Philipp Spitta (1841–94) published the first volume of his monumental biography of Bach, completed in 1880; and in 1875 the Bach Choir was founded in London, providing the first two British performances of the B Minor Mass, conducted by Otto Goldschmidt on 26 April and 8 May 1876. In the world today, Bach is probably the second most popular classical composer of all time, Mozart being the first and Beethoven the third.

******

But none the less the truth about his character and his life experiences has for two centuries been thoroughly unacknowledged or misunderstood, largely under the influence of the hagiographical account written by Forkel at the beginning of the 19th century. All the subsequent biographies have been written in the academic and musicological style, with the result that despite the huge range of available evidence he has always been understood to be a unique genius, a consummate intellectual, world-famous, profoundly religious, and frequently undermined by idiotic employers and colleagues. The account in this book strongly suggests that these prevailing assumptions are by no means wholly correct, and that his life and work, though long and hard, involved a considerable range of discords as well as harmonies.

The positive elements are significant and remarkable, and may be summarised as follows: he was certainly an exceptionally skilful musician, particularly on the organ and harpsichord; a huge range of his compositions are masterpieces which continue to move and delight audiences around the world; and he worked extremely hard throughout his life, particularly in writing music and teaching young musicians.

On the other hand, as this biography makes apparent, a close study of Bach also reveals a number of negative elements. For example, although much of his music is superb and masterly, if you explore it all you find that a lot of it is not – and indeed that Scheibe's famous but modest criticism has some truth in it, including that 'This great man would be the admiration of whole nations if he had more comfort, if he did not take away the natural element in his pieces by giving them a bombastic and confused style, and if he did not darken their beauty by an excess of artifice'.* If any of us should take the time to read or listen to all the thousands of works he composed, we would inevitably agree that many of them are boring or troublesome or over-complex; and therefore it should be understood that, although he had unique talents in the wide ranges of music performance and composition, he was neither a perfectionist nor a full-time genius.

Although Bach was commended by several aristocrats and senior employers, he was involved in a remarkable range of rows and disputes. His supporters in modern times have always maintained that people like Geyersbach, the Arnstadt consistory, Duke Wilhelm Ernst, Johann August Ernesti and Johann Adolph Scheibe were idiots or monsters, because they criticised or disputed with Bach; but there is clear evidence that at least some of them, particularly Ernesti and Scheibe, were exceptionally diligent, industrious, honest and intelligent, and their surviving criticisms clearly reveal his negative characteristics. Ernesti, for example, who looks friendly and honest in his fine portrait painted by Anton Graff, led a remarkable life as theologian, writer and teacher. After working at the Leipzig St Thomas's School for 28 years (1731–59), he was appointed professor of theology at the university, where he remained for more than 20 years until his death in September 1781, aged 74. The standard academic assumption is that he showed no liking for music, but that is most unconvincing if you read the full details of his laborious complaints about the school's cantor.

And so over two centuries the complex life of this famous composer has remained, to many general music-lovers, a mystery. Changing that has been the main purpose of this book.

---

* See page 271.

JULIAN SHUCKBURGH

In the opening Introduction, speculation is mentioned.* But that is not to imply that much of what has been related is based on theory or guesswork; over the last 125 years an impressive range of explorations and discoveries by academics throughout the world has revealed a vast amount of information about Bach. The essential conclusions in this account are that because he, despite his talents, had an exceptionally troubled life, he was unable to achieve the same fame, power and financial stability as several of his contemporaries. Moreover, connecting the events of his daily and domestic life with his compositions can lead to some striking new insights. In other words, chronology is the major source of revelation.

---

* See page 2.

Endnotes

1   Johann Mattheson, *Das beschützte Orchestre* (1717); H. T. David and A. Mendel, revised and expanded by C. Wolff (eds): *The New Bach Reader:* NBR 318.
2   Christoph Wolff, *Johann Sebastian Bach: The Learned Musician* (New York 2000).
3   *Bach-Dokumente II*, no. 429.
4   *Bach-Dokumente II*, no. 200; *NBR* 319.
5   *Bach-Dokumente II*, no. 400; *NBR* 343.
6   *Lorenz Mizlers Muzikalische Bibliothek* was published at irregular intervals from 1736. Bach's obituary appeared in its final issue.
7   Recorded in the Eisenach church register (*Bach-Dokumente II*, no. 1).
8   This family tradition is described in J. N. Forkel's 1802 biography, presumably based on information provided by Sebastian's son Carl Philipp Emanuel Bach. See *NBR*, Part VI, p. 424.
9   Phillipe Ariès's *Centuries of Childhood*, originally published in France as *L'Enfant et la familiale sous l'ancien régime* (1960), is the prime creator of these concepts, supported by many more recent works, such as Lawrence Stone's *The Family, Sex and Marriage in England 1500–1800*. (London 1977).
10 Linda A. Pollock, *Forgotten Children: Parent–Child Relations from 1500 to 1900* (Cambridge 1983).
11 *Bach-Dokumente II*, no. 2.
12 Conrad Freyse, *Eisenacher Dokumente um Sebastian Bach* (Leipzig 1933), p. 20.
13 Ditto.
14 Ditto, p. 21.
15 *Bach-Dokumente II*, no. 3.
16 See *Bach-Jahrbuch* 1985, p. 60.
17 A. F. Büsching: *A New System of Geography* (London 1762), Vol. 6, p. 52.
18 *Bach-Dokumente II*, no. 4.
19 *Bach-Jahrbuch* 1985, p. 60.
20 Werner David, *Johann Sebastian Bachs Orgeln* (Berlin 1951), p. 79.
21 J. Gagliardi, *Germany Under the Old Regime* (Harlow 1991).
22 See Spitta, Vol. 1, p. 189.
23 Konrad Küster, *Der junge Bach* (Stuttgart 1996), p. 93.
24 A. F. Büsching, Vol. 6, p. 237.
25 *NBR* 306.
26 S. F. Daw, 'Age of Boys' Puberty', *Human Biology*, Vol. 42, 1970.
27 See Spitta, vol. 1, pp. 194ff.
28 Friedrich Erhardt Niedt, *MusikalischeHandleitung*, 2nd ed. (Hamburg 1721), Vol. 2, pp. 176–7.

29 This story was recounted, many years after Sebastian's death, by Friedrich Wilhelm Marpurg, a writer on music who had known him and his two eldest sons and presumably heard it from them (*Bach-Dokumente*, III, no. 914).
30 John Mainwairing: *Memoirs of the Life of George Frederic Handel* (London 1760).
31 BWV 993. See C. Wolff, p. 75.
32 *Bach-Dokumente I*, no. 38. See *NBR* 189, Bach's letter to Herr Klemm, a Sangerhausen town councillor, written 34 years later in November 1736.
33 *Bach-Dokumente II*, no. 6.
34 *Bach-Dokumente II*, no. 7.
35 *Bach-Dokumente II*, no. 8.
36 Rutland Boughton, *John Sebastian Bach* (London 1930), p. 76; see also C. Wolff, pp. 479–80.
37 *Bach-Dokumente II*, no. 8.
38 A. F. Büsching: *A New System of Geography* (London 1762), Vol. 6, p. 118.
39 Markus Schiffner: *Der junge Bach in Arnstadt* (Arnstadt 1995).
40 A full account of these events, from the Arnstadt Consistory records, is reproduced in *Bach-Dokumente* (Leipzig and Kassel 1963–72), nos. 14, 16 and 17. See *NBR* 19–21.
41 *Bach-Dokumente II*, no. 16.
42 See page 131.
43 See pages 14–15.
44 The average age at which men married was apparently 27 or 28, and women were 25 or 26 (Michael Anderson: *Approaches to the History of the Western Family 1500–1914* (London 1980).
45 A. F. Büsching, *A New System of Geography* (London 1762), Vol. 6, p. 459.
46 *Bach-Dokumente II*, nos. 19–21.
47 *Bach-Dokumente II*, no. 28.
48 *NBR*, Part VI, p. 424.
49 *Bach-Dokumente I*, no. 83.
50 *Bach-Dokumente I*, no. 1.
51 *Bach-Dokumente I*, no. 21.
52 Konrad Küster, *Der junge Bach* (Stuttgart 1996), pp. 186ff.
53 *Bach-Dokumente II*, no. 38.
54 See C. Wolff, *Johann Sebastian Bach: The Learned Musician* (New York 2000), p. 121.
55 *Bach-Dokumente I*, no. 148.
56 *Bach-Dokumente II*, no. 49.
57 See Richard Petzoldt, *Georg Philipp Telemann, Leben und Werk* (Leipzig 1967).
58 *Bach-Dokumente II*, no. 51.
59 *Bach-Dokumente II*, no. 55.
60 *Bach-Jahrbuch* 1994, p. 32; and *Bach-Dokumente II*, no. 63.
61 *Bach-Dokumente II*, no. 63.
62 *Bach-Dokumente I*, no. 2.
63 *Bach-Dokumente I*, no. 4.
64 *Bach-Dokumente II*, no. 66.
65 *NBR* 39e.
66 *Bach-Dokumente II*, no. 67.
67 The cantatas from this period that survive are, in their probable chronological order, BWV 208, 182, 12, 172, 21, 199, 61, 63, 152, 18, 54, 31, 165, 185, 163, 132, 155, 80a, 164, 161, 162, 70a, 186a, and 147a – which includes the famous chorale known as 'Jesu, Joy of Man's Desiring'. BWV 61 (*Nun komm, der Heiden Heiland*) is regarded by many present-day Bach experts as deservedly one of the most renowned cantatas, but that is not my view.

68 *Bach-Dokumente II*, no. 74.
69 *Bach-Dokumente II*, no. 73.
70 *Bach-Dokumente I*, no. 5.
71 *Bach-Dokumente I*, no. 85.
72 Charles S. Terry, *Bach: A Biography* (London 1928), pp. 109–10.
73 *Bach-Dokumente II*, no. 84.
74 Telemann described this event in one of his autobiographies, published in Johann Mattheson, *Grundlage einer Ehrenpforte* (Hamburg 1740), p. 364.
75 *Bach-Dokumente I*, nos. 167, 87, 109.
76 A. F. Büsching, *A New System of Geography* (London 1762), Vol. 6, p. 106.
77 C. Wolff, *Johann Sebastian Bach: The Learned Musician* (New York 2000), pp. 193–4.
78 *Bach-Dokumente II*, no. 91.
79 *Bach-Dokumente II*, no. 86.
80 *Bach-Dokumente II*, no. 94.
81 *Bach-Dokumente II*, no. 95.
82 *Bach-Dokumente I*, no. 149.
83 *Bach-Dokumente II*, no. 100.
84 *Bach-Dokumente II*, no. 102.
85 *Bach-Dokumente II*, no. 150.
86 *Bach-Dokumente II*, no. 110.
87 C. Wolff, *Johann Sebastian Bach: The Learned Musician* (New York 2000), p. 218.
88 *Bach-Dokumente I*, no. 8.
89 *NBR* 88.
90 *NBR* 90.
91 B. Smallman, *The Background of Passion Music* (London 1957).
92 A number of town council and other documents referring to Bach's appointment have survived. See *NBR* 93–108.
93 *Bach-Dokumente II*, no. 124.
94 Appeals Councillor Platz: see *NBR* 94c.
95 *Bach-Dokumente I*, no. 91.
96 *Bach-Dokumente II*, no. 149.
97 *Bach-Dokumente II*, no. 139.
98 *Bach-Dokumente II*, no. 145.
99 J. G. Keysler, *Travels through Germany, Bohemia, Hungary, Switzerland, Italy, and Lorraine* (London 1756)
100 Tanya Kevorkian, 'The Rise of the Poor, Weak, and Wicked: Poor Care, Punishment, Religion, and Patriarchy in Leipzig, 1700–1730', *Journal of Social History* (Autumn 2000).
101 Tanya Kevorkian, p. 165.
102 *Bach-Dokumente II*, no. 129.
103 *Bach-Dokumente I*, no. 23.
104 *J. S. Bach*, translated by Ernest Newman, Breitkopf & Hartel (London 1911). First published in French in 1905.
105 A full account of the life and work of Christiane Mariane von Ziegler, including her brief relationship with Bach and full details of the nine cantatas he composed in 1725 using her text, is available in *A Woman's Voice in Baroque Music: Mariane von Ziegler and J. S. Bach*, by Dr Mark A. Peters, Aldershot 2008. He states that 'the Ziegler/Bach cantatas deserve detailed attention by scholars and performers alike'.
106 *Bach-Dokumente II*, no. 12.
107 *Bach-Jahrbuch* 1985, p. 85.
108 *Bach-Dokumente III*, no. 628, no. 56b.

109 *NBR* 127.
110 Throughout most of the 20th century it was believed that the first performance did not take place until 1729, but more recent research has revealed that it was almost certainly performed two years earlier.
111 *Johann Sebastian Bach: His Work and Influence on the Music of Germany, 1685–1750*, by Philipp Spitta, in three volumes, translated by Clara Bell and J. A. Fuller-Maitland (London 1889), Vol. II, p. 537.
112 BWV 193, *Ihr Tore zu Zion*. See David Schulenberg, contributor to *J. S. Bach*, ed. Malcolm Boyd, (Oxford 1999), p. 237.
113 *Christiane Eberhardine und August der Starke: Eine Ehetragödie*, by Paul Haake (Leipzig 1930).
114 *Bach-Dokumente II*, no. 227.
115 A full 34-page account of Frau Christiane Eberhardine's memorial service in Leipzig was written and published in 1727 by Christoph Ernst Sicul, entitled *Das Tränender Leipzig, oder Solennia Lipsiensia* (Leipzig 1727). It contains a brief mention of 'Herr Capellmeister Johann Sebastian Bach' as the composer of the *Trauer-musik* and the player of the harpsichord; and all 72 lines of Gottsched's poem.
116 *Bach-Dokumente II*, no. 246.
117 *Bach-Dokumente I*, no. 19. Another letter, written by the town council in February 1730 to Dr Deyling, and possibly influenced by Bach, orders that no new hymns should be introduced in any of the church services without the council's approval (*NBR* 149).
118 *Bach-Dokumente I*, no. 63.
119 *Bach-Dokumente II*, no. 262.
120 Philipp Spitta, *Johann Sebastian Bach*, Vol. 2, p. 242.
121 *Bach-Dokumente II*, nos. 280–81.
122 *Bach-Dokumente I*, no. 22.
123 *Bach-Dokumente I*, no. 23.
124 *Bach-Dokumente I*, no. 432.
125 *Bach-Dokumente II*, nos. 200, 239, 263, 268–9, 283, 304, 408, 432, 449, 463, 465–6, 469, 471 482, 514, 522, 526, 542, 575; Christian G. Gerber, *Geschichte der Kirchen-Ceremonien in Sachsen* (Leipzig 1732), p. 283; Johann Adolph Scheibe, *Critischer Musikus*, 2nd ed. (Leipzig 1745), pp. 148 and 645–6. See *NBR* 318–342.
126 *Bach-Dokumente I*, no. 166.
127 *Bach-Dokumente I*, no. 27.
128 *Bach-Dokumente II*, no. 351 and *I*, no. 119.
129 *Bach-Dokumente I*, no. 184. See *NBR* 302–03.
130 See facsimile in *Neue Bach-Ausgabe: Kritischer Bericht* II/5, p. 61 (Christoph Wolff).
131 *Bach-Dokumente I*, no. 32.
132 *Bach-Dokumente I*, no. 33.
133 *Bach-Dokumente I*, no. 34.
134 *Bach-Dokumente II*, no. 382.
135 *Bach-Dokumente I*, no. 35.
136 *Bach-Dokumente I*, no. 383.
137 *Bach-Dokumente I*, no. 37.
138 *Bach-Dokumente I*, no. 38.
139 *Bach-Dokumente I*, no. 39.
140 *Bach-Dokumente II*, no. 388.
141 *Bach-Dokumente I*, no. 39.
142 *Bach-Dokumente I*, no. 40.
143 *Bach-Dokumente I*, no. 41.
144 *Bach-Dokumente II*, no. 406.

145 Johann Adolph Scheibe, *Critischer Musikus* (Leipzig 1745), p. 148.
146 *Bach-Dokumente II*, no. 400.
147 *Bach-Dokumente I*, no. 68.
148 *Bach-Dokumente II*, no. 409.
149 *Bach-Dokumente II*, no. 413.
150 *Bach-Dokumente II*, no. 463.
151 *Bach-Dokumente I*, no. 42.
152 *Bach-Dokumente I*, no. 42.
153 *Bach-Dokumente II*, no. 439.
154 *Bach-Dokumente II*, no. 511.
155 *Bach-Dokumente II*, no. 554. The report was printed on 11 May 1747.
156 *Bach-Dokumente II*, no. 592.
157 *Bach-Dokumente II*, nos. 583–4.
158 *Bach-Dokumente II*, nos. 598–9.
159 *Bach-Dokumente II*, nos. 614–15.
160 *Bach-Dokumente II*, no. 612.
161 *Bach-Dokumente II*, no. 323.
162 *NBR*, Part VI.
163 *Bach-Dokumente II*, nos. 617, 625, 626.
164 *Bach-Dokumente II*, no. 627

Appendix 1

The compositions of J. S. Bach, listed chronologically

Notes to table head

1. BWV is the catalogue of all Bach's works (*Bach-Werke-Verzeichnis*), produced by Wolfgang Schmieder under the title *Thematisch-systematisches Verzeichnis der musikalischen Werke von Johann Sebastian Bach* in 1950, and revised in 1990. Anh. is *anhang*, appendix.

2. The scorings are abbreviated as follows: A (alto solo), B (bass solo), bc (basso continuo), bn (bassoon), cdc (corna da caccia), cdt (corna da tirarsi), cl (keyboard instrument, e.g. clavichord, harpsichord, etc.), ct (cornet), flt (flute), flp (flauto piccolo), hn (horn), hpd (harpsichord), inc (including), ob (oboe), ob d'am (oboe d'amore), ob da c (oboe da caccia), obbl (obbligato), org (organ), rec (recorder), S (soprano solo), str (violins 1 and 2, viola), T (tenor solo), timp (timpani), tb (trombone), tr (trumpet), trdt (tromba da tirarsi), v da g (viola da gamba), v d'am (viola d'amore), va (viola), vc (violoncello), vcp (violoncello piccolo), vn (violin), vnp (violino piccolo), vv (choral voices).

3. The comments are brief summaries of the works' sources and purposes, as far as they are known. 'Text' indicates the source of what is known about the vocal works. The star ratings (see Appendix 2) are the author's personal assessments: three stars for a masterpiece; two stars for a superb work; one star for an excellent work. Also included are references to accounts of the works in the main chapters.

Date	Type	BWV[1]	Title
?1702	Keyboard	992	Capriccio in B♭ major
c. 1702	Keyboard	993	Capriccio in E major
?c. 1704	Keyboard	963	Sonata in D major
?1704–07	Church Cantata	150	Nach dir, Herr, verlanget mich
Before 1705	Organ	531	Prelude & Fugue in C major
Before 1705	Organ	533	Prelude & Fugue in E minor
Before 1705	Organ	549	Prelude & Fugue in C minor/D minor
Before 1705	Organ	565	Toccata in D minor
Before 1705	Organ	568	Prelude in G major
Before 1705	Organ	569	Prelude in A minor
Before 1705	Organ	570	Fantasia in C major
Before 1705	Organ	588	Canzona in D minor
Before 1705	Organ	921	Prelude (Fantasia) in C minor
Before 1705	Organ	Anh. 205	Fantasia in C minor
Before 1705	Keyboard	965	Sonata in A minor
Before 1705	Keyboard	966	Sonata in C major
Before 1705	Organ	1090–1120	Neumeister Chorales
c. 1705	Keyboard	818	Suite in A minor
c. 1705	Keyboard	820	Ouverture in F major
c. 1705	Keyboard	967	Sonata in A minor
1705–17	Organ	535	Prelude & Fugue in G minor
Before 1707	Organ	551	Prelude & Fugue in A minor
Before 1707	Organ	574	Fugue in C major
Before 1707	Organ	578	Fugue in G minor
Before 1707	Keyboard	822	Suite in G minor
Before 1707	Keyboard	832	Partita in A major
Early 1708	Aria	524	Quodlibet
1707–08	Church Cantata	131	Aus der Tiefen rufe ich, Herr, zu dir
1707–08 (?)	Church Cantata	106	Gottes Zeit ist die allerbeste Zeit

Scoring[2]	Comment/text/rating (one to three stars)[3]
cl	*Capriccio sopra la lontananza de il fratro diletissimo* (not *fratello*, so not Johann Jacob). See p. 42.
cl	In honour of his brother Johann Christoph Bach of Ohrdruf. See pp. 42, 53 and 90.
cl	
SATB, 4vv, bn, 2vn, bc	* Some academics believe it dates c. 1708–9. Psalm 25:1–2, 5, and 15. Brahms used the theme from the final chorus in his 4th symphony. See p. 64.
org	See p. 43
org	See p. 43
org	It is believed to have been revised after 1723. See p. 24.
org	*** Regarded by some academics as doubtful and spurious. See p. 47.
org	
org	
org	
org	
org	
org	
cl	Based on J. A. Reincken's *Hortus musicus* (see pp. 40, 41 and 64).
cl	Based on J. A. Reincken's *Hortus musicus* (see pp. 40, 41 and 64).
org	A collection of organ chorales discovered in 1984, of which about 30 are attributed to Bach and believed to have been composed in this period. It was compiled by J. G. Neumeister (1757–1840).
cl	
cl	
cl	
org	
org	
org	Based on a trio sonata by Giovanni Legrenzi (1626–90).
org	
cl	
cl	
SATB, bc	Fragment, for a wedding in Mühlhausen, late October. See p. 70.
SATB, 4vv, ob, bn, str, bc, inc bn	Libretto probably by G. C. Eilmar. Psalm 130; B. Ringwaldt hymn vv.2 & 5. See pp. 72, 85.
SATB, 4vv, 2rec, 2v da g, bc	'Actus Tragicus.' 2:**. Acts 17:28; Psalm 90:12; Isaiah 38:1; Eccl. 14:17; Rev. 22:20; Psalm 31:5; Luke 23:43; v.1 Luther hymn (1524); v.7 A. (?E). Reissner (Reusner?) hymn (1533). See pp. 68-9, 189.

Date	Type	BWV[1]	Title
1707–08 (?)	Church Cantata	4	Christ lag in Todes Banden
1707–08 (?)	Church Cantata	196	Der Herr denket an uns
c. 1707–08	Church Cantata	223	Meine Seele soll Gott loben
Before 1708	Keyboard	833	Prelude & Partita in F major
Before 1708	Keyboard	913	Toccata in D minor
Before 1708	Organ	545	Prelude & Fugue in C major
Before 1708	Organ	563	Fantasia con imitazione in B minor
Before 1708	Organ	566	Prelude & Fugue in E major/C major
04/02/1708	Church Cantata	71	Gott ist mein König
1708–14	Keyboard	823	Suite in F minor
1708–17	Organ	651–68	Eighteen Chorales
1708–17	Mass	233a	Kyrie eleison – Christe, du Lamm Gottes
?1708–12	Organ	582	Passacaglia in C minor
?1708–17	Organ	536	Prelude & Fugue in A major
?1708–17	Organ	575	Fugue in C minor
?1708–17	Motet	228	Fürchte dich nicht, ich bin bei dir
04/02/1709	Church Cantata	Anh. 192	Lost
Before 1710	Organ	532	Prelude & Fugue in D major
Before 1710	Organ	550	Prelude & Fugue in G major
Before 1710	Organ	579	Fugue in B minor
Before 1710	Keyboard	896	Prelude & Fugue in A major
Before 1710	Keyboard	912	Toccata in D major
Before 1710	Keyboard	917	Fantasia in G minor
Before 1710	Keyboard	944, 946–54,	20 Fugues and Sonatas
Before 1710	Keyboard	989	Aria Variata in A minor
?1710	Organ	534	Prelude & Fugue in F minor
c. 1710	Keyboard	914	Toccata in E minor
c. 1710	Keyboard	915	Toccata in G minor
1710–1725	Organ	542	Fantasia & Fugue in G minor

Scoring[2]	Comment/text/rating (one to three stars)[3]
SATB, 4vv, 2vn, 2va, bc	* It opens with a brief but moving sinfonia (1*), followed by seven movements all based on the seven verses of Luther's Easter hymn (1524). Subsequently revised and re-performed in Leipzig (1724–8). The finest movement is the bass solo, 6**, with its dramatic expression of death (*Tode*). See p. 60.
STB, 4vv, str, bc	Psalm 115:12–15. It contains notably modest instrumentation.
Lost	Only the title survives.
cl	
cl	
org	Believed to have been revised in 1712–17.
org	
org	
SATB, 4vv, 3tpt, timp, 2rec, vc, 2ob, str, bc inc org obbl, bn	The inauguration of Mühlhausen town council. The only published cantata. Psalm 74:12, 16, 17, 19; II Samuel 19:35, 37; Deuteronomy 33:25; Genesis 21:22; v.6 J. Heermann hymn (1630) 6:*. See pp. 66, 71.
cl	
org	Revised and re-copied in 1739–42. See p. 117
5vv, bc	The original Kyrie of BWV 233 (1738–9). See p. 80.
org	
org	
org	
8vv	Believed to have been played at a memorial service for Frau Stadhauptmann Winckler, 04/02/1726 (New Grove).
Lost	Performed at the inauguration of Mühlhausen town council, but subsequently lost.
org	
org	
org	Based on Arcangelo Corelli's sonata opus 3, no. 4. See p. 64.
cl	
cl	
cl	
cl	Some are undated, or before 1705. Several are based on works by, for example, Torelli, Albinoni, and 956, 958–9, J. A. Reincken. 961, 963–8. See p. 64.
cl	
org	
cl	
cl	
org	2:*.

Date	Type	BWV[1]	Title
Before 1712	Organ	572	Pièce d'orgue in G major
Before 1712	Chamber	1026	Fugue in G minor
c. 1712	Organ	564	Toccata, Adagio, Fugue in C Major
c. 1712	Keyboard	910	Toccata in F sharp minor
?1712–17	Organ	538	Toccata & Fugue in D minor
After 1712	Chamber	996	Suite in E minor
After 1712	Organ	540	Toccata & Fugue in F major
After 1712	Organ	541	Prelude & Fugue in G major
1713–14	Organ	592–6	5 Concerto arrangements
1713–14	Keyboard	972–87	16 Concerto arrangements
Mainly 1713–15	Organ	599–644	*Orgel-Büchlein*
23/02/?1713/16	Secular Cantata	208	Was mir behagt, ist nur die muntre Jagd (Hunt Cantata)
02/08/1713	Canon	1073	Canon a 4 perpetuus
19/10/1713	Aria	?	
Before 1714	Motet	Anh. III 159	Ich laße dich nicht, du segnest mich denn
Before 1714	Keyboard	911	Toccata in C minor
Before 1714	Keyboard	916	Toccata in G major
Before 1714	Keyboard	922	Fantasia in A minor
25/03/1714	Church Cantata	182	Himmelskönig, sei willkommen
22/04/1714	Church Cantata	12	Weinen, Klagen, Sorgen, Zagen
20/05/1714	Church Cantata	172	Erschallet, ihr Lieder
17/06/1714	Church Cantata	21	Ich hatte viel Bekummernis
12/08/1714	Church Cantata	199	Mein Herze schwimmt im Blut
02/12/1714	Church Cantata	61	Nun komm, der Heiden Heiland

Scoring[2]	Comment/text/rating (one to three stars)[3]
org	
vn, hpd	
org	
cl	
org	The piece is nicknamed 'Dorian'.
lute	This piece is derived from an earlier (c. 1708) original in D minor.
org	
org	Revised in c. 1727.
org	Based on Prince Johann Ernst of Saxe-Weimar, and Vivaldi.
cl	Based on Vivaldi, Marcello, Ernst, Telemann, and Corelli.
org	See pp. 81, 97 and 130.
SSTB, 2hn, 2 rec, 2ob, ob da c, bn, str, bc	Text by Salomo Franck. The birthday of Duke Christian of Saxe-Weissenfels, ?1713. 9: 'Sheep may safely graze.'** 13: earlier version of 'My heart ever faithful,' BWV 68 (21/05/1725); 15: reused in BWV149 (1729). See pp. 90, 171.
fl, str	
S, hpd, 2vn, va, str, bc	Possibly part of a secular cantata performed for Wilhelm-Ernst's birthday. It was discovered in 2005.
8vv	Believed for many years to have been composed by the organist Johann Christoph Bach (see p. 22), but now attributed to J. S. Bach.
cl	
cl	
cl	
ATB, 4vv, rec, str, bc	* Spitta suggests the libretto was by Salomo Franck. Psalm 40:7–8; v.7 P. Stockman hymn (1633). Revived 25/03/1724, and c. 1728 with different instruments. 2:* 5:** 8:*. See p. 95.
ATB, 4vv, tr, ob, str, bc inc bn	Libretto possibly by Franck. Acts 14:22; v.6 S. Rodigast hymn (1674), reused in BWV 69a, 1723. Revived 30/04/1724. Chorus (2)*** recycled as Crucifixus in B Minor Mass. See p. 96.
SATB, 4vv, 3tr, timp, ob, str, bc inc bn	** Libretto possibly by Franck. John 14:23; v.6 P. Nicolai hymn. Revived 28/05/1724, and 13/05/1731. 4:** See p. 310, endnote 67.
STB, 4vv, 3tr, timp, 4tb, ob, str, bc	Part earlier than 1714. 4 trombones added in 1723. Text possibly by Franck. Psalm 94:19; Psalm 43:5; Rev. 5:12, 13; Psalm 116:7; vv.2, 5 Neumark hymn (1657). Played in the Hamburg job application, autumn 1720, revived in Leipzig (13/06/1723) with changes. See pp. 115, 146.
S, ob, str, bc	Text by G. C. Lehms (1711). Aria 2:*, Aria 4:*. The first example of a solo cantata (with no 4-voice ensemble). Revived in 08/08/1723. See p. 98.
STB, 4vv, str, bc	Text by Erdmann Neumeister. v.1 Luther hymn; Rev. 3:20; v.7 Nicolai hymn (1599). Revived in Leipzig, 28/11/1723.

Date	Type	BWV[1]	Title
25/12/1714 or 15	Church Cantata	63	Christen, ätzet diesen Tag
30/12/1714	Church Cantata	152	Tritt auf die Glaubensbahn
Before 1715	Keyboard	823	Suite in F minor
1715–25	Chamber	894	Sonata in A minor
1715–25	Keyboard	894	Prelude & Fugue in A minor
?24/02/1715	Church Cantata	18	Gleichwie der Regen und vom Schnee Himmel fallt
24/03/1715	Church Cantata	54	Widerstehe doch der Sünde
21/04/1715	Church Cantata	31	Der Himmel lacht! die Erde jubilieret
16/06/1715	Church Cantata	165	O heilges Geist- und Wasserbad
14/07/1715	Church Cantata	185	Barmherziges Herze der ewigen Liebe
24/11/1715	Church Cantata	163	Nur jedem das Seine
22/12/1715	Church Cantata	132	Bereitet die Wege, bereitet die Bahn
After 1715	Organ	543	Prelude & Fugue in A minor
19/01/1716	Church Cantata	155	Mein Gott, wie lang, ach lange
23/02/1716			
15/03/1716	Church Cantata	80a	Alles, was von Gott geboren
12/04/1716			
07/06/1716			
05/07/1716			
?06/09/1716	Church Cantata	164	Ihr, die ihr euch von Christo nennet
27/09/1716	Church Cantata	161	Komm, du süße Todesstunde
25/10/1716	Church Cantata	162	Ach! ich sehe, itzt, da ich zur Hochzeit gehe
06/12/1716	Church Cantata	70a	Wachet! betet! betet! wachet!
13/12/1716	Church Cantata	186a	Ärgre dich, o Seele
20/12/1716	Church Cantata	147a	Herz und Mund und Tat und Leben

Scoring[2]	Comment/text/rating (one to three stars)[3]
SATB, 4vv, 4tr, timp, 3ob, str, bc	1713–15. Organ obbligato added after c. 1729. Recitative (2)***. Text ? J. M. Heineccius. No chorale. Terry says the opening two lines are suggested by a poem by J. J. Rambach, published in 1720. 4 trumpets suggest it was composed for performance outside Weimar. Revived in Leipzig 25/12/1723. See pp. 98, 122, 151.
SB, rec, ob, v d'am, v da g, bc cl	Text by Franck, dialogue Jesus (B) and Soul (S). No chorale or 4vv ensemble (chorus). See p. 189.
v d'am, hpd cl	1708–17. This was adapted after 1729 to the Concerto for flute and violin, BWV 1044.
STB, 4vv, 4va, bc inc bn	Text by Neumeister. ?1715. 2 recorders added in 1724. Isaiah 55:10; Psalm 118:25, 4 vv. Luther German Litany (1528–29); v.8 L. Spengler hymn (1524).
A, 4vv, 2hn, 3ob, str, bc	Text by Lehms (1711). This is one of only 12 solo cantatas, and 9 with no SATB ensemble or chorus.
STB, 5vv, 3 tr, timp, 3ob, str, bc	Text by Franck. Taille added in 1724, revived 12/04/1716, plus several Leipzig revivals, 1724–31, including 09/04/1724 and 25/03/1731. See p. 122.
SATB, 4vv, str, bc inc bn	Text by Franck, from John 3:1–15. v.5 L. Hembold hymn (1575).
SATB, 4vv, ob, str, bc inc. bn	Text by Franck. Later (1723) version with trumpet da tirarsi instead of oboe; v.1 J. Agricola hymn (1529). See p. 146.
SATB, 4vv, str, bc	Text by Franck (1715), Matt. 22:15–22. 3: two obbligato cellos, low sonorities. It may have been revived in Leipzig (e.g. 31/10/1723).
SATB, 4vv, ob, str, bc org	Text by Franck (1715). 1: Isaiah 40:3; 3: John 1:19; the final chorale is lost.
SATB, 4vv, bn, str, bc	Text by Franck. 2: inc. bassoon obbligato; v.12 P. Speratus hymn (1524). See p. 158.
	Revival of BWV 208 (1713).
Lost	Text by Franck. See BWV 80 (1727–31).
	Revival of BWV 31 (1715).
	?Revival of BWV 165 (1715).
	Revival of BWV 185 (1716).
SATB, 4vv, 2fl,2ob, str, bc	See 26/08/1725.
AT, 4vv, 2rec, org obbl, str, bc	Text by Franck; v.4 C. Knoll hymn (1611). There were several Leipzig revivals. 5:*. See p. 235.
SATB, 4vv, trdt, str, bc inc. bn	Text by Franck; v.7 Rosenmüller & Albinus hymn (1652). Parts are missing, e.g. aria (3). Revived on 10/10/1723.
Lost	See 21/11/1723.
Lost	See 11/07/1723. It was probably never performed.
Lost	See 02/07/1723.

Date	Type	BWV[1]	Title
?1717–23	Orchestral	1043	Concerto for Two Violins
?1717–23	Orchestral	1041	Violin Concerto in D minor
?1717–23	Orchestral	1042	Violin Concerto in E major
1717–23	Keyboard	933–8	Six Little Preludes
1717–23	Keyboard	939–43	Five Preludes
?1718–23	Secular Cantata	202	Weichet nur, betrübte Schatten
?1718–23	Church Cantata	Anh. 197	Ihr wallenden Wolken
10/12/1718	Secular Cantata	Anh. I 5	Lobet den Herrn, alle seine Heerscharen
10/12/1718	Secular Cantata	66a	Der Himmel dacht auf Anhalts Ruhm und Glück
c. 1719–25	Organ	547	Prelude & Fugue in C major
01/01/1719	Secular Cantata	134a	Die Zeit, die Tag und Jahre macht
Before 1720	Keyboard	806–11	English Suites
Before 1720	Keyboard	968	Adagio in G major
Before 1720	Chamber	1001	Sonata No 1 in G minor
Before 1720	Chamber	1002	Partita No 1 in B minor
Before 1720	Chamber	1003	Sonata No 2 in A minor
Before 1720	Chamber	1004	Partita No 2 in D minor
Before 1720	Chamber	1005	Sonata No 3 in C major
Before 1720	Chamber	1006	Partita No 3 in E major
c. 1720	Keyboard	841–3	3 Minuets in G major, G minor and G major
c. 1720	Chamber	999	Prelude in C minor
c. 1720	Chamber	1007	Suite No 1 in G major
c. 1720	Chamber	1008	Suite No 2 in D minor
c. 1720	Chamber	1009	Suite No 3 in C major
c. 1720	Chamber	1010	Suite No 4 in Eb major
c. 1720	Chamber	1011	Suite No 5 in C minor
c. 1720	Chamber	1012	Suite No 6 in D major
01/01/1720			
01/01/1720	Secular Cantata	Anh. I 6	Dich loben die lieblichen Strahlen
22/01/1720	Keyboard	924, 926–30	Little Clavier Book for W. F. Bach
10/12/1720	Secular Cantata	184a	Lost
10/12/1720 or 22?	Secular Cantata	173a	Durchlauchtster Leopold

Scoring[2]	Comment/text/rating (one to three stars)[3]
2vn, str, bc	*** See pp. 110 and 276.
vn, str, bc	*** See p. 276.
vn, str, bc	*** See p. 276.
cl	See pp. 113 and 129.
cl	
S, ob, str, bc	Wedding cantata. It was possibly composed earlier, or later in Leipzig. 1:*; 7:* adapted elsewhere. 9: gavotte, very short!
Lost	New Year. It was cited by Forkel.
Lost	Text by C. F. Hunold. The birthday of Prince Leopold. See p. 111.
Lost	Text by C. F. Hunold. See p. 111.
org	
AT, 4vv, 2ob, str, bc	Text by C. F. Hunold: serenata tribute to the house of Anhalt-Cöthen. It contains a dialogue between Divine Providence (alto) and Time (tenor). See p. 111.
cl	
cl	
vn	See pp. 46, 110.
vn	See pp. 46, 110
vn	See pp. 46, 110
vn	5:**. See p. 46. Some academics, particularly Professor Helga Thœne, believe this movement was an epitaph to Bach's first wife, Maria Barbara, who died in July 1720 (see pp. 110, 114).
vn	See p. 46, 110.
vn	See pp. 110 and 114.
cl	From Clavierbüchlein for W. F. Bach (see below, and p. 114).
lute	See p. 110.
vc	See p. 110.
vc	See p. 110.
vc	5:* See p. 110.
vc	See p. 110.
vc	See p. 110.
vc	See p. 110.
	Revival of BWV 134a (01/01/1719).
Lost	Text by C. F. Hunold. Music lost.
cl	See pp. 113-114.
Lost	Possibly 21/01/1721. Adapted to BWV 184, 30/05/1724.
SB, 2fl, bn, str, bc	Birthday of Leopold. Adapted to BWV 173, 29/05/1724.

Date	Type	BWV[1]	Title
?10/12/1720	Secular Cantata	Anh. I 7	Heut ist gewiß ein guter Tag
After 1720	Organ	539	Prelude & Fugue in D minor
After 1720	Organ	590	Pastorella in F major
?1720s	Motet	230	Lobet den Herrn, alle Heiden
Before 1722	Orchestral	1046	Brandenburg Concerto 1
		1047	Brandenburg Concerto 2
		1048	Brandenburg Concerto 3
		1049	Brandenburg Concerto 4
		1050	Brandenburg Concerto 5
		1051	Brandenburg Concerto 6
1722	Keyboard	846–69	*The Well-Tempered Clavier* Part I
1722–25	Keyboard	812–17	French Suites
10/12/1722			
Before 1723	Keyboard	903	Chromatic Fantasia & Fugue in D minor
Before 1723	Chamber	1013	Partita in A minor
Before 1723	Secular Cantata	203	Amore traditore
Completed 1723	Keyboard	772–86	2-Part Inventions
Completed 1723	Keyboard	787–801	15 Sinfonias (3), 3-Part Inventions
1723–29	Organ	546	Prelude & Fugue in C minor
1723–29	Organ	583	Trio in D minor
01/01/1723	Secular Cantata	Anh. I 8	Lost
07/02/1723	Church Cantata	22	Jesus nahm zu sich die Zwölfe
07/02/1723	Church Cantata	23	Du wahrer Gott und Davids Sohn
30/05/1723	Church Cantata	75	Die Elenden sollen essen
06/06/1723	Church Cantata	76	Die Himmel erzählen die Ehre Gottes

Scoring[2]	Comment/text/rating (one to three stars)[3]
Lost	
org	'Fiddle' nickname.
org	
4vv, org, bc	Psalm 117.
2hn, 3ob, bn, vnp, str, bc	** 1:*; 2:**; 3:* ; 4:**. See pp. 111 and 120-121.
tr, rec, ob, vn, st, bc	* 1:*; 2:**; 3:*. See pp. 111 and 120-121.
3vn, 3va, 3vc, violone, hpd	* 1:**; 2:*. See pp. 111 and 120-121
vn, 2fl, st, bc	** 1:*; 2:***; 3:**. See pp. 111 and 120-121.
fl, vn, hpd, st	* 1:*; 2:*; 3:*. See pp. 111, 120-121 and 282.
2va, 2v da g, vc, hpd, bc	* 1:*; 2:*; 3:*. See pp. 111, 120-21 and 189.
cl	See pp. 106, 118-19, 125, 130, 304.
cl	See p. 124. The first five were included in the Clavierbüchlein for A. M. Bach (see p. 124), along with the organ chorale prelude, BWV 728, the Air and Variations in C minor (BWV 991), and the *Fantasia pro Organo* in C major (BWV 573). Possible performance of BWV 173a (see 10/12/1720 above).
cl	
fl	This possibly dates from the early 1720s.
B, hpd, bc	Sometimes this is considered unauthentic. The Italian poet is unknown. It was possibly composed for performance outside Cöthen, e.g. in Karlsbad. A message about the misery of love affairs.
cl	See p. 129.
vn, cl	See p. 129.
org	
org	*
Lost	
ATB, 4vv, ob, str, bc	Trial for the Leipzig job. Luke 18:31, 34; v.5 Creutziger hymn (1524). Several revivals in Leipzig, inc. 20/02/1724. See p. 133.
SAT, 4vv, 2 ob d'am, cornett, 3tb, str, bc	Trial for the Leipzig job. Revived 1724, and c. 1730, with 2 ob, str, bc. 1–3: ref. to Luke 18:35–43; 4: German Agnus Dei (1528). See p. 133.
SATB, 4vv, tr, 2ob, ob d'am, str, bc inc bn	Written in Cöthen, some say this was the first cantata heard in Leipzig. 1: Psalm 22:26; 7: v.5 Rodigast hymn (1674); 14: v.6 Rodigast hymn. See pp. 139 and 146.
SATB, 4vv, tr, 2ob, ob d'am, v da g, str, bc	1: Psalm 19:1, 3; 7: v.1 Luther hymn; 14: v.3 ditto. Sinfonia (8) revised in organ Trio Sonata BWV 528, and probably derived from a pre-1723 work. See pp. 146 and 189.

Date	Type	BWV[1]	Title
13/06/1723			
20/06/1723	Church Cantata	24	Ein ungefärbt Gemüte
20/06/1723			
24/06/1723	Church Cantata	167	Ihr Menschen, rühmet Gottes liebe
?24/06/1723	Mass	237	Sanctus in C major
02/07/1723	Church Cantata	147	Herz und Mund und Tat und Leben
11/07/1723	Church Cantata	186	Ärgre dich, o Seele, nicht
18/07/1723	Church Cantata	136	Erforsche mich, Gott, und erfahre mein Herz
?18/07/1723	Motet	227	Jesu, meine Freude
25/07/1723	Church Cantata	105	Herr, gehe nicht ins Gericht mit deinem Knecht
01/08/1723	Church Cantata	46	Schauet doch und sehet
08/08/1723	Church Cantata	179	Siehe zu, daß deine Gottesfurcht nicht Heuchelei sei
08/08/1723			
09/08/1723	Secular Cantata	Anh. I 20	Lost
15/08/1723	Church Cantata	69a	Lobe den Herrn, meine Seele
22/08/1723	Church Cantata	77	Du sollt Gott, deinen Herren, lieben
29/08/1723	Church Cantata	25	Es ist nichts Gesundes an meinem Leibe
30/08/1723	Church Cantata	119	Preise, Jerusalem, den Herrn
05/09/1723	Church Cantata	138	Warum betrübst du dich, mein Herz?
12/09/1723	Church Cantata	95	Christus, der ist mein Leben
19/09/1723 or 25/09/1725	Church Cantata	148	Bringet dem Herrn Ehre seines Namens

328

Scoring[2]	Comment/text/rating (one to three stars)[3]
	Revival of BWV 21 (1714). See p. 146.
ATB, 4vv, trdt, 2ob, 2ob d'am, str, bc	Text by Neumeister. 3: Matt. 7:12; 6: v.1 Heermann hymn (1630). See pp. 145.
	Second revival of BWV 185 (1715).
SATB, 4vv, trdt, ob, ob da c, str, bc	5: v.5 Graumann (or Gramann) hymn (1549). Spitta says the words of 3: have 'vapid emptiness'.
4vv, 3 tr, timp, 2ob, str, bc	Some academics believe this brief movement was performed on Christmas Day, 1724.
SATB, tr, 2ob, ob d'am, 2 ob da c, str, bc inc bn	Adapted from lost BWV 147a (20/12/1716) Text: 1*, 2*, 5, 7 by Franck; v.6 Jahn (Janus) hymn (1661); pt 2 v.17 ditto. 10:** (Jesu, joy of man's desiring). See p. 310, endnote 67.
SATB, 4vv, 2ob, taille, str, bc	Text partly by Franck (1, 3, 5). Adapted from lost BWV 186a (13/12/1716). Chorale verses 12 & 11, Sporatus hymn (1524).
ATB, 4vv, 2ob d'am, str, bc	1: Psalm 139:23; 6: v.9 J. Heermann hymn (1630). See p. 149.
5vv	** Widely believed, but not proved, to have been a memorial service for Johanna Maria Kees.
SATB, 4vv, hn, 2ob, str, bc	* 1: Psalm 143:2; 6: v.11 J. Rist hymn. See p. 149.
ATB, 4vv, 2rec, str, bc	Trumpet, horn da tirarsi, and 2 taille added later. 1**: Lam. 1:12 (first part reworked as Qui Tollis in B Minor Mass); 6: v.9 J. M. Meyfart hymn. See pp. 147 and 224.
STB, 4vv, 2ob, 2 ob da c, str, bc	1: Ecclus 1:28; 5:*; 6: v.1 C. Tietze hymn (1663). 1 and 3 reused in Mass BWV 236 and 5 reused in Mass BWV 234.
	Revival of BWV 199 (1714).
Lost	
SATB, 4vv, 3tr, timp, rec, 3ob, ob da c, str, bc	Text by J. O. Knauer. 1: Psalm 103:2; 6: v.6 Rodigast hymn (1674) – reused from BWV 12 (22/04/1714). Revived 31/08/1727, adapted into BWV 69 (08/1748). See p. 149.
SATB, 4vv, trdt, 2ob, str, bc	Text by Knauer. 1: Luke 10: 27, with chorale tune from Luther hymn; 6: no text surviving. The tune is from another Luther hymn (1524).
STB, 4vv, cornett, 3tb, 3rec, 2 ob ?d'am, str, bc	Text by J. J. Rambach *Geistliche Poesien* (Halle 1720). 1: Psalm 38:3; 6: v.12 Heermann hymn (1630). See p. 149.
SATB, 4vv, 4tr, timp, 2rec, 3ob, 2ob da c, str, bc	Inauguration of the town council. 1: Psalm 147: 12–14; 9: vv.22 & 23 Luther Te Deum.
SATB, 4vv, 2ob d'am, str, bc	Chorale, anon (1561), verbatim in 1, 2 & 6, adapted in 3–5.
STB, 4vv, hn, 2ob, ob d'am, str, bc	* Stanzas from three hymns: 1: v.1 S. Graff (1605) and tune of Luther chorale (1524); 3: v.1 V. Heiberger (1613); 7: v.4 N. Herman (1560).
AT, 4vv, tr, ob, ob d'am, ob da c, str, bc	Based on Picander's *Sammlung erbaulicher Gedanken* (Leipzig 1725). The earliest association with Picander (see p. 91). 1: Psalm 96:8.

Date	Type	BWV[1]	Title
?29/09/1723	Church Cantata	50	Nun ist das Heil und die Kraft
03/10/1723	Church Cantata	48	Ich elender Mensch, wer wird mich erlösen
10/10/1723			
17/10/1723	Church Cantata	109	Ich glaube, liebe Herr, hilf meinem Unglauben
24/10/1723	Church Cantata	89	Was soll ich aus dir machen, Ephraim?
Before 11/1723	Secular Cantata	194a	?Lost
31/10/1723			
02/11/1723	Church Cantata	194	Höchsterwünschtes Freudenfest
07/11/1723	Church Cantata	60	O Ewigkeit, du Donnerwort
14/11/1723	Church Cantata	90	Es reißet euch ein schrecklich Ende
21/11/1723	Church Cantata	70	Wachet! betet! betet! wachet!
28/11/1723			
25/12/1723			
?25/12/1723	Mass	238	Sanctus in D major
25/12/1723	Mass	243a	Magnificat in E^b major
26/12/1723	Church Cantata	40	Darzu ist erschienen der Sohn Gottes
27/12/1723	Church Cantata	64	Sehet, welch eine Liebe hat uns der Vater erzieget
After 1723	Organ	537	Prelude & Fugue in C minor
After 1723	Chamber	1023	Sonata in E minor
c.1724	Chamber	1034	Sonata in E minor
01/01/1724	Church Cantata	190	Singet dem Herrn ein neues Lied

Scoring[2]	Comment/text/rating (one to three stars)[3]
8vv, 3tr, timp, 3ob, str, bc	** Movement from a lost cantata? Text Rev. 12: 10. One movement only survives. The date is largely speculative. The 8vv version (a copy dating after 1750) may be post-Bach. A motet.
AT, 4vv, trdt, 2ob, str, bc	1: Romans 7:24; 3: v.4 Rutilius hymn (1604); 7: anon hymn (1620). 6: hemiola (cf. BWV 20).
	Revival of BWV 162 (1716).
SATB, 4vv, hn, 2ob, str, bc	** 1: Mark 9:24; 6: v.7 L. Spengler hymn (1524). Powerful musical treatment of agony of belief versus despair, based on the St Mark quote 'I believe; help thou mine unbelief'. See p. 150.
SAB, 4vv, hn, 2ob, str, bc	1: Hosea 11:8; 6: v.7 J. Heermann hymn (1630). The last line of the soprano recitative is remarkable. The choir are only in the final chorale.
Lost	See p. 151.
	Revival of BWV 80a (1716) as 80b (mostly lost).
STB, 4vv, 3ob, bn, str, bc	Consecration of Störmthal church and organ, Nov 1723. Adapted from lost BWV 194a (above). Interestingly, the organ is not included. Revived on 04/06/1724. 3:* 6: vv.6 & 7 J. Heermann hymn (1630); 12: vv.9 & 10 P. Gerhardt hymn (1647). See p. 80.
ATB, 4vv, hn, 2ob d'am, str, bc	Dialogue: Fear (A) and Christ (B). 1: v.1 Rist hymn (1642); 6: v.5 F. J. Burmeister hymn (1662). Elsewhere quotes from Psalm 119:116 and Rev. 14:13.
ATB, 4vv, tr, str, bc	** 1:**. 5: v.7 Martin Moller hymn (1584). See p. 150.
SATB, 4vv, tr, ob, str, bc inc bn	Text partly by Franck. Adapted from lost BWV 70a, 1716. 7: v.10 anon hymn (1620); 11: v.5 Keimann hymn (1655). Revived on 18/11/1731. See p. 151.
	Revival of BWV 61 (1714).
	Revival of BWV 63 (1714). See p. 151.
4vv, cornett, str, bc	Performed on Christmas Day 1723 or 1724?
SSATB, 5vv, 3 tr, timp, 2rec, 2ob, 2ob d'am, str, bc	** Revised in D major as BWV 243 (1728–31). 2*, 4*, 8**, 9*, 11*, 12**, 15*. See pp. 151-6.
ATB, 4vv, 2hn, 2ob, str, bc	1: John 3:8 (reused in the last movement of BWV 233, Missa in F major, 1738–39); 3: v.3 Caspar Fuger hymn (1592); 6: v.2 P. Gerhardt hymn (1653); 8: v.4 C. Keymann hymn (1650). The text is possibly by Bach. See p. 157.
SAB, 4vv, cornett, 3tb, ob d'am, str, bc	Text by Knauer. 1: I John 3:1; 2: v.7 Luther hymn (1524); 4: G. M. Pfefferkorn hymn (1667); 5:*; 8: v.5 J. Franck hymn, *Jesu, meine Freude* (1650). See p. 157.
org	
vn, v da g, hpd	Some sources date it 1714–17.
fl, bc	Probably for flute solo, harpsichord added by a pupil. See p. 282.
ATB, 4vv, 3tr, timp, 3ob, ob d'am, bn, str, bc	** Partly lost, i.e. incomplete. 1–3 & 5 adapted to 1730 BWV 190a, also lost. 1: Psalms 149:1 and 150:4, 6; 1 & 2: Luther Te Deum (1529); 7: v.2 T. Herman hymn (1593). Text possibly by Picander. See p. 157.

Date	Type	BWV[1]	Title
02/01/1724	Church Cantata	153	Schau, lieber Gott, wie meine Feind
06/01/1724	Church Cantata	65	Sie werden aus Saba alle kommen
09/01/1724	Church Cantata	154	Mein liebster Jesus ist verloren
16/01/1724			
23/01/1724	Church Cantata	73	Herr, wie du willt, so schicks mit mir
30/01/1724	Church Cantata	81	Jesu schläft, was soll ich hoffen
02/02/1724	Church Cantata	83	Erfreute Zeit im neuen Bunde
06/02/1724	Church Cantata	144	Nimm, was dein ist, und gehe hin
13/02/1724	Church Cantata	181	Leichgesinnter Flattergeister
13/02/1724			
20/02/1724			
20/02/1724			
25/03/1724			
07/04/1724	Passion	245	*St John Passion*
09/04/1724			
10/04/1724	Church Cantata	66	Erfreut euch, ihr Herzen
11/04/1724	Church Cantata	134	Ein Herz, das seinen Jesum lebend weiß
16/04/1724	Church Cantata	67	Halt im Gedächtnis Jesum Christ
23/04/1724	Church Cantata	104	Du Hirte Israel, höre
?27/04/1724	Church Cantata	Anh. I 15	Siehe, der Hüter Israel
30/04/1724			

Scoring[2]	Comment/text/rating (one to three stars)[3]
ATB, 4vv, str, bc	1: v.1 D. Denicke hymn (1646), ref. to Gospel, Matt. 2:13–23; 3: Isaiah 41:10; 5: v.5 P. Gerhardt hymn (1653); 9: vv.11 & 12 (as 3vv) M. Moller hymn (1587). See p. 157-158.
TB, 4vv, 2hn, 2rec, 2ob da c, str, bc	1: Isaiah 60:6; 2: J. Spangenberg translation of *Puer Natus in Bethlehem* (1545); 7: v.10 P. Gerhardt hymn (1647). See p. 158.
ATB, 4vv, 2ob d'am, str, bc	3: v.2 M. Janus (Jahn) hymn; 4: harpsichord; 5: Luke 2:49 (part of Gospel reading); 8: v.6 C. Keymann (or Keimann) hymn (1658). See p. 158. Revival of BWV 155 (1716).
STB, 4vv, hn, 2ob, str, bc	** Later version, 1730s, with organ obbligato instead of horn. 1:** v.1 Kaspar Beinemann hymn (1582); 5: v.9 L. Helmbold hymn (1563). See p. 158-159.
ATB, 4vv, 2rec, 2 ob d'am, str, bc	** Aria 1 (Jesu schläft):***, 2:*, 3:*, 4: Matt. 8:26 (part of Gospel reading, Matt. 8:23–7); 7: v.2 J. Franck hymn *Jesu meine Freude* (1650). See p. 159.
ATB, 4vv, 2hn, 2ob, str, bc	2*: including Luke 2:29–31 (Gospel of day); 3: Hebrews 4:16; 5: v.4 Luther hymn (1524). A printed copy survives. The librettist is unknown. See p. 159.
SAT, 4vv, 2ob, ob d'am, str, bc	1: Matt. 20:14; 2:* 3: v.1 Rodigast hymn (1674); 6: v.1 A von Brandenburg hymn (1548). The printed text survives. The librettist is unknown. See p. 159.
SATB, 4vv, tr, str, bc	Flute and obliggato added later. All text is original (possibly written by Bach). No chorale. See p. 159.
	Revival of BWV 18 (1715).
	Revival of BWV 22 (1723).
	Revival of BWV 23 (1723).
	Revival of BWV 182 (1714).
SATB, 4vv, 2fl, 2ob, 2ob d'am, 2ob da c, 2 v d'am, v da g, lute/org/hpd, str, bc	** Revised 30/03/1725, and in the late 1740s (including bassono grosso in basso continuo). See pp. 10, 101, 156, 160, 162-3, 172, 184, 222, 248, 304-5.
	Revival of BWV 31 (1716)
ATB, 4vv, tr, 2ob, bn, str, bc	Adapted from Secular Cantata BWV 66a, 10/12/1718, lost. 4 & 5: Hope and Fear dialogue. 6: v.3 of medieval Easter hymn 'Christ ist erstanden' (c. 1100). Revived on 26/03/1731.
AT, 4vv, 2ob, str, bc	Adapted from Secular Cantata BWV 134a, 01/01/1719.
ATB, 4vv, hn, fl, 2ob d'am, str, bc	1: 2 Tim. 2:8; 4: v.1 N. Herman chorale (1760); 6: first line from John 20:19 (Gospel); 7: v.1 J. Ebert hymn (1601).
TB, 4vv, 2ob, ob da c, 2 ob d'am, str, bc	1: Psalm 80:1; 6: v.1 C. Becker hymn.
SATB, 4vv, 3tr, timp, 2ob, st, bc	Degree ceremony, Leipzig. Lost.
	Revival of BWV 12 (1714). See p. 96.

Date	Type	BWV[1]	Title
07/05/1724	Church Cantata	166	Wo gehest du hin?
14/05/1724	Church Cantata	86	Wahrlich, wahrlich, ich sage euch
18/05/1724	Church Cantata	37	Wer da gläubet und getauft wird
21/05/1724	Church Cantata	44	Sie werden euch in den Bann tun
28/05/1724			
28/05/1724	Church Cantata	59	Wer mich liebet, der wird mein Wort halten
?29/05/1724	Church Cantata	173	Erhöhtes Fleisch und Blut
30/05/1724	Church Cantata	184	Erwünschtes Freudenlicht
04/06/1724			
04/06/1724			
11/06/1724	Church Cantata	20	O Ewigkeit, du Donnerwort
18/06/1724	Church Cantata	2	Ach Gott, vom Himmel sieh darein
24/06/1724	Church Cantata	7	Christ unser Herr zum Jordan kam
25/06/1724	Church Cantata	135	Ach, Herr, mich armen Sünder
02/07/1724	Church Cantata	10	Meine Seel erhebt den Herren
09/07/1724	Church Cantata	93	Wer nur den lieben Gott läßt walten
23/07/1724	Church Cantata	107	Was willst du dich betrüben
30/07/1724	Church Cantata	178	Wo Gott der Herr nicht bei uns hält
06/08/1724	Church Cantata	94	Was frag ich nach der Welt
13/08/1724	Church Cantata	101	Nimm von uns, Herr, du treuer Gott

Scoring[2]	Comment/text/rating (one to three stars)[3]
ATB, 4vv, ob, str, bc	* 1: 'Whither goest thou?' (John 16:5). 2**; 3*: v.3 Ringwaldt hymn; 5*; 6: v.1 E. J. von Scwarzburg-Rudolstadt hymn (1686). See p. 164.
SATB, 4vv, 2ob d'am, str, bc	1: 'Verily, verily', John 16:23 (Gospel reading); 3: v.16 G. Grunwald hymn (1530); 6: v.1 Speratus hymn (1524).
SATB, 4vv, 2ob d'am, str, bc	1: Mark 16:16; 3: v.5 Nicolai hymn (1599); 6: v.4 J. Kolross hymn (c. 1535). Revived on 03/05/1731.
SATB, 4vv, 2ob, str, bc	* 1 & 2: John 16:2 (parts of Gospel reading); 4*: v.1 M. Moller hymn (1587); 7: v.15 P. Flem(m)ing Hymn (1642). See p. 164. Revival of BWV 172 (1714).
SB, 4vv, 2tr, timp, str, bc	Libretto: Neumeister – 4 of his 7 movements, so possibly uncompleted. It may have been performed a year earlier (16/05/23). 1: John 14:23; 3: v.1 Luther hymn (1524). See p. 137 and 165.
SATB, 4vv, 2fl, str, bc	Adapted from Secular Cantata BWV 173a, 1720. Ready for 1723, and revived on 14/05/1731.
SAT, 4vv, 2fl, str, bc	Aria (2):**. Adapted from Secular Cantata BWV 184a (1720), mostly lost. Revived 15/05/1731. 5: v.8. Anark von Wildenfels hymn (1526). See p. 118.
	?Revival of BWV 165 (1715)
	Revival of BWV 194 (1723)
ATB, 4vv, trdt, 3ob, str, bc	*** Based on Johann Rist hymn (1642), vv.1, 7, 11 & 16 verbatim, 2–6, 8–10 paraphrased, with word-for-word quotations. 1:*, 3:***, 5:*, 6:***, 10:*. See p. 165.
ATB, 4vv, 4tb, 2ob, str, bc	Aria (5)* based on Luther chorale, vv.1 & 6 verbatim, 2–5 paraphrased.
ATB, 4vv, 2 ob d'am, str, bc	Text Luther baptismal hymn (1541), vv.1 & 7 verbatim, 2–6 paraphrased.
ATB, 4vv, cornett, tb, 2ob, str, bc	Text Cyriacus Schneegass hymn (1597), vv.1 & 6 verbatim, 2–5 paraphrased. See p. 235.
SATB, 4vv, tr, 2ob, str, bc	Luke 1:46–55 (Magnificat, a canticle for Vespers). 1: Luke 1:46–8, rest paraphrased, partly direct quotes. Revived in the 1740s with oboes replacing trumpets in 5. Reworked 5 as an organ chorale, including in 1748 the printed edition of 'the so-called Schübler chorales'.
SATB, 4vv, 2ob, str, bc	* G. Neumark hymn, vv.1, 4, 5 & 7 verbatim, 2, 3, 6 paraphrased. Terry says it was arranged by Picander. 1:*; 3:**.
STB, 4vv, hn, 2fl, 2ob d'am, str, bc	Johann Heermann hymn, same name (1630). The only example in the 1720s of the complete setting of a hymn.
ATB, 4vv, 2ob, 2ob d'am, str, bc	J. Jonas (1493–1555) hymn. 7: contains two chorale verses (unusual).
SATB, 4vv, fl, 2ob, ob d'am, str, bc	Balthasar Kindermann chorale, same name (1664). vv.1, 7 & 8 verbatim, 3 & 5 expanded for recitatives, 2, 4 and 6 paraphrased as arias.
SATB, 4vv, cornett, 3 tb, fl, 2ob, ob da c str, bc	Chorus (1),* rich orchestration, Aria (2),* with violin solo, also Aria (6) with cello, recorder and cornett. Martin Moller hymn (1584), same name, some verses paraphrased.

Date	Type	BWV[1]	Title
20/08/1724	Church Cantata	113	Herr Jesu Christ, du höchstes Gut
03/09/1724	Church Cantata	33	Allein zu dir, Herr Jesu Christ
10/09/1724	Church Chorale	78	Jesu, der du meine Seele
17/09/1724	Church Cantata	99	Was Gott tut, das ist wohlgetan
24/09/1724	Church Cantata	8	Liebster Gott, wenn werd ich sterben
29/09/1724	Church Cantata	130	Herr Gott, dich loben alle wir
01/10/1724	Church Cantata	114	Ach, lieben Christen, seid getrost
08/10/1724	Church Cantata	96	Herr Christ, der einger Gottessohn
15/10/1724	Church Cantata	5	Wo soll ich fliehen hin
22/10/1724	Church Cantata	180	Schmücke dich, o liebe Seele
29/10/1724	Church Cantata	38	Aus tiefer Not schrei ich zu dir
05/11/1724	Church Cantata	115	Mache dich, mein Geist, bereit
12/11/1724	Church Cantata	139	Wohl dem, der sich auf seinen Gott
19/11/1724	Church Cantata	26	Ach wie flüchtig, ach wie nichtig
26/11/1724	Church Cantata	116	Du Friederfürst, Herr Jesu Christ
03/12/1724	Church Cantata	62	Nun komm, der Heiden Heiland

Scoring[2]	Comment/text/rating (one to three stars)[3]
SATB, 4vv, fl, 2 ob d'am, str, bc	** Chorus (1**), Recitative (6)* Interesting variations on chorale cantata, some verses paraphrased with references to Gospel reading Luke 18:9–14 (6: 'Wie der bußfertge Zöllner freten'). 5: melisma. Hymn by Bartholamäus Ringwalt (1588). See p. 166.
ATB, 4vv, 2ob, str, bc	1: & 6: K. Hubert hymn (1540). 3:***. See p. 166.
SATB, 4vv, hn, fl, 2ob, str, bc	Text from J. Rist hymn (1641) of same name, vv.1 & 12 verbatim, rest paraphrased. 1: passacaglia.
SATB, 4vv, hn, fl, ob d'am, str, bc	Text from P. Rodigast hymn (1674) of same name, vv.1 verbatim, 2–5 paraphrased with reference to Gospel Matt. 6:29–34 (sermon on the mount). Revived in 1732–35. 1: rescored c. 1734 as opening chorus to BWV 100.
SATB, 4vv, hn, fl, 2ob d'am, str, bc	2–4 paraphrased. 1:* Academics say the flute represents funeral bells (*Leichenglocken*), and also in 2. It sounds secular to me. 5: harmonisation of chorale is (unusually) by Daniel Velter.
SATB, 4vv, 3tr, timp, fl, 3ob, str, bc	paraphrased. Feast of St Michael the Archangel – battle with dragon (devil) in heaven. 1: is 'Old Hundredth' hymn tune. 4: duet recitative.
SATB, 4vv, hn, fl, 2ob, str, bc	Aria (5)* J. Gigas hymn, 1, 4, 7, the rest paraphrased.
SATB, 4vv, hn, tb, fl, rec piccolo (4th fl), 2ob, vnp, str, bc	1 & 6 E. Kreuziger, 2–5 paraphrased. 1: Sopranino recorder conveys the light of the morning star. 2: refers to Gospel (Matt. 22:34–46), and the difficult question about the meaning of 'son of David'. Revived twice, around 24/10/1734, and in 1744–7, with revisions to the orchestration.
SATB, 4vv, tr, trdt, 2ob, str, bc	J. Heerman hymn (1630), verses 1 and 11 for 1 and 7, 2–10 paraphrased. 1: restless semiquaver pattern illustrates the questing subject. 3: viola obbligato (only one other case). 5:*
SATB, 4vv, 2rec, fl, ob, ob da c, vcp, str, bc	** J. Franck hymn (1652), verses 1, 4 and 7; 2, 3, 5, 8 paraphrased. The same tune is used in the organ Prelude BWV 654. 1:***, 2:* (with striking transverse flute accompaniment), 3:*, 5:* See p. 166.
SATB, 4vv, 4 tb, 2ob, str, bc	Luther chorale, vv.1 & 5, 2–4 paraphrased. Related to the 21st Sunday after Trinity Gospel reading, John 4:46–54.
SATB, 4vv, hn, fl, ob d'am, vcp, str, bc	*** J. B. Freystein hymn (1697), tune probably by Johann Rosenmüller. 2:***, 4:**. See p. 166.
SATB, 4vv, 2ob d'am, str, bc	* J. C. Rube (died c. 1748) hymn (1697) verses 1 and 6, 2–5 paraphrased, tune, re-used in BWV 156 (1729), by H. Schein, Leipzig Thomaskantor, 1628. Parts of the original score are missing. Words of the recitative 3 were newly written, ref. to the Gospel reading, Matt. 22:15–22.
SATB, 4vv, hn, fl, 3ob, str, bc	Chorale text Michael (?Melchior) Franck (1652). A crucial example of musical expression of language, frequently used by Schweitzer.
SATB, 4vv, hn, fl, ob d'am, str, bc	Text by Jacob Ebert (1601), 1 and 7 verbatim, the rest paraphrased. 3: recitative with chorale tune interspersed. 4: trio.
SATB, 4vv, hn, 2ob, str, bc	Luther chorale 1 and 8 verbatim, the rest paraphrased. 5: recitative for S and A in 3rds and 6ths. Revived in 1732–35.

Date	Type	BWV[1]	Title
25/12/1724	Church Cantata	91	Gelobet seist du, Jesu Christ
25/12/1724	Mass	232[III]	Sanctus
26/12/1724	Church Cantata	121	Christum wir sollen loben schon
27/12/1724	Church Cantata	133	Ich freue mich in dir
31/12/1724	Church Cantata	122	Das neugeborne Kindelein
Before 1725	Chamber	1014	Sonata No 1 in B minor
Before 1725	Chamber	1015	Sonata No 2 in A major
Before 1725	Chamber	1016	Sonata No 3 in E major
Before 1725	Chamber	1017	Sonata No 4 in C minor
Before 1725	Chamber	1018	Sonata No 5 in F minor
Before 1725	Chamber	1019	Sonata No 6 in G major
Before 1725	Orchestral	1066	Suite No 1 in C major
Before 1725	Keyboard	895	Prelude & Fugue in A minor
Before 1725	Keyboard	923	Prelude in B minor
After 1724	Motet	231	Sei Lob und Preis mit Ehren
c. 1725	Chamber	1000	Fugue in G minor
c. 1725	Keyboard	819	Suite in E^b major
c. 1725	Keyboard	904	Fantasia & Fugue in A minor
01/01/1725	Church Cantata	41	Jesu, nun sei gepreiset
06/01/1725	Church Cantata	123	Liebster Immanuel, Herzog der Frommen
07/01/1725	Church Cantata	124	Meinen Jesum laß ich nicht
14/01/1725	Church Cantata	3	Ach Gott, wie manches Herzeleid
21/01/1725	Church Cantata	111	Was mein Gott will, das g'scheh allzeit
28/01/1725	Church Cantata	92	Ich hab in Gottes Herz und Sinn

Scoring[2]	Comment/text/rating (one to three stars)[3]
SATB, 4vv, 2hn, timp, 3ob, str, bc inc bn	Luther hymn, 1 and 6 verbatim, the rest paraphrased. 1: expression of angels; 2: recitative/chorale; 3: dotted = French-style 'galant'; 4: 'anguish' (vale of tears). Revived in 1731/2 and after 1735 or even 1740.
6vv, 3tr, timp, 3ob, str, bc	Reused in the Mass in B Minor. See p. 166.
SATB, 4vv, cornett, 3tb, ob d'am, str, bc	Luther hymn, vv.1 & 8 verbatim, 2–7 paraphrased. 1: said by David Humphreys to be in 'archaic' style. 6: *Ewigkeit* (eternity).
SATB, 4vv, cornett, 2 ob d'am, str, bc	1 and 6 Caspar Ziegler hymn (1697), 2–5 anon, paraphrased. 4:**. Probably revived at least once. See p. 166.
SATB, 4vv, 3rec, 2ob, taille, str, bc	* C. Schneegass hymn (1597), vv.1, 3 & 7; 2, 4–6 paraphrased to fit 6-movement cantata format. Surprisingly gloomy music for Christmas! 3 is an unusual trio (soprano, alto and tenor) aria.
vn, hpd	1717–23. Other versions.
vn, hpd	1717–23. Other versions.
vn, hpd	1717–23. Other versions.
vn, hpd	1717–23. Other versions.
vn, hpd	1717–23. Other versions.
2ob, bn, str, bc	Believed to be late Cöthen or early Leipzig, by 1724–5.
cl	
cl	
8vv	Based on BWV 28 (1725) and Telemann.
lute	Arrangement of fugue from the violin sonata BWV 1001 (before 1720).
cl	
cl	
SATB, 4vv, 3tr, timp, 3ob, vcp, str, bc	J. Hermann hymn of three 14-line verses, verbatim in 1 and 6, paraphrased 2–5. 1: complex; 2*. 6 music reused in BWV 171 (1729).
ATB, 4vv, 2fl, 2ob d'am, str, bc	A. Fritsch hymn, 1 and 6 verbatim, 2–5 paraphrased. 1: gigue; 3: 'hard journey of the cross' expressed in tune and key (3 sharps etc); 5: 'scorn', and 'lonely' unaccompanied.
SATB, 4vv, tpt da tirarsa, ob d'am, str, bc	C. Keymann hymn, 1 and 6 verbatim, the rest paraphrased. The first line of the first verse is repeated at the end of almost every movement (3, 6): 'My Jesus leave I not.'
SATB, 4vv, hn, tb, 2ob d'am, str, bc	M. Moller hymn (1587), some verbatim some paraphrased. 4: 'mein Kreuz hilft Jesus tragen' ends in G sharp minor.
SATB, 4vv, 2ob, str, bc	Margrave Albrecht of Brandenburg hymn (1587), always sung on that day in Leipzig. Some verses are verbatim, some paraphrased. 1:* 2: bass and continuo only, austere; 4:*
SATB, 4vv, 2ob d'am, str, bc	*** Paul Gerhardt 1647 hymn partly paraphrased, 5 verses verbatim. 9 movements, almost all very dramatic. 2:*, 3:*. See p. 167.

Date	Type	BWV[1]	Title
02/02/1725	Church Cantata	125	Mit Fried und Freud ich fahr dahin
04/02/1725	Church Cantata	126	Erhalt uns, Herr, bei deinem Wort
11/02/1725	Church Cantata	127	Herr Jesu Christ, wahr' Mensch und Gott
12/02/1725	Church Cantata	Anh. I 14	Sein Segen fließt daher wie ein Strom
23/02/1725	Secular Cantata	249a	Entfliehet, verschwindet entweichet, ihr Sorgen
25/03/1725	Church Cantata	1	Wie schön leuchtet der Morgenstern
30/03/1725			
Apr–Jul/1725	Secular Cantata	36c	Schwingt freudig euch empor
01/04/1725	Oratorio	249	Easter Oratorio
01/04/1725			
02/04/1725	Church Cantata	6	Bleib bei uns, denn es will Abend werden
03/04/1725			
08/04/1725	Church Cantata	42	Am Abend aber desselbigen Sabbaths
15/04/1725	Church Cantata	85	Ich bin ein guter Hirt
22/04/1725	Church Cantata	103	Ihr werdet weinen und heulen
29/04/1725	Church Cantata	108	Es ist euch gut, daß ich hingehe
06/05/1725	Church Cantata	87	Bisher habt ihr nichts gebeten in meinem Namen

Scoring[2]	Comment/text/rating (one to three stars)[3]
ATB, 4vv, hn, fl, ob, ob d'am, str, bc	** Luther chorale, 'Lord now lettest thou… (Luke 2:29ff, Simeon). Ruth Tatlow says 'A response of joy at the prospect of death is almost offensive to modern ears…' See p. 167.
ATB, 4vv, tr, 2ob, str, bc	Hymn, 4vv.1*–3, 6 by Luther, 2 (4 and 5) by Jonas, 1 (7) by Walther. 1: trumpet sounds warlike, and needed a virtuoso trumpeter; 2: melisma ; 4: powerful; 6: long Amen.
STB, 4vv, tr, 2rec, 2ob, str, bc	** P. Eber hymn (1562), 1 and 7 verbatim, the rest paraphrased. The last cantata before Lent (no music until Good Friday, six weeks away). 3 and 4: word painting. The subject is death. 1:*, 3:*. See p. 167.
Lost	Wedding. Only an anonymous text survives.
SATB, 4vv, 3tr, timp, 2rec, fl, 2ob, str, bc	Lost. Text by Picander.
STB, 4vv, 2hn, 2ob da c, 2vn, str, bc	Philipp Nicolai hymn (1599), 1 and 6 verbatim, the rest paraphrased. 5:* includes text mentioning 'sounding strings', pleasantly portrayed by a violin duet; and in 6 the second horn plays an independent part in the closing chorale. Revival of *St John Passion* (BWV 245, 07/04/1724), with changes – and again in the late 1740s.
SATB, ob da c, str, bc	Text probably by Picander, for a Leipzig academic's birthday. Tenor aria 5:*. See pp. 168-9, 172.
SATB, 4vv, 3tr, timp, 2rec, fl, 2 ob (d'a), str, bc	Text probably by Picander. Largely based on BWV 249a (above). See p. 171, 244.
	Adapted revival of BWV 4 (1707–08).
SATB, 4vv, 2ob, ob da c, vcp, str, bc	** 1:** inspired by the Luke 24:29 story of Jesus' resurrection; 2:* similar to the last chorus of *St John Passion*, and in the same key; 3: Selnecker hymn (1572); 5:***; 6: Luther hymn (1543). See p. 167. Easter Sunday repeat performance of BWV 4 (1707–08), with changes.
SATB, 4vv, 2ob, str, bc inc bn	1: sinfonia; 2: John 20:19. 3:*, alto aria, is by far the longest movement, based on Matt. 18:20; 4: based on Fabricius hymn (1632) is an unusual chorale for soprano and tenor duet; 7: two hymn verses, by Luther and Johann Walther, the latter with a political issue: peaceful life under the authority of all princes and magistrates. Revived in 1731, and c. 1742.
SATB, 4vv, 2ob, vcp, str, bc	Based on Gospel reading John 10:11–16. 1: verse 1 Cornelius Becker hymn (1598); 6: verse 4 E. C. Homburg hymn (1658).
ATB, 4vv, fl p, 2 ob d'am, tr, bn, str, bc	First text by Mariane von Ziegler (b. 30/6/95). 1:*, accompanied by descant recorder, based on Gospel reading John 16:20–22. See pp. 167–8. Revived 15/04/31.
ATB, 4vv, 2 ob d'am, str, bc	2nd Ziegler text. 1: John 16:17; 4: John 16:13; 6: v.8 Gerhardt hymn.
ATB, 4vv, 2ob, 2ob da c, str, bc	3rd Ziegler text. 1: John 16:24; 4: not Ziegler; 5: John 16:33; 6:**; 7: v.9 H. Müller hymn (1659). It is very gloomy, all in minor keys.

Date	Type	BWV[1]	Title
10/05/1725	Church Cantata	128	Auf Christi Himmelfahrt allein
13/05/1725	Church Cantata	183	Sie werden euch in den Bann tun
20/05/1725	Church Cantata	74	Wer mich liebet, der wird mein Wort halten
21/05/1725	Church Cantata	68	Also hat Gott die Welt geliebt
22/05/1725	Church Cantata	175	Er rufet seinen Schafen mit Namen
27/05/1725	Church Cantata	176	Es ist ein trotzig und verzagt Ding
29/07/1725	Church Cantata	168	Tue Rechnung! Donnerwort
03/08/1725	Secular Cantata	205	Zerreißet, zersprenget, zertrümmert die Gruft
19/08/1725	Church Cantata	137	Lobe den Herren, den mächtigen König der Ehren
26/08/1725	Church Cantata	164	Ihr, die ihr euch von Christo nennet
31/10/1725	Church Cantata	79	Gott, der Herr, ist Sonn
27/11/1725	Secular Cantata	Anh. 196	Auf! süß-entzüchende Gewalt
25/12/1725	Church Cantata	110	Unser Mund sei voll Lachens

Scoring[2]	Comment/text/rating (one to three stars)[3]
ATB, 4vv, tr, 2hn, 2ob d'am, taille, str, bc	4th Ziegler text, but much altered by Bach. 1: verse 1 Wegelin & Sonnemann hymn; 3: aria with recitative in the middle; 5: verse 4 of M. Arenarius hymn.
SATB, 4vv, 2ob d'am, 2ob da c, vcp, str, bc	** 5th Ziegler text. 1: recitative, John 16:2; 5: verse 5 Gerhardt hymn (1653). See p. 168.
SATB, 4vv, 3tmpt, timp, 2ob, ob da c, str, bc	6th Ziegler text. The first two movements were reworked from the first two movements of BWV 59 (28/04/1724). 1: John 14:23; 4: John 14:28.
SB, 4vv, hn, cornett, 3trbn, 2ob, taille, vcp, str, bc	*** 7th Ziegler text, based on Gospel reading John 3:16–21. 1***: verse 1: Salomo Liscow hymn (1675), tune by G. Vopelius (1682); 2:*** is the famous 'My heart ever faithful', gently scored. 5: John 3:18. Both of the arias (2 and 4) are linked to BWV 208 (1713). See p. 168.
ATB, 4vv, 2tpt, 3rec, vcp, str, bc	8th Ziegler text, based on John 10:1–11. 1: John 10:3; 2**, accompanied by three recorders; 4: a revision of BWV173a (?1720); 5: John 10:6; 7: J. Rist hymn v.9.
SAB, 4vv, 2ob, ob da c, str, bc	9th Ziegler text. 3:**; 6: v.8 P. Gerhardt hymn.
SATB, 4vv, 2ob d'am, str, bc	Text by Franck, based on Luke 16:1–19. It was possibly first composed in Weimar. 5: *Kelte* (chains) contains a long interlocked melisma; 6: v.8 B. Ringwaldt hymn (1688).
SATB, 4vv, 3tr, timp, 2hn, 2fl, 2ob, ob d'am, v d'am, v da g, str, bc	Text by Picander. Performed on the name day of Dr A. F. Muller (1684–1761), professor at Leipzig, Dean of Philosophy faculty, probably played by torchlight outside his house in Katherinenstraße. It is the best and biggest secular cantata, 40 minutes long, the largest orchestration he ever assembled, involving at least 24 players. 9: adapted in 4:, BWV 171 (1729). See pp. 172 and 189.
SATB, 4vv, 3tr, timp, 2ob, str, bc	J. Neander hymn (1680), all 5 verses, i.e. old method of chorale cantatas, viz. Buxtehude, & BWV. 4. Tune: 'Praise to the Lord, the Almighty, the king of creation', 4, trumpet, and 5. 1: hemiola; 2: reused as organ Schübler chorale no. 6. Chorus, 3 arias, chorale. Revived several times, inc. 1746/7.
SATB, 4vv, 2fl, 2ob, str, bc	Text by Franck. May have been composed in 1715 and performed on 06/09/1716. 2: recitative includes quotes from sermon on the mount (Matt. 5:7 and 7:7); 4:*; 5:* S and B duet; 6: verse 6 Elizabeth Creuziger hymn (1524).
SAB, 4vv, 2hn, timp, 2fl, 2ob, str, bc	Reformation Festival. 1: Psalm 84:11; 3: v.1 M. Rinkart hymn 'Nun danket und Schild alle Gott' (Now thank we all our God) tune; 5:* soprano and bass duet; 6: v.8 L. Hembold hymn. 1 and 5 reused in Mass BWV 236 (c. 1738–9), 2 reused in Mass BWV 234 (c. 1738). Revived on 31/10/1730.
Lost	Text by J. C. Gottsched.
SATB, 4vv, 3 tr, timp, 2fl, 3ob, ob d'am, ob da c, str, bc inc bn	* G. C. Lehms libretto (1711). Cf. BWV 1069 – unclear which was written first. Christmas Day. 1:* relevant to dispute about choruses, Psalm 126:2–3; 5: Luke 2:14. See p. 169.

Date	Type	BWV[1]	Title
26/12/1725	Church Cantata	57	Selig ist der Mann
27/12/1725	Church Cantata	151	Sußer Trost, mein Jesus kömmt
30/12/1725	Church Cantata	28	Gottlob! nun geht das Jahr zu Ende
Before 1726	Keyboard	900	Prelude & Fughetta in E minor
1726–31	Keyboard	825–30	Clavier-Übung 1
1726–31	Keyboard	906	Fantasia & Fugue in C minor
1726–30	Church Cantata	36(1)	Schwingt freudig euch empor
1726–27	Secular Cantata	204	Ich bin in mir vergnügt
1726–27	Motet	225	Singet dem Herrn ein neues Lied
01/01/1726	Church Cantata	16	Herr Gott, dich loben wir
13/01/1726	Church Cantata	32	Liebster Jesu, mein Verlangen
20/01/1726	Church Cantata	13	Meine Seufzer, meine Tränen
27/01/1726	Church Cantata	72	Alles nur nach Gottes Willen
?03/1726	Church Cantata	34a	O ewiges Feuer, o Ursprung der Liebe
12/05/1726 or 13/04/1728	Church Cantata	146	Wir müssen durch viel Trübsal
30/05/1726	Church Cantata	43	Gott fähret auf mit Jauchzen

Scoring[2]	Comment/text/rating (one to three stars)[3]
SB, 4vv, 2ob, taille, str, bc	G. C. Lehms libretto (1711). A dramatic dialogue between Soul (S) and Jesus (B). 1: James 1:12; 3:* 'I wish for death without Jesus's love' – gloomy; 7: fine soprano aria ends unusually suddenly; 8: tune of *Lobe den Herren* (Praise to the Lord).
SATB, 4vv, fl, str, bc	G. C. Lehms libretto (1711). 1:*** Great soprano aria on the comfort of the birth of Jesus; 5: N. Herman hymn verse 8 (ob d'am added c. 1727). See p. 169.
SATB, 4vv, cornett, 3tb, 2ob, taille, str, bc	E. Neumeister libretto. 2: verse 1 Johann Gramann hymn (1530); 3: Jeremiah 32:41; 6: verse 6 Paul Eber hymn (1580).
cl	
cl	Keyboard partitas published in Leipzig, No. 1 in 1726, Nos. 2 and 3 in 1727, No. 4 in 1728, Nos. 5 and 6 in 1730. See p. 184.
cl	The fugue is incomplete.
Lost	For Advent Sunday. Four other versions, 36c (1725), 36a (1726), 36(2) (1731) and 36b (1735).
S, fl, 2ob, str, bc	Text by C. F. Hunold, apart from some lines. Contentment not available from friends or possessions. 8:** See BWV 84 (09/02/1727). Possibly Bach himself altered the Hunold text.
8vv	*** Debates continue over this well-known work's sources, what event it was composed for, whether it should be accompanied, and other issues. The text is mainly Psalm 149:1–3, Psalm 103:13–16 and Psalm 150:2 and 6.
ATB, 4vv, hn, 2ob, ob da c, str, bc	* G. C. Lehms (1711) plus 6: v.6 P. Eber hymn. 3:* 'Let us exult, rejoice' is a whooping dialogue between the chorus and the bass soloist. The horn was changed to corno da caccia or viola in later performances. 5:* (Beloved Jesus) conveys meditative text. Revived on 01/01/1731, after 1745 and on 01/01/1749.
SB, 4vv, ob, str, bc	G. C. Lehms (1711) dialogue between Soul (S) and God (B) (see BWV 57, 26/12/25), based on Luke 2:41–52, 12-year-old Jesus preaching in temple; 2: Psalm 84 (set by Brahms in his German Requiem). 1:**; 5:*, a tenor and bass duet. See p. 169.
SATB, 4vv, 2rec, ob da c, str, bc	* G. C. Lehms (1711) plus 6: P. Fleming hymn. Almost all the movements are in minor keys, conveying 'my sighs, my tears'. 5:*, the bass solo, is described by Malcolm Boyd as 'perhaps the most grief-laden aria that Bach ever wrote'.
SAB, 4vv, 2ob, str, bc	Text by Salomo Franck, so probably written in Weimar for 27/01/15 and rewritten. Subject: charity. 1: reused, adapted, in BWV 235 Mass in G minor; 6: hymn by Margrave Albrecht (1547).
SATB, 4vv, 3tpt, timp, 2fl, 2ob, str, bc	Incomplete. It was produced for the wedding of a Leipzig clergyman. Reworked as BWV 34 (c. 1746). Gospel: John 14:23–31.
SATB, 4vv, 2ob, 2ob d'am, taille, org obbl, str, bc	** The first cantata with organ obbligato (also 35, 169, 49). The opening sinfonia (1:***) later, c. 1738, became the opening movement of BWV 1052. 4:*, 7:*. See pp. 169 and 276.
SATB, 4vv, 3tpt, timp, 2ob, str, bc	Later performed without trumpets. 1: Psalm 47:5–6; 4: Mark 16:19.

Date	Type	BWV[1]	Title
16/06/1726			
23/06/1726	Church Cantata	39	Brich dem Hungrigen dein Brot
21/07/1726	Church Cantata	88	Siehe, ich will viel Fischer aussenden
28/07/1726	Church Cantata	170	Vergnügte Ruh, beliebte Seelenlust
04/08/1726	Church Cantata	187	Es wartet alles auf dich
11/08/1726	Church Cantata	45	Es ist dir gesagt, Mensch, was gut ist
25/08/1726	Church Cantata	102	Herr, deine Augen sehen nach dem Glauben
25/08/1726	Secular Cantata	249b	Verjaget, zerstreuet, zerrüttet ihr Sterne: Die Feie des Genius
26/08/1726 or 30/08/1727	Church Cantata	Anh. I 4	Wünschet Jerusalem Glück
08/09/1726	Church Cantata	35	Geist und Seele wird verwirret
22/09/1726	Church Cantata	17	Wer Dank opfert, der preiset mich
29/09/1726	Church Cantata	19	Es erhub sich ein Streit
06/10/1726	Church Cantata	27	Wer weiß, wie nahe mir mein Ende?
13/10/1726	Church Cantata	47	Wer sich selbst erhöhet
20/10/1726	Church Cantata	169	Gott soll allein mein Herze haben

Scoring[2]	Comment/text/rating (one to three stars)[3]
	Second revival of BWV 194 (1723).
SAB, 4vv, 2rec, 2ob, str, bc	1: Isaiah 58:7–8, helping the poor; 4: Hebrews 13:16.
SATB, 4vv, 2hn, 2 ob d'am, taille, str, bc	Text maybe written by Duke Ernst Ludwig of Saxe-Meiningen. 1 is, unusually, an aria (Jeremiah 16:16), involving hunting in the second half; 3 is also used in BWV 236 (c.1738–9); 5 is also used in BWV 234 (c. 1738); 7: C. Tierse hymn, v.1.
A, ob d'am, org obbl, str, bc	Text by Lehms (1711). 1:** Aria only, no choir; 3: odd, organ and strings, no bass. 5:** Revived in 1746 or 1747. See p. 170.
SAB, 4vv, 2ob, str, bc	1: Psalm 104:27–8; 4: Matt. 6:31–32. Reused for BWV 235 (c. 1738): 1: for Gloria; 4: for Gratias agimus; 3: for Domine filii; 5: for Qui tollis.
ATB, 4vv, 2fl, 2ob, str, bc	Text possibly by Christoph Helm. 1:** Micah 6:8; 3:**; 4: Matt. 7:22–3; 7: J. Heerman hymn v.2. See p. 170.
ATB, 4vv, fl, 2ob, vcp, str, bc	Meiningen libretto. 1:** Jeremiah 5:3, adapted in BWV 235 (1738–9); 3: adapted as Qui tollis in BWV233 (1738–9); 5: adapted as Quoniam in BWV 233 (1738–9); 7: vv.7 & 8 of S. Heerman hymn. See p. 170.
Lost	Lost. Text by Picander.
Lost	Text by Picander. Change of town council.
A, 2ob, taille, org obbl, str, bc	1 and 5 are thought to be partly adapted from a lost oboe concerto. Lehms libretto (1711). 2:* may be adapted from a Weimar slow movement from a concerto; 4: may also be a so-called parody.
SATB, 4vv, 2ob ?d'am, str, bc	Text maybe by C. Helm, Meiningen. 1: Psalm 50:23; 3: Psalm 36:6; 4: Luke 17:15–16. 5:*. The subject is gratitude. 1: re-used for Cum sancto spiritu in Mass BWV235 (1738–9), transposed down a tone.
STB, 4vv, 3tpt, timp, 2ob, 2 ob d'am, taille, str, bc	Anonymous adaptation of a Picander poem: 1:* 'there arose a great strife' between St Michael and the Devil. 5:** includes Martin Schallang tune (1571) for hymn, normal for St Michael's Day; 7: v. from c. 1600 hymn. See p. 170.
SATB, 5vv, hn, 2ob, ob da c, hpd obbl (later org obbl), str, bc	Unusually diverse sources: 1:* Neumann hymn (also used in BWV 93, 1723), chorus inc. S, A & T solos, words from Amelie Juliane, Countess of Schwarzburg-Rudolfstadt hymn (1656); 2: echo of Neumeister hymn (1700) 4: *Flügel her!*; 5:*, *Gute Nacht*; 6: v.1 J. G. Albinus hymn (1649), tune and harmonisation by the former Nikolaikirche organist Johann Rosenmüller (1650s).
SB, 4vv, 2ob, org obb, vcp, str, bc	Text by J. F. Helbig, a poet much used by Telemann, only this one time by Bach. 1: Luke 14:11; 5: v.11 of the chorale *Warum betrübst du dich, mein Herz*.
A, 4vv, 2ob d'am, taille, org obbl, str, bc	Partly adapted from a lost oboe concerto reworked as harpsichord concerto BWV 1053 (c. 1738), of which the last movement became 1: of BWV 49 (see below). The libretto 'shows signs of the composer's intervention' (David Schulenberg). 1:*, an organ-based sinfonia; 5:***. See pp. 170.

Date	Type	BWV[1]	Title
27/10/1726	Church Cantata	56	Ich will den Kreuzstab gerne tragen
?31/10/1726	Church Cantata	129	Gelobet sei der Herr, mein Gott
03/11/1726	Church Cantata	49	Ich geh und suche mit Verlangen
10/11/1726	Church Cantata	98	Was Gott tut, das ist wohlgetan
17/11/1726	Church Cantata	55	Ich armer Mensch, ich Sündenknecht
24/11/1726	Church Cantata	52	Falsche Welt, dir trau ich nicht
30/11/1726	Secular Cantata	36a	Steigt freudig in die Luft
11/12/1726	Secular Cantata	207	Vereinigte Zweitracht der wechselnden Saiten
1727	Canon	1074	Canon a 4
1727–31	Mass	242	Christe eleison
1727–31	Church Cantata	80	Ein feste Burg ist unser Gott
1727–31	Church Cantata	195	Dem Gerechten muß das Licht
1727–31	Organ	544	Prelude & Fugue in B minor
05/01/1727	Church Cantata	58	Ach Gott, wie manches Herzeleid
02/02/1727	Church Cantata	82	Ich habe genug
02/02/1727			
09/02/1727	Church Cantata	84	Ich bin vergnügt mit meinem Glücke
11/04/1727	Passion	244	*St Matthew Passion*

Scoring[2]	Comment/text/rating (one to three stars)[3]
B, 4vv, 2ob, taille, str, bc	* One of the unusual solo bass cantatas. Text possibly by Picander, drawing on Erdmann Neumeister's libretto. 2: about travelling by sea. The final chorale (5) was probably for one voice per part.
SAB, 4vv, 3tpt, timp, fl, 2ob, ob d'am, str, bc	Johann Olearius 5-verse hymn (1655). No recitatives. 1:* festive, re God; 2: re Jesus; 3:* re the Holy Spirit, in E minor; 4: re nature (6/8); 5:* a chorale with fanfare.
SB, ob d'am, org obbl, vc piccolo, str, bc	* No choruses. Text possibly by Picander, a dialogue between Soul (soprano) and Jesus (bass). 1:* is a sinfonia, from a lost work later revised as harpsichord concerto BWV 1053, c. 1738. See p. 171.
SATB, 4vv, ob, ob d'am, taille, str, bc	Gospel reading John 4:47–54. 1: Samuel Rodigast hymn (1674).
T, 4vv, fl, ob d'am, str, bc	The only surviving cantata for solo tenor, 'relatively little known'. 1:** influenced by the words *Er ist gerecht, ich ungerecht* (He is just, I am unjust); 5: v.6 of Johann Rist hymn. See p. 171.
S, 4vv, 2hn, 3ob, str, bc	* The opening sinfonia,*, is from Brandenburg Concerto No 1 (BWV 1046). 5:* See p. 121.
Lost	Four other versions, 36c (1725), 36(1) (1726–30), 36(2) (1731) and 36b (1735). See p. 180.
SATB, 4vv, 3tpt, timp, 3fl, 2ob(da c), str, bc	The celebration of Dr Gottlieb Kortte's appointment as professor of jurisprudence in Leipzig. See pp. 121 and 246.
hpd, org	Dedicated to law student Ludwig Friedrich Hudemann.
SA, bc	A brief duet inserted in Mass in C minor by Francesco Durante (1684–1755).
SATB, 4vv, 2ob, taille, str, bc	Adapted from lost 1715 BWV80a. Huge and ambitious, technically skilled, but earning no stars.
SB, 4vv, 3tpt, timp, 2hn, 2fl, 2ob, 2ob d'am, str, bc	Wedding cantata. This version is lost, the second version, c. 1742 is incomplete, and the final version was c. 1748–9. Performed in Ohrdruf c. 1736, and again c. 1742, and on 11/09/1741 for the wedding of Johanna Eleonora Schütz in the Thomaskirche.
org	
SB, 2ob, taille, str, bc	Duet dialogue between God and Soul. 1: v.1 M. Moller hymn; 5: v.2 M. Behm hymn.
B, ob, str, bc	*** Several other versions, including for soprano, plus oboe da caccia, the last done in c. 1749. Anna Magdalena Bach copied two movements into her book. See p. 171. Revival of BWV 83 (1724).
S, 4vv, ob, str, bc	Text by Picander. 5: v.12 Ämilie Juliana, Countess of Schwarzburg-Rudolstadt hymn (1686). It is believed that the choir was probably one voice per part.
S in ripieno, Ch 1:	*** Libretto by Picander. See pp. 2, 9, 10, 184-192, 195, 201, 235, 239, 248, 295 and 304-5..
SATB, 4vv, 2 rec, 2fl, 2ob, 2 ob d'am, 2 ob da	

Date	Type	BWV[1]	Title
?15/04/1727	Church Cantata	158	Der Friede sei mit dir
12/05/1727	Secular Cantata	Anh. I 9	Entfernet euch, ihr heitern Sterne
03/08/1727	Secular Cantata	193a	Ihr Häuser des Himmels ihr scheinenden Lichter
25/08/1727	Church Cantata	193	Ihr Tore zu Zion
?31/08/1727			
17/10/1727	Secular Cantata	198	Laß, Fürstin, laß noch einen Strahl
1728–31	Church Cantata	117	Sei Lob und Ehr dem höchsten Gut
1728–31	Mass	243	Magnificat in D major
05/02/1728	Secular Cantata	216	Vergnügte Pleißenstadt
06/02/1728	Church Cantata	157	Ich laße dich nicht, du segnest mich denn
17/10/1728	Church Cantata	188	Ich habe meine Zuversicht
?25/10/1728	Church Cantata	197a	Ehre sei Gott in der Höhe
after 1728	Secular Cantata	216a	Erwählte, Pleißenstadt: Apollo et Mercurius
?1729	Church Cantata	120a	Herr Gott, Beherrscher aller Dinge
1729–41	Orchestral	1044	Concerto in A minor

350

Scoring[2]	Comment/text/rating (one to three stars)[3]
c, v da g, str, bc; Ch 2: SATB, 4vv, 2fl, 2ob, 2ob d'am, v da g, str, bc	
B, 4vv, ob, vn, bc	v.1 Albinus hymn (1649); v.5 Luther hymn. Spitta suggests the text is by Franck. 2* is an aria with the chorus, accompanied by solo violin (or possibly flute). Some movements may be missing.
Lost	Text by C. F. Haupt.
Lost	Text by Picander. Music lost. Reused as BWV 193 (25/08/1727).
SA, 4vv, 2ob, str, bc	Probably performed for the inauguration of the town council. See pp. 102 and 170. Revival of BWV 69a (1723) with changes, 3: transposed up a fifth, tenor to alto. Further revised as BWV 69, 1748.
SATB, 4vv, 2fl, 2ob d'am, 2v da g, 2 lutes, str, bc	*** Memorial service for Electress Christiane Eberhardine, known as the *Trauer Ode*. Text by J. C. Gottsched. 1:***; 4:* funeral bells; 5:** the longest movement, a very intense statement about her death; 8:** eternity; 10:** several bars with all four voices in unison. See p. 194-5.
ATB, 4vv, 2fl, 2ob d'am, str, bc	* Text entirely from the J. J. Schutz nine-verse hymn (1637), verbatim. It was not written for a specific Sunday, so it is hard to assign its date. 9 repeats the music of 1, with Schutz's 9th verse.
SSATB, 5vv, 3tr, timp, 2rec/fl, 2ob, bn, st, bc	A version of BWV 243a (25/12/1723).
SA, ?	This survives only in fragmentary form, including a 'parody' of movement 13 in BWV 205 (1725).
TB, 4vv, fl, ob d'am, str, bc	** Funeral cantata for Johann Christoph von Ponickau, eminent lawyer. Text by Picander. 5: v.6 C. Keymann hymn (1658). See p. 196.
SATB, 4vv, 2ob, taille, org obbl, str, bc inc. bn	** Text by Picander. 1***: sinfonia adapted from the lost violin concerto which was re-used for the harpsichord concerto BWV 1052. 2:**. The manuscript was broken up for sale in the 19th century. See pp. 197 and 276.
SATB, 2fl, ob(da c), vc/bn, str, bc	The earlier version of BWV 197, 1736/7. Text by Picander.
Lost	
SATB, 4vv, 3tr, timp, 2ob, 2 ob d'am, org obbl str, bc	A wedding cantata, partly lost, and mostly derived from earlier lost compositions. Reworked as BWV 120b (26/06/1730) and BWV 120 (27/08/1742).
fl, vn, str, bc	See p. 282.

Date	Type	BWV[1]	Title
1729–41	Orchestral	1069	Suite No 4 in D major
01/01/?1729	Church Cantata	171	Gott, wie dein Name, so ist auch dein Ruhm
12/01/1729	Secular Cantata	210a	O angenehme Melodei
?23/01/1729	Church Cantata	156	Ich steh mit einem Fuß im Grabe
?27/02/1729	Church Cantata	159	Sehet, wir gehn hinauf gen Jerusalem
24/03/1729	Church Cantata	244a	Klagt, Kinder, klagt es aller Welt
15/04/1729			
18/04/1729	Church Cantata	Anh. 190	Ich bin ein Pilgrim auf der Welt
?19/04/1729	Church Cantata	145	Ich lebe, mein Herze, zu deinem Ergötzen
06/06/1729	Church Cantata	174	Ich liebe den Höchsten von ganzem Gemüte
26/06/1729	Church Cantata	120b	Gott, man lobet dich in der Stille
?29/09/1729	Church Cantata	149	Man singet mit Freuden vom Sieg
20/10/1729	Motet	226	Der Geist hilft unser Schwachheit
1729 (?autumn)	Secular Cantata	201	Geschwinde, ihr wirbelnden Winde
After 1729	Secular Cantata	209	Non sa che sia dolore
Before 1730	Keyboard	901	Prelude & Fughetta in F major
Before 1730	Keyboard	902	Prelude & Fughetta in G major
1730–34	Chamber	1031	Sonata in E^b major
1730–45	Organ	562	Fantasia & Fugue in C minor

Scoring[2]	Comment/text/rating (one to three stars)[3]
3tr, timp, 3ob, bn, str, bc	Probably composed for the *collegium musicum* (see p. 106). 1 (overture) derived from the opening chorus of Cantata BWV 110 (Christmas Day, 1725).
SATB, 4vv, 3tr, timp, 2ob, str, bc	Text by Picander. 1:* Psalm 48:10, adapted in B Minor Mass as Patrem omnipotentem; 6: v.2 J. Hermann hymn (1593), music also derived from BWV 41 (01/01/1725).
Mostly lost	Homage to Duke of Saxe-Weißenfels. Reused as BWV 210 (c. 04/1742). See pp. 199 and 286.
ATB, 4vv, str, bc	Text by Picander. 1: sinfonia from a lost concerto movement, later used as Largo in harpsichord concerto BWV 1057 (c. 1738). 2: combined tenor aria and soprano chorale (J. H. Schein hymn, 1628), as used in earlier Weimar cantatas; 6: v.1 K. Beinemann hymn, 1582.
SATB, 4vv, ob, str, bc inc. bn	Text by Picander. 1: dialogue between Soul (S) and Jesus (B); 4:* 5: P. Stockmann hymn, used three times in the *St John Passion*, and in BWV 182 (25/03/1714). See p. 235.
Lost	Funeral of Prince Leopold of Anhalt-Cöthen. Text by Picander, partly similar to the *St Matthew Passion* (BWV 244) and *Traue Ode* (BWV 198). Music lost. See p. 198.
	Revival of *St Matthew Passion* BWV 244 (1727).
4vv, str, bc	Text by Picander. A fragment of 4 is extant, the rest lost.
SATB, 4vv, tr, fl, 2ob da c, str, bc	Text by Picander. Possibly the opening movement is missing.
ATB, 4vv, 2hn, 2ob, taille, str, bc	Text by Picander. 1:** sinfonia based on Brandenburg 3.1; 2:*; 5: v.1 M Schalling hymn (1589). See p. 121.
Lost	Music lost. Text by Picander, for the 200th anniversary of the Augsburg Confession. See BWV 120a (?1729) and BWV 120 (27/08/1742).
SATB, 4vv, 3tpt, timp, 3ob, bn, str, bc	Text by Picander. 1728 or 1729. Gospel reading re St Michael and all Angels was one of his favourites (see other cantatas for this day, inc. *Nun ist das Heil*, BWV 50). 1: from the last movement of BWV 208 (1713), and reused in the lost Anh. 193 (1740); 3:*; 7: M. Schalling hymn (1571), with trumpets and timpani in the last few bars.
8vv	* Romans 8:26–27, and a Luther hymn. For the funeral of J. H. Ernesti. See p. 203.
SATTBB, 6vv, 3tpt, timp, 2fl, 2ob, ob d'am, str, bc	* A Picander poem about the competition between Phoebus and Pan, *dramma per musica*. 5:*. See p. 201.
S, fl, str, bc	* A rather operatic cantata, probably composed for the *collegium musicum*, about the departure of a scholar or sailor. 1:* sinfonia; 3:*; 5*.
cl	
cl	
fl, hpd	Leipzig, before 09/09/1734. See pp. 221 and 282.
org	

Date	Type	BWV[1]	Title
c. 1730	Organ	525	Sonata in E♭ major
c. 1730	Organ	526	Sonata in C minor
c. 1730	Organ	527	Sonata in D minor
c. 1730	Organ	528	Sonata in E minor
c. 1730	Organ	529	Sonata in C major
c. 1730	Organ	530	Sonata in G major
c. 1730	Solo Instrumental	995	Suite in G minor
25/06/1730	Church Cantata	190a	Singet dem Herrn ein neues Lied
28/08/1730	Church Cantata	Anh. I 3	Gott, gib dein Gerichte dem Könige
17/09/1730	Church Cantata	51	Jauchzet Gott in allen Landen
1730 (?autumn)	Church Cantata	192	Nun danket alle Gott
31/10/1730			
c. 1731	Orchestral	1068	Suite No 3 in D major
01/01/1731			
02/02/1731			
23/03/1731	Passion	247	St Mark Passion
25/03/1731			
26/03/1731			
27/03/1731			
08/04/1731	Church Cantata	112	Der Herr ist mein getreuer Hirt
15/04/1731			
03/05/1731			
13/05/1731			
14/05/1731			
15/05/1731			
20/05/1731			
20/05/1731			
25/08/1731	Secular Cantata	Anh. I 10	So kämpfet nur, ihr mintern Töne

Scoring[2]	Comment/text/rating (one to three stars)[3]
org	
org	
org	
org	Arranged from BWV 76 (06/06/1723).
org	
org	
lute	See p. 281.
Lost	Picander's printed libretto shows that it was at least partly based on BWV 190 (1/1/1724).
Lost	Celebrating the change of town council. Only the text survives.
S, tpt, str, bc	** 1:*, 2:*, 4.*, J. Gramann hymn (1530), ending with Alleluja. No chorus. See pp. 211–12.
SB, 4vv, 2 fl, 2ob, str, bc	*** Three verses of M. Rinckart hymn (1636), 'Now thank we all our God' tune, in all three movements. 2: soprano and bass duet; 3: 12/8, is reminiscent of Suite BWV 1068 (see below). See p. 215. Revival of BWV 79 (1725).
3tpt, timp, 2ob, str, bc	2:*** (Air on a G String). See pp. 220-221.
	Revival of BWV 16 (01/01/26).
	?Revival of BWV 82 (1727).
Lost	Text by Picander. See pp. 156, 219 and 304.
	Revival of BWV 31 (1715).
	Revival of BWV 66 (1724).
	Revival of BWV 134 (11/04/24) with changes.
SATB, 4vv, 2hn, 2ob d'am, str, bc	* All five verses of W. Meuslin hymn (1530), a paraphrase of Psalm 23:3:* bass ariosi and recitative, 'Though I walk through the valley of death'; 4:** soprano and tenor duet. See pp. 218–19. Revival of BWV 103 (1725).
	Revival of BWV 37 (1724).
	Second revival of BWV 172 (1714).
	Revival of BWV 173 (1724).
	Revival of BWV 184 (1724).
	Revival of BWV 59 (1723 or 1724).
	Revival of BWV 194 (1723).
Lost	Text by Picander. Music lost.

Date	Type	BWV[1]	Title
27/08/1731	Church Cantata	29	Wir danken dir, Gott
18/11/1731			
25/11/1731	Church Cantata	140	Wachet auf, ruft uns die Stimme
02/12/1731	Church Cantata	36(2)	Schwingt freudig euch empor
1732–35	Chamber	1021	Sonata in G major
1732–35	Chamber	1038	Trio Sonata in G major
1732–35	Church Cantata	100	Was Gott tut, das ist wohlgetan
1732–35	Orchestral	1061	Harpsichord Concerto in C major
11/04/1732			
05/06/1732	Secular Cantata	Anh. I 18	Froher Tag, verlangte Stunden
06/07/1732	Church Cantata	177	Ich ruf zu dir, Herr Jesu Christ
?20/07/1732	Church Cantata	9	Es ist das Heil uns kommen her
03/08/1732	Secular Cantata	Anh. I 11	Es lebe der König, der Vater im Lande
Before 1733	Motet	229	Komm, Jesu, komm!
03/08/1733	Secular Cantata	Anh. I 12	Frohes Volk, vergnügte Sachsen
05/09/1733	Secular Cantata	213	Laßt uns sorgen, laßt uns wachen

Scoring[2]	Comment/text/rating (one to three stars)[3]
SATB, 4vv, 3tpt, timp, 2ob, org obbl, str, bc	** Installation of Leipzig city council. 1: sinfonia arrangement of the violin Partita BWV 1006 (before 1720); 2: Psalm 75:1, reworked as 'Gratias agimus tibi' in Mass in B minor BWV 232; 3: tenor aria, repeated in 7: (alto); 5: probably derived from an earlier siciliana; 6: Amen in unison for all 8 singers; 8: v.5 J. Gramann hymn (1549), with trumpets. Unknown text. Revivals on 31/08/39 and 25/08/49, and possibly others. See pp. 221-2 and 224. Revival of BWV 70 (1723).
STB, 4vv, hn, 2ob, taille, vn piccolo, str, bc	Text and tune from the Philipp Nicolai hymn (1599) ('Wake, O wake'), plus text for recitatives and arias by an unknown author, based on the Song of Solomon. 1: ecstatic 'Allelulia' fugue; 3 and 6 arias are dialogues between bride and bridegroom. 4: reused in BWV 645, the Schübler chorale 1 (c. 1748), and in numerous other arrangements.
SATB, 4vv, 2ob da c, str, bc	Text by Picander, plus 3 chorales based on Luther hymn (1524), and Nicolai hymn (1599). See three previous versions, from 1725 on, and one to come (1735). This is the main surviving version.
vn, v da g, hpd	Some experts believe this dates from before 1720.
fl, vn, bc	Constructed on bass of BWV 1021, probably by one of Bach's sons or pupils. See p. 282.
SATB, 4vv, 2hn, timp, fl, ob d'am, str, bc	Text by S. Rodigast (1674), the same hymn as BWV 98 and 99. There are no recitatives. 1:* is a reuse of 1: BWV 99 (17/9/1724); 3: a soprano aria, assumes virtuoso flautist; 6:* is a reuse of the chorale used twice in BWV 75 (30/5/1723), added with instruments.
2 hpd, str, bc	
	The third performance of *St John Passion* BWV 245 (1724).
Lost	Text by J. H. Winckler. Music lost.
SATB, 4vv, 2ob (da c), bn, vn, str, bc	* J. Agricola hymn (c.1530), all 5 verses. No recitatives. Revived at least once, in 1742. 1:*. See p. 223.
SATB, 4vv, fl, ob d'am, str, bc	P. Speratus hymn (1523/4), 1 and 7 verbatim, the rest paraphrased. It also refers to the Gospel (Matt. 5:20-6) and Epistle (Rom. 6:3-11). 3:*, tenor aria. See p. 223.
Lost	Text by Picander. Music lost.
8vv	** The text is a poem by Paul Thymich (1684), probably obtained from his Wagner hymnal.
Lost	Text by Picander. Music lost.
SATB, 4vv, 3tr, timp, 2hn, 2fl, 2ob, ob d'am, v d'am, v da g, str, bc	** Text by Picander, a *dramma per musica* for the birthday of Prince Friedrich Christian, Sept 1733, performed in Gottfried Zimmermann's coffee shop in Leipzig. 3:***. Several movements were reused in the Christmas Oratorio BWV 248 (12/1734), which makes it hard to appreciate the virtues of this fine secular work, about whether life should be about pleasure or virtue. See pp. 226, 234-6 and 238.

Date	Type	BWV[1]	Title
08/12/1733	Secular Cantata	214	Tönet, ihr Pauken! Erschallet, Trompeten!
?25/12/1733	Mass	232[I]	Missa
1734	Canon	1075	Canon a 2 perpetuus
c. 1734	Secular Cantata	211	Coffee Cantata
?19/02/1734	Secular Cantata	205a	Blast Lärmen, ihr Feinde Verstärket die Macht
?25/07/1734	Church Cantata	97	In allen meinen Taten
10/1734	Secular Cantata	206	Schleicht, spielende Wellen
05/10/1734	Secular Cantata	215	Preise dein Glücke, gesegnetes Sachsen
24/10/1734			
21/11/1734	Secular Cantata	Anh. I 19	Thomana saß annoch betrübt
25–27/12/1734	Oratorio	248[1]	Christmas Oratorio
1735	Secular Cantata	36b	Die Freude reget sich
1735	Keyboard	831, 971	Clavier-Übung 2
c. 1735–46	Mass	239	Sanctus in D minor
c. 1735–46	Mass	240	Sanctus in G major
30/01/1735	Church Cantata	14	Wär Gott nicht mit uns dieser Zeit
11/04/1735			
12/04/1735			
19/05/1735	Oratorio	11	Ascension Oratorio (Lobet Gott in seinen Reichen)
03/08/1735	Secular Cantata	207a	Auf, schmetternde Töne der muntern Trompeten

Scoring[2]	Comment/text/rating (one to three stars)[3]
SATB, 4vv, 3tr, timp, 2fl, 2ob, ob d'am, str, bc	* A *dramma per musica* for the birthday of Electress Maria Josepha, Dec 1733. Most movements were reused in the Christmas Oratorio, BWV 248 (12/1734). 1:** See pp. 228-32, 234-6
SSATB, 5vv, 3tr, timp, cdc, 2fl, 2ob da c, str, bc	Composed for the Dresden Court. Reused for BWV 191 (Christmas 1745) and the Mass in B Minor (1748–49). See p. 224.
fl, vn	Dedicated to J. M. Gesner.
STB, ?4vv, fl, str, bc	Text by Picander, 9 and 10 possibly by Bach. See p. 240.
Lost	See p. 233.
SATB, 4vv, 2ob, str, bc	** Paul Fleming hymn (1642), all 9 movements. 4:* is a violin solo with double stopping; 6:**, the alto aria, about how Jesus can comfort you throughout weakness and bondage. See p. 239.
SATB, 4vv, 3tr, timp, 3fl, 2ob, 2ob d'am, Str, bc	Composition of BWV 206, first performed 07/10/1736 (see below), postponed because of BWV 215 (see below). See p. 239.
STB, 8vv, 3tr, timp, 2fl, 2ob, 2ob d'am, str, bc inc. bn	Text by J. C. Clauder, a teacher at Leipzig university. Anniversary election of Augustus III, king of Poland. 1:***, taken from BWV Anh. 11 (lost), reused as Osanna in the B Minor Mass (BWV 232). 7: reused in the Christmas Oratorio BWV 248 (see below). See pp. 233-4, 238 and 240.
	?Revival of BWV 96 (1724).
Lost	Text by J. A. Landvoigt. Music lost.
SATB, 4vv, 3tr, timp, 2fl, 2ob, 2ob d'am, str, bc	** Adapted from secular cantatas BWV 213–15. Parts 1, 2 and 3 performed 25–27/12/1734. 31:**, one of few original compositions. See pp. 10, 233-39, 244.
SAT, 4vv, fl, ob d'am, str, bc	Text probably by Picander. Performed to celebrate the birthday of Professor J. F. Rivinus. See four other versions, 36c, 36a, 36(1), and 36(2).
cl	Date of composition unknown (see below). See pp. 184, 244 and 274.
4vv, str, bc	
vv, 2ob, str, bc	Performed 1735–46. Some experts say it is spurious, not by Bach.
STB, 4vv, hn/tr, 2ob, str, bc	Composed to fill the gap in his second *jahrgang*. Based on a 3-verse Luther hymn (1524) paraphrasing Psalm 124. Gloomy, but modern academics refute Spitta's theory that it was affected by the War of Polish Succession. 2:*. See pp. 243-4.
	?Revival of BWV 66 (1724).
	?Revival of BWV 134 (1724).
SATB, 4vv, 3tr, timp, 2fl, 2 ob, str, bc	** Unknown librettist, from Luke 24:50–52 and Acts 1:9–12. 1:**; 4:***, from a lost wedding cantata, is reused in B Minor Mass as Agnus dei; 11**: 1697 hymn by G. W. Sacer. See pp. 244–5.
SATB, 4vv, 3tr, timp, 2fl, 2ob d'am, ob da c, str, bc	*Dramma per musica*, for Friedrich August II of Saxony & Poland's name-day. 1, 3, 5 and 7–9 are taken from BWV 207 (11/12/1726). The librettist is unknown. See p. 246.

Date	Type	BWV[1]	Title
c. 1736	Chamber	1030	Sonata in B minor
c. 1736	Chamber	1032	Sonata in A major
c. 1736	Chamber	1033	Sonata for Flute and BC
1736–37	Chamber	1006a	Suite in E major
1736–37	Church Cantata	197	Gott ist unsre Zuversicht
1736–37	Motet	118	O Jesu Christ, mein Lebens Licht
c. 1736–41	Chamber	1039	Trio Sonata in G major
30/03/1736			
07/10/1736	Secular Cantata	206	Schleicht, spielende Wellen, und murmelt gelinde
28/09/1737	Secular Cantata	30a	Angenehmes Wiederau, freue dich in deinen Auen
?1738–39	Mass	233	Mass in F major
?1738–39	Mass	235	Mass in G minor
1738–39	Orchestral	1067	Suite No 2 in B minor
c. 1738	Mass	234	Mass in A major
c. 1738–39	Mass	236	Mass in G major
c. 1738	Orchestral	1052	Harpsichord Concerto in D minor
c. 1738	Orchestral	1053	Harpsichord Concerto in E major
c. 1738	Orchestral	1054	Harpsichord Concerto in D major
c. 1738	Orchestral	1055	Harpsichord Concerto in A major
c. 1738	Orchestral	1056	Harpsichord Concerto in F minor
c. 1738	Orchestral	1057	Harpsichord Concerto in F major
c. 1738	Orchestral	1058	Harpsichord Concerto in G minor

Scoring[2]	Comment/text/rating (one to three stars)[3]
fl, hpd, bc	** See pp. 246 and 282.
fl, hpd	Possibly dating from before 9/9/1734. See pp. 246 and 282.
fl, bc	Probably composed for unaccompanied flute, with the harpsichord added later by a pupil. See pp. 246 and 282.
lute	An arrangement of the E major solo violin partita BWV 1006 (before 1720), possibly not for lute.
SATB, 4vv, 3tr, timp, 2ob, 2ob d'am, str, bc inc bn	A wedding cantata for (according to Spitta) 'people of rank'. 5: v.3 Luther hymn *Nun bitten wir den Heiligen Geist* (1524). 10: v. from Neumark hymn *Wer nur den lieben Gott läßt walten* (1657).
4vv, 2 litui, cdt, 3 tb	The term *lituus* means a brass instrument not exactly known, probably horns or trumpets. Possibly for outdoor performance. Revised 1746–7 with altered instruments.
2fl, bc	** Some sources date this work circa 1720. See pp. 282.
	Good Friday, second revival of *St Matthew Passion*, BWV 244 (1737), revised. See p. 248.
SATB, 4vv, 3tr, timp, 3fl, 2ob, 2 ob d'am, str, bc	*Dramma per musica* for the birthday of Augustus III. Poet unknown (possibly Picander). Four personifications of rivers of Saxony, Poland and the Habsburg Empire: Pleiße (S), Danube (A), Elbe (T) & Vistula (B). Composed in October 1734 (see above). Performed indoors at Zimmermann's café. Revived 03/08/1740 for August III's name-day, out-of-doors. Composed in October 1734 (see above). See p. 240.
SATB, 4vv, 3tr, timp, 2fl, 2ob, ob d'am, str, bc	*** Text by Picander, celebrating the ennoblement of J. C. von Hennicke (1681–1752). Time (S), Fortune (A), R. Elster (T) and Fate (B). Reused (except 11) as BWV 30 a year or two later, without trumpets. 1:***; 2:*; 5:**; 7:**; 9:**; 12:* ('lightning'); 13: repeat of 1. See pp. 269 and 281.
SAB, 4vv, 2hn, 2ob, 2bn, str, bc	Parts taken from BWV 11 (1735), 40 (1723), 102 (1726), 233a (1708–17). 3:*. See pp. 80 and 281.
ATB, 4vv, 2ob, str, bc	Parts taken from BWV 72 (1726), 102 (1726), 187 (1726). See p. 281.
fl, str, bc	** 1:*, 2:**, 4:**, 5:*, 6:*, 7:**. See pp. 275 and 281.
SAB, 4vv, 2fl, str, bc	From BWV 67 (1724), 79 (1725), 136 (1723), 179 (1723). 4:*. See p. 281.
SAB, 4vv, 2ob, str, bc	From BWV 17 (1726), 79 (1725), 138 (1723), 179 (1723). See p. 281.
hpd, str, bc	** See pp. 169, 197, 276 and 281.
hpd, str, bc	Adapted from a lost ?oboe concerto. See pp. 170, 276 and 281.
hpd, str, bc	Adapted from Violin Concerto BWV 1042 (1717–23). See pp. 276 and 281.
hpd, str, bc	See p. 276.
hpd, str, bc	See p. 281.
hpd, 2rec, str, bc	Adapted from Brandenburg Concerto BWV 1049 (before 1722). See p. 281.
hpd, str, bc	Adapted from Violin Concerto BWV 1041 (1717–23). See p. 276, 281.

Date	Type	BWV[1]	Title
c. 1738	Orchestral	1059	Harpsichord Concerto
c. 1738	Orchestral	1060	Harpsichord Concerto in C minor
c. 1738	Orchestral	1062	Harpsichord Concerto in C minor
c. 1738	Orchestral	1063	Harpsichord Concerto in D minor
c. 1738	Orchestral	1064	Harpsichord Concerto in C major
c. 1738	Orchestral	1065	Harpsichord Concerto in A minor
28/04/1738	Secular Cantata	Anh. I 13	Willkommen! Ihr herrschenden Götter der Erden!
1738–42	Church Cantata	30	Freue dich, erlöste Schar
1739	Organ	552, 669–89, 802–05	Clavier-Übung 3
31/08/1739			
1739–42	Organ	651–68	Eighteen Chorales
c. 1740–45	Chamber	998	Prelude, fugue and allegro in E^b major
c. 1740	Chamber	997	Suite in C minor
c. 1740	Keyboard	870–93	*The Well-Tempered Clavier* Part II
c. 1740	Chamber	1025	Suite in A major
c. 1740–42	Latin church music	1082	Suscepit Israel
03/08/1740			
29/08/1740	Church Cantata	Anh. 197	Herrscher des Himmels König der Ehren
Before 1741	Chamber	1027	Sonata in G major
Before 1741	Chamber	1028	Sonata in D major
Before 1741	Chamber	1029	Sonata in G minor
After 1740	Keyboard	918	Fantasia in C minor
c. 1741	Chamber	1035	Sonata in E major
1741	Keyboard	988	Goldberg Variations
11/09/1741			
1742–49	Keyboard	1080	The Art of Fugue
c. 1742	Church Cantata	200	Bekennen will ich seinen Namen
23/03/1742			

Scoring[2]	Comment/text/rating (one to three stars)[3]
hpd, ob, str, bc	Partly lost. See p. 281.
2hpd, str, bc	See p. 281.
2hpd, str, bc	Adapted from Violin Concerto BWV 1043 (1717–23).
3hpd, str, bc	See p. 221.
3hpd, str, bc	See p. 221.
4hpd, str, bc	Adapted from Vivaldi's concerto for four violins, op. 3, no. 10. See p. 221.
Lost	Text by J. C. Gottsched. Music lost. See p. 279.
SATB, 4vv, 2fl, 2ob, ob d'am, str, bc	*** 1738 or later, adapted from BWV 30a (28/091735). Text maybe by Picander, without trumpets and timpani. But still a joyous welcome of St John the Baptist. 6: v. from J. Olarius hymn *Tröstet, tröstet, meine Leben*. See pp. 270 and 281.
org	Printed in 1739. Date of composition unknown (see below). See pp. 184, 247 and 282.
	Revival of BWV 29 (1731).
org	Revised and re-copied from 1708–17. See p. 281.
lute	* Probably composed in the early to mid 1740s. See pp. 280-1.
lute	Possibly dated from 1737–41. Original in a different key. See p. 280-281.
cl	Forty-eight more preludes and fugues, in all twenty-four keys. See pp. 106, 118, 125, 130, 280 and 304.
vn, hpd	This seven-movement piece is thought not to be by Johann Sebastian Bach, but by his son Johann Christoph Friedrich Bach (1732–95). It is derived from a work by Silvius Leopold Weiß (1686–1750).
SATB, ?2vn, bc	Adjustment of a movement in the Magnificat in C major by Antonio Caldara.
	Revival of BWV 206 (1736).
Lost	Change of town council. The last chorus is adapted from BWV 208 (1713), otherwise lost.
V da g, hpd	Some sources date this c. 1720–39. See pp. 281–2.
V da g, hpd	Some sources date this c. 1720–39.
V da g, hpd	Some sources date this c. 1720–39.
cl	
fl, bc	Possibly in July or August 1741, this was performed in Leipzig or Potsdam. See p. 282.
cl	Published in autumn 1741 as *Clavier-Übung* 4. See pp. 184 and 284.
	? Third revival of BWV 195 (1727).
cl	This was largely complete by 1742, but further changes were made up to 1749. See p. 285.
A, 2vn, bc inc bn	1 (aria) is a fragment of a lost cantata. Based on Luke 2:22–32, 'for the Lord is the light of my life'.
	Third revival of *St Matthew Passion*, BWV 244 (1727).

Date	Type	BWV[1]	Title
?03/04/1742	Secular Cantata	210	O holder Tag, erwünschte Zeit
27/08/1742	Church Cantata	120	Gott, man lobet dich in der Stille
30/08/1742	Secular Cantata	212	Peasant Cantata
25/12/1745	Mass	191	Gloria in excelsis Deo
After 1745	Canon	1087	14 Canons
c. 1745–47	Church Cantata	1083	Tilge, Höchster, meine Sünden
c. 1746–47	Church Cantata	34	O ewiges Feuer, o Ursprung der Liebe
c. 1746–47 Before 1747	Canon	1076	Canon triplex a 6
1747	Canon	1077	Canon doppio sopr'il soggetto
1747	Studies in Counterpoint	1079	Musical Offering
1747	Canon	769	Canonic Variation on Vom Himmel hoch
01/10/1747 1747–48	Mass	241	Sanctus in D major
1747–48	Mass	1081	Credo in unum Deum
26/08/1748	Church Cantata	69	Lobe den Herrn, meine Seele
c. 1748	Organ	645–50	Schübler Chorales
1748/49	Mass	232	Mass in B minor

Scoring[2]	Comment/text/rating (one to three stars)[3]
S, fl, ob d'am, str, bc	* Reuse of BWV 210a (1729), for a wedding. Text about the value of music, and its relation to life and death. Some experts speculate that Anna Magdalena Bach might have sung it. 10:*. See pp. 199 and 286.
SATB, 4vv, 3tr, timp, 2rec, 3ob, 2 ob da c, str, bc	** Text probably by Picander. Inauguration of town council. Reuse of several sources, including BWV 120a (1729): 1:* Psalm 65:1; 2:* partly reused in B Minor Mass 'Et expecto'; 3: about Leipzig's lime trees; 4:** already reused in violin sonata BWV 1019a, 3rd movement. Arias 1and 4 are both in ¾ time. See p. 287.
SB, hn, fl, str, bc	* Text by Picander, celebrating the manorial accession of C. H. von Dieskau. An unusual, 24-movement popular work, much of it echoing trendy and familiar songs and tunes. Only two arias (14, soprano, and 20, bass) are substantial, the latter a reuse of BWV 201.7 (1729). 24:* See p. 287.
ST, 5vv, 3tpt, timp, 2fl, 2ob, str, bc	Adapted from Missa BWV 232[1] (1733), reused in the Mass in B Minor.
cl	Manuscript additions to the Goldberg Variations, BWV 988 (1741). See pp. 184 and 284.
SA, str, bc	An arrangement of Pergolesi's *Stabat mater*.
ATB, 4vv, 3tmpt, timp, 2fl, 2ob, str, bc	** Possibly dating from early 1740s, adapted from a wedding cantata of March 1726, BWV 34a. Words (by an unknown librettist) are from Acts 2:1–13 (Epistle) and John 14:23–31 (Gospel). 1:*; 3:***; 5*.
	Revival of BWV 118 (1736–7), with instrumental changes.
str, fl	3 simultaneous canons a 2, each in contrary motion, written for the Haußmann portrait. See p. 290.
str, fl	2 simultaneous canons a 2, each in contrary motion, dedicated to J. G. Fulder.
vn, fl, vc, hpd, org	See pp. 291–2.
org	See p. 293.
	?Second revival of BWV 96 (1724).
8vv, 2ob d'am, bn, str, bc	Arranged from *Missa Superba* by J. C. Kerll (1627–93).
vv, bc	Insert in Mass in F major by G. B. Bassani.
SATB, 4vv, 3tpt, timp, 3ob, ob d'am, str, bc	Adapted from BWV 69a, 08/1723 and 08/1727, for the Leipzig town council inauguration. Text partly by J. O. Knauer, 1: Psalm 103:2; 5:*; 6:* Luther hymn.
org	BWV 645 was transcribed from BWV 140 (25/11/1731); BWV 647 from BWV 93 (9/07/1724), BWV 648 from BWV 10 (2/07/1724), BWV 649 from BWV 6 (2/04/1725) and BWV 650 from BWV 137 (19/08/1725). The source of BWV 646 is unknown.
SATB, 6vv, 3tpt, timp, 2fl, 3ob, cdc, str, bc	*** See pp. 10, 148, 166, 222, 224, 233, 244, 293-5 and 305-6.

Date	Type	BWV[1]	Title
1749	Canon	1078	Canon sup. Fa Mi a 7 post tempum musicum
01/01/1749			
04/04/1749			
25/08/1749			

Undated

N/D	Choral	439-507	Schemielli Hymns
N/D	Choral	302–342	Four-part Chorales
N/D	Organ	552	Prelude & Fugue in E^b
N/D	Organ	548	Prelude & Fugue in E minor
N/D	Organ	571	Fantasia in G major
N/D	Organ	577	Fugue in G major
N/D	Organ	589	Alla breve in D major
N/D	Organ	645–50	Schübler Chorales
N/D	Organ	669–89	Choral-based organ works
N/D	Organ	690–770	Choral-based organ works
N/D	Organ	802–05	Duets
N/D	Keyboard	821	Suite in B^b minor
N/D	Keyboard	831	Overture in the French Style
N/D	Keyboard	904	Fantasy & Fugue in A minor
N/D	Keyboard	944	Fantasy & Fugue in A minor
N/D	Keyboard	964	Sonata in D minor
N/D	Keyboard	971	Italian Concerto in F major
N/D	Canon	1072	Canon trias harmonica
N/D	Canon	1086	Canon, Concordia discors
N/D	Chamber	1040	Canonic Trio in F major

Scoring[2]	Comment/text/rating (one to three stars)[3]
str, fl	Dedicated to 'Schmidt', alias Benjamin Faber.
	Second or third revival of BWV 16 (01/01/26).
	Fourth revival of *St John Passion*, BWV 245 (1724).
	Second revival of BWV 29 (1731 and 1739). See p. 299.
4vv, vn, vc, org	Edited by J. P. Kirnberger and C. P. E. Bach, Leipzig 1784–87.
org	In *Clavier-Übung III*, 1739.
org	Wedge. Revised 1727–31.
org	
org	Jig.
org	
org	See 1748.
org	In *Clavier-Übung III*, 1739.
org	71 chorale-based organ pieces, dating from before 1700 to c. 1723, many undated, some revised c. 1740. See pp. 247 and 280.
org	In *Clavier-Übung III*, 1739.
cl	
cl	In *Clavier-Übung II*, 1735
cl	
cl	After Torelli.
cl	
cl	In *Clavier-Übung II*, 1735. 1:*. See p. 244.
fl, hpd	
cl	
vn, ob, bc	Movement based on material from Cantata BWV 208, later used in Cantata BWV 68.
4vv, org	Schemelli's *Musicalisches Gesangbuch*, 1736. See pp. 246-7.

Appendix 2

Works and movements: a personal choice

In the course of studying the long and complex life of Bach, particularly finding contacts between his compositions and the events taking place at all the different times, the author inevitably came to a number of conclusions about the musical qualities in the huge range of surviving works. The first motivation is that in virtually all the existing biographies this does not occur, probably because experts for more than two centuries have been outraged by the Johann Adolph Scheibe criticism, which reads: 'This great man would be the admiration of whole nations if he had more comfort, if he did not take away the natural element in his pieces by giving them a bombastic and confused style, and if he did not darken their beauty by an excess of artifice.' Even though Bach did indeed become admired by whole nations 180 years ago, the author believes Scheibe's observation to be largely true. Secondly, although Bach is indeed one of the greatest composers of all time, there is no doubt that some of his works are more moving and beautiful than others, whether or not they can be connected with the events in his life. The list that follows, showing the author's personal assessments chronologically, allots **three stars for masterpieces, two stars for further superb works, and one star for further excellent works**. This is not to imply that the works and movements not listed are poor, or are not worth playing or listening to, or involve bombast, confusion and darkness. The purpose is to encourage readers to listen to works (all of which are listed in Appendix 1) that they have not heard before, and come to their own conclusions.

Year	Date	BWV	Ratings[1]	Mentions in biography
1704	?1704–07	150	*	pp. 64, 316
	Before 1705	565	***	pp. 47, 316
1707	1707–08 (?)	106	2**	pp. 68-9, 189, 316
	1707–08 (?)	4	*, 1*, 6**	pp. 60, 318
	04/02/1707	71	6*	pp. 66, 71, 318
1710	1710–25	542	2*	p. 318
1713	23/02/?1713 or 16	208	9**	pp. 90, 171, 320
1714	25/03/1714	182	*, 2*, 5**, 8*	pp. 95, 320
	22/04/1714	12	2***	pp. 96, 320
	20/05/1714	172	**, 4**	pp. 310, 320
	12/08/1714	199	2*, 4*	pp. 98, 320
	25/12/1714 or 15	63	2***	pp. 98, 122, 322
1716	27/09/1716	161	5*	pp. 235, 322
1717	?1717–23	1043	***	pp. 110, 276, 324
	?1717–23	1041	***	pp. 276, 324
	?1717–23	1042	***	pp. 276, 324
1718	?1718–23	202	1*, 7*	p. 324
	Before 1720	1004	5**	pp. 46, 110, 114, 324
1720	c. 1720	1009	5*	pp. 110, 324
1721	Before 1722	1046	**, 1*, 2**, 3*. 4**	pp. 111, 120-21, 326
	Before 1722	1047	*, 1*, 2**, 3*	pp. 111, 120-21, 326
	Before 1722	1048	*, 1**, 2*	pp. 111, 120-21, 326
	Before 1722	1049	**, 1*, 2*, 3*	pp. 111, 120-21, 326
	Before 1722	1050	*, 1*, 2*, 3*	pp. 111, 120-21, 282, 326
	Before 1722	1051	*, 1*, 2*, 3*	pp. 111, 120-21, 189, 326
1723	1723–9	583	*	p. 326
	02/07/1723	147	1*, 2*, 10**	p. 328
	?18/07/1723	227	**	p. 328
	25/07/1723	105	*	pp. 149, 328
	1/08/1723	46	1**	pp. 147, 224, 328
	8/08/1723	179	5*	p. 328
	12/09/1723	95	*	p. 328
	?29/09/1723	50	**	p. 330
	17/10/1723	109	**	pp. 150, 330

1 The star ratings are from three to one. Where preceding numbers are listed, they are the specific movements in the work.

Year	Date	BWV	Ratings[1]	Mentions in biography
	2/11/1723	194	3*	pp. 151, 330
	14/11/1723	90	**, 1**	pp. 150, 330
	25/12/1723	243a	**, 2*, 4*, 8**, 9*, 11*, 12**, 15*	pp. 151-5, 330
	27/12/1723	64	5*	pp. 157, 330
1724	1/01/1724	190	**	pp. 157, 330
	23/01/1724	73	**, 1**	pp. 158-9, 332
	30/01/1724	81	**, 1***, 2*, 3*	pp. 159, 332
	2/02/1724	83	2*	pp. 159, 332
	6/02/1724	144	2*	pp. 159, 332
	7/04/1724	245	**	pp. 10, 101, 156, 160, 162-3, 172, 184, 222, 248, 304-5, 332
	7/05/1724	166	*, 2**, 3*, 5*	pp. 164, 334
	21/05/1724	44	*, 4*	pp. 164, 334
	30/05/1724	184	2**	pp. 118, 334
	11/06/1724	20	***, 1*, 3***, 5*, 6***, 10*	pp. 165, 334
	18/06/1724	2	5*	p. 334
	9/07/1724	93	*, 1*, 3**	p. 334
	13/8/1724	101	1*, 2*	p. 334
	13/08/1724	113	**, 1**, 6*	pp. 166, 336
	3/09/1724	33	3***	pp. 166, 336
	24/09/1724	8	1*	p. 336
	29/09/1724	130	1*	p. 336
	1/10/1724	114	5*	p. 336
	15/10/1724	5	5*	p. 336
	22/10/1724	180	**, 1***, 2*, 3*, 5*	pp. 166, 336
	5/11/1724	115	***, 2***, 4**	pp. 166, 336
	12/11/1724	139	*	pp. 336
	27/12/1724	133	4**	pp. 166, 336
	31/12/1724	122	*	p. 338
1725	1/01/1725	41	2*	p. 338
	21/01/1725	111	1*, 4*	p. 338
	28/01/1725	92	***, 2*, 3*	pp. 167, 338
	2/02/1725	125	**	pp. 167, 340
	4/02/1725	126	1*	p. 340
	11/02/1725	127	**, 1*, 3*	pp. 167, 340
	25/03/1725	1	5*	p. 340

Year	Date	BWV	Ratings[1]	Mentions in biography
	Apr–July 1725	36c	5*	pp. 168-9, 340
	2/04/1725	6	**, 1**, 2*, 5***	pp. 167, 340
	8/04/1725	42	3*	pp. 340
	22/04/1725	103	1*	pp. 167-8, 340
	6/05/1725	87	6**	p. 340
	13/05/1725	183	**	pp. 168, 342
	21/05/1725	68	***, 1***, 2***	pp. 168, 342
	22/05/1725	175	2**	p. 342
	27/05/1725	176	3**	p. 342
	26/08/1725	164	4*, 5*	p. 342
	31/10/1725	79	5*	p. 342
	25/12/1725	110	*, 1*	pp. 169, 342
	26/12/1725	57	3*	p. 344
	27/12/1725	151	1***	pp. 169, 344
1726	1/01/1726	16	*, 3*, 5*	p. 344
	13/01/1726	32	1**, 5*	pp. 169, 344
	21/01/1726	13	*, 5*	p. 344
	12/05/1726	146	**, 1***, 4*, 7*	pp. 169, 276, 344
	28/01/1726	170	1**, 5**	pp. 170, 346
	11/08/1726	45	1**, 3**	pp. 170, 346
	25/08/1726	102	1**	pp. 170, 346
	8/09/1726	35	2*	p. 346
	22/09/1726	17	5*	p. 346
	29/09/1726	19	1*, 5**	pp. 170, 346
	6/10/1726	27	1*, 5*	pp. 346
	20/10/1726	169	1*, 5***	pp. 170. 346
	27/10/1726	56	*	p. 348
	?31/10/1726	129	1*, 3*, 5*	p. 348
	3/11/1726	49	*, 1*	pp. 171, 348
	17/11/1726	55	1**	pp. 171, 348
	24/11/1726	52	*, 1**, 5*	pp. 121, 348
	1726–7	204	8**	p. 344
	1726–7	225	***	p. 344
1727	2/02/1727	82	***	pp. 171, 348
	11/04/1727	244	***	pp. 2, 9-10, 184-192, 195, 198, 201, 235, 239, 248, 295, 304-5, 348
	?15/04/1727	158	2*	p. 350

372

Year	Date	BWV	Ratings[1]	Mentions in biography
	17/10/1727	198	***, 1***, 4*, 5**, 8**, 10**	pp. 194-5, 350
	1727–31	117	*	p. 350
1728	6/02/1728	157	**	pp. 196, 350
	17/10/1728	188	**, 1***, 2**	pp. 197, 276, 350
1729	1/01/?1729	171	1*	p. 352
	?27/02/1729	159	4*	p. 352
	6/06/1729	174	1**, 2*	pp. 121, 352
	?29/09/1729	149	3*	p. 352
	20/10/1729	226	*	pp. 203, 352
	1729 (autumn?)	201	*, 5*	pp. 201, 352
1730	After 1729	209	*, 1*, 3*, 5*	p. 352
	17/10/1730	51	**, 1*, 2*, 4*	pp. 211-12, 354
	1730 (autumn?)	192	***	pp. 215, 354
1731	c. 1731	1068	2***	pp. 220-21, 354
	8/04/1731	112	*, 3*, 4**	pp. 218-19, 354
	27/08/1731	29	**	pp. 221-2, 224, 356
1732	?20/07/1732	9	3*	pp. 223, 356
	1732–35	100	1*, 6*	p. 356
	6/07/1732	177	*, 1*	pp. 223, 356
	Before 1733	229	**	p. 356
1733	5/09/1733	213	**, 3***	pp. 226, 234-6, 238, 356
	8/12/1733	214	*, 1**	pp. 228-32, 234-6, 358
1734	?25/07/1734	97	**, 4*, 6**	pp. 239 358
	5/10/1734	215	1***	pp. 233-4, 238, 240, 358
	25–27/12/1734	248	**, 31**,	pp. 10, 233-9, 244, 358
1735	30/01/1735	14	2*	p. 358
	19/05/1735	11	**, 1**, 4***, 11**	pp. 244-5, 358
1736	c. 1736	1030	**	pp. 256, 282, 360
	c. 1736–41	1039	**	pp. 282, 360
1737	28/09/1727	30a	***, 1***, 2*, 5**, 7**, 9**, 12*	pp. 269, 281, 360
1738	c. 1738	234	4*	pp. 281, 360
	c. 1738	1052	**	pp. 169, 197, 276, 281, 360
	1738–9	233	3*	pp. 80, 281, 360
	1738–9	1067	**, 1*, 2**, 4**, 5*, 6*, 7**	pp. 275, 281, 360
	1738–42	30	***	pp. 270, 281, 362

Year	Date	BWV	Ratings[1]	Mentions in biography
1740	c. 1740–45	998	*	pp. 280-1, 362
1742	?3/04/1742	210	*, 10*	pp. 199, 286, 364
	27/08/1742	120	**, 1*, 2*, 4**	pp. 287, 364
	30/08/1742	212	*, 24*	pp. 287, 364
1746	1746–7	34	**, 1*, 3***, 5*	p. 364
1748	26/08/1748	69	5*, 6*	p. 364
1748–9		232	***	pp. 10, 148, 166, 222, 224, 233, 244, 293-5, 305-6, 364
No date		971	1*	pp. 184, 244, 366

Select bibliography

Anderson, M.: *Approaches to the History of the Western Family 1500–1914*, London 1980

Anon.: *Hymns Ancient and Modern*, Norwich 1994

Anon.: *Introduction to the Knowledge of Germany*, London 1789

Anon.: *The Holy Bible: Authorized King James Version*, Oxford 1953

Ariès, P.: *Centuries of Childhood*, London 1962

Baselt, B.: 'Handel and his Central German Background', *Handel Tercentenary Collection*, ed. S. Sadie and A. Hicks, London 1987

Boughton, R.: *Johann Sebastian Bach*, London 1930

Boyd, M.: *Bach*, third edition, New York 2000

Boyd, M. (ed.): *J. S. Bach*, Oxford 1999

Bruford, W. H.: *Germany in the 18th Century: The Social Background of the Literary Revival*, Cambridge 1965

Buelow, G. J.: 'In Defence of J. A. Scheibe against J. S. Bach', *Proceedings of the Royal Musical Association*, 101 (1974-5), London 1975

Büsching, A. F.: *A New System of Geography*, London 1762

Butt, J.: *Das Alte Leipzig*, Leipzig 1985

Chiapusso, J.: *Bach's World*, Bloomington 1968

David, H. T. and A. Mendel, revised and expanded by C. Wolff (eds): *The New Bach Reader*, New York 1999

David, W.: *Johann Sebastian Bachs Orgeln*, Berlin 1951

Daw, S. F.: 'Age of Boys' Puberty in Leipzig, 1727–49', *Human Biology*, 42, 1970, pp. 87-9

Edwards, F. G.: 'Bach's Music in England', *Musical Times*, Sept-Dec 1896

Eidam, K.: *The True Life of J. S. Bach*, New York 2001

Ehrenzweig, A.: *The Hidden Order of Art*, London 1993

Fischer, H. C.: *Johann Sebastian Bach: His Life in Pictures and Documents*, Holzgerlingen, 2000

Fock, G.: *Der junge Bach in Lüneburg*, Hamburg 1950

Forkel, J. N.: *On Johann Sebastian Bach's Life, Genius, and Works*, London 1820

Freyse, C.: *Eisenacher Dokumente um Sebastian Bach*, Leipzig 1933

Gagliardi, J.: *Germany Under the Old Regime*, Harlow 1991

Gaines, J.: *Evening in the Palace of Reason*, London 2005

Geck, M.: Bach: *Leben und Werk*, Reinbeck 2000

Geiringer, K: *The Bach Family*, London 1954

Godman, S.: 'The History of Bach: A Recent German Assessment', *Musical Opinion* 71, 1948

Haake, Paul: *Christiane Eberhardine und August der Starke: Eine Ehetragödie*, Leipzig 1930

Hogwood, C.: *Handel*, revised edition, London 2007

Howitt, N.: *The Rural and Domestic Life of Germany*, London 1842

Jacob, W.: *A view of the agriculture, manufactures, statistics and state of society, of Germany, and parts of Holland and France*, London 1820

Kevorkian, T.: 'The Rise of the Poor, Weak, and Wicked: Poor Care, Punishment, Religion, and Patriarchy in Leipzig, 1700–1730', *Journal of Social History*, Fall 2000, pp. 163–181

Keysler, J. G.: *Travels through Germany, Bohemia, Hungary, Switzerland, Italy, and Lorraine*, London 1756

Kivy, P.: *Authenticities: Philosophical Reflections on Musical Performance*, London 1995

Kivy, P.: *The Possessor and the Possessed*, London 2001

Kollmann, A. F. C.: 'Of John Sebastian Bach, and His Works', *The Quarterly Musical Register*, No. 1, January 1, 1812

Küster, K.: *Der junge Bach*, Stuttgart 1996

Mainwaring, J.: *Memoirs of the Life of George Frederic Handel*, London 1760

Marshall, J.: *Travels through Holland, Flanders, Germany, Denmark, Sweden,*

Lapland, Russia, the Ukraine and Poland, in the Years 1768, 1769, and 1770, London 1772–76

Mattheson, J.: *Das beschützte Orchestre*, Leipzig 1717

Mattheson, J.: *Grundlage einer Ehrenpforte*, Hamburg 1740

Monk, W. H. (ed.): *Hymns Ancient & Modern*, Norwich 1916

Montagu, Lady M. W.: *Letters from the Right Honourable Lady Mary Wortley Montagu 1709–1762*, London 1906

Moore, Dr J.: *A view of society and manners in France, Switzerland, and Germany*, 2 vols, London 1789

Neumann, W. and H-J Schulze (eds): *Bach-Dokumente I*, Leipzig 1963

Neumann, W. and H-J Schulze (eds): *Bach-Dokumente II*, Leipzig 1969

Niedt, F. E.: *Musikalische Handleitung*, second edition, Hamburg 1721

Ovid: *Metamorphoses* (tr. A. D. Melville), Oxford 1998

Owen, J.: *Travels (into different parts of Europe in the years 1791 and 1792)*, London 1796

Parry, C. H. H.: *Johann Sebastian Bach*, London 1909

Peters, M. A.: *A Woman's Voice in Baroque Music*, Aldershot 2008

Petzoldt, R.: *Georg Philipp Telemann, Leben und Werk*, Leipzig 1967

Picken, L.: 'Bach Quotations from the 18th Century', *Music Review*, May 1944

Pollock, L. A.: *Forgotten Children: Parent-Child Relations from 1500 to 1900*, Cambridge 1983

Rastall, A.: *The Heaven Singing*, Vol. 1, Cambridge 1996

Russell, J.: *A Tour in Germany and Some of the Southern Provinces of the Austrian Empire in the Years 1820, 1821, 1822*, London 1828

Safley, T. M.: *Matheus Miller's Memoir*, Basingstoke 2000

Schiffner, M.: *Der junge Bach in Arnstadt*, Arnstadt 1995

Schlosser, F. C.: *History of the 18th Century*, tr. D. Davison, 8 vols, London 1843–52

Schulze, H-J. (ed.): *Bach-Dokumente III*, Leipzig 1972

Schulze, H-J. and C. Wolff (eds): *Bach-Jahrbuch*, Leipzig 1975–2009

Schweitzer, A.: *J. S. Bach*, 2 vols, London 1911

Schwendowius, B. & W. Dömling (eds): *J. S. Bach: Life, Times, Influence*, Yale University Press, 1977

Sicul, Christoph Ernst: *Das Tränender Leipzig, oder Solennia Lipsiensia*, Leipzig 1727

Simonton, D. K.: *Origins of Genius: Darwinian Perspectives on Creativity*, Oxford 1999

Sloboda, J. A.: *The Musical Mind: The Cognitive Psychology of Music*, Oxford 1985

Smallman, B.: *The Background of Passion Music: J. S. Bach and His Predecessors*, London 1957

Spence, K. and G. Swayne (eds): *How Music Works*, London 1981

Spitta, P.: *Johann Sebastian Bach*, 3 vols, London 1884–5

Stone, L.: *The Family, Sex and Marriage in England 1500–1800*, London 1977

Terry, C. S.: *Bach: A Biography*, London 1928, revised edition, 1933

Wraxall, N. W.: *Memoirs*, London 1799

Wheeler, O.: *Sebastian Bach, the Boy from Thuringia*, London 1939

Williams, P.: *J. S. Bach: A Life in Music*, Cambridge 2007

Wolf, A.: *A History of Science, Technology, and Philosophy in the 18th Century*, London 1952

Wolff, C.: *Johann Sebastian Bach: The Learned Musician*, New York 2000

Wraxall, N. W.: *Memoirs*, London 1799

Index

Abel, Christian Ferdinand, 109
Agricola, Johann Friedrich, 7, 302
Ahle, Johann Georg, 65
Ahle, Johann Rudolf, 65
Albinoni, Tomaso, 40, 64, 77, 151, 201, 319
Altenburg, 281
Altes Rathaus, Leipzig, 253, 290
Altmann, Catharina Dorothea, 95
Altnickol, Johann Christoph, 296
Anderson, Michael, 310, 375
Anderson, Nicholas, 166
Andisleben, 242
Anhalt, 108, 112
Anhalt-Zerbst court, 132
Anna Ivanovna, Empress of Russia, 182
Anne, Queen, 202-3
Ansbach, 88, 204
Anton Günther II, Count of Schwarzburg-Arnstadt, 47
Ariès, Phillipe, 309, 375
Arnold, Johann Heinrich, 32
Arnstadt, 7, 17, 19, 27, 28, 46-7, 49, 54, 57, 64-6, 74, 77, 82, 99, 101, 117, 130, 136, 242-3, 307
Augsburg, 88-9
Augustus Ludwig, Prince, of Anhalt-Cöthen, 111

Bach, Anna Magdalena, 2, 121-6, 130, 138, 143, 145, 160, 165, 172, 180, 195-7, 204, 218-19, 222-3, 227, 246, 248, 269-70, 281, 284, 304, 327, 349, 365
Bach, Anna Schmied, 242
Bach, Barbara Catharina, 50-2, 57, 59
Bach, Barbara Margaretha, 26, 27-8
Bach, Carl Philipp Emanuel, 2, 4, 6-9, 31, 42, 95, 103, 108, 113, 115, 117, 130, 138, 160, 172, 195, 218, 222-3, 240, 242, 246, 269, 276, 280, 284-5, 288, 290-2, 296, 302-3, 305, 309, 367
Bach, Caspar, 242
Bach, Catharina, 57, 59
Bach, Catharina Dorothea, 84, 108, 113, 138, 160, 172, 195, 218, 220, 223, 248, 284
Bach, Christian Gottlieb, 172, 195-6
Bach, Christiana Benedicta, 204, 218
Bach, Christiana Dorothea, 218, 223
Bach, Christiana Sophia Henrietta, 130, 138, 172, 181
Bach, Elisabeth, 15, 17-18, 20, 25, 195
Bach, Elisabeth Juliana Friderica, (Lieschen), 180, 195, 218, 223, 246, 269, 284, 296
Bach, Ernestus Andreas, 144, 195
Bach, Friedelena Margaretha, 59, 85, 108, 114, 138, 143, 160, 203, 220
Bach, Georg Christoph, 19, 242

Bach, Gottfried Heinrich, 160, 172, 195, 218, 223, 246, 269, 284
Bach, Hans, 19
Bach, Heinrich, 19, 28, 57-8
Bach, Johann Aegedius, 19
Bach, Johann Ambrosius, 14, 16-20, 22, 25-7, 44, 47, 53, 57, 101, 122, 195, 269
Bach, Johann Andreas, 242
Bach, Johann August, 289
Bach, Johann August Abraham, 227, 240, 246
Bach, Johann Balthasar, 15, 16, 17, 19, 25
Bach, Johann Bernhard (1676-1749), 85, 87, 99, 242
Bach, Johann Bernhard (1700-43), 99, 108, 120, 242
Bach, Johann Christian, 4, 246, 269, 284, 289
Bach, Johann Christoph (1676-?), 59
Bach, Johann Christoph (1685-1740), 242
Bach, Johann Christoph (1671-1721), 8, 15-18, 28-33, 36, 37, 42, 47, 53, 57, 90, 99, 115, 120, 242, 303, 317
Bach, Johann Christoph (1645-93), 17, 19, 20
Bach, Johann Christoph (1642-1703), 19, 21-2, 46, 58-9, 75, 81, 85, 279
Bach, Johann Christoph (1702-56), 242
Bach, Johann Christoph (1713), 90, 195
Bach, Johann Christoph Friederich, 222-3, 269, 289, 363
Bach, Johann Elias, 242, 269, 280, 284, 287-8
Bach, Johann Egidius, 242
Bach, Johann Ernst (1683-1739), 53-5, 242
Bach, Johann Friedrich, 59, 75, 242, 246
Bach, Johann Gottfried Bernhard, 98, 108, 113, 138, 160, 172, 195, 218, 223, 243, 245, 261-2, 269, 276-80
Bach, Johann Günther, 26, 28, 242
Bach, Johann Heinrich, 19, 242
Bach, Johann Jacob (1682-1722), 15, 16, 20, 28, 30, 42, 123, 130, 195, 243
Bach, Johann Jacob (1668-92), 17, 25
Bach, Johann Lorenz, 242
Bach, Johann Michael (1648-94), 19, 46, 57-9
Bach, Johann Michael (1685-?), 59, 243
Bach, Johann Nicolaus (1682-?), 16-18, 20, 26, 115
Bach, Johann Nikolaus (1669-1753), 59, 242, 279
Bach, Johann Sebastian (1685-1750), 1-369
Bach, Johann Sebastian (1713), 90
Bach, Johann Stephan, 37
Bach, Johann Valentin, 269
Bach, Johanna Carolina, 270, 284, 289
Bach, Johanna Dorothea, 26, 42, 84
Bach, Johanna Juditha, 15, 16, 18, 25
Bach, Johanna Maria, 288
Bach, Johannes (Hans), 241-2
Bach, Johannes Jonas, 15, 16-18
Bach, Johann Rudolf, 65
Bach, Leopold Augustus, 111, 113,

195
Bach, Maria Barbara, 57, 59, 65, 71, 78, 84-5, 88-90, 95, 98, 108, 110-11, 113, 123, 181, 195, 304, 325
Bach, Maria Elisabeth, 58
Bach, Marie Salome, 15, 16, 27, 28, 70, 198
Bach, Maria Sophia, 90, 195
Bach, Regina Johanna, 196-7, 218, 223, 227
Bach, Regina Susanna, 284, 289
Bach, Tobias Friedrich, 29, 30, 242
Bach, Vitus (Veit), 14, 241-2, 303
Bach, Wilhelm Friedemann, 6, 88, 108, 113, 120, 124-5, 138, 160, 172, 195, 199-200, 202-3, 218, 222-4, 242-3, 246, 263, 269, 276, 280, 289, 291, 305, 325
Bach Choir, 306
Bach Society, 305
Barabbas, 191
Bassani, Giovanni Battista, 293, 365
Becker, Augustus, 92, 94
Beethoven, Ludwig van, 306
Bell, Clara, 312
Bellstedt, Johann Gottfried, 58-9
Bellstedt, Johann Hermann, 58
Bellstedt, Susanna Barbara, 58-9
Berlin, 2, 9-10, 14, 77, 102, 109, 112, 120-1, 240, 276, 280, 284, 288, 290, 292, 295, 299-300, 305
Beyer, Heinrich Christian, 207
Biedermann, Johann Gottlieb, 297-8
Bienemann, Kaspar, 158, 333
Birnbaum, Johann Abraham, 272-3, 288, 290
Böhm, Georg, 39-40

Börner, Andreas, 50
Bösen park, Leipzig, 143
Boughton, Rutland, 310, 375
Boyd, Malcolm, 166, 312, 345, 375
Brahms, Johannes, 317, 345
Braun, August, 37
Breitkopf, Bernhard Christoph, 228, 247, 292
Brockes, Barthold Heinrich, 156
Brückner, Tobias David, 66
Brühl, A. R. von, 263
Brühl, Count Heinrich von, 299
Brühl Street, Leipzig, 143
Brunner, Heinrich, 34
Brunswick, 37, 111, 132
Brunswick-Lüneburg, Duke of, 37
Büsching, A. F., 309-11, 375
Buxtehude, Anna Margaretha, 54
Buxtehude, Dietrich, 40, 47, 52-4, 63-4, 343

Cadolzburg, 88
Caiaphas, 189
Calvin, Jean, 108
Carl IV, King of Sicily, 279
Carlsbad, 110, 114
Cassel, 14
Charlotte Dorothea Sophia, Duchess of Saxe-Weimar, 79, 111
Charlotte Friederike Wilhelmine, Princess, of Anhalt-Cöthen, 169, 180
Charlotte Marie of Saxe-Jena, Princess, 45
Christian, Duke of Saxe-Weißenfels, 89, 171, 199, 321
Christian VI, King of Denmark, 288

381

Christian Ludwig, Margrave of Brandenburg, 112, 120
Christiane Eberhardine, Electress, 193, 195, 312, 351
Cicero, 226
Cologne, 77
Copenhagen, 275, 288
Corelli, Arcangelo, 3, 40, 77, 319, 321
Corresponding Society of Musical Sciences, 290, 293, 297
Cöthen, 9, 102-3, 106, 108-12, 114, 117-18, 121-22, 125, 129-31, 133-4, 138, 140, 144, 147, 151, 163, 165, 180-1, 195, 197, 199, 212-3, 221, 243, 276, 302, 327, 339
Couperin, François, 40, 201
Crüger, Johann, 214
Cuntzius, Christoph, 91

Danzig, 35, 182, 212, 214
Darmstadt, 97-8, 133, 169
David, Werner, 309, 375
Daw, S. F., 309, 375
Decius, Nikolaus, 219
Deyling, Dr Salomon, 139-40, 163, 196, 252, 257, 264, 267-8, 312
Dieskau, Carl Heinrich von, 287, 365
Disney, Walt, 47
Doles, Johann Friedrich, 296-7
Donndorf, Dr Christoph, 218, 222
Dornheim, 58, 66
Dresden, 14, 102-3, 107, 115, 132, 137, 173, 176, 185, 209, 222-6, 228, 243, 259, 263, 273, 275-7, 280, 288-9, 295, 297, 299, 359
Drese, Johann Samuel, 46, 78-9, 83, 87, 99, 101-3, 105-6
Drese, Johann Wilhelm, 78-9, 94, 103, 106
Durante, Francesco, 293, 349
Duve, Andreas Christoph, 132-3

Effler, Johann, 44, 73
Eidam, Klaus, 50, 375
Eilmar, Georg Christian, 72, 85, 88, 317
Effler, Johann, 46, 79,
Einicke, Georg Friedrich, 297-8
Eisenach, 7, 14, 15-19, 28-30, 35, 85, 87, 95, 99, 106, 138, 200, 242-3, 279
Eitelwein, Johann Friedrich, 226
Elias, 280
Elbe river, 37
Eleonore Wilhelmine, Princess, of Anhalt-Cöthen, 101-2
Elmenhorst, Heinrich, 40-1
Elster river, 270
Emanuel Leberecht, Prince, of Anhalt-Cöthen, 108
Emanuel Ludwig, Prince, of Anhalt-Cöthen, 108, 184
Emmerling, Sophia Dorothea, 99
England, 13, 38, 45, 109, 209
Erdmann, Georg, 35-6, 39, 42, 53, 181-2, 212-4, 219
Erfurt, 7, 15, 17-19, 26, 27, 101-2, 115, 123-4, 242-3, 290
Ernesti, Johann August, 240, 246, 248-61, 263-7, 288, 296-7, 298, 307
Ernesti, Johann Heinrich, 131, 160, 201, 203, 266
Ernesti, Regina Maria, 160

Ernst August, Duke of Saxe-Weimar, 79, 82-3, 99, 101, 105-6
Ernst Ludwig, Count, of Darnstadt, 133

Fasch, Johann Friedrich, 132-3
Feldhaus, Martin, 46-7, 57-9, 65
Feldhaus, Margaretha, 46, 58, 65
Fleming, Paul, 239
Flemming, Joachim Friedrich, Count von, 102
Florence, 109
Forkel, Johann Nikolaus, 5-9, 11, 31, 36, 71, 130, 291, 304, 306, 309, 325, 376
France, 6, 7, 13, 35, 38, 45, 102, 109, 209
Franck, Johann, 159, 337
Franck, Salomo, 89, 95-7, 117, 144, 321, 323, 329, 331, 343, 345, 351
Franconia, 243
Frankenhausen, 297
Frankfurt on the Main, 13, 77, 87, 95, 105-6, 125-6, 132
Frankfurt on the Oder, 9, 240, 242, 246, 276, 280
Frederick Wilhelm, Elector of Brandenburg, 102
Frederick Wilhelm I, King of Prussia, 112, 291-2
Frescobaldi, Girolamo, 40
Freyse, Conrad, 309, 376
Frieberg, 297
Friederica Henrietta, Princess of Anhalt-Bernburg, 125-6
Friedrich II, King of Prussia (Frederick the Great), 276, 284, 288
Friedrich August, Elector of Saxony, King August II of Poland, 7, 102, 148, 173-5, 193, 223
Friedrich August II, Elector of Saxony, King August III of Poland, 193, 224-5, 233, 240, 246, 263-4, 267-8, 279, 288, 293-4, 359, 361
Friedrich Christian, Prince of Saxony, 226-7, 357
Frobenius, Michael Ernst, 49
Fuller-Maitland, John Alexander, 312

Gabrieli, Andrea, 40
Gaffurius, Franchinus, 119
Gagliardi, John G., 309, 376
Gardiner, Sir John Eliot, 1
Gaudlitz, Rev. Gottlieb, 196
General History of Music (Forkel), 6
Gentzmer, Johann Cornelius, 207
George I, King, 77, 203
George II, King, 299
George House, Leipzig, 143-4
Gera river, 49
Gerber, Ernst Ludwig, 106, 312
Gerlach, Carl Gotthelf, 200, 260, 264-5
Gerstenbüttel, Joachim, 117
Gesner, Elisabeth Charitas, 240
Gesner, Johann Matthias, 204, 211, 217-8, 226, 240, 248, 250, 261, 359
Gethsemane, 188
Geyersbach, Johann Heinrich, 50-2, 54, 307
Gisela Agnes, Princess, of Anhalt-Cöthen, 108

383

Gleditsch, Johann Caspar, 207
Gleichen, counts of, 28, 29
Goldberg, Johann Gottlieb, 284
Golden Ring Inn, Halle, 91
Goldschmidt, Otto, 306
Görner, Johann Gottlieb, 172-4, 177-8, 193-4, 201, 272
Gotha, 17, 30, 32-3, 101-2, 106, 182, 200, 241-2, 260
Göttingen University, 5, 217, 240
Gottsched, Johann Christoph, 193-4, 312, 343, 351, 363
Graff, Heinrich, 160
Graupner, Christoph, 133
Greece, 119, 232
Großenmunra, 242
Günther, Count Anton, 65

Haake, Paul, 312, 376
Habsburg, 288
Hagedorn, Anna Dorothea, 88
Hague, The, 109
Hahn, Christian, 122
Hainstraße, Leipzig, 218
Halle, 41, 86, 90-3, 100, 102-3, 106, 112, 115, 126, 132, 136, 144, 202, 289-90
Halle University, 132
Hamburg, 9, 13, 37, 39-41, 52, 54, 77, 107-8, 110-11, 115, 117, 125-6, 132-3, 137, 176, 270, 275, 305, 321
Handel, Georg Frideric, 3-4, 5, 9, 41, 54, 77, 86, 88, 90, 97, 107-8, 110, 112, 115, 118, 144, 163, 201-3, 243, 271, 289, 290, 301, 305
Hanover, 14, 37, 77, 203

Harrer, Johann Gottlob, 299, 301-2
Harz mountains, 37
Haßler, Hans Leo, 188, 191, 235, 239
Haußmann, Elias Gottlob, 289-90, 365
Haymarket Theatre, 203
Heermann, Johann, 66, 146, 329, 331, 335, 347
Heilbronn, 242
Heindorff, Ernst Dietrich, 50
Heineccius, Johann Michael, 93, 144, 323
Heitmann, Johann Joachim, 118
Hennicke, Johann Christian von, 269-70, 361
Henrici, Christian Friedrich (Picander), 172, 184-5, 189, 193, 196-7, 201, 219, 226-8, 233-4, 236, 240, 270, 287, 329, 341, 343, 347, 349, 351, 353, 355, 357, 359, 361, 363, 365
Henrici, Johanna Elisabeth, 270
Herda, Elias, 32-4, 36
Herod the Great, 238-9
Herthum, Christoph, 47, 49
Heße-Darmstadt, 133
Hetzehenn, Johann Gottfried, 245
Hildesheim, 86
Hoffmeister & Kühnel, publishers, 5, 280, 304
Holland, 109, 142
Höltzel, Dr Johann August, 162
Hübner, Jacob Ernst, 183
Hungary, 241
Hunold, Christian Friedrich (Menantes), 111, 144, 325, 345
Hutter, Leonhard, 33

Ilm river, 44
Italy, 13, 45, 97, 109, 209

Jagemann, Adam von, 83
Jena, 33, 132, 242, 279
Jena University, 33, 181, 280
Jerusalem, 187, 190
Jesus Christ, 21, 33, 69-70, 72, 95-6, 98, 137, 149, 159, 164, 167-8, 171, 185-191, 219, 223, 234-5, 237, 243, 323, 333, 349
Johann Adolf II, Duke, of Weißenfels, 281
Johann Ernst, Prince of Saxe-Weimar, 99, 101, 321
Johann Ernst I, Duke of Saxe-Weimar, 44
Johann Ernst II, Duke of Saxe-Weimar, 44-6, 79
Joseph of Arimathea, 192
Joseph I, Holy Roman Emperor, 53, 67
Judas Iscariot, 187-8, 190

Katharinenstraße, Leipzig, 200, 240, 343
Kauffmann, Georg Friedrich, 132-4
Keiser, Reinhard, 156
Keul, Caspar, 26
Kevorkian, Tanya, 311, 376
Keyserlingk, Count Hermann Carl von, 263, 283
Keysler, Johann Georg, 142-3, 311, 376
Kiesewetter, Johann Christoph, 32
Kirchbach, Hans Carl von, 193-4
Kirnberger, Johann Philipp, 10, 305, 367
Kleinzschocher, 287

Klemm, Anna Margarete, 278-9
Klemm, Johann Friedrich, 261-2, 277, 310
Knauer, Johann Oswald, 329, 331, 365
Kobelius, Johann Augustin, 44
Koch, Johann Georg, 17
Kolof, Lorenz Christoph Mizler von, 7, 275, 282
Kornagel, Johann Gottfried, 207
Krause, Gottfried Theodor, 248-50, 258, 263
Krause, Johann Gottlieb, 248-52, 254-60, 263-4
Kräuter, Philipp David, 88-9
Krebs, Johann Ludwig, 253, 257
Krebs, Johanna, 197
Kregel, Johann Ernst, 144
Kriegel, Abraham, 205, 260
Kropffgans, Johann, 280
Kuhnau, Johann, 100-1, 106-7, 126, 132, 134, 137, 156, 176-7, 179, 183, 208, 210, 244
Küster, Konrad, 309-10, 376
Küttler, Samuel, 248-50, 252, 257

Lahm, 242
Lämmerhirt family, 15, 28
Lämmerhirt, Martha Catharina, 84, 123
Lämmerhirt, Tobias, 65, 85, 123
Lange, Gottfried, 133-4, 139, 141, 160, 205, 211
Laucha an der Unstrut, 132
Lazarus, 139
Legrenzi, Giovanni, 64, 317
Lehmann, Gottfried Conrad, 140, 163
Lehms, Georg Christian, 97-8, 144,

169-70, 321, 323, 343, 345, 347
Leipzig, 2, 9, 13, 69, 77, 86-89, 106-8, 125-7, 131, 133-4, 142-4, 146, 148, 151, 156, 161, 163, 167, 174, 183, 185, 192-3, 195, 197, 199, 202, 204, 210, 213-4, 222-6, 233, 240, 243, 248, 256-7, 261, 263-5, 267-8, 270, 273, 279, 281, 284, 288, 290, 291, 295-6, 298-9, 303-5, 307, 321, 323, 327, 339, 341, 353, 357, 363, 365
Leipzig University, 4, 9, 86, 106, 132-3, 136-7, 140, 143, 161, 172, 178-9, 199-200, 222, 240, 242, 264, 296, 307
Lenck, George, 132-3
Leopold, Prince, of Anhalt-Cöthen, 102, 106, 108-11, 114, 122, 125, 134, 165, 180, 195, 197, 325, 353
Leopold I, Holy Roman Emperor, 53, 65
Liebe, Andreas, 122
Liebe, Johann Siegmund, 122
Liebfrauenkirche, Halle, 289
Löbau, 183
Lohenstein, Daniel Cooper von, 272
London, 86, 110, 203
Lower Church, Arnstadt, 50
Lower Church, Sangerhausen, 261
Lübeck, 52-4
Lully, Jean-Baptiste, 40, 201
Ludwig, Margrave Christian, 112, 120
Ludwig, Prince, of Anhalt-Cöthen, 108
Lüneburg, 5, 32, 36-7, 39, 41-2, 43, 53, 57, 63, 115, 181
Luther, Martin, 8, 14, 30, 33, 60, 64, 70, 80-1, 86, 97, 108, 131, 134, 137, 150, 152, 156, 224, 241, 243, 246, 317-18, 321, 327, 331, 335, 339, 341, 353, 359
Lyceum, Ohrdruf, 29, 30, 32-3
Lyncker, Wilhelm Ferdinand, Baron von, 88

Macfarren, Sir George, 239
Magdeburg, 86, 132, 134
Mainwairing, John, 310, 376
Marcello, Benedetto, 321
Marchand, Louis, 7-8, 102-3, 303
Marshall, Joseph, 142, 376-7
Maria Amalia, Princess, of Saxony, 279
Maria Josepha, Electress of Saxony, Queen of Poland, 228, 359
Marpurg, Friedrich Wilhelm, 310
Mary Magdalene, 192
Mary the mother of James and Joses, 192
Mattheson, Johann, 4, 54, 218, 270, 298, 309, 311, 377
Meckbach, Conrad, 88
Meckbach, Friedemann, 88
Meissner, Katharina, 197
Mendelssohn-Bartholdy, Felix, 2, 9-10, 305
Menser, Carl Friedrich, 140
Meuslin, Wolfgang, 219
Meyfart, Johann Matthäus, 149
Mietke, Michael, 112
Milan, 77
Mizler, Lorenz Christoph, 7, 290, 292-3, 297, 302
Mount of Olives, 188
Mozart, Wolfgang Amadeus, 5, 306
Mühlhausen, 7, 46, 58, 61, 63-4, 66, 70, 73-4, 77-8, 82, 85, 88, 126, 130, 139,

243, 245-6, 261, 277, 317, 319
Müller, August Friedrich, 172, 233, 343

Nagel, Maximilian, 254, 260
Nagel, Sebastian, 17
Naumburg, 132, 288, 291, 296
Neideck Castle, Arnstadt, 49, 57
Neumeister, Erdmann, 97, 137, 144-5, 321, 323, 329, 335, 345, 349
Neumeister, J. G., 317
Newman, Ernest, 311
New Church, Arnstadt, 46, 47, 49-50, 56, 65, 71
New Church, Leipzig, 87, 132, 136, 141, 206, 265
Niedt, Friedrich Erhardt, 309, 377
Nienburg Palace, Cöthen, 101
Nostiz, Gottlob von, 111
Nostiz, Juliana Magdalena, 111
Nuremberg, 30, 88, 244, 283

Ohr river, 28
Ohrdruf, 28-31, 34, 36-7, 39, 43, 49, 53, 84, 99, 115, 181, 242, 317, 349
Öhringen, 242
Orr Mountains, 142
Ottoman Empire, 115
Our Lady Church, Halle, 90, 100
Ovid, 201, 377

Pachelbel, Johann, 18, 28, 30-1, 33-4, 63, 81,
Palestrina, Giovanni Pierluigi da, 293
Paris, 77, 102
Pegau, 270
Peru, 32

Peter the Great, Tsar of Russia, 182
Peters, Dr Mark A., 311, 377
Petzoldt, Richard, 310, 377
Pezold, Carl Friedrich, 141, 201, 204-5
Picander, see Henrici, Christian Friedrich
Pisendel, Johann Georg, 88
Platz, Abraham Christoph, 311
Plaußig, 226
Pleißen Castle, Leipzig, 143
Poland, 87, 102, 142, 181, 193, 209, 229, 231, 240, 264, 302
Pollock, Linda A., 309, 377
Ponickau, Johann Christoph von, 196, 351
Pontius Pilate, 190
Potsdam, 290, 363
Prague, 109
Pretzsch Castle, 193
Princeton, New Jersey, USA, 290
Promitz, Count Erdmann von, 87
Prussia, 26, 109, 112, 276, 284, 288, 290
Pythagoras, 119

Quedlinburg, 100

Rambach, Johann Andreas, 55-6, 329
Ramos de Pareja, Bartolomeo, 119
Rechenberg, Carl Otto, 106-7
Red Castle, Weimar, 45-6, 79, 83, 99, 105
Reiche, Gottfried, 161, 207
Reimann, Johann Balthasar, 4
Reincken, Johann Adam, 40-1, 47, 63-4, 107, 115, 117-18, 317, 319
Relationscourier, Hamburg: 133

Repnin, Prince Anikita Ivanovi☐, 181–2

Richter, Johann Moritz, 79, 201

Riemschneider, Johann Gottfried, 110

Riga, 181

Rinckart, Martin, 214, 355

Ringwalt, Bartholomäus, 166, 317, 335, 337

Rist, Johann, 165, 335, 337

Rolle, Christian Friedrich, 100, 132–3

Romanus, Dr Franz Conrad, 86

Rome, 77, 109, 232

Roth, 204

Rothe, Christian, 34

Rother, Christian, 207

Russia, 142, 181, 212

Saale river, 90

St Agnus's Church, Cöthen, 108

St Anne's Church, Augsburg, 89

St Blasius's Church, Mühlhausen, 63, 65, 71, 73, 75

St Boniface's Church, Arnstadt, 46

St Catherine's Church, Hamburg, 40, 115

St George's Church, Eisenach, 25, 86

St George's Latin School, Eisenach, 20-1, 27

St Godehard Church, Hildesheim, 86

St Jacobi's Church, Hamburg, 115, 117

St John's Church, Leipzig, 2, 288, 300, 301

St John's Church, Lüneburg, 39

St John's Church, Magdeburg, 132

St Martin's Church, Brunswick, 132

St Mary and Magdalen School, Mühlhausen, 71

St Mary's Cathedral, Zwickau, 132

St Mary's Church, Lübeck, 53-4

St Mary's Church, Mühlhausen, 64, 66, 72, 85, 245

St Michael's Church, Ohrdruf, 28-9, 33, 181

St Michael's School, Lüneburg, 36-8, 42, 77, 86

St Nicholas's Church, Leipzig, 133, 135, 139-40, 143, 161-3, 173-4, 177, 196, 200, 206, 218, 224, 226, 234, 248, 250, 252, 257, 289

St Nicholas's School, Leipzig, 161

St Paul's Church, Leipzig, 106, 137, 139, 141, 143, 172-5, 177-9, 193

St Peter and Paul's Church, Weimar, 85

St Peter's Church, Leipzig, 141, 143, 206

St Sophia's Church, Dresden, 176, 222, 224

St Thomas's Church, Erfurt, 15, 28

St Thomas's Church, Leipzig, 86, 100, 106, 126, 131, 133, 135, 140, 156, 161-2, 173-4, 184-5, 201, 206, 234, 248, 252, 257, 272, 288-9, 296, 301, 349

St Thomas's School, Leipzig, 9, 131-3, 137-8, 143, 172, 200-2, 204-10, 213, 217-8, 222, 240, 242, 246, 251, 262–3, 268, 280, 284, 290, 302, 307

Salzungen, 34

Sangerhausen, 43–4, 261, 276–7, 279

Saxe-Eisenach, Duke of, 14, 86

Saxe-Weißenfels, Duke of, 44, 353

Saxe-Weimar, Duchy of, 44, 47–8,

Saxony, 7, 16, 45, 102, 107, 115, 173, 193, 224, 229-33, 242-3, 288, 290, 302

Scarlatti, Domenico, 293
Schanert, Johann Andreas, 99
Scheibe, Johann, 107, 161
Scheibe, Johann Adolph, 4, 161, 270-5, 282, 288, 290, 296-7, 306-7, 312-13, 369
Scheide, William H., 290
Schelle, Johann, 176-7, 179, 208, 210
Schellhafer Hall, 201
Schemelli, Georg Christian, 246, 367
Schieferdecker, Johann Christian, 54
Schott, Georg Balthazar, 132-4, 200, 260
Schiffner, Markus, 310, 377
Schmieder, Wolfgang, 10, 315
Schneider, Johann, 226
Schröter, Christoph Gottlieb, 290, 297-8
Schubart, Johann Martin, 82, 85, 89, 103, 130
Schübler company, Zella, 292
Schulenberg, David, 312, 347
Schultze, Friedrich, 246-7
Schütz, Heinrich, 40, 156
Schweinfurt, 242
Schweitzer, Albert, 8, 165, 228, 337, 378
Shakespeare, William, 2
Sicul, Christoph Ernst, 312, 378
Silbermann, Gottfried, 224, 291
Silesia, 87, 288, 296
Simon Peter, 190
Simon the leper, 187
Smallman, Basil, 311, 378
Sophienstraße, Dresden, 224
Sorau, 87
Spengler, Lazarus, 150, 323, 331
Speiß, Joseph, 109-10

Spitta, Philipp, 8, 185, 192, 202, 306, 309, 312, 321, 329, 351, 361, 378
Sporck, Count Franz Anton, 184
Stauber, Johann Lorenz, 58-9, 65-6
Stauber, Regina, 58-9, 66
Steger, Adrian, 144
Steinbach, Georg Adam, 66
Steindorff, Johann Martin, 132-3
Stertzing, Georg Christoph, 22-3
Stieglitz, Dr Christian Ludwig, 202, 249, 251, 256-7, 301
Stockholm, 130, 243
Stolpen, 185
Stone, Laurence, 309, 378
Störmthal, 151
Strattner, Georg Christoph, 46
Strecker, Adolf, 66
Sweden, 142, 181-2

Taylor, Dr John, 299-300
Telemann, Amalie Louise Julianne, 87, 95
Telemann, Georg Philipp, 3, 9, 86-8, 95, 97, 99, 105-6, 118, 125-6, 131-4, 144, 151, 163, 200-1, 220, 243, 270, 290, 301, 311, 321, 339, 347
Telemann, Maria, 86
Terry, Charles Stanford, 6, 8, 311, 323, 335, 378
Thilo, Valentin, 247
Thuringia, 4, 14, 18, 22, 28, 29, 35-7, 42, 43, 49, 64-5, 70, 78, 101, 106, 112-13, 115, 120, 122, 183, 213-4, 220, 242-3, 245, 261, 303
Torelli, Guiseppe, 64, 319, 367
Trebs, Heinrich Nicolaus, 34, 80

Tunder, Franz, 54

Udestädt, 242
Unstrut river, 64,
Uthe, Justus Christian, 57

Versailles, 102
Vienna, 77, 114
Venice, 109
Vivaldi, Antonio, 40, 77, 151, 200, 221, 321, 363
Vogler, Johann Caspar, 82, 85, 130
Volumier, Jean Baptiste, 102-3
Vonhoff, Johann Bernhard, 34
Vonhoff, Johanna Dorothea, 26, 29
Vulpius, Melchior, 96

Waldenburg, 183
Walter, Johann, 156
Walther, Johann Gottfried, 78
Warsaw, Poland, 223
Wechmar, 241-2
Wedemann, Johann, 57, 59
Weigel, Christoph, 244
Weimar, 4, 17, 44-8, 72, 75, 77-9, 81-2, 87-94, 99, 102-3, 105-8, 115, 117, 122-3, 130, 144, 146-7, 151, 156, 158, 163, 180-1, 204, 213, 218, 221, 270, 276, 281, 294, 303, 323, 343, 345, 347
Weiß, Christian, 140
Weiß, Silvius Leopold, 280, 363
Weiße, Johann Anton, 101
Weißenfels, 89-90, 97, 121, 171-2, 199, 222, 281, 290, 302
Weldig, Adam Immanuel, 78, 85, 89, 95
Wender, Johann Friedrich, 46, 71-2,

Werckmeister, Andreas, 120
Westhoff, Johann Paul von, 45, 78-9
Wiederau, 270
Wiegand, Johann Andreas, 28
Wilhelm Ernst, Duke of Saxe-Weimar, 44-5, 72-4, 78-9, 88-9, 99, 101, 103, 105-6, 130, 134, 180, 307, 321
Wilhelmj, August, 221
Wilhelmsburg Palace, Weimar, 45, 78-9, 83, 88, 103
Winckler, Johann Gottfried, 251, 319, 357
Winkworth, Catherine, 214
Witt, Christian Friedrich, 101, 105
Wittenberg University, 185
Wolff, Christoph, 1, 2, 8, 32, 50, 160, 228, 309-12, 377-8
Wolle, Christoph, 300
Wortley Montagu, Lady Mary, 142
Wülcken, Margarethe Elisabeth, 122, 290
Wülcken, Johann Caspar, 121, 222
Wülcken, Johann Caspar II, 122, 197

Zachow, Friedrich Wilhelm, 90-1
Zanthier, Christoph Jost von, 111
Zeitz, 121, 197, 246-7
Zella, 292
Zelter, Carl Friedrich, 10, 305
Zerbst, 122
Zerbst, Johann Christoph, 17
Ziegler, Christiane Mariane von: 168, 311, 341, 343
Zimmermann, Gottfried, 200, 220, 240, 264, 275, 357, 361
Zöschau, 287
Zschortau, 288
Zwickau, 132